ON LANGUAGE

Chomsky's Classic Works
Language and Responsibility and
Reflections on Language in One Volume

NOAM CHOMSKY

THE NEW PRESS • NEW YORK
1998

Language and Responsibility ©1977 by Flammarion.
English translation and revisions of Language and Responsibility ©1979 by Noam
Chomsky. Reflections on Language ©1975 by Noam Chomsky. All rights reserved.

ISBN 1-56584-475-0

Published in the United States by The New Press, New York
Distributed by W. W. Norton & Company, Inc.

The New Press was established in 1990 as a not-for-profit alternative to the large,
commercial publishing houses currently dominating the book publishing industry.
The New Press operates in the public interest rather than for private gain, and is committed to publishing, in innovative ways, works of educational, cultural, and community value that are often deemed insufficiently profitable.

Printed in the United States of America

9 8 7 6

Contents

Language and Responsibility

Translator's Note

That my name appears as translator of a book by Noam Chomsky into English obviously requires an explanation.

The origin of this book lies in conversations between Chomsky and the French linguist Mitsou Ronat, carried on in English on his part, in French on hers. The conversations were recorded on tape, and Mitsou Ronat published them in France after translating Chomsky into French (Noam Chomsky, *Dialogues avec Mitsou Ronat,* Paris, 1977).

When Pantheon then planned publication of this book in the United States, Chomsky asked me to prepare an "English version." As the passages contributed by Mitsou Ronat were originally in French, these constituted a straightforward task of translation. However, the French translation of Chomsky presented quite a different problem. The original tapes were no longer available. I felt a bit as if, say, one of Shakespeare's plays had been lost and only the (very excellent) German translation of Schlegel and Tieck had survived, and the problem now was to prepare an English text on that basis. The task was rendered somewhat less formidable by Chomsky's willingness to go over my "translation" very carefully and to correct it. As it turned out, in doing so he also made substantial revisions in the text.

Thus, as far as this portion of the book—the major portion by far—is concerned, what the title page should actually say is: "reconstructed with the aid of . . ." rather than "translated by . . . ." Of course, it is possible that in spite of the great pains he took, some errors still escaped Chomsky's notice; for these, I'm afraid, I must accept entire responsibility.

In spite of these difficulties, I enjoyed the work more than any translation I have ever undertaken: because of the content—the

first chapter on political questions and on the student movement of the 1960s said so many things which needed to be said
—and also because I believe the book presents the clearest
exposition yet of Chomsky's basic conceptions in linguistics and
related issues in philosophy, psychology, and social studies. It
offers an excellent introduction to those not familiar with
Chomsky's linguistic work and the generative grammar approach. At the same time, it provides a comprehensive overview
of the various aspects of generative grammar and the present
state of research that should be of interest to linguists, philosophers, and others who have more familiarity with these questions.

Introductory Comment

The material that follows is based on conversations held in January 1976, conducted partly in French, partly in English. The transcript was published in French translation in 1977. Retranslation into English posed a number of problems, among them, the difficulty of reconstructing the original. In the course of reviewing the translation I introduced a number of stylistic and sometimes substantive changes, adding passages to clarify or extend what was said. Thus the present book, while preserving the basic structure of the original, is not simply a translation of the French translation of my remarks, but is rather an elaboration and in some cases modification of the French version.

Noam Chomsky
Cambridge, Mass.
April 1978

PART I

Linguistics and Politics

CHAPTER 1

Politics

M.R.: Paradoxically, your political writings and your analyses of American imperialist ideology appear to be better known, in France as well as in the United States, than the new discipline which you have created: generative grammar. That poses the question: Do you see a link between your scientific activities—the study of language—and your political activities? For example, in the methods of analysis?

N.C.: If there is a connection, it is on a rather abstract level. I don't have access to any unusual methods of analysis, and what special knowledge I have concerning language has no immediate bearing on social and political issues. Everything I have written on these topics could have been written by someone else. There is no very direct connection between my political activities, writing and others, and the work bearing on language structure, though in some measure they perhaps derive from certain common assumptions and attitudes with regard to basic aspects of human nature. Critical analysis in the ideological arena seems to me to be a fairly straightforward matter as compared to an approach that requires a degree of conceptual abstraction. For the analysis of ideology, which occupies me very much, a bit of open-mindedness, normal intelligence, and healthy skepticism will generally suffice.

For example, take the question of the role of the intelligentsia in a society like ours. This social class, which includes historians and other scholars, journalists, political commentators, and so on, undertakes to analyze and present some picture of social reality. By virtue of their analyses and interpretations, they serve as mediators between the social facts and the mass of the population: they create the ideological justification for social practice. Look at the work of the specialists in contemporary affairs and compare their interpretation with the events, compare what they say with the world of fact. You will often find great and fairly systematic divergence. Then you can take a further step and try to explain these divergences, taking into account the class position of the intelligentsia.

Such analysis is, I think, of some importance, but the task is not very difficult, and the problems that arise do not seem to me to pose much of an intellectual challenge. With a little industry and application, anyone who is willing to extricate himself from the system of shared ideology and propaganda will readily see through the modes of distortion developed by substantial segments of the intelligentsia. Everybody is capable of doing that. If such analysis is often carried out poorly, that is because, quite commonly, social and political analysis is produced to defend special interests rather than to account for the actual events.

Precisely because of this tendency one must be careful not to give the impression, which in any event is false, that only intellectuals equipped with special training are capable of such analytic work. In fact that is just what the intelligentsia would often like us to think: they pretend to be engaged in an esoteric enterprise, inaccessible to simple people. But that's nonsense. The social sciences generally, and above all the analysis of contemporary affairs, are quite accessible to anyone who wants to take an interest in these matters. The alleged complexity, depth, and obscurity of these questions is part of the illusion propagated by the system of ideological control, which aims to make the issues seem remote from the general population and to persuade them of their incapacity to organize their own affairs or to understand the social world in which they live without the tutelage of intermediaries. For that reason alone one should be careful not to link the analysis of social issues with scientific topics which, for their part, do require special training and techniques, and thus a special intellectual frame of reference, before they can be seriously investigated.

In the analysis of social and political issues it is sufficient to face the facts and to be willing to follow a rational line of argument. Only Cartesian common sense, which is quite evenly distributed, is needed . . . if by that you understand the willingness to look at the facts with an open mind, to put simple assumptions to the test, and to pursue an argument to its conclusion. But beyond that no special esoteric knowledge is required to explore these "depths," which are nonexistent.

M.R.:   In fact I'm thinking of the work which has been able to reveal the existence of "rules" of ideology, inaccessible to the consciousness of those caught up in history; for example, the study which Jean Pierre Faye has devoted to the rise of Nazism. This type of work shows that the critique of ideology can attain intellectual profundity.

N.C.:   I do not say that it is impossible to create an intellectually interesting theory dealing with ideology and its social bases. That's possible, but it isn't necessary in order to understand, for example, what induces intellectuals often to disguise reality in the service of external power, or to see how it is done in particular cases of immediate importance. To be sure, one can treat all of this as an interesting topic of research. But we must separate two things:

1. Is it possible to present a significant theoretical analysis of this? Answer: Yes, in principle. And this type of work might attain a level at which it would require special training, and form, in principle, part of science.

2. Is such a science necessary to remove the distorting prism imposed by the intelligentsia on social reality? Answer: No. Ordinary skepticism and application is sufficient.

Let us take a concrete example: When an event occurs in the world, the mass media—television, the newspapers—look for someone to explain it. In the United States, at least, they turn to the professionals in social science, basing themselves on the notion, which seems superficially reasonable and in some instances is reasonable within limits, that these experts have a special competence to explain what is happening. Correspondingly, it is very important for the professionals to make everyone believe in the existence of an intellectual frame of reference which they alone possess, so that they alone have the right to comment on these affairs or are in a position to do so. This is one of the ways in which the professional intelligentsia serve a useful and effective function within the apparatus of social control. You don't ask the man in the street how to build a bridge, do you? You turn to a professional expert. Very well, in the same way you should not ask this man in the street: Must we intervene in Angola? Here one needs professionals—very carefully selected, to be sure.

To make all of this more concrete, let me comment in a very personal way: in my own professional work I have touched on a variety of different fields. I've done work in mathematical linguistics, for example, without any professional credentials in mathematics; in this subject I am completely self-taught, and not very well taught. But I've often been invited by universities to speak on mathematical linguistics at mathematics seminars and colloquia. No one has ever asked me whether I have the appropriate credentials to speak on these subjects; the mathematicians couldn't care less. What they want to know is what I have to say. No one has ever objected to my right to speak, asking whether I have a doctor's degree in mathematics, or whether I have taken advanced courses in this subject. That would never have entered their minds. They want to know whether I am right or wrong, whether the subject is interesting or not, whether better approaches are possible—the discussion dealt with the subject, not with my right to discuss it.

But on the other hand, in discussion or debate concerning social issues or American foreign policy, Vietnam or the Middle

East, for example, the issue is constantly raised, often with considerable venom. I've repeatedly been challenged on grounds of credentials, or asked, what special training do you have that entitles you to speak of these matters. The assumption is that people like me, who are outsiders from a professional viewpoint, are not entitled to speak on such things.

Compare mathematics and the political sciences—it's quite striking. In mathematics, in physics, people are concerned with what you say, not with your certification. But in order to speak about social reality, you must have the proper credentials, particularly if you depart from the accepted framework of thinking. Generally speaking, it seems fair to say that the richer the intellectual substance of a field, the less there is a concern for credentials, and the greater is the concern for content. One might even argue that to deal with substantive issues in the ideological disciplines may be a dangerous thing, because these disciplines are not simply concerned with discovering and explaining the facts as they are; rather, they tend to present these facts and interpret them in a manner that conforms to certain ideological requirements, and to become dangerous to established interests if they do not do so.

To complete the picture I should note a striking difference, in my personal experience at least, between the United States and other industrial democracies in this regard. Thus I have found over the years that although I am often asked to comment on international affairs or social issues by press, radio, and television in Canada, Western Europe, Japan, Australia, that is very rare in the United States.

(I exclude here the special pages of the newspapers in which a range of dissenting view is permitted, even encouraged, but encapsulated and identified as "full expression of a range of opinion." I am referring rather to the commentary and analysis that enters into the mainstream of discussion and interpretation of contemporary affairs, a crucial difference.)

The contrast was quite dramatic through the period of the Vietnam war, and remains so today. If this were solely a personal experience, it would not be of any significance, but I am quite sure it is not. The United States is unusual among the industrial democracies in the rigidity of the system of ideological control—"indoctrination," we might say—exercised through the mass media. One of the devices used to achieve this narrowness of perspective is the reliance on professional credentials. The universities and academic disciplines have, in the past, been successful in safeguarding conformist attitudes and interpretations, so that by and large a reliance on "professional expertise" will ensure that views and analyses that depart from orthodoxy will rarely be expressed.

Thus, when I hesitate to try to link my work in linguistics to analyses of current affairs or of ideology, as many people suggest, it is for two reasons. In the first place, the connection is in fact tenuous. Furthermore, I do not want to contribute to the illusion that these questions require technical understanding, inaccessible without special training. But I don't want to deny what you say: one can approach the nature of ideology, the role of ideological control, the social role of the intelligentsia, etc., in a sophisticated fashion. But the task which confronts the ordinary citizen concerned with understanding social reality and removing the masks that disguise it is not comparable to Jean Pierre Faye's problem in his investigation of totalitarian language.

M.R.:   In your analyses of ideology you have pointed to a "curious" fact: At times certain journals practice a policy of "balance," which consists of presenting contradictory reports or interpretations side by side. You said, however, that only the official version, that of the dominant ideology, was retained, even without proof, while the version of the opposition was rejected in spite of the evidence presented and the reliability of the sources.

N.C.:   Yes, in part because, obviously, privileged status is accorded to the version that conforms better to the needs of power and privilege. However, it is important not to overlook the tremendous imbalance as to how the social reality is presented to the public.

To my knowledge, in the American mass media you cannot find a single socialist journalist, not a single syndicated political commentator who is a socialist. From the ideological point of view the mass media are almost one hundred percent "state capitalist." In a sense, we have over here the "mirror image" of the Soviet Union, where all the people who write in *Pravda* represent the position which they call "socialism"—in fact, a certain variety of highly authoritarian state socialism. Here in the United States there is an astonishing degree of ideological uniformity for such a complex country. Not a single socialist voice in the mass media, not even a timid one; perhaps there are some marginal exceptions, but I cannot think of any, off-hand. Basically, there are two reasons for this. First, there is the remarkable ideological homogeneity of the American intelligentsia in general, who rarely depart from one of the variants of state capitalistic ideology (liberal or conservative), a fact which itself calls for explanation. The second reason is that the mass media are capitalist institutions. It is no doubt the same on the board of directors of General Motors. If no socialist is to be found on it—what would he be doing there!—it's not because they haven't been able to find anyone who is qualified. In a capitalist society the mass media are capitalist institutions. The fact that these institutions reflect the ideology of dominant economic interests is hardly surprising.

That is a crude and elementary fact. What you speak of points to more subtle phenomena. These, though interesting, must not make one forget the dominant factors.

It is notable that despite the extensive and well-known record of government lies during the period of the Vietnam war, the press, with fair consistency, remained remarkably obedient, and quite willing to accept the government's assumptions, framework of thinking, and interpretation of what was happening. Of course, on narrow technical questions—is the war succeeding? for example—the press was willing to criticize, and there were always honest correspondents in the field who described what they saw. But I am referring to the general pattern of interpretation and analysis, and to more general assumptions about what is right and proper. Furthermore, at times the press simply concealed easily documented facts—the bombing of Laos is a striking case.

But the subservience of the media is illustrated in less blatant ways as well. Take the peace treaty negotiations, revealed by Hanoi radio in October 1972, right before the November presidential elections. When Kissinger appeared on television to say that "peace is at hand," the press dutifully presented his version of what was happening, though even a cursory analysis of his comments showed that he was rejecting the basic principles of the negotiations on every crucial point, so that further escalation of the American war—as in fact took place with the Christmas bombings—was inevitable. I do not say this only with the benefit of hindsight. I and others exerted considerable energy trying to get the national press to face the obvious facts at the time, and I also wrote an article about it before the Christmas bombings,[1] which in particular predicted "increased terror bombing of North Vietnam."

The exact same story was replayed in January 1973, when the peace treaty was finally announced. Again Kissinger and the White House made it clear that the United States was rejecting every basic principle in the treaty it was signing, so that continued war was inevitable. The press dutifully accepted the official version, and even allowed some amazing falsehoods to stand unchallenged. I've discussed all of this in detail elsewhere.[2]

Or to mention another case, in an article written for *Ramparts*,[3] I reviewed the retrospective interpretations of the war in Vietnam presented in the press when the war came to an end in 1975—the liberal press, the rest is not interesting in this connection.

Virtually without exception, the press accepted the basic principles of government propaganda, without questioning them. Here we're talking about that part of the press which considered itself as opposed to the war. That's very striking.

The same is often true of passionate critics of the war; presumably, to a large extent they aren't even conscious of it.

That applies particularly to those who are sometimes considered the "intellectual élite." There is, in fact, a curious book called *The American Intellectual Elite* by C. Kadushin, which presents the results of an elaborate opinion survey of a group identified as "the intellectual élite," undertaken in 1970. This book contains a great deal of information on the group's attitudes toward the war at the time when opposition to the war was at its peak. The overwhelming majority considered themselves to be opponents of the war, but in general for what they called "pragmatic" reasons: they became convinced at a given moment that the United States could not win at an acceptable cost. I imagine a study of the "German intellectual élite" in 1944 would have produced similar results. The study indicates quite dramatically the remarkable degree of conformity and submission to the dominant ideology among people who considered themselves informed critics of government policy.

The consequence of this conformist subservience to those in power, as Hans Morgenthau correctly termed it, is that in the United States political discourse and debate has often been less diversified even than in certain Fascist countries, Franco Spain, for example, where there was lively discussion covering a broad ideological range. Though the penalties for deviance from official doctrine were incomparably more severe than here, nevertheless opinion and thinking was not constrained within such narrow limits, a fact that frequently occasioned surprise among Spanish intellectuals visiting the United States during the latter years of the Franco period. Much the same was true in Fascist Portugal, where there seem to have been significant Marxist groups in the universities, to mention just one example. The range and significance of the ideological diversity became apparent with the fall of the dictatorship, and is also reflected in the liberation movements in the Portuguese colonies—a two-way street, in that case, in that the Portuguese intellectuals were influenced by the liberation movements, and conversely, I suppose.

In the United States the situation is quite different. As compared with the other capitalist democracies, the United States is considerably more rigid and doctrinaire in its political thinking and analysis. Not only among the intelligentsia, though in this sector the fact is perhaps most striking. The United States is exceptional also in that there is no significant pressure for worker participation in management, let alone real workers' control. These issues are not alive in the United States, as they are throughout Western Europe. And the absence of any significant socialist voice or discussion is again quite a striking feature of the United States, as compared to other societies of comparable social structure and level of economic development.

Here one saw some small changes at the end of the sixties; but in 1965 you would have had great difficulty in finding a Marxist professor, or a socialist, in an economics department at a major university, for example. State capitalist ideology dominated the social sciences and every ideological discipline almost entirely. This conformism was called "the end of ideology." It dominated the professional fields—and still largely does—as well as the mass media and the journals of opinion. Such a degree of ideological conformity in a country which does not have a secret police, at least not much of one, and does not have concentration camps, is quite remarkable. Here the range of ideological diversity (the kind that implies lively debate on social issues) for many years has been very narrow, skewed much more to the right than in other industrial democracies. This is important. The subtleties to which you alluded must be considered within this framework.

Some changes did take place at the end of the sixties in the universities, largely due to the student movement, which demanded and achieved some broadening of the tolerated range of thinking. The reactions have been interesting. Now that the pressure of the student movement has been reduced, there is a substantial effort to reconstruct the orthodoxy that had been slightly disturbed. And constantly, in the discussions and the literature dealing with that period—often called "the time of troubles" or something of that sort—the student left is depicted as a menace threatening freedom of research and teaching; the student movement is said to have placed the freedom of the universities in jeopardy by seeking to impose totalitarian ideological controls. That is how the state capitalist intellectuals describe the fact that their near-total control of ideology was very briefly brought into question, as they seek to close again these slight breaches in the system of thought control, and to reverse the process through which just a little diversity arose within the ideological institutions: the totalitarian menace of fascism of the left! And they really believe this, to such an extent have they been brainwashed and controlled by their own ideological commitments. One expects that from the police, but when it comes from the intellectuals, then that's very striking.

It is certainly true that there were some cases in the American universities when the actions of the students went beyond the limits of what is proper and legitimate. Some of the worst incidents, as we know now, were instigated by government provocateurs,[4] though a few, without doubt, represented excesses of the student movement itself. Those are the incidents on which many commentators focus their attention when they condemn the student movement.

The major effect of the student movement, however, was quite different, I believe. It raised a challenge to the subservience of the universities to the state and other external powers —although that challenge has not proven very effective, and this subordination has remained largely intact—and it managed to provoke, at times with some limited success, an opening in the ideological fields, thus bringing a slightly greater diversity of thought and study and research. In my opinion, it was this challenge to ideological control, mounted by the students (most of them liberals), chiefly in the social sciences, which induced such terror, verging at times on hysteria, in the reactions of the "intellectual élite." The analytic and retrospective studies which appear today often seem to me highly exaggerated and inexact in their account of the events that took place and their significance. Many intellectuals are seeking to reconstruct the orthodoxy and the control over thought and inquiry which they had institutionalized with such success, and which was in fact threatened—freedom is always a threat to the commissars.

M.R.:   The student movement was first mobilized against the war in Vietnam, but did it not quite soon involve other issues?

N.C.:   The immediate issue was the Vietnam war, but also the civil rights movement of the preceding years—you must remember that the activists in the vanguard of the civil rights movement in the South had very often been students, for example, SNCC (Student Non-violent Coordinating Committee), which was a very important and effective group with a largely black leadership, and supported by many white students. Furthermore, some of the earlier issues had to do with opening up the campus to a greater range of thought and to political activity of diverse tendencies, as in the Berkeley free speech controversy.

It did not seem to me at the time that the student activists were really trying to "politicize" the universities. During the period when the domination of faculty ideologues was not yet at issue, the universities were highly politicized and made regular and significant contributions to external powers, especially to the government, its programs and its policies; this continued to be true during the period of the student movement, just as it is today. It would be more exact to say that the student movement, from the beginning, tried to open up the universities and free them from outside control. To be sure, from the point of view of those who had subverted the universities and converted them to a significant extent into instruments of government policy and official ideology this effort appeared to be an illegitimate form of "politicization." All of this seems obvious as regards university laboratories devoted to weapons production or social science programs with intimate connections to counterinsurgency, government intelligence services and propaganda, and social control. It is less obvious, perhaps, but nevertheless true, I think, in the domain of academic scholarship.

To illustrate this, take the example of the history of the cold war, and the so-called revisionist interpretation of the period following World War II. The "revisionists," as you know, were those American commentators who opposed the official "orthodox" version. This orthodoxy, quite dominant at the time, held that the cold war was due solely to Russian and Chinese aggressiveness, and that the United States played a passive role, merely reacting to this. This position was adopted by even the most liberal commentators. Take a man like John Kenneth Galbraith, who within the liberal establishment has long been one of the most open, questioning, and skeptical minds, one of those who tried to break out of the orthodox framework on many issues. Well, in his book *The New Industrial State,* published in 1967—as late as that!—where he lays much stress on the open and critical attitude of the intelligentsia and the encouraging prospects this offers, he says that "the undoubted historical source" of the cold war was Russian and Chinese aggressiveness: "the revolutionary and national aspirations of the Soviets, and more recently of the Chinese, and the compulsive vigor of their assertion."[5] That is what the liberal critics were still saying in 1967.

The "revisionist" alternative was developed in various conflicting versions by James Warburg, D. F. Fleming, William Appleman Williams, Gar Alperovitz, Gabriel Kolko, David Horowitz, Diane Clemens, and others. They argued that the cold war resulted from an interaction of great power designs and suspicions. This position not only has prima facie plausibility, but also receives strong support from the historical and documentary record. But few people paid much attention to "revisionist" studies, which were often the object of scorn or a few pleasantries among "serious" analysts.

By the end of the sixties, however, it had become impossible to prevent serious consideration of the "revisionist" position, in large part because of the pressures of the student movement. Students had read these books and wanted to have them discussed. What resulted is quite interesting.

In the first place, as soon as the revisionist alternative was seriously considered, the orthodox position simply dissolved, vanished. As soon as the debate was opened, it found itself lacking an object, virtually. The orthodox position was abandoned.

To be sure, orthodox historians rarely admitted that they had been in error. Instead, while adopting some of the revisionist views, they attributed to the revisionists a stupid position, according to which—to take a not untypical characterization—"the Soviet Government . . . was merely the hapless object of our vicious diplomacy." This is Herbert Feis's rendition of the position of Gar Alperovitz, whose actual view was that "the Cold War cannot be understood simply as an American response to a Soviet challenge, but rather as the insidious interaction of mutual suspicions, blame for which must be shared by all." Quite typically, the view attributed to the revisionists was a nonsensical one that takes no account of interaction of the superpowers. Orthodox historians took over some elements of the revisionist analysis, while attributing to them an idiotic doctrine that was fundamentally different from what had actually been proposed, and in fact was the mirror image of the original orthodox position. The motivation for this mode of argument is of course obvious enough.

Starting from this slightly revised basis, many orthodox historians have sought to reconstruct the image of American benevolence and passivity. But I do not want to go into this development here. As for the impact of the revisionist analysis, Galbraith again provides an interesting example: I have already quoted his book, which appeared in 1967. In a revised edition, in 1971, he replaced the word "the" by the word "an" in the passage quoted: "the revolutionary and national aspirations of the Soviets, and more recently of the Chinese, and the compulsive vigor of their assertion, were *an* undoubted historical source [of the cold war]" (my emphasis). This account is still misleading and biased, because he does not speak of the *other* causes; it would also be interesting to see in just what way the initiatives of China were "an undoubted source" of the cold war. But the position is at least tenable, in contrast to the orthodox position, which he gave in the previous edition four years earlier—and prior to the general impact of the student movement on the universities.

Galbraith is an interesting example just because he is one of the most open, critical, and questioning minds among the liberal intelligentsia. His comments on the cold war and its origins are also interesting because they are presented as a casual side remark: he does not attempt in this context to give an original historical analysis, but merely reports in passing the doctrine accepted among those liberal intellectuals who were somewhat skeptical and critical. We are not talking here about an Arthur Schlesinger or other ideologues who at times present a selection of historical facts in a manner comparable to the party historians of other faiths.

One can understand why so many liberal intellectuals were terrified at the end of the sixties, why they describe this period as one of totalitarianism of the left: for once they were compelled to look the world of facts in the face. A serious threat, and a real danger for people whose role is ideological control. There is a recent and quite interesting study put out by the Trilateral Commission—*The Crisis of Democracy,* by Michel Crozier, Samuel Huntington, and Joji Watanuki—in which an international group of scholars and others discuss what they see as contemporary threats to democracy. One of these threats is posed by "value-oriented intellectuals" who, as they correctly point out, often challenge the institutions that are responsible for "the indoctrination of the young"—an apt phrase. The student movement contributed materially to this aspect of "the crisis of democracy."

By the late sixties the discussion had gone beyond the question of Vietnam or the interpretation of contemporary history; it concerned the *institutions* themselves. Orthodox economics was very briefly challenged by students who wanted to undertake a fundamental critique of the functioning of the capitalist economy; students questioned the institutions, they wanted to study Marx and political economy.

Perhaps I can illustrate this once again with a personal anecdote:

In the spring of 1969 a small group of students in economics here in Cambridge wanted to initiate a discussion of the nature of economics as a field of study. In order to open this discussion, they tried to organize a debate in which the two main speakers would be Paul Samuelson, the eminent Keynesian economist at MIT (today a Nobel laureate), and a Marxist economist. But for this latter role they were not able to find anyone in the Boston area, no one who was willing to question the neo-classical position from the point of view of Marxist political economy. Finally I was asked to take on the task, though I have no particular knowledge of economics, and no commitment to Marxism. Not one professional, or even semi-professional, in 1969! And Cambridge is a very lively place in these respects. That may give you some idea of the prevailing intellectual climate. It is difficult to imagine anything comparable in Western Europe or Japan.

The student movement changed these things to a small extent: what was described, as I told you, as terror at the university . . . the SS marching through the corridors . . . the academic intelligentsia barely survived these terrifying attacks by student radicals . . . of course, due solely to their great courage. Unbelievable fantasies! Although, to be sure, there were incidents, sometimes instigated by provocateurs of the FBI, as we know now, which stimulated that paranoid interpretation. What a devastating thing, to have opened up the university just a little! But the mass media were hardly touched at all, and now orthodoxy has been reestablished, because the pressure is no longer there. For example, a serious diplomatic historian like Gaddis Smith can now describe Williams and Kolko as "pamphleteers" in the *New York Times Book Review*.

M.R.: To what do you attribute this "falling off" of the pressure?

N.C.: To many things. When the New Left developed within the student movement in the United States, it could not associate itself with any broader social movement, rooted in any important segment of the population. In large part this was the result of the ideological narrowness of the preceding period. Students form a social group that is marginal and transitory. The student left constituted a small minority, often confronted by very difficult circumstances. A living intellectual tradition of the left did not exist, nor a socialist movement with a base in the working class. There was no living tradition or popular movement from which they could gain support. Under these circumstances, it is perhaps surprising that the student movement lasted as long as it did.

M.R.: And the new generation?

N.C.: It is faced with new forms of experience. Students today seem to find it easier to adapt to the demands imposed from the outside, though one should not exaggerate; in my experience at least, colleges are quite unlike the fifties and early sixties. The economic stagnation and recession have a lot to do with student attitudes. Under the conditions of the sixties students could suppose that they would find means of subsistence, no matter what they did. The society seemed to have sufficient interstices, there was a sense of expansiveness and optimism, so that one could hope to find a place somehow. Now that is no longer the case. Even those who are "disciplined" and well prepared professionally may become well-educated taxi drivers. Student activism has felt the effect of all this.

Other factors have also played a role. There is evidence that certain universities, perhaps many of them, have explicitly sought to exclude leftist students. Even in liberal universities, political criteria have been imposed to exclude students who might "cause problems." Not entirely, of course, otherwise they would have excluded all the good students. Leftist students also have had serious difficulties in working at the universities, or later, in gaining appointments, at least in the ideological disciplines, political science, economics, Asian studies, for example.

M.R.:   At the time of the French publication of your book *Counterrevolutionary Violence (Bains de Sang)* there was much talk in France about the fact that the English original had been censored (that is, distribution was blocked) by the conglomerate to which the publishing house belonged; the publishing house itself was closed and its personnel dismissed. The chief editor became a taxi driver and now is organizing a taxi-drivers' union. French television has cast doubt on this story.

N.C.:   That "censorship" by the conglomerate did take place, as you describe, but it was a stupid act on their part. At that level censorship isn't necessary, given the number of potential readers on the one hand, and on the other, the weight exerted by the enormous ideological apparatus. I have often thought that if a rational Fascist dictatorship were to exist, then it would choose the American system. State censorship is not necessary, or even very efficient, in comparison to the ideological controls exercised by systems that are more complex and more decentralized.

M.R.:   Within this framework, how do you interpret the Watergate affair, which has often been presented in France as the "triumph" of democracy?

N.C.:   To consider the Watergate affair as a triumph of democracy is an error, in my opinion. The real question raised was not: Did Nixon employ evil methods against his political adversaries? but rather: Who were the victims? The answer is clear. Nixon was condemned, not because he employed reprehensible methods in his political struggles, but because he made a mistake in the choice of adversaries against whom he turned these methods. *He attacked people with power.*

The telephone taps? Such practices have existed for a long time. He had an "enemies list"? But nothing happened to those who were on that list. I was on that list, nothing happened to me. No, he simply made a mistake in his choice of enemies: he had on his list the chairman of IBM, senior government advisers, distinguished pundits of the press, highly placed supporters of the Democratic Party. He attacked the Washington *Post,* a major capitalist enterprise. And these powerful people defended themselves at once, as would be expected. Watergate? Men of power against men of power.

Similar crimes, and others much graver, could have been charged against other people as well as Nixon. But those crimes were typically directed against minorities or against movements of social change, and few ever protested. The ideological censorship kept these matters from the public eye during the Watergate period, although remarkable documentation concerning this repression appeared at just this time. It was only when the dust of Watergate had settled that the press and the political commentators turned toward some of the real and profound cases of abuse of state power—still without recognizing or exploring the gravity of the issue.

For example, the Church Committee has published information, the significance of which has not really been made clear. At the time of its revelations, a great deal of publicity was focused on the Martin Luther King affair, but still more important revelations have hardly been dealt with by the press to this day (January 1976). For example, the following: In Chicago there was a street gang called the Blackstone Rangers, which operated in the ghetto. The Black Panthers were in contact with them, attempting to politicize them, it appears. As long as the Rangers remained a ghetto street gang—a criminal gang, as depicted by the FBI, at least—the FBI were not much concerned; this was also a way of controlling the ghetto. But radicalized into a political group, they became potentially dangerous.

The basic function of the FBI is not to stop crime. Rather, it functions as a political police, in large measure. An indication is given by the FBI budget and the way it is apportioned. Some suggestive information on this subject has been revealed by a group calling themselves the "Citizens' Commission to Investigate the FBI," who succeeded in stealing from the FBI's Media, Pennsylvania, office a collection of documents which they attempted to circulate to the press. The breakdown of these documents was approximately the following: 30 percent were devoted to routine procedures; 40 percent to political surveillance involving two right-wing groups, ten groups concerned with immigrants, and more than two hundred liberal or left-wing groups; 14 percent to AWOLs and deserters; 1 percent to organized crime—mostly gambling—and the rest to rape, bank robbery, murder, etc.

Faced with the potential alliance of the Rangers and the Black Panthers, the FBI decided to take action, in line with the national program of dismantling the left in which it was engaged, the national Counter-Intelligence Program known as Cointelpro. They sought to incite conflict between the two groups by means of a forgery, an anonymous letter sent to the leader of the Rangers by someone who identified himself as "a black brother." This letter warned of a Panther plot to assassinate the leader of the Rangers. Its transparent purpose was to incite the Rangers—described in FBI documents as a group "to whom violent type activity, shooting, and the like, are second nature"—to respond with violence to the fictitious assassination plot.

But it didn't work, perhaps because at that time the relations between the Rangers and the Panthers were already too close. The FBI had to take on the task of destroying the Panthers itself. How?

Though there has been no systematic investigation, we can reconstruct what seems to be a plausible story:

A few months later, in December 1969, the Chicago police conducted a pre-dawn raid on a Panther apartment. Approximately one hundred shots were fired. At first the police claimed that they had responded to the fire of the Panthers, but it was quickly established by the local press that this was false. Fred Hampton, one of the most talented and promising leaders of the Panthers, was killed in his bed. There is evidence that he may have been drugged. Witnesses claim that he was murdered in cold blood. Mark Clark was also killed. This event can fairly be described as a Gestapo-style political assassination.

At the time it was thought that the Chicago police were behind the raid. That would have been bad enough, but the facts revealed since suggest something more sinister. We know today that Hampton's personal bodyguard, William O'Neal, who was also chief of Panther security, was an FBI infiltrator. A few days before the raid, the FBI office turned over to the Chicago police a floor plan of the Panther apartment supplied by O'Neal, with the location of the beds marked, along with a rather dubious report by O'Neal that illegal weapons were kept in the apartment: the pretext for the raid. Perhaps the floor plan explains the fact, noticed by reporters, that the police gunfire was directed to inside corners of the apartment rather than the entrances. It certainly undermines still further the original pretense that the police were firing in response to Panther gunshots, confused by unfamiliar surroundings. The Chicago press has reported that the FBI agent to whom O'Neal reported was the head of Chicago Cointelpro directed against the Black Panthers and other black groups. Whether or not this is true, there is direct evidence of FBI complicity in the murders.

Putting this information together with the documented effort of the FBI to incite violence and gang warfare a few months earlier, it seems not unreasonable to speculate that the FBI undertook on its own initiative the murder that it could not elicit from the "violence-prone" group to which it had addressed a fabricated letter implicating the Panthers in an assassination attempt against its leader.

This one incident (which, incidentally, was not seriously investigated by the Church Committee) completely overshadows the entire Watergate episode in significance by a substantial margin. But with a few exceptions the national press or television have had little to say on the subject, though it has been well covered locally in Chicago. The matter has rarely been dealt with by political commentators. The comparison with coverage of such "atrocities" as Nixon's "enemies list" or tax trickery is quite striking. For example, during the entire Watergate period, the *New Republic,* which was then virtually the official organ of American liberalism, found no occasion to report or comment on these matters, although the basic facts and documents had become known.

The family of Fred Hampton brought a civil suit against the Chicago police, but up to the present the FBI involvement has been excluded from the courts, although much relevant information is available in depositions made under oath.

If people offended by "Watergate horrors" were really concerned with civil and human rights, they should have pursued the information released by the Church Committee with regard to the affair of the Blackstone Rangers, and considered the possible relevance of this information to what is known concerning FBI involvement in the murder of Fred Hampton by the Chicago police. At least a serious inquiry should have been initiated to examine what seem to be possible connections, and to bring to light the FBI role under Nixon and his predecessors. For what was at issue here was an assassination in which the national political police may have been implicated, a crime that far transcends anything attributed to Nixon in the Watergate investigations. I should recall that the Watergate inquiry did touch on one issue of extraordinary importance, the bombing of Cambodia, but only on very narrow grounds—it was the alleged "secrecy" of the bombings, not the fact itself, that was charged to Nixon as his "crime" in this regard.

There are other cases of this kind. For example, in San Diego the FBI apparently financed, armed, and controlled an extreme right-wing group of former Minute Men, transforming it into something called the Secret Army Organization specializing in terrorist acts of various kinds. I heard of this first from one of my former students, who was the target of an assassination attempt by the organization. In fact, he is the student who had organized the debate on economics that I told you about a little while ago, when he was still a student at MIT. Now he was teaching at San Diego State College and was engaged in political activities—which incidentally were completely nonviolent, not that this is relevant.

The head of the Secret Army Organization—a provocateur in the pay of the FBI—drove past his house, and his companion fired shots into it, seriously wounding a young woman. The young man who was their target was not at home at the time. The weapon had been stolen by this FBI provocateur. According to the local branch of the ACLU, the gun was handed over the next day to the San Diego FBI Bureau, who hid it; and for six months the FBI lied to the San Diego police about the incident. This affair did not become publicly known until later.

This terrorist group, directed and financed by the FBI, was finally broken up by the San Diego police, after they had tried to fire-bomb a theater in the presence of police. The FBI agent in question, who had hidden the weapon, was transferred outside the state of California so that he could not be prosecuted. The FBI provocateur also escaped prosecution, though several members of the secret terrorist organization were prosecuted. The FBI was engaged in efforts to incite gang warfare among black groups in San Diego, as in Chicago, at about the same time. In secret documents, the FBI took credit for inciting shootings, beatings, and unrest in the ghetto, a fact that has elicited very little comment in the press or journals of opinion.

This same young man, incidentally, was harassed in other ways. It appears that the FBI continued to subject him to various kinds of intimidation and threats, by means of provocateurs. Furthermore, according to his ACLU attorneys, the FBI supplied information to the college where he was teaching that was the basis for misconduct charges filed against him. He faced three successive inquiries at the college, and each time was absolved of the charges brought against him. At that point the chancellor of the California state college system, Glenn Dumke, stated that he would not accept the findings of the independent hearing committees and simply dismissed him from his position. Notice that such incidents, of which there have been a fair number, are not regarded as "totalitarianism" in the university.

The basic facts were submitted to the Church Committee by the ACLU in June 1975 and also offered to the press. As far as I know, the committee did not conduct any investigation into the matter. The national press said virtually nothing about these incidents at the time, and very little since.

There have been similar reports concerning other government programs of repression. For example, Army Intelligence has been reported to have engaged in illegal actions in Chicago. In Seattle, fairly extensive efforts were undertaken to disrupt and discredit local left-wing groups. The FBI ordered one of its agents to induce a group of young radicals to blow up a bridge; this was to be done in such a manner that the person who was to plant the bomb would also be blown up with it. The agent refused to carry out these instructions. Instead, he talked to the press and finally testified in court. That is how the matter became known. In Seattle FBI infiltrators were inciting arson, terrorism, and bombing, and in one case entrapped a young black man in a robbery attempt, which they initiated and in the course of which he was killed. This was reported by Frank Donner in the *Nation,* one of the few American journals to have attempted some serious coverage of such matters.

There is a good deal more of this. But all these isolated cases only take on their full meaning if you put them into the context of the policies of the FBI since its origins during the post–World War I Red scare, which I will not try to review here. The Cointelpro operations began in the 1950s, with a program to disrupt and destroy the Communist Party. Although this was not officially proclaimed, everybody knew something of the sort was going on, and there were very few protests; it was considered quite legitimate. People even joked about it.

In 1960 the disruption program was extended to the Puerto Rican independence movement. In October 1961, under the administration of Attorney-General Robert Kennedy, the FBI initiated a disruption program against the Socialist Workers Party (the largest Trotskyist organization); the program was later extended to the civil rights movement, the Ku Klux Klan, black nationalist groups, and the peace movement in general; by 1968 it covered the entire "New Left."

The rationale given internally for these illegal programs is quite revealing. The program for disrupting the Socialist Workers Party, which came directly from the central office of the FBI, presented its rationale in essentially these terms:

> We launch this program for the following reasons:
> (1) the Socialist Workers Party is openly running candidates in local elections throughout the country;
> (2) it supports integration in the South;
> (3) it supports Castro.

What does this actually indicate? It means that SWP political initiative in running candidates in elections—*legal* political activity—their work in support of civil rights, and their efforts to change U.S. foreign policy justify their destruction at the hands of the national political police.

This is the rationale behind these programs of government repression: they were directed against civil rights activities and against legal political action that ran counter to the prevailing consensus. In comparison with Cointelpro and related government actions in the 1960s, Watergate was a tea party. It is instructive, however, to compare the relative attention accorded to them in the press. This comparison reveals clearly and dramatically that it was the improper choice of targets, not improper acts, that led to Nixon's downfall. The alleged concern for civil and democratic rights was a sham. There was no "triumph of democracy."

M.R.:   It appears that a proposal, containing passages from the Constitution of the United States and the Bill of Rights, was distributed in the streets at one time and people refused to sign them, believing them to be left-wing propaganda.

N.C.:   Such incidents have been reported from the 1950s, if I recall. People have been intimidated for many years. Liberals would like to believe that all of this is due to a few evil men: Joe McCarthy and Richard Nixon. That is quite false. One can trace the postwar repression to security measures initiated by Truman in 1947, and efforts by Democratic liberals to discredit Henry Wallace and his supporters at that time. It was the liberal senator Hubert Humphrey who proposed detention camps in case of a "national emergency." He did finally vote against the McCarran Act, but said at the time that he found it not sufficiently harsh in some respects; he was opposed to the provision that prisoners in the detention camps should be protected by the right of habeas corpus: that was not the way to treat Communist conspirators! The Communist Control Act introduced by leading liberals a few years later was so patently unconstitutional that no one actually tried to enforce it, to my knowledge. This law, incidentally, was specifically directed in part against trade unions. And together with these senators, many liberal intellectuals implicitly supported the fundamental aims of "McCarthyism," though they objected to his methods —particularly when they too became targets. They carried out what amounted to a partial "purge" in the universities, and in many ways developed the ideological framework for ridding American society of this "cancer" of serious dissent. These are among the reasons for the remarkable conformism and ideological narrowness of intellectual life in the United States, and for the isolation of the student movement that we discussed earlier.

If these liberals opposed McCarthy, it was because he went too far, and in the wrong way. He attacked the liberal intelligentsia themselves, or mainstream political figures like George Marshall, instead of confining himself to the "Communist enemy." Like Nixon, he made a mistake in choosing his enemies when he began to attack the Church and the Army. Commonly, if liberal intellectuals criticized him, it was on the grounds that his methods were not the right ones for ridding the country of real communists. There were some notable exceptions, but depressingly few.

Similarly, Justice Robert Jackson, one of the leading liberals on the Supreme Court, opposed the doctrine of "clear and present danger" (according to which freedom of speech could be abridged in cases affecting the security of the state) when applied to Communist activities, because it was not harsh enough. If you wait until the danger becomes "clear and present," he explained, it will be too late. You must stop Communists *before* their "imminent actions." Thus he supported a truly totalitarian point of view: We must not permit this kind of discussion to begin.

But these liberals were very shocked when McCarthy turned his weapons against them. He was no longer playing according to the rules of the game—the game that they invented.

M.R.: Similarly, I've noticed that the scandal involving the CIA did not concern the main activities of the agency, but the fact that it did work which in principle was the assigned sphere of the FBI.

N.C.: In part, yes. And look at the furor that has arisen over the attempts at political assassination organized by the CIA. People were shocked because the CIA tried to assassinate foreign leaders. Certainly, that is very bad. But these were only abortive attempts; at least in most cases—in some it is not so clear. Consider in comparison the Phoenix program in which the CIA was involved, which, according to the Saigon government, exterminated forty thousand civilians within two years. Why doesn't that count? Why are all these people less significant than Castro or Schneider or Lumumba?

The official who was responsible for this, William Colby, who headed the CIA, is now a respected columnist and lecturer on university campuses. The same thing happened in Laos, though even worse. How many peasants were killed as a result of CIA programs? And who speaks of this? Nobody. No headlines.

It's always the same story. The crimes that are exposed are significant, but they are trivial as compared to the really serious criminal programs of the state, which are ignored or regarded as quite legitimate.

M.R.:   How do you find all this information? If the newspapers don't report it . . .

N.C.:   This information is accessible, but only for *fanatics:* in order to unearth it, you have to devote much of your life to the search. In that sense the information is accessible. But this "accessibility" is hardly significant in practice. It is politically more or less irrelevant. All the same, on the personal level, the situation for someone like me is of course incomparably preferable in the United States to the totalitarian societies. In the Soviet Union, for example, someone who tried to do what I do here would probably be in prison. It is interesting, and typical, that my political writings critical of U.S. policies are never translated in the so-called Communist countries, though they are, quite widely, in many other parts of the world. But one must be cautious in assessing the political significance of the relative freedom from repression—at least for the privileged—in the United States. Exactly what does it mean, concretely?

For example, last year I was invited to give a lecture at Harvard before a group of journalists called the Nieman Fellows, who come there each year from all over the United States and foreign countries in order to further their education, so to speak. They asked me to discuss Watergate and related topics —the press generally was quite proud of its courageous and principled behavior during the Watergate period, for very little reason, as I've just tried to explain. Instead of discussing Watergate, I spoke about the things to which I've just alluded, because I wondered to what extent these journalists, who are quite sophisticated and well informed compared to the general population, might know about these matters. Well, none of them had any idea of the scale of the FBI programs of repression, except for one journalist from Chicago, who knew all about the Hampton affair. That had indeed been discussed in detail in the Chicago press. If there had been someone from San Diego in the group, he would have known about the Secret Army Organization, and so forth . . .

That is one of the keys to the whole thing. Everyone is led to think that what he knows represents a local exception. *But the overall pattern remains hidden.* Information is often given in the local papers, but its general significance, the patterns on the national level, remain obscured. That was the case during the entire Watergate period, although the information appeared just at that time, in its essentials, and with extensive documentation. And even since then the discussion has rarely been analytic or anywhere near comprehensive, and has not accounted for what happened in a satisfactory manner. What you face here is a very effective kind of ideological control, because one can remain under the impression that censorship does not exist, and in a narrow technical sense that is correct. You will not be imprisoned if you discover the facts, not even if you proclaim them whenever you can. But the results remain much the same as if there were real censorship. Social reality is generally concealed by the intelligentsia. Of course matters were quite different during the period when there was an enormous popular anti-war and student movement. Within the structure of popular movements there were many possibilities for expressing views that departed from the narrow limits of more or less "official" ideology, to which the intelligentsia generally conform.

M.R.: What was the reaction of Americans to the statements of Solzhenitsyn?

N.C.: Very interesting—at least in the liberal press, which is what primarily concerns me. Some criticized his extravagances. He went well beyond what they could tolerate. For example, he called for direct intervention by the United States in the USSR—of a sort that could very well lead to war and, far short of that, is likely to harm the Russian dissidents themselves. Also, he denounced American weakness in abandoning the struggle to subdue the Vietnamese resistance, publicly opposed democratic reforms in Spain, supported a journal that called for censorship in the United States, and so on. Nonetheless, the press never ceased marveling at what an absolute moral giant this man was. In our petty lives, we can barely imagine such heights of moral grandeur.

In fact, the "moral level" of Solzhenitsyn is quite comparable to that of many American Communists who have fought courageously for civil liberties here in their own country, while at the same time defending, or refusing to criticize, the purges and labor camps in the Soviet Union. Sakharov is not as outlandish in his views as Solzhenitsyn, certainly, but he too says that it was a great setback for the West not to have pursued the Vietnam war to an American victory. The United States did not act with sufficient resolution, and delayed too long in sending a large expeditionary force, he complains. Every fabrication of the U.S. propaganda apparatus is repeated, just as American Communists who have struggled for civil rights here parrot Russian propaganda. The easily documented fact of American aggression in South Vietnam is not part of history, for example. One must admire Sakharov's great courage and his fine work in defense of human rights in the Soviet Union. But to refer to such people as "moral giants" is quite remarkable.

Why do they do this? Because it is extremely important for mainstream American intellectuals to make people believe that the United States does not confront any real moral problems. Such problems only arise in the Soviet Union, and the "moral giants" are there to respond to them.

Compare Solzhenitsyn to many thousands of Vietnam war resisters and deserters; many of them acted at a moral level that is incomparably superior to his. Solzhenitsyn resolutely defends his own rights and those of people like him—which is certainly admirable. The resisters and many deserters defended the *rights of others*—namely, the victims of American aggression and terror. Their actions were on a much higher moral plane. Furthermore, their actions were not merely a response to their own persecution; for the most part they undertook these actions, which led to imprisonment or exile, of their own free will, when they could have easily lived in comfort. Yet we read in the American liberal journals that we can hardly conceive of the moral grandeur of Solzhenitsyn in our society, and surely can find no one like him. A very interesting pretense, with many implications.

It is quite generally claimed now that the American resistance had as its cause the young men's fear of being drafted; that's a very convenient belief for the intellectuals who confined themselves to "pragmatic" opposition to the war. But it is an enormous lie. For most of those who were in the resistance from its origins, nothing would have been easier than to escape the draft, with its class bias, as many others actually did. In fact, many of the activists already had deferments. Many of the deserters too chose a difficult and painful course for reasons of principle. But for those who supported the war initially, and who only raised their whisper of protest when the costs became too great, it is impossible to admit the existence of a courageous and principled resistance, largely on the part of youth, to the atrocities which they themselves had readily tolerated. The mainstream of American liberalism does not wish to hear anything about all that. It would raise too many embarrassing questions: What were they doing when the war resisters were facing prison or exile? And so on. So Solzhenitsyn comes to them as a gift of God, which permits them to evade moral questions, "exporting them," so to speak, and to conceal their own role as people who remained silent for so many years, or finally objected on narrow and morally repugnant grounds of cost and U.S. government interest.

Moynihan, when he was ambassador to the United Nations, produced the same effect when he attacked the Third World.

These attacks aroused great admiration here; for example, when he denounced Idi Amin of Uganda as a "racist murderer." The question is not whether Idi Amin is a racist murderer. No doubt the appelation is correct. The question is, what does it mean for Moynihan to make this accusation and for others to applaud his honesty and courage in doing so? Who is Moynihan? He served in four administrations, those of Kennedy, Johnson, Nixon, and Ford—that is to say, administrations that were guilty of racist murder on a scale undreamed of by Idi Amin. Imagine that some minor functionary of the Third Reich had correctly accused someone of being a racist murderer. This manner of shifting moral issues to others is one of the ways to reconstruct the foundations of moral legitimacy for the exercise of American power, shaken during the Vietnam war. Solzhenitsyn is exploited to this end in a natural and predictable way, though of course one cannot on those grounds draw any conclusions in regard to his charges against the Soviet system of oppression and violence.

Think of someone like Angela Davis: she defends the rights of American blacks with great courage and conviction. At the same time she refused to defend Czech dissidents or to criticize the Russian invasion of Czechoslovakia. Is she regarded as a "moral giant"? Hardly. Yet I believe she is superior to Solzhenitsyn on the moral level. At least she did not reproach the Soviet Union for not having conducted its atrocities with sufficient vigor.

M.R.: After what you have said, and what is said about the U.S. intervention in Chile in Uribe's book,[6] there apparently exists a veritable policy of *vaccination*. Deliberately a major scandal is exploded about a minor event—Watergate, the ITT case in 1973—in order to better hide and render more *acceptable* (according to Faye's definition) the true scandals: political assassinations, the coup d'état of September. You inoculate the public with a minor scandal; then when more serious things happen, the subject has already been deprived of most of its sensation value, its topical importance no longer has the aspect of novelty—the two fundamental criteria for big headlines in the newspapers.[7]

N.C.:   Yes, that is in keeping with what I've just said about the liberal press since the end of the war. The government has great need now to restore its credibility, to make people forget history, and to rewrite it. The intelligentsia have to a remarkable degree undertaken this task. It is also necessary to establish the "lessons" that have to be drawn from the war, to ensure that these are conceived on the narrowest grounds, in terms of such socially neutral categories as "stupidity" or "error" or "ignorance" or perhaps "cost."

Why? Because soon it will be necessary to justify other confrontations, perhaps other U.S. interventions in the world, other Vietnams.

But this time, these will have to be successful interventions, which don't slip out of control. Chile, for example. It is even possible for the press to criticize successful interventions—the Dominican Republic, Chile, etc.—as long as these criticisms don't exceed "civilized limits," that is to say, as long as they don't serve to arouse popular movements capable of hindering these enterprises, and are not accompanied by any rational analysis of the motives of U.S. imperialism, something which is complete anathema, intolerable to liberal ideology.

How is the liberal press proceeding with regard to Vietnam, that sector which supported the "doves"? By stressing the "stupidity" of the U.S. intervention; that's a politically neutral term. It would have been sufficient to find an "intelligent" policy. The war was thus a tragic error in which good intentions were transmuted into bad policies, because of a generation of incompetent and arrogant officials. The war's savagery is also denounced; but that too is used as a neutral category . . . Presumably the goals were legitimate—it would have been all right to do the same thing, but more humanely . . .

The "responsible" doves were opposed to the war—on a pragmatic basis. Now it is necessary to reconstruct the system of beliefs according to which the United States is the benefactor of humanity, historically committed to freedom, self-determination, and human rights. With regard to this doctrine, the "responsible" doves share the same presuppositions as the hawks: they do not question the right of the United States to intervene in other countries. Their criticism is actually very convenient for the state, which is quite willing to be chided for its errors, as long as the fundamental right of forceful intervention is not brought into question.

Take a look at this editorial in the *New York Times,* offering a retrospective analysis of the Vietnam war as it came to an end. The editors feel that it is too early to draw conclusions about the war:

> Clio, the goddess of history, is cool and slow and elusive in her ways. . . . Only later, much later, can history begin to make an assessment of the mixture of good and evil, of wisdom and folly, of ideals and illusions in the long Vietnam story. . . . There are those Americans who believe that the war to preserve a non-Communist, independent South Vietnam could have been waged differently. There are other Americans who believe that a viable, non-Communist South Vietnam was always a myth. . . . A decade of fierce polemics has failed to resolve this ongoing quarrel.

You see, they don't even mention the logical possibility of a third position: namely, that the United States did not have the right, either the legal or the moral right, to intervene by force in the internal affairs of Vietnam. We leave to history the task of judging the debate between the hawks and the respectable doves, but the third position, opposed to the other two, is excluded from discussion. The sphere of Clio does not extend to such absurd ideas as the belief that the United States has no unique right to intervene with force in the internal affairs of others, whether such intervention is successful or not. The *Times* published many letters responding to its editorial, but no letter questioning the alternatives presented. I know for certain that at least one such letter was sent to them* . . . quite possibly many others.

April 8, 1975

To the Editor
New York Times
229 West 43d St.
New York, N.Y. 10036

Dear Sir:

An editorial in the *Times,* April 5, observes that "a decade of fierce polemics has failed to resolve this ongoing quarrel" between two contending views: that "the war to preserve a non-Communist, independent South Vietnam could have been waged differently," and that "a viable, non-Communist South Vietnam was always a myth." There has also been a third position: That apart from its prospects for success, the United States has neither the authority nor competence to intervene in the internal affairs of Vietnam. This was the position of much of the authentic peace movement, that is, those who opposed the war because it was wrong, not merely because it was unsuccessful. It is regrettable that this position is not even a contender in the debate, as the *Times* sees it.

On a facing page, Donald Kirk observes that "since the term 'bloodbath' first came into vogue in the Indochinese conflict, no one seems to have applied it to the war itself— only to the possible consequences of ending the war." He is quite wrong. Many Americans involved in the authentic peace movement have insisted for years on the elementary point that he believes has been noticed by "no one," and it is a commonplace in literature on the war. To mention just one example, we have written a small book on the subject (*Counterrevolutionary Violence: Bloodbaths in Fact and*

---

*Translator's note: Noam Chomsky has made available the letter he and Professor Edward S. Herman sent to the *New York Times.* I would like to take the opportunity to make this letter public at this late date, both for its intrinsic interest and to illustrate the limits imposed on public discussion in our leading newspaper.

Propaganda, 1973), though in this case the corporation (Warner Brothers) that owned the publisher refused to permit distribution after publication. But quite apart from this, the observation has been made repeatedly in discussion and literature on the war, by just that segment of opinion that the *Times* editorial excludes from the debate.

Sincerely yours,

Noam Chomsky
Professor, MIT

Edward S. Herman
Professor, University
of Pennsylvania

NC/ESH: lt

Note that as the *Times* sets the spectrum of debate, the position of much of the peace movement is simply excluded from consideration. Not that it is wrong, but rather unthinkable, inexpressible. As the *Times* sets the ground rules, the basic premises of the state propaganda system are presupposed by all participants in the debate: the American goal was to preserve an "independent" South Vietnam—perfect nonsense, as is easy to demonstrate—and the only question that arises is whether this worthy goal was within our grasp or not. Even the more audacious propaganda systems rarely go so far as to put forth state doctrine as unquestionable dogma, so that criticism of it need not even be rejected, but may simply be ignored.

Here we have a marvelous illustration of the functioning of propaganda in a democracy. A totalitarian state simply enunciates official doctrine—clearly, explicitly. Internally, one can think what one likes, but one can only express opposition at one's peril. In a democratic system of propaganda no one is punished (in theory) for objecting to official dogma. In fact, dissidence is encouraged. What this system attempts to do is to fix the limits of possible thought: supporters of official doctrine at one end, and the critics—vigorous, courageous, and much admired for their independence of judgment—at the other. The hawks and the doves. But we discover that all share certain tacit assumptions, and that it is these assumptions that are really crucial. No doubt a propaganda system is more effective when its doctrines are insinuated rather than asserted, when it sets the bounds for possible thought rather than simply imposing a clear and easily identifiable doctrine that one must parrot—or suffer the consequences. The more vigorous the debate, the more effectively the basic doctrines of the propaganda system, tacitly assumed on all sides, are instilled. Hence the elaborate pretense that the press is a critical dissenting force—maybe even too critical for the health of democracy—when in fact it is almost entirely subservient to the basic principles of the ideological system: in this case, the principle of the right of intervention, the unique right of the United States to serve as global judge and executioner. It is quite a marvelous system of indoctrination.

Here is still another example along the same lines. Look at this quotation from the Washington *Post,* a paper that is often regarded as the most consistent critic of the war among the national media. This is from an editorial of April 30, 1975, entitled "Deliverance":

> For if much of the actual conduct of Vietnam policy over the years was wrong and misguided—even tragic—it cannot be denied that some part of the purpose of that policy was right and defensible. Specifically, it was right to hope that the people of South Vietnam would be able to decide on their own form of government and social order. The American public is entitled, indeed obligated, to explore how good impulses came to be transmuted into bad policy, but we cannot afford to cast out all remembrance of that earlier impulse.

What were the "good impulses"? When precisely did the United States try to help the South Vietnamese choose their own form of government and social order? As soon as such questions are posed, the absurdity becomes evident. From the moment that the American-backed French effort to destroy the major nationalist movement in Vietnam collapsed, the United

States was consciously and knowingly opposed to the organized political forces within South Vietnam, and resorted to increasing violence when these political forces could not be crushed. But these facts, easily documented, must be suppressed. The liberal press cannot question the basic doctrine of the state religion, that the United States is benevolent, even though often misguided in its innocence, that it labors to permit free choice, even though at times some mistakes are committed in the exuberance of its programs of international goodwill. We must believe that we "Americans" are always good, though, to be sure, fallible:

> For the fundamental "lesson" of Vietnam surely is not that we as a people are intrinsically bad, but rather that we are capable of error—and on a gigantic scale. . . .

Note the rhetoric: "we as a people" are not intrinsically bad, even if we are capable of error. Was it "we as a people" who decided to conduct the war in Vietnam? Or was it something that had rather more to do with our political leaders and the social institutions they serve? To pose such a question is of course illegitimate, according to the dogmas of the state religion, because that raises the question of the institutional sources of power, and such questions are only considered by irrational extremists who must be excluded from debate (we can raise such questions with regard to other societies, of course, but not the United States).

It is not out of pessimism that I believe in the effectiveness of such techniques of legitimation of U.S. interventions, as a basis for future actions. One must not forget that while the U.S. government suffered a setback in Vietnam, it succeeded only too well in Indonesia, in Chile, in Brazil, and in many other places during the same period.

The resources of imperialist ideology are quite vast. It tolerates—indeed, encourages—a variety of forms of opposition, such as those I have just illustrated. It is permissible to criticize the lapses of the intellectuals and of government advisers, and even to accuse them of an abstract desire for "domination," again a socially neutral category, not linked in any way to concrete social and economic structures. But to relate that abstract "desire for domination" to the employment of force by the United States government in order to preserve a certain system of world order, specifically, to ensure that the countries of the world remain open insofar as possible to exploitation by U.S.-based corporations—that is extremely impolite, that is to argue in an unacceptable way.

In the same way, the respectable members of the academic world must ignore the substantial documentation concerning the principles that guide U.S. foreign policy, and its concern to create a global economic order that conforms to the needs of the U.S. economy and its masters. I'm referring, for example, to the crucial documentation contained in the *Pentagon Papers*, covering the late 1940s and early 1950s, when the basic policies were clearly set, or the documents on global planning for the postwar period produced in the early 1940s by the War-Peace Studies groups of the Council on Foreign Relations, to mention only two significant examples. Quite generally, the question of the influence of corporations on foreign policy, or the economic factors in policy formation, are reserved for the barest mention in a footnote in respectable studies of the formation of policy, a fact that has been occasionally studied, and is easily documented when studied.

M.R.: To reveal the profits of "philanthrophy," that is hardly in good taste.

In fact, all that you have been saying suggests to me a curious convergence, in the form of a provisional conclusion, that goes back to the initial question: What can the links be between a theory of ideology and the concepts of your linguistic theory, generative grammar?

The imperialist ideology, you say, can readily tolerate a quite large number of contradictions, infractions, and criticisms—all these remain acceptable, *except one:* to reveal the economic motives. You have a situation of the same kind in generative poetics. I am thinking of the analysis which Halle and Keyser[8] proposed for English iambic pentameter.

The verse has a structure of alternating strong and weak stresses:

WS, WS, WS, WS, WS,
(where *W* = weak and *S* = strong)

But if one studies the corpus of English poetry, one finds an enormous number of contradictions to the meter, of "infractions" of the dominant schema, and these verses are not only acceptable but often even the most beautiful. *One thing only is forbidden:* to make a weak position in the meter (in the abstract verse schema) correspond to a stressed vowel surrounded by two unstressed vowels. (Halle and Keyser's concept of "maximum stress.")

The observation of this kind of forbidden statement in the media permits the hope that the theory of ideology can reveal the objective laws which underlie political discourse; but for the time being all that is only a metaphor.

CHAPTER 2

Linguistics and the
Human Sciences

M.R.: There has been a good deal of question during these last years about "interdisciplinary studies," about establishing closer links between neighboring disciplines. What do you think of the way in which the relationship between linguistics and psychology has been presented?

N.C.: In my opinion one should not speak of a "relationship" between linguistics and psychology, because linguistics is *part of* psychology; I cannot conceive of it in any other way.

In general, the following distinction is often made: linguistics is the study of language, and psychology the study of the acquisition or utilization of language. This distinction does not seem to me to make much sense. No discipline can concern itself in a productive way with the acquisition or utilization of a form of knowledge, without being concerned with the *nature* of that system of knowledge.

If psychology were to limit itself to the study of models of learning or perception or speech while excluding from its field of investigation the system itself that is thus acquired or utilized, it would condemn itself to sterility. That kind of delimitation of psychology would be quite pointless.

At this point, linguistics understood as the study of the system of language seems to fill a conceptual gap in the manner in which psychology is often conceived. In effect, it makes possible a psychology of language which is concerned at the same time with the system that is acquired *and* the ways in which it is acquired and used. This direction offers great hopes. At the same time, a linguistics which concerns itself solely with the system that is acquired and not with the manner in which it is acquired or the ways in which it is put to use confines itself within too narrow limits, and omits the consideration of issues that may have great importance for its narrower goals, which are of great interest in themselves.

Psychology of language, properly understood, is a discipline which embraces the study of the acquired system (the grammar), of the methods of acquisition (linked to universal grammar), and models of perception and production, and which also studies the physical bases for all of this. This study forms a coherent whole. Results obtained in the study of one of the parts may contribute to the understanding of the others. Take the work of Jerry Fodor in psycholinguistics . . .

Mr.R.:   If my memory is correct, he conducts experiments that consist of inserting noises or "clicks" at precise places on a magnetic tape on which sentences have been recorded, and then asking the subjects of the experiment the exact location in the sentence where they have perceived, or heard, these "clicks."

N.C.:   Yes. And in principle this work might help to resolve controversial problems of linguistic structure. Take the case of the grammatical transformation called "raising." This is an operation which has been postulated for such constructions as *John expected Bill to leave.* This operation takes the subject of the embedded clause *Bill leaves* and "raises" it to the position of object of the main verb (*John expected that—Bill leaves* thus becomes *John expected—Bill—to leave*). Let us take another sentence, which superficially resembles *John expected Bill to leave: John persuaded Bill to leave.* The click experiments might in principle tell us whether these sentences have the same structure. Suppose that in the recording of the two sentences, a click is inserted over the word *Bill.* If the click is perceived before *Bill* in the case of *expected* and after *Bill* in the case of *persuaded,* and if furthermore it is established that the perceptual displacement of the clicks depends on the surface syntactic structure, then one could conclude that the respective structures are:

(John expected (Bill to leave))

and *(John (persuaded Bill) (to leave)).*

If, on the other hand, the relevant experiments show that the perceived displacement of the clicks is the same in both cases, that is to say, if the click placed over *Bill* is displaced perceptually to the right (i.e., after *Bill*), that would indicate that "raising" has taken place, and that the subject of the embedded phrase has become the object of *expect.*

Such results might contribute to resolving the problem of whether "raising" takes place in these structures. To be sure, it is too early to hope for definitive answers from such experiments. But the logic of the situation is sufficiently clear. It is possible that significant relationships between perception and sentence structure will be experimentally demonstrated. In fact, anyone who is interested in the structure of language will hope for the development of such experimental techniques, because then one would have means for empirically testing theories of language structure through the study of models of perception, and vice versa.

Furthermore, we might expect that any progress made in the psychology of language will furnish suggestive models for other aspects of cognitive psychology (such as visual perception, formation of theories about the external world, whether those of common sense or of scientific research, etc.), which might be studied profitably in a similar manner: that is, by determining the basic properties of the acquired cognitive systems *and* by investigating the processes of acquisition and use of these systems.

Cognitive psychology would thus study each cognitive system as a particular "mental organ," having its own structure, and subsequently investigating their modes of interaction. For such modes of interaction exist: when we see something, we are in general capable of speaking about it, and command of appropriate terminology may play some role in sharpening visual perception. There is the possibility for a kind of "translation" between visual representation and spoken language. The same is true for other systems. Linguistics is one part of cognitive psychology: a part that is relatively easy to isolate. Language is a system (very rich, to be sure), but easy to isolate, among the various mental faculties.

M.R.:   It is clear that the psychology you founded, by filling the conceptual "gap" that inheres in the sciences of behavior with the theory of generative grammar, is very different from that experimental psychology which has been presented to us for a long time now, be it by Skinner or by Piaget. We are far removed from intelligence quotients and the absolute faith in tests.

N.C.:   Many people tend to think of psychology in terms of its tests and experimental methods. But one should not define a discipline by its procedures. It should be defined, in the first place, by the object of its investigation. Experimental or analytic procedures must be devised in order to shed light on this object. Behaviorist psychology, for example, excels in its experimental techniques, but it has not properly defined its object of inquiry, in my opinion. Thus it has excellent tools, very good tools . . . but nothing very much to study with them.

M.R.:   It was with this critique of behaviorism that you began your philosophic work. In your review article on Skinner, which appeared in *Language* in 1959, you rejected the scientific pretensions of the experimental methods which proceed by stimulus-response reinforcement and "operant conditioning," used to study animal behavior. For example, Skinner considers it of interest to ask *X* number of subjects what a painting of the Flemish School evokes for them. The elicited response that would be judged "good" by Skinner is: "For me it evokes Holland." However, you have pointed out that one could reply: "I feel the painting is hung too low," or "In my opinion the painting clashes with the flowered wallpaper." These experiments, you wrote, are as simple as they are empty.

N.C.: I must add that quite similar critiques were made by Wolfgang Köhler and by other Gestalt psychologists many years before, but with little effect. And we must not forget that, as I've just said, many of the experiments that have been developed show considerable ingenuity and elegance. Certainly one must preserve the experimental sophistication of behaviorist psychology, but in order to employ it rationally. The same thing is true in physics: perhaps there are more sophisticated experimental techniques than those devised by physicists to answer interesting questions, but which have no relevance to questions of scientific interest. It would then be senseless to define physics in terms of this technology of experimentation. In itself this technology has no interest, apart from its possible relevance to significant questions.

In the same way, psychological experiments have no interest, unless they can be put to use to sharpen our understanding of significant theories that can be developed concerning some significant object of study.

M.R.: Are there many psychologists who are working in the direction you have just defined, who are interested at the same time in the linguistic system and in the principles of its acquisition?

N.C.: Quite a few in this country. In France you have Jacques Mehler, for one. It is becoming an important field, and I hope to remain in close contact with it.

M.R.: But does experimental psycholinguistics always serve solely to verify linguists' hypotheses, or do you consider it a field with its own goals?

N.C.: As I mentioned before, there is in principle an interplay between the study of the structure of language (that part of psychology called "linguistics") and experimental psycholinguistics, which is largely concerned with models of perception and production. I am personally interested in the possibility of testing linguistic hypotheses. Certain questions cannot be resolved by sole reliance on the customary methods of linguistics. For example: the study of temporal processes, constraints on memory, the interactions between cognitive systems. Furthermore, the abstract study of grammar, and the kinds of data utilized by linguists, are simply insufficient to resolve certain questions concerning language. Linguistics can hope to characterize the class of possible grammars, that is, establish the abstract properties which every language must satisfy. Similarly, study of a particular language can at best specify abstract properties of its grammar. It is something like the study of algebra: every abstract algebra can be realized by many different real systems. The theory of groups can be realized by the number system, or by the rotation of objects. In a similar way the formal systems of the linguists can correspond to different real systems . . .

M.R.:   Just as in metrics, according to Morris Halle, the same abstract representation—XXXXXX, for example—can correspond to six vowels for the poet, to six roses for the gardener, or to six steps for the dancer . . .

N.C.:   And if the linguist is interested in the real nature of human beings—which is what I suppose—then he will seek to discover the system that is really utilized. The data of linguistics are not rich enough to answer these fascinating questions beyond a certain point. Therefore, the linguist must hope for further insight from the study of process models and neurological structures.

M.R.:   The linguistic model is a model of what is termed *competence.* You have just mentioned process models or models of *performance.* This opposition, *competence-performance,* was first clearly stated around 1964–5. You defined linguistic *competence* as that knowledge internalized by a speaker of a language, which, once learned and possessed, unconsciously permits him to understand and produce an infinite number of new sentences. *Generative grammar* is the explicit theory proposed to account for that competence. In performance, other cognitive systems, aside from competence (memory, etc.), intervene.

In *Language and Mind* you indicate that the other branches of psychology—dealing with vision, memory, and so on—must, in order to become scientific, define an equivalent concept of competence. Now it is evident that most psychologists oppose just that concept.

N.C.:   In my opinion, many psychologists have a curious definition of their discipline. A definition that is destructive, suicidal. A dead end. They want to confine themselves solely to the study of performance—behavior—yet, as I've said, it makes no sense to construct a discipline that studies the manner in which a system is acquired or utilized, but refuses to consider the nature of this system.

In my opinion, in order to do good psychology one must start by identifying a cognitive domain—vision, for example—that is to say, a domain which can be considered as a system, or a mental organ, that is more or less integrated. Once that system is identified, one can try to determine its nature, to investigate theories concerning its structure. To the extent that such a theory can be formulated, it is possible to ask on what basis the system is acquired, what are the analogues in it to universal grammar, its biologically given principles. Similarly, study of performance presupposes an understanding of the nature of the cognitive system that is put to use. Given some level of theoretical understanding of some cognitive system, we may hope to study in a productive way how the cognitive system is used, and how it enters into interaction with other cognitive systems. Something like that should be the paradigm for psychology, I think. Of course, this is an oversimplification. One cannot legislate the "order of discovery." But this paradigm seems to me basically correct.

M.R.:   That is the approach which you have followed in linguistics. You have identified the system: the *competence—*

and you have proposed a theory, that of *generative grammar*. Universal grammar is the set of hypotheses that bear on the acquisition of the system and so on. But such is not the customary path of psychology.

N.C.:   No, because until fairly recently psychologists have tried to leap over the initial stages; and going directly to the subsequent stages, they have been unable to accomplish as much as they could. Because you cannot study the acquisition or use of language in an intelligent manner without having some idea about this language which is acquired or utilized. If all you know of language is that it consists of words, or if you have a theory of the Saussurean type that tells you: "Here is a sequence of signs, each having a sound and a meaning," that limits very greatly the type of process model you can investigate. You must work with performance models, which produce word-by-word sequences, with no higher structure. You can only work with acquisition models, which acquire a system of concepts and sounds, and with the relations between these systems. That would be a primitive psychology, limited by the conception of language that was the point of departure. The same holds quite generally.

Psychologists often say that they don't presuppose a model of competence, that is to say, a theory of language. But that is not true; they could not do anything without having a conception of the nature of language. Every psychologist presupposes at least that language is a system of words: that is a model of competence. A very bad model of competence, but a model just the same. If they want to do better psychology, they must choose a better model of competence.

Why are many psychologists reluctant to consider richer and more abstract models of competence? Many linguists too, for the matter. In my opinion, because they are still under the influence of empiricist doctrines that are restricted in principle to quite elementary models of competence. These doctrines maintain that all learning, including language acquisition, proceeds by the accumulation of specific items, by the development of associations, by generalization along certain stimulus dimensions, by abstracting certain properties from a complex of properties. If this is the case, the models of competence are so trivial that it is possible to ignore them.

M.R.: When looked at this way, the Saussurean system of signs, conceived as a *store* slowly deposited in memory, corresponds very well, in effect, with the trivial empiricist model.

Do you know Gregory's experiments on vision? They prove that vision is produced by an interaction between an innate system and experience.

N.C.: Gregory is one of those who are trying to construct a model of *competence* for vision. That is interesting work, and it seems a logical way to treat these questions. Apparently, the visual cortex of mammals is predetermined in part, with a certain margin of indeterminacy. There exist, for example, cells of the visual cortex which are designed to perceive lines at a certain angle, and others at another angle; but the development of these receptors, their *density,* in particular, or their precise orientation within a predetermined range of potential orientation, all this depends on the visual environment, so it appears.

M.R.: Vision is thus a construction, like grammar?

N.C.: It seems that the general structure of the visual system is fixed, but the particular detailed realization remains open. For example, it is supposedly virtually impossible to determine precise binocular coordination genetically. It seems that visual experience is required to solve this engineering problem in a precise way, though binocular vision is genetically determined.

In general, serious psychology will be concerned primarily with domains in which human beings excel, where their capacities are exceptional. Language is one such case. There one is sure to find rich structures to study. In the domain of visual perception, for example, one of the most extraordinary abilities is to identify faces. How can one, after having seen a face from a certain angle, recognize it from another angle? That involves a remarkable geometric transformation. And to distinguish two faces! It would be no small task to design a device to match human performance in these respects.

It is possible that the theory of face perception resembles a generative grammar. Just as in language, if you suppose that there are base structures and transformed structures, then one might imagine a model which would generate the possible human faces, and the transformations which would tell you what each face would look like from all angles. To be sure, the formal theories would be very different from those of language . . .

M.R.: . . . because we are passing from linear sequence to volume.

N.C.:   There has also been very interesting work recently on the perceptual system of infants. During the past few years experimental methods have been devised that permit one to work with very young infants, even just a few days old, or a few weeks, and to determine some aspects of their perceptual systems, which exist, evidently, prior to relevant experience. It has been reported, for example, that infants distinguish the phonetic categories P, T, and K, which acoustically form a continuum: there is no line of demarcation between these categories, and no physical necessity to divide the acoustic continuum just this way. But perceptually they do not form a continuum. Particular stimuli along this dimension will be perceived as P or T or K. It seems that infants already make this categorial distinction, which indicates that it must reflect part of the human perceptual system that is not learned, but is rather an innate capacity, perhaps specifically related to language, though this is debated.

There is other work, on surprise reflexes, for example: if you present a small circle to a baby, which becomes a large circle, the infant will be startled. But if you present a circle, the size of which diminishes, there is no startle response. Such results have been reported informally, but I'm not sure that they have already been published or how firm they are. If they are correct, they suggest that there exists a mechanism, in effect innate, to recognize an approaching object. At the time this reflex does not have any function: the baby cannot move away in any fashion. That reflex would be built into the human perceptual system, and to find a functional explanation for it one would perhaps have to go back millions of years, to arrive at some evolutionary explanation.

M.R.:   Can they see when they are that young?

N.C.:   Again until recently, it was not known to what extent infants could see. One did not have any means of establishing that. Apparently, there is fairly complex visual perception well before the child can move. In any case, very early. One can also perhaps study linguistic capacities—as well as deficiencies, aphasia, and so forth—by similar methods.

There has been quite a bit of interesting work on the neurology of language, for example, on lateralization or the functions of the two hemispheres of the brain. Language is normally a left-hemisphere function primarily, and current work aims to clarify the specific functions of the two hemispheres. For instance, Bever has reported some work suggesting that musical analysis is carried out by the left side of the brain, which is concerned with analytic processing, while the right side keeps a sort of sensory account. That would be interesting if correct. While the phenomenon of lateralization does not occur solely among humans, it is in them that it is most highly developed.

These different lines of research are mutually supportive. In the coming years they may constitute one of the most exciting parts of science.

M.R.:   You do not mention sociology. However, sociolinguistics seem to have been widely accepted. This discipline seeks to look at the facts of language as realities produced by social classes. I'm thinking particularly of Labov's[1] work on non-standard English of the ghettos. In my opinion, that is also linguistics.

N.C.:   The study of various dialects certainly falls squarely within linguistics. But I do not see in what way the study of ghetto dialects differs from study of the dialects of university-trained speakers, from a purely linguistic point of view. On the theoretical level that is much the same thing. In fact, there are some who claim at times that there are certain theories concerning the study of language in society. Perhaps so, but I have not as yet *seen* such theories, or any specific account of the principles involved. Very few theoretical proposals have been made about these questions, to my knowledge.

Certainly, it is true that no individual speaks a well-defined language. The notion of language itself is on a very high level of abstraction. In fact, each individual employs a number of linguistic systems in speaking. How can one describe such an amalgam? Linguists have generally, and quite properly, proceeded in terms of an idealization: Let us assume, they say, the notion of a homogeneous linguistic community. Even if they don't admit it, that is what they do. It is the sole means of proceeding rationally, so it seems to me. You study ideal systems, then afterwards you can ask yourself in what manner these ideal systems are represented and interact in real individuals. Perhaps sociolinguistics might come up with some sort of principle concerning the variety of such systems, though I know of no results of this sort. It has been suggested that the language system of an individual does not consist in the interaction of ideal systems, but in a single system with some margin of variation. If that is it, then it's not very interesting.

I agree with what you say: that is part of linguistics. A linguistics that takes the idealization of ordinary linguistics one step closer to the complexity of reality. Fine.

M.R.: I think it is very important for Labov to show that the language of the ghetto has a grammar of its own, which is not defined as a collection of errors or infractions of standard English . . .

N.C.: . . . But who could doubt that? No linguist could possibly doubt that.

M.R.: All right, because linguists know that this is a linguistic principle. But Labov is primarily addressing teachers, pedagogues who do not recognize, in general, the legitimacy of the spoken language, and who, besides, have the ideological task of inculcating a feeling of inferiority in those who do not speak the standard dialect.

N.C.:   He is doing something very useful on the level of educational practice, in attempting to combat the prejudices of the society at large—and that is very good. But on the linguistic level, this matter is evident and banal. Stone Age man spoke a language similar to ours, so far as we know. It is evident that the language of the ghettos is of the same order as that of the suburbs. The study of Black English, from a linguistic point of view, is on a par with the study of Korean or of American Indian languages, or of the difference between the English of Cambridge, England, and Cambridge, Massachusetts. That is very useful work. But what disturbs me are the theoretical pretensions. We have here good descriptive linguistics, but it takes no sophistication in linguistics to establish the socially relevant conclusion. The same ideological aim is attained, for example, by Theodore Rosengarten in his book, *All God's Dangers,* which is the autobiography of Nate Shaw. Rosengarten transcribed the narrative of an old black man, who was illiterate and who had preserved an astonishing memory of his entire life. He was a sort of natural storyteller, whose life, involved in historic social struggles, is fascinating. Rosengarten, transcribing the spoken narration of this old man, is saying much the same thing as what you attribute to Labov: this man is also a human being, in fact, a human being who was altogether remarkable.

Perhaps some confusion arises from one of my statements, which has provoked more controversy than I had foreseen: I spoke of the necessity to conceive of a homogeneous linguistic community . . .

M.R.:   . . . As an idealization necessary for scientific work. Which, as you wrote, does not mean that reality is homogeneous; but such an idealization is necessary, in fact, automatic even, when one studies the language of the ghettos.

N.C.:   Of course. And all dialects. In my opinion, this is the rational way to approach the study of dialect variations: we are still always speaking of idealized systems. Only such systems have interesting properties. Combinations of systems rarely have interesting properties. Let me take an example: as a small child, my friend Morris Halle spoke five languages. Taken together these five languages do not have interesting properties. Individually, they do. In the same way, if someone speaks a collection of dialects, you will only discover a great confusion if you do not separate the elements of which this ensemble is composed.

M.R.:   Nevertheless, it seems important to me to confront the progressive work of Labov with the position in psycholinguistics of someone like Bernstein,[2] who reinforces and justifies social discrimination.

N.C.:   The work of Bernstein may very well be reactionary in its implications, and perhaps hardly worth discussing as a specimen of the rational study of language. I had believed it should no longer be necessary to say that the spoken language of an urban ghetto is a real language. But perhaps that's not the case. Some educators, and others, seem to take seriously the hypothesis about the severe limitations of competence among the children of the "lower classes." But the existence of a discipline called "sociolinguistics" remains for me an obscure matter.

M.R.:   More generally, what does sociology mean to you today?

N.C.:   Again, a discipline is defined in terms of its object and its results. Sociology is the study of society. As to its results, it seems that there are few things one can say about that, at least at a fairly general level. One finds observations, intuitions, impressions, some valid generalizations perhaps. All very valuable, no doubt, but not at the level of explanatory principles. Literary criticism also has things to say, but it does not have explanatory principles. Of course ever since the ancient Greeks people have been trying to find general principles on which to base literary criticism, but, while I'm far from an authority in this field, I'm under the impression that no one has yet succeeded in establishing such principles. Very much as in other human sciences. That is not a criticism. It is a characterization, which seems to me to be correct. Sociolinguistics is, I suppose, a discipline that seeks to apply principles of sociology to the study of language; but I suspect that it can draw little from sociology, and I wonder whether it is likely to contribute much to it.

M.R.: In general one links a social class to a set of linguistic forms in a manner that is almost bi-unique.

N.C.: You can also collect butterflies and make many observations. If you like butterflies, that's fine; but such work must not be confounded with research, which is concerned to discover explanatory principles of some depth and fails if it does not do so.

M.R.: Certain sociologists accuse linguistics of participating in the legitimation of the dominant language, in particular because of the concept of "competence," which is often confused, more or less, with skill in handling the language. But above all, they reproach linguistics for its idealization, which removes it from social reality.

N.C.: Opposition to idealization is simply objection to rationality; it amounts to nothing more than an insistence that we shall not have meaningful intellectual work. Phenomena that are complicated enough to be worth studying generally involve the interaction of several systems. Therefore you *must* abstract some object of study, you must eliminate those factors which are not pertinent. At least if you want to conduct an investigation which is not trivial. In the natural sciences this isn't even discussed, it is self-evident. In the human sciences, people continue to question it. That is unfortunate. When you work within some idealization, perhaps you overlook something which is terribly important. That is a contingency of rational inquiry that has always been understood. One must not be too worried about it. One has to face this problem and try to deal with it, to accommodate oneself to it. It is inevitable.

There are no simple criteria that provide the correct idealization, unless it is the criterion of obtaining meaningful results.

If you obtain good results, then you have reason to believe that you are not far from a good idealization. If you obtain better results by changing your point of view, then you have improved your idealization. There is a constant interaction between the definition of the domain of research and the discovery of significant principles. To reject idealization is puerile. It is particularly strange to hear such criticism from the left. Marxist political economy furnishes a classic and familiar example, with its idealizations and its far-reaching abstractions.

M.R.:   Aren't sociologists seeking to preserve the methods they use at present, their interviews, surveys, statistics, and so on, which take the place of scientific practice?

N.C.:   Again, in itself this type of approach is neither good nor bad. The question is whether it leads to the discovery of principles that are significant. We are back to the difference between natural history and natural science. In natural history, whatever you do is fine. If you like to collect stones, you can classify them according to their color, their shape, and so forth. Everything is of equal value, because you are not looking for principles. You are amusing yourself, and nobody can object to that. But in the natural sciences, it is altogether different. There the search is for the discovery of intelligible structure and for explanatory principles. In the natural sciences, the facts have no interest in themselves, but only to the degree to which they have bearing on explanatory principles or on hidden structures that have some intellectual interest. I think this whole discussion comes down to a confusion between two senses of the word *interesting.* Certain things are interesting in themselves—for example: human action. When a novelist deals with human actions, that's interesting; the flight of a bird, a flower, that's interesting. In this sense, natural history and descriptive sociology are interesting, just like a novel. Both deal with interesting phenomena, and display these to our view, perhaps even yield insight into them, somehow.

But there is another meaning of the word *interesting,* in physics, for example. A phenomenon in itself does not have interest for a physicist. In fact, physicists are generally interested, at least in the modern period, in "exotic" phenomena, of virtually no interest in themselves, in the first sense of the word *interesting*. What happens under the conditions of a scientific experiment is of no importance in itself. Its interest lies in its relation to whatever theoretical principles are at stake. Natural science, as distinct from natural history, is not concerned with the phenomena in themselves, but with the principles and the explanations that they have some bearing on. There is no right or wrong in the choice of one of these definitions of the word *interesting* (or some other sense, relating to utility, for example). It is not wrong to be interested in human actions or right to be interested in particle accelerators. There are simply two entirely different things. The attraction of sociology should not be based on a confusion between the two senses of the word.

In the study of language, too, you find strange phenomena. In English you cannot say:

John seems to the men to like each other

meaning that John seems to each of the men to like the others. There is nothing wrong with the intended meaning; it is just that this sentence doesn't express it. In itself that does not have any interest; no one ever says it, and that's all there is to the matter. But it happens that the phenomenon has intellectual interest, because it is linked to significant principles of linguistic theory.

The problem in the human sciences is that practitioners can easily find themselves in the position of describing phenomena of little interest and having nothing interesting to say about their subject. That is the worst of all; presenting, say, statistical analyses on subjects that are without interest ... To be sure, anthropology and sociology often achieve very interesting results. Take the work of my colleague Kenneth Hale, for example. He has been studying the "cultural wealth" of indigenous cultures and languages of Australia. These people can be characterized as among the most "primitive" in the world, at least from the point of view of technology. But they have developed intellectual systems which are extraordinarily complex, and language games which are incomparable . . .

M.R.: I remember reading his study of a game of antonyms, where each speaker must replace words by their opposites, according to certain rules . . .

N.C.: Yes, that is one example. What emerges from his work is very interesting, undoubtedly. These games could not have been invented simply to pass the time: they respond to fundamental intellectual needs. It has also been suggested that the proliferation of the extraordinarily complex and intricate systems of kinship may have no explanation in terms of social function . . .

M.R.: Thus he is opposed to the functionalism of Lévi-Strauss, which links the kinship system to exchange . . .

N.C.: Perhaps these kinship systems satisfy an intellectual need. They may be the kind of mathematics you can create if you don't have formal mathematics. The Greeks made up number theory, others make up kinship systems. Hale and others report informants who are exceptionally gifted in kinship systems, just as mathematicians can be gifted. These discoveries belong to anthropology, but naturally to psychology as well. They show how human beings create cultural richness under conditions of material privation. As far as these language games are concerned, children are said to have no difficulty at all in learning them. They seem to be linked to rites of puberty. All very strange and fascinating.

M.R.: These discoveries are "interesting" in both senses of the word.

It seems to me that the facts of language also offer these two ways of being interesting.

N.C.: Yes. Take a good traditional grammar: it presents those phenomena which have a "human" interest; for example, irregular verbs. Irregular verbs, that's amusing. But traditional grammar does not take interest in what some generative grammarians term the *specified subject condition,* * because the phenomena which are excluded by this condition have no "human interest."

For example, the sentence I mentioned earlier, *John seems to the men to like each other,* is excluded by the specified subject condition. But I doubt that any traditional grammar, even the most comprehensive one, would trouble to note that such sentences must be excluded. And that is quite legitimate, as far as traditional grammars of English are concerned; these grammars appeal to the intelligence of the reader instead of seeking explicitly to characterize this "intelligence." One can suppose that the specified subject condition—or any other principle which excludes this phrase—is simply an aspect of the intelligence of the speaker, an aspect of universal grammar; consequently, it does not require explicit instruction to the person who reads a traditional grammar.

For the linguist, the opposite is true. The linguist is interested in what the traditional grammars *don't say;* he is interested in the principles—or at least that is what should interest him, in my opinion.

M.R.:   The typical reaction one encounters in the human sciences, against idealization, thus seems linked to the fact that people are not interested in what they have in common, but . . .

N.C.:   . . . but in what differentiates them, yes. And in their normal human lives, this is the right decision. The same thing must be true of frogs. No doubt, they would not be interested

---

*This is a condition which forbids both the extraction of an element belonging to an embedded phrase, and also its association with an element that is outside this phrase, if the embedded phrase contains a "specified" subject—"specified" in a meaning of the term which must be defined precisely. For example, in the sentence, *We expected John to like each other,* the phrase *each other* cannot be associated with the antecedent *we,* so that the sentence does not express the meaning, "Each of us expected that John would like the other." The specified subject condition prevents this association, because of the presence of the subject *John* in the embedded clause, *John to like each other.* The same condition operates in the example given above: *John seems to the men to like each other.* Here the subject of *like* is not phonetically present, but is "understood" to be *John.* For a discussion of these questions, see Chomsky, *Reflections on Language* (New York: Pantheon, 1975), chapter 3.

in what makes them frogs, but in what makes them different from one another: whether one jumps further, etc.; anything that makes a frog remarkable for other frogs. The frogs assume that it is perfectly natural to be a frog. They are not preoccupied by "frogness."

M.R.:   Among Americans, "frogs" is also used to designate the French . . .

N.C.:   I did not have that in mind.

CHAPTER 3

A Philosophy of Language

M.R.: Your linguistic discoveries have led you to take positions in philosophy of language and in what is called "philosophy of knowledge." In particular, in your last book (*Reflections on Language*), you were induced to determine the limits of what is *knowable in thought;* as a result, the reflections on language became transformed virtually into a philosophy of science . . .

N.C.: Of course, it is not the study of language that determines what is to count as a scientific approach; but in fact this study provides a useful model to which one can refer in the investigation of human knowledge.

In the case of language, one must explain how an individual, presented with quite limited data, develops an extremely rich system of knowledge. The child, placed in a linguistic community, is presented with a set of sentences that is limited and often imperfect, fragmented, and so on. In spite of this, in a very short time he succeeds in "constructing," in internalizing the grammar of his language, developing knowledge that is very complex, that cannot be derived by induction or abstraction from what is given in experience. We conclude that the internalized knowledge must be limited very narrowly by some biological property. Whenever we encounter a similar situation, where knowledge is constructed from limited and imperfect data in a manner that is uniform and homogeneous among all individuals, we can conclude that a set of initial constraints plays a significant role in determining the cognitive system which is constructed by the mind.

We find ourselves faced with what may seem a paradox, though it is in fact not a paradox at all: where rich and complex knowledge can be constructed in a uniform way, as in the case of knowledge of language, there must exist constraints, limitations imposed by biological endowment on the cognitive systems that can be developed by the mind. The scope of attainable knowledge is linked in a fundamental way with its limits.

M.R.:   If all kinds of grammatical rules were possible, then the acquisition of these rules would become impossible; if all combinations of phonemes were possible, there would no longer be language. The study of language shows, on the contrary, to what extent the sequential combinations of words, of phonemes, are limited, that these combinations form only a small subset of the set of imaginable combinations. Linguistics must render explicit the rules which limit these combinations. But on the basis of these limits one obtains an infinity of language forms . . .

N.C.:   If sharp limits on attainable knowledge did not exist, we could never have such extensive knowledge as that of language. For the simple reason that without these prior limitations, we could construct an enormous number of possible systems of knowledge, each compatible with what is given in experience. So the uniform attainment of some specific system of knowledge that extends far beyond experience would be impossible: we might adopt different cognitive systems, with no possibility of determining which of these systems is in fact the right one. If we have a considerable number of theories that are comparable in credibility, that is virtually the same as having no theory at all.

Let us suppose that we discover a domain of intelligence where human beings excel. If someone has developed a rich explanatory theory in spite of the limitations of available evidence, it is legitimate to ask what the general procedure is that has permitted this move from experience to knowledge—what is the system of constraints that has made possible such an intellectual leap.

The history of science might provide some relevant examples. At certain times, rich scientific theories have been constructed on the basis of limited data, theories that were intelligible to others, consisting of propositions linked in some manner to the nature of human intelligence. Given such cases, we might try to discover the initial constraints that characterize these theories. That leads us back to posing the question: What is the "universal grammar" for intelligible theories; what is the set of biologically given constraints?

Suppose we can answer this question—in principle that might be possible. Then, the constraints being given, we can inquire into the kinds of theories that can in principle be attained. This amounts to the same thing as when we ask, in the case of language: Given a theory of universal grammar, what types of languages are in principle possible?

Let us refer to the class of theories made available by the biological constraints as *accessible theories.* It may be that this class will not be homogeneous, that there will be degrees of accessibility, accessibility relative to other theories, etc. In other words, the theory of accessibility may be more or less structured. The "universal grammar" for theory construction is then a theory of the structure of accessible theories. If this "universal grammar" is part of the biological endowment of a person, then given appropriate evidence, the person will, in some cases at least, have certain accessible theories available. Admittedly, I'm simplifying greatly.

Consider then the class of *true* theories. We can imagine that such a class exists, expressed, let us say, in some notation available to us. Then we can ask: What is the *intersection* of the class of accessible theories and the class of true theories, that is to say, which theories belong at the same time to the class of accessible theories and to the class of true theories? (Or we can raise more complex questions about degree of accessibility and relative accessibility.) Where such an intersection exists, a human being can attain real knowledge. And conversely, he cannot attain real knowledge beyond that intersection.

Of course, this is on the assumption that the human mind is part of nature, that it is a biological system like others, perhaps more intricate and complex than others that we know about but a biological system nevertheless, with its potential scope and its intrinsic limits determined by the very factors that provide its scope. Human reason, on this view, is not the universal instrument that Descartes took it to be but rather a specific biological system.

M.R.:   We come back again to the idea according to which scientific activity is not possible except within the biological limits of the human being . . .

N.C.:   But notice that there is no particular biological reason why such an intersection should exist. The capacity to invent nuclear physics provides an organism with no selectional advantage, and was not a factor in human evolution, it is reasonable to assume. The ability to solve algebra problems is not a factor in differential reproduction. There is, to my knowledge, no credible version of the view that these special capacities are somehow continuous with practical abilities, toolmaking and the like—which is not to deny, of course, that these special capacities developed for unknown reasons as a concomitant of evolution of the brain that may have been subject to selectional pressures.

In a sense, the existence of an intersection of the class of accessible theories and the class of true theories is a kind of biological miracle. It seems that this miracle took place at least in one domain, namely, physics, and the natural sciences that one might think of loosely as a kind of "extension" of physics: chemistry, biochemistry, molecular biology. In these domains, progress has been extremely rapid on the basis of limited data, and in a manner intelligible to others. Perhaps we are confronted here with a unique episode in human history: there is nothing to lead one to believe that we are a universal organism. Rather, we are subject to biological limitations with respect to the theories we can devise and comprehend, and we are fortunate to have these limitations, for otherwise we could not construct rich systems of knowledge and understanding at all. But these limitations may well exclude domains about which we would like very much to know something. That's too bad. Perhaps there is another organism with a differently organized intelligence that would be capable of what we are not. This is, as a first approximation, a reasonable one in my opinion, a way to think about the question of acquisition of conscious knowledge.

Going a step further, it is not unimaginable that a particular organism might come to examine its *own* system of acquiring knowledge; it might thus be able to determine the class of intelligible theories which it can attain. I don't see any contradiction in that. A theory which is found to be unintelligible, an "inaccessible theory" in the sense just given, does not thereby become intelligible or accessible.

It would simply be identified. And if in some domain of thought the accessible theories turn out to be remote from the true theories, that's too bad. Then human beings can, at best, develop a kind of intellectual technology, which for inexplicable reasons predicts certain things in these domains. But they won't truly *understand* why the technology is working. They will not possess an intelligible theory in the sense that an interesting science is intelligible. Their theories, though perhaps effective, will be intellectually unsatisfying.

Looking at the history of human intellectual endeavor from this point of view, we find curious things, surprising things. In mathematics certain areas seem to correspond to exceptional human aptitudes: number theory, spatial intuition. Pursuit of these intuitions determined the main line of progress in mathematics, until the end of the nineteenth century, at least. Apparently our mind is capable of handling the abstract properties of number systems, abstract geometry, and the mathematics of the continuum. These are not the absolute limits, but it is probable that we are confined to certain branches of science and mathematics.

Presumably, all that I have just said would be rejected by a strict empiricist, or even regarded as senseless.

M.R.:   That is to say by someone who believes in the proposition according to which man proceeds by induction and generalization in the acquisition of knowledge, starting from "empty" or "blank" minds, without a priori biological limitations. Within that framework, knowledge is no more determined by the structure of the mind than is the form of a design by the wax tablet . . .

N.C.:   Yes. These empiricist hypotheses have very little plausibility, in my opinion; it does not seem possible to account for the development of commonsense understanding of the physical and social world, or science, in terms of processes of induction, generalization, abstraction, and so on. There is no such direct path from data that are given to intelligible theories.

The same is true in other domains, music, for example. After all, you can always imagine innumerable musical systems, most of which will seem to the human ear to be just noise. There too, biological factors determine the class of possible musical systems for human beings, though what exactly this class may be is an open and currently debated question.

In this case as well, no direct functional explanation seems available. Musical ability is not a factor in reproduction. Music does not improve material well-being, does not permit one to function better in society, etc. Quite simply, it responds to the human need for aesthetic expression. If we study human nature in a proper way, we may discover that certain musical systems correspond to that need, while others do not.

M.R.:   Among those fields in which the scientific approach has not made any progress in two thousand years you list the study of human behavior.

N.C.:   Behavior, yes, that is one such case. The basic questions have been posed since the beginning of historical memory:

the question of causation of behavior seems simple enough to pose, but virtually no theoretical progress has been made in answering it. One might formulate the basic question as follows: Consider a function of certain variables such that, given the values of the variables, the function will give us the behavior that results under the conditions specified by these values, or perhaps some distribution over possible behaviors. But no such function has been seriously proposed, even to a weak approximation, and the question has remained without issue. In fact, we don't know of any reasonable way to approach the problem. It is conceivable that this persistent failure is to be explained on the grounds that the true theory of behavior is beyond our cognitive reach. Therefore we can make no progress. It would be as if we tried to teach a monkey to appreciate Bach. A waste of time . . .

M.R.: Then the question of behavior would be different from the question of syntax: that too had never been posed before the development of generative grammar.

N.C.: But in this case, once the question is posed, everyone comes up with answers that are similar or comparable. When certain questions are posed, sometimes the answer is impossible to imagine, sometimes answers begin to appear quite widely. And when an answer is proposed, those who have an adequate understanding of the question will also regard the answer as intelligible. It is often the case that a question cannot yet properly be posed, or posed with the requisite degree of sophistication; but then it can sometimes be posed properly, and still seem to lie beyond our intellectual grasp.

Another analogue to the case of language, perhaps, is our comprehension of the social structures in which we live. We have all sorts of tacit and complex knowledge concerning our relations to other people. Perhaps we have a sort of "universal grammar" of possible forms of social interaction, and it is this system which helps us to organize intuitively our imperfect perceptions of social reality, though it does not follow necessarily that we are capable of developing conscious theories in this domain through the exercise of our "science-forming faculties." If we succeed in finding our place within our society, that is perhaps because these societies have a structure that we are prepared to seek out. With a little imagination we could devise an artificial society in which no one could ever find his place . . .

M.R.:   Then you can compare the failure of artificial languages with the failure of utopian societies?

N.C.:   Perhaps. One cannot learn an artificial language constructed to violate universal grammar as readily as one learns a natural language, simply by being immersed in it. At most, one might conceive of such a language as a game, a puzzle . . . In the same way we can imagine a society in which no one could survive as a social being because it does not correspond to biologically determined perceptions and human social needs. For historical reasons, existing societies might have such properties, leading to various forms of pathology.

Any serious social science or theory of social change must be founded on some concept of human nature. A theorist of classical liberalism such as Adam Smith begins by affirming that human nature is defined by a propensity to truck and barter, to exchange goods: that assumption accords very well with the social order he defends. If you accept that premise (which is hardly credible), it turns out that human nature conforms to an idealized early capitalist society, without monopoly, without state intervention, and without social control of production.

If, on the contrary, you believe with Marx or the French and German Romantics that only social cooperation permits the full development of human powers, you will then have a very different picture of a desirable society. There is always some conception of human nature, implicit or explicit, underlying a doctrine of social order or social change.

M.R.:   To what degree can your discoveries about language and your definitions of fields of knowledge lead to the emergence of new philosophic questions? To which philosophy do you feel closest?

N.C.:   In relation to the questions we have just been discussing, the philosopher to whom I feel closest and whom I'm almost paraphrasing is Charles Sanders Peirce. He proposed an interesting outline, very far from complete, of what he called "abduction" . . .

M.R.: Abduction is, I believe, a form of inference which does not depend solely on a priori principles (like deduction), nor solely on experimental observation (like induction). But that aspect of Peirce is very little known in France.

N.C.: Or here in the United States either. Peirce argued that to account for the growth of knowledge, one must assume that "man's mind has a natural adaptation to imagining correct theories of some kinds," some principle of "abduction" which "puts a limit on admissible hypothesis," a kind of "instinct," developed in the course of evolution. Peirce's ideas on abduction were rather vague, and his suggestion that biologically given structure plays a basic role in the selection of scientific hypotheses seems to have had very little influence. To my knowledge, almost no one has tried to develop these ideas further, although similar notions have been developed independently on various occasions. Peirce has had an enormous influence, but not for this particular reason.

M.R.: More in semiology . . .

N.C.: Yes, in that general area. His ideas on abduction developed Kantian ideas to which recent Anglo-American philosophy has not been very receptive. As far as I know, his approach in epistemology has never been followed up, even though there has been much criticism of inductivist approaches —Popper, for example.

Russell, for his part, was much preoccupied in his later work (*Human Knowledge*) with the inadequacy of the empiricist approach to the acquisition of knowledge. But this book has generally been ignored. He proposed various principles of *non-demonstrative inference* with the aim of accounting for the knowledge which in reality we possess.

M.R.: Non-demonstrative inference differs from the deductions of mathematical logic to the degree where, in spite of the truth of the premises and the rigorous character of the reasoning, the truth of the conclusions is not guaranteed; they are only rendered *probable*. Is that it?

N.C.:   In substance, yes: one might say that his approach here was Kantian to a certain degree, but with fundamental differences. In some way, Russell remained an empiricist. His principles of non-demonstrative inference are *added* one by one to the fundamental principle of induction, and do not offer a radical change in perspective. But the problem is not quantitative, it is qualitative. The principles of non-demonstrative inference do not fulfill the need. I believe a radically different approach is necessary, which takes a starting point that is quite remote from empiricist presuppositions. This is true not only for scientific knowledge, where it is generally accepted today, but also for what we can call the constructions of "common-sense understanding," that is, for our ordinary notions concerning the nature of the physical and social world, our intuitive comprehension of human actions, their ends, their reasons, and their causes, etc.

These are very important issues, which would demand much more analysis than I can give here. But to return to your question, a great deal of the work of contemporary philosophers on language and the nature of scientific research has been very stimulating for me. My own work, from the very beginning, was greatly influenced by developments in philosophy (as the published acknowledgments of indebtedness indicate; particularly, to Nelson Goodman and W. V. Quine). And that continues to be true. To mention only a few examples, the work of John Austin on speech acts proved very fruitful, as well as that of Paul Grice on the logic of conversation. At present very interesting work is being pursued on the theory of meaning along various lines. One can cite the contributions of Saul Kripke, Hilary Putnam, Jerrold Katz, Michael Dummett, Julius Moravcsik, Donald Davidson, and many others. Certain of the work on model-theoretic semantics—the study of "truth in possible worlds"—seems promising. In particular, I would mention the work of Jaakko Hintikka and his colleagues, which deals with questions that are central to quite a range of topics in syntax and semantics of natural languages, particularly with regard to quantification. Such work has also been extended to pragmatics, that is to the study of the manner in which language is used to accomplish certain human ends; for example, the work of the Israeli philosopher Asa Kasher. As these few brief references indicate, this work is being done on an international scale and is not just Anglo-American.

I should also mention work on history and philosophy of science, which has begun to furnish a richer and more exact understanding of the manner in which ideas develop and take root in the natural sciences. This work—for example, that of Thomas Kuhn or Imre Lakatós—has gone well beyond the often artificial models of verification and falsification, which were prevalent for a long time and which exercised a dubious influence on the "soft sciences," as the latter did not rest on the foundations of a healthy intellectual tradition that could guide their development. It is useful, in my opinion, for people working in these fields to become familiar with ways in which the natural sciences have been able to progress; in particular, to recognize how, at critical moments of their development, they have been guided by radical idealization, a concern for depth of insight and explanatory power rather than by a concern to accommodate "all the facts"—a notion that approaches meaninglessness—even at times disregarding apparent counterexamples in the hope (which at times has proven justified only after many years or even centuries) that subsequent insights would explain them. These are useful lessons that have been obscured in much of the discussion about epistemology and the philosophy of science.

M.R.:   What do you think of European philosophers, of the French in particular?

N.C.:   Outside of Anglo-American philosophy, I do not know enough about contemporary philosophers to discuss them at all seriously.

M.R.:   Have you ever met any French Marxist philosophers?

N.C.:   Rarely. Here some distinctions are necessary. Contemporary Marxist philosophy has been linked in large part to Leninist doctrine, at least until recently. European Marxism after World War I developed unfortunate tendencies, in my opinion: the tendencies associated with Bolshevism, which has always seemed to me an authoritarian and reactionary current. The latter became dominant within the European Marxist tradition after the Russian Revolution. But much more to my taste, at least, are quite different tendencies, for example, that range of opinion that extends roughly from Rosa Luxemburg and the Dutch Marxist Anton Pannekoek and Paul Mattick to the anarcho-syndicalist Rudolf Rocker and others.

These thinkers have not contributed to philosophy in the sense of our discussion; but they have much to say about society, about social change, and the fundamental problems of human life. Though not about problems of the sort that we have been discussing, for example.

Marxism itself has become too often a sort of church, a theology.

Of course, I'm generalizing far too much. Work of value has been done by those who consider themselves Marxists. But up to a certain point this criticism is justified, I'm afraid. In any case, I do not believe that Marxist philosophy, of whatever tendency, has made a substantial contribution to the kind of questions we have been discussing.

For the rest, what I know has not impressed me greatly and has not encouraged me to seek to know more.

M.R.:   But you met Michel Foucault, I believe, during a television broadcast in Amsterdam?

N.C.:   Yes, and we had some very good discussions before and during the broadcast. On Dutch television, we spoke for several hours, he in French and I in English; I don't know what the Dutch television viewers made of all that. We found ourselves in at least partial agreement, it seemed to me, on the question of "human nature," and perhaps not as much on politics (the two basic points about which Fons Elders interviewed us).

As far as the concept of human nature and its relation to scientific progress was concerned, it seemed that we were "climbing the same mountain, starting from opposite directions," to repeat a simile which Elders suggested. In my view, scientific creativity depends on two facts: on the one hand, on an intrinsic property of mind, and on the other, on a combination of social and intellectual conditions. There is no question of choosing between these. In order to understand a scientific discovery, it is necessary to understand the interaction between these factors. But personally I am more interested in the first, while Foucault stresses the second.

Foucault considers the scientific knowledge of a given epoch to be like a *grid* of social and intellectual conditions, like a system the rules of which permit the creation of new knowledge. In his view, if I understand him correctly, human knowledge is transformed due to social conditions and social struggles, with one grid replacing the other, thus bringing new possibilities to science. He is, I believe, skeptical about the possibility or the legitimacy of an attempt to place important sources of human knowledge within the human mind, conceived in an ahistorical manner.

His position also involves a different usage of the term *creativity.* When I speak of creativity in this context, I am not making a value judgment: creativity is an aspect of the ordinary and daily use of language and of human action in general. However, when Foucault speaks of creativity he is thinking more of the achievements of a Newton, for example—although he stresses the common social and intellectual base for the creations of scientific imagination, rather than the achievements of an individual genius—that is to say, he is thinking of the conditions for radical innovation. His use of the term is a more normal one than mine. But even if contemporary science may find some solution to problems relating to ordinary, normal creativity—and I am rather skeptical even about this—still it cannot hope, certainly, to be able to come to grips with true creativity in the more usual sense of the word, or, say, to foresee the achievements of great artists or the future discoveries of science. That seems a hopeless quest. In my opinion, the sense in which I am speaking of "normal creativity" is not unlike what Descartes had in mind when he made the distinction between a human being and a parrot. In the historical perspective of Foucault, one no longer seeks to identify the innovators and their specific achievement or the obstacles which stand in the way of the emergence of truth, but to determine how knowledge, as a system independent of individuals, modifies its own rules of formation.

M.R.:   In defining the knowledge of an epoch as a grid or system, doesn't Foucault draw near to structuralist thought, which also conceives of language as a system?

N.C.:   To reply properly it would be necessary to study this matter in depth. In any case, while I have been speaking of the limitations imposed on a class of accessible theories—linked to the limitations of the human mind that permit the construction of rich theories in the first place—he is more interested in the proliferation of theoretical possibilities resulting from the diversity of social conditions within which human intelligence can flourish.

M.R.:   In the same way, structuralist linguistics stresses the differences between languages.

N.C.:   I have to be cautious in response, because the expression "structural linguistics" can cover a great variety of positions. It is certainly true that American "neo-Bloomfieldian" linguists, who sometimes call themselves "structuralists," have been impressed above all by the diversity of languages, and that some of them, like Martin Joos, have gone so far as to declare, as a general proposition of linguistic science, that languages can differ from one another in an arbitrary manner. When they speak of "universals," this involves a characterization of a very limited nature, perhaps some statistical observations. On the other hand, such a characterization would be very wide of its mark in the case of other schools of structural linguistics; for example, the work of Roman Jakobson, who has always been concerned with linguistic universals which narrowly constrain the class of possible languages, especially in phonology.

As far as Foucault is concerned, as I've said, he seems skeptical about the possibility of developing a concept of "human nature" that is independent of social and historical conditions, as a well-defined biological concept. I don't believe that he would characterize his own approach as "structuralist." I don't share his skepticism. I would be in agreement with him in saying that human nature is not as yet within the range of science. Up to the present, it has escaped the reach of scientific inquiry; but I believe that in specific domains such as the study of language, we can begin to formulate a significant concept of "human nature," in its intellectual and cognitive aspects. In any case, I would not hesitate to consider the faculty of language as part of human nature.

M.R.: Did you and Foucault speak of the Port-Royal *Grammaire Générale*?

N.C.: More precisely, about my relationship to the work on the history of ideas. There are a number of misunderstandings on this subject.

These questions can be approached in various ways. My approach to the early modern rationalist tradition, for example, is not that of a historian of science or of philosophy. I have not attempted to reconstruct in an exhaustive manner what people thought at that time, but rather to bring to light certain important insights of the period that have been neglected, and often seriously distorted, in later scholarship, and to show how at that time certain persons had already discerned important things, perhaps without being fully aware of it. These specific intentions are spelled out quite explicitly in my book *Cartesian Linguistics,* for example.

I was interested in earlier stages of thought and speculation relating to questions of contemporary significance. And I tried to show in what ways and to what extent similar ideas were formulated, anticipations of later developments, perhaps from rather different perspectives. I think that we can often see, from our current vantage point in the progress of understanding, how a thinker of the past was groping toward certain extremely significant ideas, frequently in a very constructive and remarkable manner, and perhaps with only a partial awareness of the nature of his quest.

Let me offer an analogy. I am not proceeding in the manner of an art historian so much as that of an art lover, a person who looks for what has value to him in the seventeenth century, for example, that value deriving in large measure from the contemporary perspective with which he approaches these objects. Both types of approach are legitimate. I think it is possible to turn toward earlier stages of scientific knowledge, and by virtue of what we know today, to shed light on the significant contributions of the period in a way in which the most creative geniuses could not, because of the limitations of their time. This was the nature of my interest in Descartes, for example, and in the philosophical tradition that he influenced, and also Humboldt, who would not have considered himself a Cartesian: I was interested in his effort to make sense of the concept of free creativity based on a system of internalized rules, an idea that has certain roots in Cartesian thought, I believe.

The kind of approach I was taking has been criticized, but not on any rational grounds, so far as I can see. Perhaps I should have discussed the nature and legitimacy of such an approach in more detail, though it seemed to me (and still seems to me) obvious. What I have been saying is quite familiar in the history of science. For example, Dijksterhuis, in his major work on the origins of classical mechanics, points out, with reference to Newton, that "Properly speaking, the whole system can only be understood in the light of the subsequent development of the science."[1] Suppose that the insights of classical mechanics had been lost, and there had been a reversion to something more akin to "natural history"—the accumulation and organization of large amounts of data and phenomenal observations, perhaps a kind of Babylonian astronomy (though even this reference is probably unfair). Then suppose that in some new phase of science, questions similar to those of the period of classical mechanics had reemerged. It would then have been entirely appropriate, quite important in fact, to try to discover significant insights of an earlier period and to determine in what ways they were anticipations of current work, perhaps to be understood properly in the light of subsequent developments. This it seems to me is more or less what happened in the study of language and mind, and I think it is quite interesting to recover insights that have long been neglected, approaching earlier work (which has often been grossly misrepresented, as I showed) from the standpoint of current interests and trying to see how questions discussed in an earlier period can be understood, and sometimes reinterpreted, in the light of more recent understanding, knowledge, and technique. This is a legitimate approach, not to be confused with efforts (like those of Dijksterhuis in physics) to reconstruct exactly how the issues appeared and how ideas were constructed at an earlier time. Of course, one must be careful not to falsify earlier discussion, but I am aware of no critical analysis of my work that shows this to be the case. There has, I am sorry to say, been a good deal of outright misrepresentation of what I wrote, in what is called "the scholarly literature," and I have been surprised to find sharp criticism of my alleged views even on topics that I did not discuss at all. I have commented occasionally on some of these falsifications, as have others, but by no means exhaustively, and I won't pursue it here.

Any person engaged in intellectual work can do the same thing with himself: you can try to reconsider what you understood twenty years ago, and thus see in what direction, in a confused manner, you were striving to go, toward what goal that perhaps became clear and intelligible only much later . . .

M.R.: What were the political disagreements between you and Foucault?

N.C.: For my part, I would distinguish two intellectual tasks. One is to imagine a future society that conforms to the exigencies of human nature, as best we understand them; the other, to analyze the nature of power and oppression in our present societies. For him, if I understand him rightly, what we can imagine now is nothing but a product of the bourgeois society of the modern period: the notions of justice or of "realization of the human essence" are only the inventions of our civilization and result from our class system. The concept of justice is thus reduced to a pretext advanced by a class that has or wants to have access to power. The task of a reformer or revolutionary is to gain power, not to bring about a more just society. Questions of abstract justice are not posed, and perhaps cannot even be posed intelligibly. Foucault says, again if I understand him correctly, that one engages in the class struggle to win, not because that will lead to a more just society. In this respect I have a very different opinion. A social struggle, in my view, can only be justified if it is supported by an argument—even if it is an indirect argument based on questions of fact and value that are not well understood—which purports to show that the consequences of this struggle will be beneficial for human beings and will bring about a more decent society. Let us take the case of violence. I am not a committed pacifist, and thus do not say that it is wrong to use violence in all circumstances, say in self-defense. But any recourse to violence must be justified, perhaps by an argument that it is necessary to remedy injustice. If a revolutionary victory of the proletariat were to lead to putting the rest of the world into crematoria, then the class struggle is not justified. It can only be justified by an argument that it will bring an end to class oppression, and do so in a way that accords with fundamental human rights. Complicated questions arise here, no doubt, but they should be faced. We were in apparent disagreement, because where I was speaking of justice, he was speaking of power. At least, that is how the difference between our points of view appeared to me.[2]

CHAPTER 4

Empiricism and Rationalism

M.R.: On many occasions you have criticized philosophic and scientific empiricism. Can you state your objections more precisely?

N.C.: In a sense, empiricism has developed a kind of mind-body dualism, of a quite unacceptable type, just at the time when, from another point of view, it rejected such dualism. Within an empiricist framework, one approaches the study of the body as a topic in the natural sciences, concluding that the body is constructed of varied and specialized organs which are extremely complex and genetically determined in their basic character, and that these organs interact in a manner which is also determined by human biology. On the other hand, empiricism insists that the brain is a tabula rasa, empty, unstructured, uniform at least as far as cognitive structure is concerned. I don't see see any reason to believe that; I don't see any reason to believe that the little finger is a more complex organ than those parts of the human brain involved in the higher mental faculties; on the contrary, it is not unlikely that these are among the most complex structures in the universe. There is no reason to believe that the higher mental faculties are in some manner dissociated from this complexity of organization.

One can say that the dualism introduced by empiricist dogma is methodological rather than substantive. That is to say, it is taken for granted that the body must be studied by the ordinary methods of science, but in the case of the mind certain preconceptions have been imposed which have virtually removed this study from the domain of scientific inquiry. In fact, this dogmatism seems to be even more striking in the most recent period. Hume, for example, really did his best to show that his elementary principles concerning the acquisition of human knowledge were sufficient to cover an interesting class of cases and challenged his opponents to produce a legitimate "idea" that could not be derived from sense impression by his principles. There is a certain kind of ambiguity in his procedure here, since in part he seems to be engaged in a kind of scientific inquiry, trying to show that certain principles he proposed were in fact adequate to cover the crucial cases, while at other times he relies on these principles to demonstrate that some notion is "illegitimate," since it cannot be derived by them—an argument that rests on our accepting his not very plausible principles concerning the nature of the mind. Hume regarded the principle of inductive reasoning as a kind of "animal instinct," which would appear to be an empirical assumption. In modern versions, his assumptions have often been converted into dogma presupposed without serious effort to show them to be valid, or to reply to classical criticisms that were raised against these principles.

There is no reason to believe today that Hume's principles or anything resembling them are adequate to account for our "ideas" or our knowledge and beliefs, nor to think that they have any particular significance. There is no place for any a priori doctrine concerning the complexity of the brain or its uniformity as far as the higher mental functions are concerned. We must proceed to the investigation of the diverse cognitive structures developed normally by human beings in the course of their maturation and their relation to the physical and social environment, seeking to determine, as best we can, the principles which govern these cognitive structures. Once a certain understanding of the nature of these systems has been obtained, then we can reasonably study the basis on which they are acquired. In my opinion, the little that we know about these questions suggests that the mind, like the body, is in effect a system of organs—we could call them "mental organs" by analogy—that is to say, highly specific systems organized according to a genetic program that determines their function, their structure, the process of their development, in quite a detailed manner; the particular realization of these fundamental principles naturally depends on their interaction with the environment, as in the case of the visual system which we mentioned previously. If that is correct, the mind is a complex system of interacting faculties, which do not develop by means of uniform principles of "general intelligence"; it is constituted of "mental organs" just as specialized and differentiated as those of the body.

M.R.: It is for that reason, doubtless, that you insist on the autonomy of grammar, on the fact that grammatical structures do not depend on other cognitive systems. Does it seem impossible to you to think of language and the structure of knowledge in terms of the same model?

N.C.: I have nothing against comparisons, but I wonder whether we are likely to learn very much by proceeding in this direction. Note that one never tends toward that kind of proposal in physiology; no one suggests that we study the structure of the eye and the heart, and then search for analogies between them. One does not expect to find meaningful analogies. If the mind consists of a system of "mental organs," in interaction, certainly, but fundamentally different in their structure, we need not expect to find fruitful analogies among them.

To make myself clear, I am not about to propose all this as a new dogma, to replace empiricist doctrine. On the contrary, just as in studying the body, we must simply retain an open mind on this subject. We know a little about a number of cognitive systems, language being the most interesting case at the moment. That small degree of insight seems to me to suggest the preceding conclusions. The important thing, of course, is to determine the deeper principles and the detailed structure of various cognitive systems, their modes of interaction, and the general conditions which each system satisfies. If one finds that these systems are acquired in a uniform manner with very little specific structure, very well. But for the present at least it seems to me that quite different conclusions are indicated. That is what I mean when I say that one need not expect to find analogies.

M.R.:   Nor phenomena of interdependence. However, certain psychologists assert that perception exerts an influence on the potential structure of sentences. An essential aspect of your critique of empiricism is the rationalist hypothesis: the structure of the brain is determined a priori by the genetic code, the brain is programmed to analyze experience and to construct knowledge out of that experience. That may seem shocking . . .

N.C.:   I don't see anything shocking in that proposition. In physiology no one has ever accepted anything analogous to empiricist dogma with regard to the mind. No one finds it outlandish to ask the question: What genetic information accounts for the growth of arms instead of wings? Why should it be shocking to raise similar questions with regard to the brain and mental faculties? We are back to the methodological dualism of the empiricists.

M.R.:   That position does not suit contemporary "human sciences."

N.C.:   Especially not behaviorist psychology, or perhaps even Piaget, though his position seems to me obscure in crucial respects. Piaget considers himself to be an anti-empiricist; but some of his writings suggest to me that he is mistaken in this conclusion. Piaget develops a certain "constructive interactionism": new knowledge is constructed through interaction with the environment. But the fundamental question is evaded: *How* is this knowledge constructed, and why *just this kind* of knowledge and not some other? Piaget does not give any intelligible answer, as far as I can make out. The only answer that

I can imagine is to suppose an innate genetic structure which determines the process of maturation. Insofar as he considers it wrong to give such an answer, he falls back into something like the empiricism that he wants to reject. What he postulates is nowhere near sufficient, it seems to me, to account for the specific course of cognitive development.

That is not to deny the very great importance of the research that has been conducted by Piaget and his group at Geneva; it has opened up entirely new perspectives in the study of human knowledge. It is primarily the interpretation of their results which seems extremely doubtful to me, in particular their attitude toward what Piaget calls "innéisme," which seems to me altogether wrong.

In philosophy, the same problems appear in some of the work of Quine, for example.[1] At times he asserts that theories are developed by induction, which he identifies with conditioning. At other times he says the opposite: theories are not determined solely by conditioning or induction, but involve abstract hypotheses ultimately originating from some innate capacity.

In recent years he has oscillated between these two positions.[2]

Functionalism

M.R.: The tendency of thought which has fought hardest against the independence of grammar as a "mental organ" is without doubt functionalism. It tends to explain the form of language by attributing a determining role to its function. This function is presumed to be *communication:* everything in language must contribute to communication, to a better communication, and inversely, nothing is linguistic which does not contribute to communication. Isn't that a fairly accurate portrait?

N.C.: Functionalism holds that the use of language influences its form. This might be understood as a variant of empiricist doctrine about language learning, one that makes very little sense, as far as I can see. But we might understand the fundamental ideas quite differently. For example, George Miller and I suggested about fifteen years ago that there may be a "functional explanation" for the organization of language with grammatical transformations, which would be a well-designed system corresponding to a certain organization of short- and long-term memory, for example.

If one could demonstrate that, it would be interesting. But what does that mean basically? What would the analogous observation mean for some physical organ, say the heart? To be sure, the heart has a function: to pump blood. One may sensibly say that the structure of the heart is determined by that function. But suppose we ask the ontogenetic question: How does our heart become what it is? How does it grow in the individual from the embryo to its final form in the mature organism? The answer is not functional: the heart does not develop in the individual because it would be useful to carry out a certain function, but rather because the genetic program determines that it will develop as it does.

Every organ has certain functions, but these functions do not determine the ontogenetic development of the organism. Nobody would suggest that a group of cells decides that perhaps it would be a good idea to become a heart because such an organ is necessary to pump blood. If this group of cells becomes a heart, it is due to the information present in the genetic code, which determines the structure of the organism.

There is a place for functional explanation, but it is on the level of evolution. It is possible that a heart develops in the course of evolution in order to satisfy a certain function. Of course, I'm simplifying enormously. But this is a point that is useful to keep in mind: functional explanation does not relate to the way organs develop in the individual.

Let's go back to linguistics: here comparable remarks can be made. To my knowledge, no functional principle with very great plausibility has yet been proposed. But suppose that someone proposes a principle which says: The form of language is such-and-such because having that form permits a function to be fulfilled—a proposal of this sort would be appropriate at the level of evolution (of the species, or of language), not at the level of acquisition of language by an individual, one would suppose.

M.R.: As a consequence, insofar as your linguistics is a theory of language *and* of the acquisition of language by an individual, functionalism cannot be retained as a fundamental principle. Inversely, one might note that the legitimacy of the dependency relation between function and structure is not even a problem for functionalist linguists, because their aim is not to explain the acquisition of language but to *describe* a linguistic corpus.

N.C.: I doubt that functionalist linguists would accept that characterization. If they mean that ontogenetic development is directed by functional considerations, that seems just as plausible to me as suggesting that the development of the heart in the individual is guided by the utility of having an organ that pumps blood, and about as well supported by the factual evidence. Or, they might say that questions touching on the basis of language acquisition do not concern them. The crucial point, however, seems to me to be that there is no real debate about the validity of functionalism at the generally vague level on which we discuss the hypothetical evolution of the species, or in the study of language change; and there is no sensible way to invoke functional notions as explanatory concepts at the synchronic or ontogenetic level, so far as I can see.

It also seems to me important to avoid a certain vulgarization with respect to the use of language. There is no reason to believe —to repeat myself once again—that language "essentially" serves instrumental ends, or that the "essential purpose" of language is "communication," as is often said, at least if we mean by "communication" something like transmitting information or inducing belief. Someone who claims that this is *the* essential purpose of language must explain just what he means by it, and why he believes this function, and no other, to be so uniquely significant.

Language is used in many different ways. Language can be used to transmit information, but it also serves many other purposes: to establish relations among people, to express or clarify thought, for play, for creative mental activity, to gain understanding, and so on. In my opinion, there is no reason to accord privileged status to one or the other of these modes. Forced to choose, I would have to say something quite classical and rather empty: language serves essentially for the expression of thought.

I know of no reason to suppose that instrumental ends, or transmission of information about one's beliefs, or other actions that might reasonably be called "communication" (unless, of course, the term is used quite vacuously), have some unique significance compared with other characteristic uses of language. In fact, what is meant by the assertion that such-and-such is *the* goal of language, or its essential purpose, is far from clear.

Once again, this plurality of modes is characteristic of the most banal and normal use of language.

It is hard to know just what people mean when they say that language is "essentially" an instrument of communication. If you press them a bit and ask them to be more precise, you will often find, for example, that under "communication" they include communication with oneself. Once you admit that, the notion of communication loses all content; the expression of thought becomes a kind of communication. These proposals seem to be either false, or quite empty, depending on the interpretation that is given, even with the best of will. It is all so vague that discussion remains mystifying. I have no idea why such proposals are so often made, frequently with such fervor, or what on earth they are supposed to signify.

The real question is: How does this organism function, and what is its mental and physical structure?

M.R.: Empiricism (and, in particular, functionalism) has enjoyed an enormous success. In spite of all the demonstrations that have been made of its errors, today it still remains the dominant philosophy. To what do you attribute that success, that power to survive? To a conjunction of ideology and politics?

N.C.: On that point we must be careful, because here we enter into speculation. When certain ideas are dominant, it is very reasonable to ask why. The reason could be that they are plausibly regarded as true, they have been verified, etc. But in the case where they are without empirical foundations, and have little initial plausibility, the question arises more sharply: the answer may actually lie in the domain of ideology. Of course the argument here must be indirect, because we don't have any direct means of determining the ideological basis for the acceptance gained by a certain doctrine.

Perhaps the instrumentalist conception of language is related to the general belief that human action and its creations, along with the intellectual structure of human beings, are designed for the satisfaction of certain physical needs (food, well-being, security, etc.). Why try to reduce intellectual and artistic achievement to elementary needs?

Is the attraction of the several variants of empiricist doctrine based on experimental verification? Hardly. There is no such verification. Does it derive from their explanatory power? No, because they can explain very little. Is it due to some analogy to other systems about which we know more? No. Again, the systems known to biology are totally different. Animal intelligence seems to be quite different. So too the physical structures of the human organism. The rational hypotheses which we can propose to explain the dominance of empiricist doctrines do not apply.

It should be noted that empiricist doctrine has not merely been "accepted" for a long period, it was hardly even questioned, but rather simply assumed, tacitly, as the framework within which thinking and research must proceed.

Perhaps, then, some sociological factor might explain in a natural way why this point of view has been so widely adopted. We can ask ourselves, who accepts and disseminates these doctrines? Essentially, the intelligentsia, including scientists and non-scientists. What is the social role of the intelligentsia? As I have said, it has been quite characteristically manipulation and social control in all its varied forms. For example, in those systems called "socialist," the technical intelligentsia belong to the élite that designs and propagates the ideological system and organizes and controls the society, a fact that has long been noted by the non-Bolshevik left. Walter Kendall, for example, has pointed out that Lenin, in such pamphlets as *What Is To Be Done?*, conceived of the proletariat as a tabula rasa upon which the "radical" intelligentsia must imprint a socialist consciousness. The metaphor is a good one. For the Bolsheviks, the radical intelligentsia must bring a socialist consciousness to the masses from the outside; as Party members, the intelligentsia must organize and control society in order to bring "socialist structures" into existence.

This set of beliefs corresponds very well to the demands of the technocratic intelligentsia: it offers them a very important social role. And in order to justify such practices, it is very useful to believe that human beings are empty organisms, malleable, controllable, easy to govern, and so on, with no essential need to struggle to find their own way and to determine their own fate. For that empiricism is quite suitable. So from this point of view, it is perhaps no surprise that denial of any "essential human nature" has been so prominent in much of left-wing doctrine.

Analogously, the modern intelligentsia in the capitalist societies—that of the United States, for example—have a certain access to prestige and power by serving the state. So, much the same is true for the liberal intelligentsia in the West. Service to the state includes social manipulation, preservation of capitalist ideology and capitalist institutions, within the framework of state capitalism. In this case as well, the concept of an empty organism is useful. It is plausible that statist ideologues and administrators are attracted by this doctrine because it is so convenient for them, in eliminating any moral barrier to manipulation and control.

These remarks apply only for the last century, more or less. Before that the situation is rather different. Without doubt, at an earlier period empiricism was associated with progressive social doctrine, in particular, with classical liberalism; although, as we were discussing, that was not always the case. One may recall the ideas of the young Marx, who was far from empiricist doctrine in spirit. Why this link between progressive social thought and empiricist doctrine? Perhaps because empiricism seemed to have—and in a certain way did have—progressive social implications in contrast to reactionary and determinist doctrines, according to which the existing social structures, slavery, autocracy, the feudal hierarchy, the role of women, were founded on unchanging human nature. Against that doctrine, the idea that human nature is a historical product had a progressive content, as it also did, one might argue, throughout the early period of capitalist industrialization.

The determinist doctrines in question maintained that certain people were born to be slaves, by their very nature. Or consider the oppression of woman, which was also founded on such concepts. Or wage labor: willingness to rent oneself through the market is considered one of the fundamental and immutable human properties, in a version of the "human essence" characteristic of the era of capitalism.

In the face of such doctrines as these, it is natural for advocates of social change to adopt the extreme position that "human nature" is a myth, nothing but a product of history. But that position is incorrect. Human nature exists, immutable except for biological changes in the species.

M.R.: But that is not the same definition of human nature, it is no longer a matter of defining a psychology of individual character.

N.C.: Certainly, we can distinguish between theories that assign a determinate social status to particular individuals or groups by virtue of their alleged intrinsic nature (e.g., some are born to be slaves), and theories that hold that there are certain biological constants characteristic of the species, which may, of course, assume very different forms as the social and material environment varies. There is much to be said about all of these matters. It seems to me that one might suggest, in a very speculative manner, that such factors as the ones I have mentioned entered into the success of empiricism among the intelligentsia. I have discussed this question a bit in *Reflections on Language,* stressing the crucial and sometimes overlooked point that speculation about these matters of ideology is quite independent of the validity of the specific doctrines in question; it is when doctrines of little merit gain wide and unquestioned credence that such speculations as these become particularly appropriate.

In *Reflections,* I also mentioned that even at the earliest stages it is not so obvious that empiricism was simply a "progressive" doctrine in terms of its social impact, as is very widely assumed. There has been some interesting work in the past few years, for example, on the philosophical origins of racism, particularly by Harry Bracken, which suggests a much more complex history. It seems that racist doctrine developed in part as a concomitant of the colonial system, for fairly obvious reasons. And it is a fact that some leading empiricist philosophers (Locke, for example) were connected to the colonial system in their professional lives, and that racist attitudes were commonly advanced during this period by major philosophers, among others. It is perhaps not unreasonable to speculate that the success of empiricist beliefs, in some circles at least, might be associated with the fact that they offer a certain possibility for formulating racist doctrine in a way that is difficult to reconcile with traditional dualist concepts concerning "the human essence."

Bracken has suggested, plausibly it seems to me, that racist doctrine raises conceptual difficulties within the framework of dualist beliefs, that is, if they are taken seriously. Cartesian dualism raises what he has called "a modest conceptual barrier" to racist doctrine. The reason for that is simple. Cartesian doctrine characterizes humans as thinking beings: they are metaphysically distinct from non-humans, possessing a thinking substance *(res cogitans)* which is unitary and invariant—it does not have color, for example. There are no "black minds" or "white minds." You're either a machine, or else you're a human being, just like any other human being in essential constitution. The differences are superficial, insignificant: they have no effect on the invariant *human essence.*

I think it is not an exaggeration to see in Cartesian doctrine a conceptual barrier—a modest one, as Bracken carefully explains—against racism. On the other hand, the empiricist framework does not offer an analogous characterization of the human essence. A person is a collection of accidental properties, and color is one of them. It is thus somewhat easier to formulate racist beliefs in this framework, although it is not inevitable.

I don't want to exaggerate the importance of these speculations. But it is worth investigating the question whether colonial ideology did in fact exploit the possibilities made available by empiricist doctrine to formulate more easily the kind of racist beliefs that were employed to justify conquest and oppression. It is unfortunate that the carefully qualified speculations that have been proposed for investigation have evoked a rather hysterical response, and some outright falsification, on the part of a number of philosophers—who are, as Bracken has observed, quite willing to consider, and even advance, very explicit proposals concerning a possible relation between rationalism and various oppressive doctrines, racism among them, thus indicating that it is not the nature of the inquiry but rather its object that they consider intolerable.

I must emphasize again that these speculations, or any others concerning the ideological or social factors that contribute to the success of any doctrine, must be recognized for what they are: speculations which are at best suggestive. Again, questions of this kind arise especially when a doctrine enjoys a great deal of attraction and success among the intelligentsia in spite of little factual support or explanatory value. This is the case with empiricism, in my opinion.

M.R.:   Empiricism thus finds support both from the right and the left . . . That explains why generative grammar is often attacked by the progressive intelligentsia, precisely because of your reference to the hypothesis of "innate ideas," as it is called, that is, the genetic limitations imposed on language. This hypothesis is accused of idealism.

N.C.:   That is true, as you say. But the characterization is quite irrational. A consistent materialist would consider it as self-evident that the mind has very important innate structures, physically realized in some manner. Why should it be otherwise? As I have already mentioned, if we assume that human beings belong to the biological world, then we must expect them to resemble the rest of the biological world. Their physical constitution, their organs, and the principles of maturation are genetically determined. There is no reason for supposing the mental world to be an exception. The hypothesis which naturally comes to mind is that these mental systems, unusual in the biological world because of their extraordinary complexity, exhibit the general characteristics of known biological systems.

I would emphasize once again that even qualitative considerations of the most evident kind suggest this conclusion: it is difficult to see any other explanation for the fact that extremely complicated and intricate structures are acquired, in a like manner among all individuals, on the basis of very limited and often imperfect data.

M.R.:   Certain psychologists still are trying to make apes talk; as a result, they deny the qualitative difference between human beings and animals, a difference which you have adopted from Cartesianism and restated in the light of modern biology. Do those who are opposed to "innéism" take the same position as these psychologists?

N.C.:   I don't want to speak for others. Let's consider this question of human uniqueness. Imagine a Martian scientist who studies human beings from the outside, without any prejudice. Suppose that he has a great deal of time at his disposal, say, thousands of years. He notices immediately that there exists on earth a unique organism, whose conditions of life change considerably without corresponding changes in his constitution; that is, modern man. Apes and monkeys live as they lived millions of years ago, while human life changes radically and very rapidly. It is extremely varied, yet there is no corresponding diversity within the human species. Take a child from a Stone Age culture and raise him in New York: he will become a New Yorker. Raise an American baby in New Guinea, and he will become a Papuan "native." The genetic differences one finds are superficial and trivial, but human beings have the extraordinary characteristic of being able to live in very different ways. Human beings have history, cultural evolution, and cultural differentiation. Any objective scientist must be struck by the qualitative differences between human beings and other organisms, as much as by the difference between insects and vertebrates. If not, he is simply irrational.

Take an even more elementary criterion: proliferation. In that regard human beings are a species with remarkable biological success. Perhaps not if you compare them to insects—or chickens (but here the proliferation in fact results from human intervention)—but compared to higher organisms, monkeys or chimpanzees, for example, they are much more numerous. Thus, in the most elementary respects, human beings are quite different. No scientist could fail to see that.

Even the most superficial observation suffices to show that there are qualitative differences between humans and other complex organisms which must be explained. If our hypothetical Martian observer searches a bit further, he will find that human beings are unique in many respects, one of these being their ability to acquire a rich and varied linguistic system, which can be used freely and in the most subtle and complicated ways, merely by immersion in a linguistic community in which the system is used. It seems to me that a rational observer would conclude that specific qualities of "intelligence," proper to this species, must be assumed. If he is of an inquiring mind and enterprising, he will seek to determine the genetically fixed mental structures which underlie the unique achievements of this species.

M.R.: I believe the rejection of "innate ideas" also springs from their association with the Cartesian notion of *soul* (âme) . . .

N.C.: That may well be true. But consider this ancient problem of the human soul in its historical context. For Descartes, for example, the existence of the soul is assumed in quite a rational way as a scientific principle. In some respects his argument for the existence of the soul is not very different from Newton's argument for gravity, as a force of nature. Descartes was wrong, no doubt, but his procedure in itself was not at all unreasonable.

To see this, it is sufficient to pursue the analogy to Newton, though I don't want to exaggerate its importance. Newton showed that Cartesian mechanics could not account for the movement of heavenly bodies. To explain this movement he postulated a new force: gravity, attraction at a distance; that is, a force which by the criteria of his time was considered to be occult, mystical, because action at a distance violated basic assumptions of mechanics. Newton showed that in this way one could account for the facts, though he too was quite uncomfortable with the "occult force" he was postulating. This postulate became the common sense of following generations, with Laplace and others. An inconceivable idea for pre-Newtonian physics subsequently became part of science because of its remarkable explanatory power.

For his part, Descartes believed—wrongly—that "push-pull" mechanics could explain all phenomena of the natural world, except such things as consciousness and human creativity. Thus to explain what was beyond the scope of his mechanics, he postulated another substance; little else was open to him, given the metaphysics of substance and accident to which he was committed. One can now imagine all sorts of other things, which are not part of his mechanics. But let us suppose that Descartes or the Cartesians could have gone further and invented a mathematics of the mind, a successful explanatory theory. Then their belief would have become part of the science of subsequent generations, like the physics of Newton.

To repeat, the existence of the soul, Descartes's second substance, is a scientific proposition: it is false, but it is not irrational. Had he elaborated his theory of the soul to an explanatory theory, he might have created a new science to supplement his speculative physiology. He was completely right to propose new principles and to seek out their consequences.

One might say that Descartes's belief that the soul is a simple substance which cannot be analyzed created an obstacle to the development of an explanatory theory of the mind, a theory which in principle might be assimilated to a suitably extended physics—but that is an altogether different question.

A convincing rejection of his dualism requires a demonstration that his postulate is useless, or unnecessary because we can explain the properties of the human mind in other ways. Let us then look for such an explanation . . . It might turn out that we are led to new principles when we inquire into the nature of the mind. It is conceivable, though not demonstrated, that principles entirely different from those of contemporary physics enter into the explanation of mental phenomena. In all these matters one must guard against dogmatism.

M.R.: To make precise what you are opposing to empiricism, I think it is important to remember that for you the mental organ is that which corresponds to the *grammar* and not to the language. The structuralists think that one memorizes extended sentences, that is to say, the language (de Saussure's *langue*), and that this represents the grammar. But for you, what is constructed in memory as grammar is quite another thing. It is necessary to insist on this difference because so often the set of rules which makes the sentences of a language possible is confused with the language as a set of memorized sequences.

For de Saussure, on the contrary, it was the language—
langue—which was deposited in memory. He could not distinguish the memory which we can have of this or that extended
sentence from the "memory"—of the grammatical form. The
situation is quite different here. The two kinds of memory are
different. The construction of the grammar is due to the language faculty. But don't you think that another confusion can
arise because of the ambiguity of the English word *language*
(both *langue* and *langage*)? Therefore, one could understand
that it is the language as *langue* which is innate . . .

N.C.:   . . . Which would be absurd, of course; if French were
innate, I would speak it . . .

It is the mechanism of language acquisition that is innate. In
a given linguistic community, children with very different experience arrive at comparable grammars, indeed almost identical
ones, so far as we know. That is what requires explanation.
Even within a very narrow community—take the élite in Paris
—the experiences are varied. Each child has a different experience, each child is confronted by different data—but in the end
the system is essentially the same. As a consequence we have
to suppose that all children share the same internal constraints
which characterize narrowly the grammar they are going to
construct.

M.R.:   This hypothesis also explains why, when the moment of maturation is passed—adolescence—it is no longer
possible to learn a language; the wolf-children never learn to
speak, and we speak a foreign language which we have learned
late in life with an accent. Without these biological constraints,
foreign accent would be inexplicable.

N.C.:   Yes, there seems to be a critical age for learning a
language, as is true quite generally for the development of the
human body. Patterns of growth are determined genetically, for
example, sexual maturation, to take a case that occurs long
after birth. It would evidently be absurd to maintain that only
what one sees at birth is determined genetically.

Even death, to a certain degree, is genetically determined. To say that the genetically determined properties of an organism cannot manifest themselves before the appropriate conditions exist, and that in general the genetic program is spelled out in a way that is partly predetermined and partly influenced by environmental factors, is a virtual truism. In the study of physical development it is a commonplace, and once again, if the methodological dualism of empiricist dogma is abandoned, there is no reason to be surprised by the discovery of similar phenomena in the study of higher mental functions.

PART II
Generative Grammar

CHAPTER 5

The Birth of Generative Grammar

Mitsou Ronat

The subject of this chapter is what distinguishes Chomsky's approach fundamentally from structuralism. Let us just briefly recall—in greatly simplified form—some properties of his generative model. A generative grammar, he says, must render explicit the implicit knowledge of the speaker, or the "intelligence" of the reader (the term intelligence *receives a special definition here). Even the most complete traditional grammars "forget" to mention the simplest characterizations. For example, with their instructions as the sole indication, one would have been unable to generate any of the above sentences. In French, nothing would prevent a priori the production of the sequence,* La grammaire est très générative *(The grammar is very generative) on the model of* La grammaire est très intéressante *(The grammar is very interesting), if we start with the definitions that the traditional French grammar of, say, Grevisse gives of the adjective. Grevisse did not specify this because the speaker of French "knows" intuitively that one does not say this. On the other hand, the French speaker must learn by heart the formation of the plural that distinguishes* loyal/loyaux *from* naval/navals; *those are irregularities . . .*

Furthermore, Chomsky proposes the construction of a formal model. Starting from an axiom and a set of well-defined rules, the desired sequences are generated "mechanically." What was termed the base component *of the grammar was conceived in the beginning as a finite set of* rewriting rules, *that is, rules having the form* φ →ψ, *which can be translated as follows: Each time you encounter the element   , which is to the left of the arrow, you can replace it by ψ, which is to the right of the arrow. I will not go into further detail here, but see Adrian Akmajian and Frank Heny's* Introduction to the Principles of Transformational Syntax, *or C. L. Baker's* Introduction to Generative Transformational Syntax.[1]

I will, however, give an idea of what the base component of a grammar is with a very simple example. Imagine a language that has only three words: Jules, Chloe, *and* loves. *The speakers of this language know "spontaneously" that certain combinations (without repetition) of these three words belong to the language, while others do not; for example*

> * Jules Chloe loves
> OK Jules loves Chloe
> * loves Jules Chloe
> * loves Chloe Jules
> OK Chloe loves Jules
> * Chloe Jules loves

> where * = does not belong to the language;
> OK = belongs to the language

The problem is to render this "knowledge" explicit. One can propose the following grammar:

$$
\{G\}
\begin{vmatrix}
S \to N\ VP \\
VP \to V\ N \\
N \to \begin{Bmatrix} Jules \\ Chloe \end{Bmatrix} \\
V \to loves
\end{vmatrix}
=
\begin{cases}
G = \text{grammar} \\
\text{"Sentence" is rewritten: noun + verb phrase} \\
\text{"Verb phrase"}\ (VP)\ \text{is rewritten: verb + noun} \\
\text{"Noun" is rewritten: } Jules \text{ or } Chloe \\
\text{"Verb" is rewritten: } loves
\end{cases}
$$

Following these "deductions" mechanically (if S, *then* N + VP, *etc.), one will arrive at the desired sequences; furthermore, one can never deduce undesirable sequences. Let us construct a* derivation:

S is replaced by: *N VP*
Replacing *VP* by *V N: N V N*
Replacing the first *N* by Jules: *Jules V N*
Replacing *V* by *loves: Jules loves N*
Replacing the second *N* by *Chloe: Jules loves Chloe*
(One cannot go further, the string is terminal)

We can equally well represent the derivation by a tree or phrase marker. *This tree describes the structure of the terminal elements of the sentence. Thus, we see that the relation of* Jules *and of* Chloe *with respect to the verb is not symmetrical:*

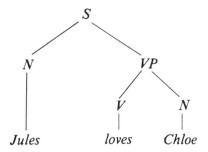

One can hardly doubt that the grammar of a natural language is incomparably more complicated. Chomsky has shown that rewriting rules, no matter how complex they may be, are not sufficient for describing the natural languages.

The grammar of a language is thus a model that must include several other components in addition to the rewriting rules of the base component. In his earliest writings, Chomsky showed that it is necessary to incorporate in the grammar at least two other levels. The rewriting rules give the structure of the sequences of words; it is necessary to add a morphophonological component and a transformational component. The transformational rules are rules of a different type, which transform the syntactic struc-

tures generated by the rewriting rules into other structures, according to precise principles. The relation between the active and the passive has usually been cited as an example involving transformation. *

The evolution of this theory has led to the complication of the model at certain points and to its simplification at others. Later, I will indicate the points at which the model has evolved.

The history of generative grammar seems to fall into three main periods, which successively have placed in the foreground one of the essential aspects of the new theory. The first, which lasted from the beginning of the 1950s to the middle of the 1960s, sought to make linguistics a science: physics seemed to be the model of reference. This is the period of The Logical Structure of Linguistic Theory *(or* LSLT, *as it will be cited).*

After that, from 1965 to 1970, the question of semantics became more central: must the meaning *of words and sentences be accounted for in the grammar, and if so, in what fashion? Very lively controversy accompanied the different answers given.*

Finally, after 1970, research became oriented more toward the problems posed by universal grammar. To comply with the formal exigencies of these discussions, I have asked Noam Chomsky to follow this thematic chronology.   **M.R.**

The History of Generative Grammar:
Opposition to Structuralism

M.R.:   Generative grammar is born of the break with and in opposition to structuralism. The latter, in general, conceived of linguistics as a classificatory activity. You have given the discipline a *logical structure,* a scientific structure . . .

N.C.:   The term *science* is perhaps honorific. My own inclination is to attach less importance to the precise description of some domain of linguistic data than to the explanatory power and depth of underlying principles.

---

*In French an example is the transformation which displaced *tous* in *Tous les garçons sont partis*—*Les garçons sont tous partis.* See Richard Kayne, *French Syntax* (Cambridge, Mass.: MIT Press, 1975).

I take for granted that in something as complex as the actual utilization of language and the judgments about language, many systems enter into interaction. No matter how careful our observations, how objective our methods, and how replicable our "experiments," the facts presented are, in my opinion, of little interest in themselves. What is of interest is their bearing on explanatory theories that seek to formulate the fundamental principles of the language faculty. Speaking just for myself, organizing the "facts of language" does not interest me very much. The notion "facts of language" has little sense outside of at least an implicit theory of language. One can perfectly well have different interests; I am simply trying to make clear what interests me. Frankly, I do not believe that seeking to account for "all the facts" constitutes a reasonable goal. In contrast, what seems important to me is the discovery of facts that are crucial for determining underlying structure and abstract hidden principles. If such principles do not exist, the enterprise is not worth undertaking. If they do exist, then facts are interesting (to me, at least) insofar as they bear on the truth of these principles. The discovery of such facts is often a creative achievement in itself, and very much "theory-related." "The facts," in any interesting sense of that notion, are not simply presented to us, nor is it of great interest, in my opinion, to present "the facts" in an exact manner, although of course the *pertinent* facts (again a notion that is linked to theory) must be presented in as precise a manner as possible . . .

M.R.:   . . . as in physics.

N.C.:   . . . If you like. That is how it seems to me. At each stage in the development of physics there have been innumerable unexplained "facts," or facts that seemed totally incompatible with the theories being actively pursued. To take a classic example, consider the "facts" of sorcery or of astrology, which seemed very well established by the standards of empirical research in the period when classical Galilean physics became established scientific doctrine. Or to take a less exotic example, consider the problems encountered by seventeenth-century physics in dealing with observations by telescope, many of which were not understood until quite recently. Or simply the problem of explaining why the apparent size and brightness of the planets did not vary as predicted by Copernican theory, as the distance between the planets changes. Or consider Galileo's inability to explain why objects don't fly off the earth, if it is indeed revolving on its axis—the explanation only came later. Without going into a detailed discussion, it is certainly true that throughout the history of the serious sciences many problems in explaining facts were put aside, in the hope that they would be explained some day. To account for "all the facts" in the physical world has never been the goal of physics in the modern period, in the sense that some linguists think that a grammar must account for "all the facts" of language and the utilization of language. The great success of physics is due in part to the willingness to restrict attention to the facts that seem crucial at a particular level of understanding, and perhaps to look for quite exotic facts that will be crucial for the theory, without taking into account even evident facts when these do not seem pertinent to physical theory (and to be quite honest, sometimes even when they appear inconsistent with it).

As for those varieties of "structuralism" or of "descriptive linguistics" that are interested primarily in the arrangement of "facts," one can doubtless say that my own goals are not necessarily incompatible with theirs, but that we are dealing with different intellectual enterprises. In my *Logical Structure of Linguistic Theory,* which contains my doctoral thesis, I tried to discuss these questions.

I suggested there that for the purposes of linguistic theory, we should be concerned with certain phenomena that were pretty much excluded from the descriptive linguistics of that period: those facts relating to what has sometimes been called the "creative" use of language, conceived as *normal* usage of language. These facts have not been treated systematically by traditional grammar or by structural linguistics although, as I have frequently pointed out, they were a classical concern, for example, in work by Humboldt, Paul, Jespersen, and others.

The traditional grammars, even those of great scope like Jespersen's,[2] present innumerable examples of complex structures, but do not give explicit principles for determining that these structures—and others which somehow "resemble" them —belong to the language, while other imaginable structures do not.

In fact, this question was not really raised. Jespersen, I suppose, did not have the impression that there was something fundamental missing in his presentation, despite his recognition of the importance of what he called "free expressions." In presenting his innumerable examples he thought that he had given an account of the language, so it appears. In reality his commentaries were not sufficient, because they appealed implicitly to the "intelligence" of the reader—to understand them and to use these examples and his often insightful commentary in the creation and comprehension of new forms, the reader had to add his own intuitive knowledge of language.

Structural grammars did not undertake the task of studying a range of highly complex syntactic structures, as the traditional grammars did.

This contribution of the intelligent reader, presupposed by previous grammars, must be made explicit if we hope to discover the basic principles of language. This is the first goal of generative grammar. In psychological terms: What is the nature of the intuitive, unconscious knowledge, which (in particular) permits the speaker to use his language?

At the time that question had not been squarely faced, though it had occasionally been put forth, and it remains a serious question today, in many crucial respects an unanswered one.

The second goal is to construct an explanatory theory. We have an at least potential explanation when we can deduce certain phenomena from general principles, that is, when we can provide a deductive chain of reasoning departing from these principles, given certain particular facts considered as "boundary conditions."

To be more concrete, let us take a well-known example, the behavior of the English auxiliary system.* One can, I think, explain some aspects of this system on the basis of a certain theory of transformational grammar and certain given facts: among them, the elementary examples of the auxiliary system in simple declarative sentences. Starting from these principles and empirical facts, I tried to show that one could explain the behavior of the auxiliary in a variety of constructions—interrogative, negative, and so on.

The rules that deal with the behavior of the English auxiliary are quite complicated, but can be simplified by the use of transformations—See Syntactic Structures, *chapter 5.*

Starting with a rewriting rule (see above, p. 104) which describes the behavior of the declarative sentence, we have:

$$Verb \rightarrow AUX + V$$
$$Aux \rightarrow C \ (M) \ (have + en) \ (be + ing) \ (be + en)$$

where the elements in ( ) are optional;
where C corresponds either to a grammatical zero

element ϕ, or to an element S which belongs to the third person singular, or to the element *past;*
where M corresponds to *will, can, may, shall, must,* i.e., the English modals.

(There is furthermore an operation affix-movement, *which attaches the grammatical affixes S, -en, -ing, ϕ, etc., to the verbs that follow them: for example, the sequence* Aux + V *is rewritten first as* C + V, *then as* S + V, *and as result of* affix-movement, *one obtains* V + S; *thus* S + leave *is turned into* leave + S, *etc.)*

The negative transformation introduces the element not *after the second element of the* Aux *rule. If* M *is not realized, a transformation inserts the element* do, *giving* He didn't leave, *etc.*

The interrogative transformation inverts the subject noun phrase and the sequence C + (M): Will he leave?

If M *is missing,* do *is introduced as before:* Did they leave?

Thus the deep structure of negative and interrogative sentences resembles that of declarative sentences, and the same properties show up in other constructions as well. If we were to describe the phenomena directly without such rules as these, we would have a very complex system of rewriting rules and the basic regularities would remain unexpressed.

A third goal appeared clearly only later, at the end of the fifties (before that it was implicit). It had to do with considering the general principles of language as the properties of a biologically given system that underlies the acquisition of language. From this point of view, one might think of the "boundary conditions" as the facts encountered by someone who learns a language; what one tries to explain, then, is essentially the knowledge of the language attained by the speaker presented with such facts. To go back to the preceding example, if we assume that the speaker possesses as part of his biological make-up the general principles of transformational grammar, and is presented with some subset of the forms of the English auxiliary, then he would *know*, because he could deduce it, the behavior of these elements in other cases, that is, the other cases would follow from the simplest permissible rule compatible with the given cases. This, at least, is the general pattern of a possible explanation.

Thus my work sought to answer two questions: first, what is the system of linguistic knowledge that has been attained, and is internally represented, by a person who knows some language? And second, how can we account for the growth and attainment of such knowledge? The second question can be thought of in psychological terms—how can knowledge be acquired?—or alternatively as the question of how we explain the phenomena of language.

M.R.: When did you think for the first time of proposing an explanatory theory in linguistics?

N.C.: That was what interested me about linguistics in the first place. As an undergraduate at the University of Pennsylvania in the late 1940s I did an undergraduate thesis called "Morphophonemics of Modern Hebrew," later expanded to a master's thesis with the same title in 1951. That work, which has not been published, was a "generative grammar" in the contemporary sense; its primary focus was what is now called "generative phonology," but there was also a rudimentary generative syntax. I suppose one might say that it was the first "generative grammar" in the contemporary sense of the term. Of course there were classical precedents: Panini's grammar of Sanskrit is the most famous and important case, and at the level of morphology and phonology, there is Bloomfield's *Menomini Morphophonemics,* published only a few years earlier, though I did not know about it at the time. Anyway, the central part of this project was an attempt to demonstrate in painstaking detail that the generative grammar I presented was the "simplest possible" grammar in a well-defined technical sense: namely, given a certain framework for the formulation of rules and a precise definition of "simplicity," the grammar was "locally optimal" in the sense that any interchange of order of rules in a tightly ordered system of many rules would lead to a less simple grammar. Reading back into this work the explicit concerns of a later period, one might say, then, that the goal was to show exactly how this grammar with its empirical consequences would be constructed by someone initially equipped with the framework for rules and the definition of simplicity (the evaluation measure), and given a sufficient sample of the data. Actually, this was done in far greater detail and scale than anything I've attempted since, and was far too ambitious, I suppose.

That grammar did, as I said, contain a rudimentary generative syntax. The grammar associated phonetic representation with what we would now call "base-generated" syntactic structure. Parenthetically, this was a pre-transformational grammar. Harris's early work on transformations was then under way and as a student of his I was familiar with it, but I did not see then how this work could be recast within the framework of generative grammar that I was trying to work out. In place of transformations, the grammar had a complex system of indices assigned to syntactic categories, which indicated syntactic relations inexpressible within the framework of segmentation and classification that was later constructed, in somewhat different terms, as the theory of phrase structure grammar.

Since that time my major interest has been to make precise the basic principles which enter into the knowledge of language that has been attained by the speaker-hearer; and beyond that, to try to discover the general theoretical principles which account for the fact that this system of knowledge, rather than something else, develops in the mind when a person is placed in a certain linguistic environment. In a general way, I might say that I am still working very much within the framework of that early unpublished work. That is, I think the right approach to the fundamental theoretical issues is the one attempted there: to make precise a certain format and schematism for grammars, and to provide an evaluation procedure (or simplicity measure) that leads to the choice of a particular system, a particular grammar that is of the required form, namely, the optimal, most highly valued system of the required form that is compatible with the presented data. Then what the "language learner" comes to know is that most highly valued system; it is that system that underlies the actual use of language by the person who has gained this knowledge. I'll come back to this point.

I continued this early work in *The Logical Structure of Language Theory (LSLT)*—which was published in part only in 1975, twenty years after it was essentially completed. The psychological point of view did not begin to appear until the end of the fifties, especially with a very important review article by Lees written for *Language.** This was a review of *Syntactic Structures,* which appeared in 1957, almost the same time as the book. In it Lees brought up the issue of language learning.

I wrote on similar questions in the years that followed, but we had been thinking about these issues for some time—Morris Halle[3] and Eric Lenneberg,[4] among others.

One of the things that most interested us was the critique of the behavioral sciences. We were trying to work out a rather

---

*See below, p. 133.

different approach to cognitive psychology. Little of this appears in *LSLT* because it seemed to me too audacious and premature. There is a more detailed discussion in the introduction to the 1975 edition of *LSLT.*

M.R.: Your theoretical positions were accorded a mixed reception in linguistic circles ... I remember reading review articles on the first colloquia in which you participated, the Texas Conference. The discussion was an epic confrontation. You opposed *evaluation procedures* (mechanisms that would tell which of two grammars, proposed to account for the facts, is the better one) to the *discovery procedures* of the structuralists, which were designed to construct the grammar directly from the facts.

N.C.: On this point one must distinguish carefully among the several tendencies that have been called "structuralist." American descriptive linguistics is one of these. Its chief contribution, in my opinion, was to raise for the first time a problem that one could readily interpret as that of explanation, or of the acquisition of language. What I mean is that the development of "discovery procedures" could have been understood as an approach to a theory of language acquisition, and also as an explanatory theory, considered from the dual perspective of psychology and epistemology. It is interesting to see that that was not the case; the linguists who were developing discovery procedures did not say: "Here is the corpus, the empirical conditions imposed by the data. Our discovery procedures constitute the theory which, applied to the corpus, produces the grammar. That grammar represents linguistic knowledge. In presenting this theory we have given an explanation for the fact that a speaker, having learned a language, knows this and that; the discovery procedure is part of his genetic equipment, and in applying it to the data of experience, he constructs this grammar, which represents his knowledge of language."

That would have been a reasonable way of interpreting what they were doing. But they did not give such an interpretation, for various reasons. However, that approach, implicit in their work, seems to me the most important contribution of this variety of structuralism. I repeat, this is not their interpretation. But I believe it to be legitimate as a reconstruction, even though it conflicts with what most of the people who did this work actually had in mind, to the best of my knowledge.

In work that I was doing in the late 1940s and early 1950s I tried to overcome some crucial deficiencies in the discovery procedures that had been developed and to make these procedures explicit, while assuming in the back of my mind a position concerning the so-called psychological reality of these procedures that was sharply in conflict with prevailing assumptions in the field, as I understood them, assumptions that might be called "fictionalist." It seems to have been generally assumed that the discovery procedures could be justified only in "pragmatic" terms, as providing an organization of the corpus that would be useful for one or another purpose. There were exceptions, for example, Charles Hockett, who put forth an explicitly "realistic" interpretation of discovery procedures in an important brief article in 1948, in the *International Journal of American Linguistics*. I was also taking for granted that the discovery procedures were basically true, in the sense that one might think of them as a representation of the procedures that were actually employed to provide the knowledge we have from the data we are given. For a long time I thought that the discovery procedures appearing in the literature were correct in their essentials—that is, that the methods employed by structural linguists like Zellig Harris,[5] with whom I was studying, were in principle correct, and that only some refinements were necessary to make them work. I spent quite a lot of time and energy, for about five or six years, I guess, trying to overcome some obvious defects of these procedures so that they would be able to produce a correct grammar with infinite descriptive scope from a finite corpus of the language; that, evidently, is the proper formulation of the task, if we think of these procedures as in effect a "learning theory" for human language.

There were thus two interrelated questions:

—Is it correct to give a psychological interpretation to these methods?

—Are these discovery procedures the ones which express correctly the biological given that makes the acquisition of language possible?

Note that we cannot properly pose the second question unless we accept a positive reply to the first. We cannot inquire into the "correctness" of methods without considering them to be an expression—more precisely, an intended expression—of some psychological reality. It is only under this "realist" interpretation that the question of correctness or truth arises. But again, this realist interpretation was not that of Harris and most others who had worked out the more elaborate procedures of analysis.

More and more I began to realize that the answer to the second question was negative. These procedures had insurmountable defects; they were wrong, in principle. The right approach seemed to involve principles that were more abstract, more indirect. I slowly came to believe that it was necessary to assume general principles, a general abstract schematism, which, when confronted with the given data, would yield a grammar representing linguistic knowledge, along the lines I mentioned earlier.

On the psychological level, structuralist discovery procedures correspond essentially to the empiricist view, according to which the acquisition of knowledge requires operations of classification and induction . . .

M.R.:   It is in that sense that structural linguistics is linked to empiricism . . .

N.C.:   In either the European version (with Troubetskoy,[6] who was quite concerned with these questions) or the American version, the procedures are essentially taxonomic, based on techniques of segmentation and classification that proceed gradually toward ever larger linguistic units.

The principles must be totally different—today I am convinced of that. One must begin by characterizing potential systems of knowledge with the help of principles which express the biological given. These principles determine the type of grammars that are available in principles. They are associated with an evaluation procedure which, given possible grammars, selects the best one. The evaluation procedure is also part of the biological given. The acquisition of language thus is a process of selection of the best grammar compatible with the available data. If the principles can be made sufficiently restrictive, there will also be a kind of "discovery procedure"—in some sense there must be such a "procedure," since knowledge is attained —but of a very different sort from what was contemplated in structuralist theory.

This conception of the nature of human knowledge, and particularly of language, is very different from the empiricist conception because one assumes the general form of the resulting system of knowledge to be given in advance. The system is not constructed gradually, step by step, by induction, segmentation and classification, generalization and abstraction, and so on.

Consequently, I think we might identify three fundamental issues that arise in comparing structuralist linguistics to generative grammar. First, with regard to the goal of explicit characterization of the attained linguistic knowledge. Second, the interpretation of the procedures: are the analytic procedures of B. Bloch,[7] of Harris, of Troubetskoy,[8] simply ways of organizing a corpus? Or do they constitute empirical hypotheses that are strong and interesting, with respect to psychological reality, and specifically to biologically given innate structure?

On this point work in generative grammar has characteristically taken a very explicit position. Yes, we propose such empirical hypotheses. Consequently, we consider pertinent all data that have any bearing on the validity of these hypotheses. At least in my opinion, it has always seemed evident that only the "realist" interpretation of linguistic theory, whether procedural or not, provides the basis for a significant discipline, one that is worth pursuing.

Trends in structuralist linguistics have varied on this question, and there are also some problems of interpretation. I believe that Jakobson and Troubetskoy did take a position close to that later adopted within generative grammar. They speak of psychological reality, it seems to me, as did Edward Sapir, for example, quite explicitly. Furthermore, at least in phonology, they postulated universal structural principles and even, in a sense, evaluation procedures in the form of considerations of symmetry, minimizing redundancy, and so on. Harris, on the contrary, rejected the realist psychological interpretation quite explicitly, at least in his early work—I am not sure that this is also true of his more recent work since the late sixties. In his *Methods* and other works up to the early sixties, he presented his theory as providing various alternatives for organizing data. The same is true of Bloch and others, though not of Hockett.

Finally, the third question deals with the nature of correct procedure. Is this a discovery procedure, inductive and taxonomic? Or is the proper approach of something like the rationalist type, that is, a characterization of the general form of knowledge (knowledge of language, in this case), with methods for choosing among alternative realizations of this general system under the empirical conditions given by experience?

I think it is proper to conceive of the theory of distinctive features in phonology and the various proposals concerning relative preference ("markedness") as a schema for a system of knowledge—if not an acquisition model. Though it is worth noting that Troubetskoy, in his phonological work, sought to furnish taxonomic procedures.

M.R.:   In relation to the second point, I've noted that there are many divergences over the definition given to the activity of linguists. The analyses, the theories they present, are these simply intellectual games or do they seek to establish the truth (even partially) of an objective law imposed upon something real?

N.C.:   The question is, how does one interpret a discovery procedure? Is it solely a matter of organizing linguistic data, or a way of expressing a psychological reality?

It is interesting to look more closely at the *practice* of the linguists, who argued explicitly that they were simply providing techniques for compact organization of data. That practice rests upon a tacit belief to the contrary, and this holds throughout the entire development of structural linguistics. Constantly, whenever someone proposed a method or procedure, someone else would point out that this procedure leads to "undesirable results." Then certain corrections and improvements were proposed. In this way procedures were constantly refined.

But what meaning can we give to the notion "undesirable result"? There is no such notion, at least in any interesting sense, if all that is at stake is a way of organizing data; then there can only be results that are neither good nor bad, apart from minimal considerations of redundancy or consistency. One cannot be right or wrong in classifying data in a theoretical vacuum. Consequently, to the degree that one recognizes tacitly the existence of such notions as "good results" versus "unwanted results," it becomes evident that one is committed to some notion of psychological reality, that is, of truth, no matter how much the commitment is denied.

However, the explicit rejection of such a commitment makes it very difficult to arrive at such an interpretation of much of this work—which might find its rationale in this interpretation.

Two Definitions of Transformation

M.R.: The concept of "transformation" is a fundamental one in your theory. It is also one of its principal innovations. In your model, the transformational component operates on the "output" of the base component (the rewriting rules): it takes phrase structures (trees) and transforms them into other phrase structures (trees).*

---

*See the example given above, p. 110.

But the linguist Zellig Harris had already used the term *transformation*. The distinction between the two uses of the term has often been poorly understood. Could you state it precisely?

N.C.: Harris's concept of "transformation" was not strictly speaking "linguistic" in its origin—or, more precisely, not a concept that belongs to the theory concerned with the grammatical structure of sentences. Harris developed this concept as part of his study of discourse in the late 1940s. The linguistic theory he had presented in his *Methods* offered only tools for describing units that do not exceed the length of a single sentence. When he attempted to extend these methods to the structure of discourse, he observed at once that the methods of segmentation and classification devised for the grammar of sentences did not lead to any useful result. He therefore sought a way to reduce the set of complex sentences of discourse to a form in which they would be susceptible to analysis by the methods devised for sentences and their parts. He proposed the use of certain "transformations" to "normalize" the discourse, to transform complex sentences into uniform simple structures to which the methods of structural linguistics might apply: segmentation of sequences, substitution of elements, classification, and so on. For Harris, transformations were systematic relations between sentences, between "surface structures." Technically, a transformation in this sense is an unordered pair of linguistic structures, taken to be structurally equivalent in a certain sense. To give a concrete example, think of two linguistic structures, each on one side of a double arrow, each structure described by a succession of grammatical categories of which it is composed. Here is how one formulates the active-passive relation within this framework:

$$N_x V N_y \leftrightarrow N_y \text{ is } Ved \text{ by } N_x$$

which is read as:

Noun X + Verb + Noun Y is equivalent to
Noun Y + *is* + Verb in past participle + *by* + Noun X

The two structures on either side of the arrow in such formulas are held to be equivalent in the following sense: If we choose a particular noun (say *John*) for N_x and a particular noun (say *Mary*) for N_y and a particular verb (say *see*) for V, then the two substitution instances—that is, *John sees Mary* on the left and *Mary is seen by John* on the right—have the same degree of acceptability as sentences. Such "equivalences" can be used to normalize a discourse in the following manner: If we are given a sentence in a discourse in one of the two forms, then we can replace it by the corresponding sentence in the other form. By continuing to apply these equivalence transformations to a discourse, we can reduce the sentences to similar forms, to which the substitution procedures developed for the grammar of sentences can be applied, and we can construct substitution classes of words that play more or less the same role in discourse; these discourse categories must not be confused with the lexical or phrase categories of the language. This is the basic idea of "discourse analysis," as Harris has developed it in various publications since about 1950. What is relevant in this context is that transformational relations in Harris's sense were developed in the course of an attempt to extend structural methods to the analysis of discourse.

On the theoretical level, one essential characteristic of Harris's transformations is that each is established independently of other aspects of grammar, as Harris has emphasized. Each transformation is established once and for all from observation and evidence, on the basis of the distributional conditions I have just described; each transformational relation exists independently of what is true or false for the rest of the language. A transformation is in effect a generalization about the acceptability of instances of two sentence forms, and that factual generalization is true or false quite apart from anything we may subsequently discover about the language in question or the theory of language, or from any other source—say psychological experiment. This account is a natural one within the general approach of Harris's *Methods*—a nonpsychological conception of linguistics.

Harris rejects the idea that the language of a particular person or community can be regarded as a well-defined set of sentences with structures characterized by grammatical principles that are true or false. At least in the framework of his *Methods,* which provided the background for the development of the notion "transformation," a grammatical description is, as he put it, a compact account of a collection of data, and thus can be incorrect only through inadvertence—for example, if it states that some element in the data set has an observable property that it does not have. Transformational analysis, in his sense, is simply another way of describing the given collection of observations, and it is therefore quite natural to describe a transformation as a generalization stating that the data exhibit some property, in this case the property of equal acceptability under systematic substitution, as described a moment ago. A grammatical description in this sense is quite different from a (partial) theory in some natural science, for example. In the natural sciences, two theories may be in conflict even if they agree on available data, and the scientist will then search for new data to choose between them, proceeding on the "realist" assumption that what the theories allege about the entities postulated in them is true or false, and therefore susceptible to further test. But Harris, at least through the early sixties, took the position that alternative linguistic descriptions cannot be in conflict in this sense. At least, that is what I take him to be maintaining in work up to the time of his paper on transformational analysis in *Language.*[9]

In *LSLT* and subsequent work in generative grammar, transformations are defined in a very different manner. Perhaps I should have used a different term instead of adapting Harris's to the quite different context of generative grammar. In *LSLT,* for example, a transformation is not a relation between two sets of sentences or between two surface structures;* it is a rule within a system of rules that assigns structural descriptions to an infinite class of sentences. In the derivation of a particular sentence, a transformational rule applies to an abstract representation of this sentence and transforms it into another abstract representation. The initial representation is the so-called deep structure, which is transformed step by step into terminal (or surface) structure.

In the framework of generative grammar, equivalence relations of the kind that Harris uses to establish a transformation can only suggest the existence of a transformation, but not establish it. For example, in English it is true that the appropriate substitution relations between the active and the passive hold by and large: *Sincerity frightens Paul* is just as good a sentence as *Paul is frightened by sincerity,* while *Paul frightens sincerity* is just as bizarre as *Sincerity is frightened by Paul.* But no matter how precisely such substitution relations hold, they do not suffice to establish the existence of a transformation relating active and passive forms. Rather, empirical arguments are needed to show that within the schematism of permissible rule systems, the optimal grammar includes such a transformation. Furthermore, even if such a transformation is postulated on the basis of some empirical argument, it would not relate *Sincerity frightens Paul* and *Paul is frightened by sincerity.* Rather, the postulated passive transformation would figure in the derivation of *Paul is frightened by sincerity* from its abstract deep structure, but not in the derivation of *Sincerity frightens Paul* from its abstract deep structure; the two deep structures might be similar or even identical and the derivations identical apart from this transformation, but that is the only sense in

---

*The term *surface* must be understood as a technical one here. It does not signify that this structure cannot possess properties that are "intellectually profound." See below, p. 171.

which one might say that the two sentences are "related" by this transformation. Thus the notion "transformation" is quite different from the one that Harris developed.

Furthermore, within the theoretical framework of generative grammar a transformation is never "incorrigible" in Harris's sense. No matter how powerful the empirical evidence in favor of a grammar containing some transformation, subsequent evidence might indicate that the grammar is wrong and some other grammar permitted by the same general theory is right, or that the general theory is wrong and some different set of principles with a different schematism for grammar is right. Nor is it possible to determine, a priori, what kinds of evidence will prove relevant to such conclusions. A grammar is essentially like a hypothesis in the natural sciences concerning some subject matter—never finally established, no matter how strong the empirical evidence—and the same is true of a particular subhypothesis of the grammar to the effect that it contains a certain transformational rule.

I hope this helps to clarify the difference between the two conceptions.

Mathematics and Linguistics

M.R.:   Generative grammars were born of a meeting between mathematics and linguistics. Can you give more precise information about this birth?

N.C.:   I should distinguish between two questions. The first relates to a problem that has already been raised: How can linguistic knowledge be explicitly characterized? An explicit characterization must ultimately be a formalized theory. This remark may also be extended to the problem of acquisition of language and the related matter of explanatory theory, in the sense of our earlier discussion. Explanations exist to the degree that the general principles are precise—in principle, formalized; starting from such principles, one can construct a deductive argument leading to the phenomena that are to be explained.

Thus a certain quasi-mathematical mode of expression is presupposed in the overall program, but one that is quite unsophisticated. We want to formulate precise principles and precise rules within a formalized system. It turns out that the way to "speak precisely" is by formalization, but it would not be correct to consider that as mathematics. For example, some variety of recursive function theory provides the means, in principle, to express linguistic rules. But up to that point, this is formalization, not mathematics. Mathematical linguistics begins when one studies abstract properties of the formalization, abstracting away from particular realizations. The subject exists in a serious sense only insofar as nontrivial theorems can be proven, or at least considered. The viewpoint is very different.

M.R.: Certain mathematical theories have seduced many linguists. I'm thinking of their "historic" encounters with telecommunications engineers . . .

N.C.: Well, at the end of the forties and the beginning of the fifties, there were important developments in the mathematical theory of communication, information theory, and the theory of automata. Technically, models such as finite state Markov sources were proposed* . . .

Very often it was supposed that these models were appropriate for the description of language. Jakobson referred to this vaguely, but Hockett utilized them quite explicitly. In 1955 he proposed a theory of language structure based on a Markov source model borrowed from the mathematical theory of communication. Similar theories were developed by psychologists, engineers, mathematicians.

All these theories left me very skeptical. I became interested in the relevant mathematics at first largely because I wanted to

---

*Briefly, formal devices with a finite number of configurations (states) that produce sequences of symbols, one after the other, in a linear order, where the next symbol produced depends only on the present state and perhaps some input. In a linguistic application, the device might produce a sentence from left to right—first *The,* then *men,* then *arrived,* etc.—using the resources of a strictly finite memory to determine the next symbol.

prove that these models were not appropriate for the grammar of natural language.

M.R.:   What was the a priori reason for your skepticism? An intuition?

N.C.:   An intuition again founded on the same anti-empiricism. In my view, a finite state Markov source model might reasonably be considered as characterizing something like the outer limits of empiricist learning theory. In fact, a mathematical psychologist and logician, Patrick Suppes, gave precise expression to this intuition, or one version of it, a few years ago. He proved that a certain very rich version of stimulus-response learning theory must remain within the limits of finite state sources of the kind we have been discussing.

He considered this to be a positive result. To me it seemed to be a negative result. The reason is this. As has been known for a long time, even elementary systems of knowledge cannot be represented in terms of finite state Markov sources—for example, our knowledge of English, or even much simpler systems, such as propositional calculus. As a consequence, Suppes's result showed that knowledge which we possess cannot even be approached at the limit (a fortiori, not attained) by the learning theory he was considering. This constituted a final step in a complete refutation of this learning theory, and consequently, less powerful theories.

I did not believe in theories of language based on the Markov source model, which seemed to me to inherit the defects of empiricist learning theory. However, to know whether they were correct or not, it was necessary to wait until they were presented in a precise manner. Then the essential question could be posed:

Do properties of natural languages exist which cannot be expressed in any of these systems?

And such properties do exist.

M.R.:   When did you demonstrate that?

N.C.:   After *LSLT* was completed. The first version of this manuscript, completed in 1955, involved a good deal of formalization but no mathematics. Shortly after, I moved from the Society of Fellows at Harvard to the Research Laboratory of Electronics at MIT. There, there was a great deal of quite justified interest in the mathematical theory of communication, and also a great deal of—less justified—faith in the potential for the study of language offered by Markov source models and the like, which had aroused considerable enthusiasm among engineers, mathematical psychologists, and some linguists. As soon as the question was clearly formulated, it was immediately obvious that these models were not adequate for the representation of language. This observation was published in *Syntactic Structures,* and along with some other material, in a more technical article in 1956.

After that a certain branch of mathematical linguistics developed, which occupied itself primarily with the formal properties of systems that were considerably richer, called "phrase structure grammars." The most interesting class of these systems turned out to be what are called technically "context-free phrase structure grammars." Since the end of the fifties there has been quite a lot of work on the formal properties of various types of grammars, on their generative power, their properties and relations, and so on, and today this study constitutes a small branch of mathematics. The French mathematician M. P. Schützenberger made quite interesting contributions to this field . . .

M.R.:   Which developed independently of linguistics . . .

N.C.:   Yes, and I hope that these studies[10] will continue to be pursued, as well as the mathematical investigation of transformational grammars. There has been some interesting recent work by Stanley Peters and Robert Ritchie on this latter topic.

Returning to the earlier point, it seems clear that empiricist learning theories are much too limited to be adequate; and it is even possible to demonstrate this if we accept the assumption that finite state Markov sources are the richest systems that can be attained by such theories, at the limit. This conclusion does not seem to be unreasonable to me, although naturally it is not a precise conclusion because the notion "empiricist theory" is not well defined.

M.R.:   Did you link your critique of these theories right away to the critique of structural linguistics?

N.C.: Well, indirectly. These theories were then very much in fashion, and they even aroused a certain degree of euphoria, I think it is fair to say. In the intellectual milieu of Cambridge there was a great impact of the remarkable technological developments associated with World War II. Computers, electronics, acoustics, mathematical theory of communication, cybernetics, all the technological approaches to human behavior enjoyed an extraordinary vogue. The human sciences were being reconstructed on the basis of these concepts. It was all connected. As a student at Harvard in the early 1950s all of this had a great effect on me. Some people, myself included, were rather concerned about these developments, in part for political reasons, at least as far as my personal motivations were concerned.

M.R.:   For political reasons?

N.C.:   Yes, because this whole complex of ideas seemed linked to potentially quite dangerous political currents: manipulative, and connected with behaviorist concepts of human nature.

M.R.:   Thus your skepticism had political causes . . .

N.C.:   Yes, in part. But of course these motivations were irrelevant to showing that all this was wrong, as I thought it was. I believed that these theories could not really offer what they promised. As soon as they were analyzed carefully, they unraveled, though not without leaving substantive and important contributions.

M.R.:   We have seen vast programs of research on artificial intelligence develop, based on the apparently infinite capacities of computers . . .

N.C.   Artificial intelligence came a little later as an outgrowth of what was then called cybernetics . . .

M.R.: The situation in this respect is paradoxical. In general, physics and technology permit the growth of human capacities and performance, sometimes with the aid of quite simple instruments. With artificial intelligence, the most advanced technology is developed to obtain the most limited results, well below the capacity of the most stupid creature . . .

N.C.: I'm afraid that much of the work in this field relies on ideas that are too elementary and superficial to shed light on the question of human intelligence. This need not be the case, and perhaps some day will not be the case. But it has been true so far, by and large, and the field has also suffered from quite irresponsible claims. The same is true in the behavioral sciences, for example, Skinner's work on verbal behavior. That work, published in 1957, was presented ten years earlier as the William James Lectures. It immediately gained great influence. W. V. Quine, George Miller, and many others wrote and talked about it with considerable enthusiasm. It was quite the rage at about the time that I came to Cambridge, in 1951, at Harvard.

One could have thought—in fact, some people did think—that computers were going to permit the automation of discovery procedures in linguistics. The idea would be to present a corpus of material to the computer so that it would work out the grammar of this text, on the assumption that the taxonomic procedures of analysis that had been developed were in essence sufficient and adequate to determine grammatical structure. It was quite generally supposed, at least in the intellectual environment here in Cambridge, that the Skinnerian theory of behavior approached adequacy, and that the notions developed within the theory of communication, in particular the Markov source model, furnished a general framework for the study of language. But when I began to study these topics, I was quickly convinced that the prevailing assumptions were false and the popular models inadequate, for reasons which were not independent but had significant links, as I've already said, with empiricist dogma.

First Steps

M.R.:   What were your first contacts with the linguistic community? Hostile? Full of conflict?

N.C.:   Not exactly. In the beginning we ignored each other. For example, almost no one paid any attention to that first work I mentioned to you, on the generative grammar of Modern Hebrew. But that was the work of a student, and I did not expect that anyone would pay attention to it. As far as I know, only two linguists showed any interest in it: Henry Hoenigswald, an Indo-Europeanist with whom I studied at the University of Pennsylvania, and Bernard Bloch, the well-known Yale phonologist.

However, outside the field of linguistics proper the work attracted the attention of Yehoshua Bar-Hillel, who was then here in Cambridge—we became very close friends. He made some excellent suggestions. For example, he suggested very persuasively that I should be much more radical and should postulate much more abstract underlying representations, similar to those postulated for earlier stages of the language, to explain contemporary forms. That turned out to be a very good idea. The significance of his suggestion became apparent much later in generative phonology. I recast the Hebrew grammar completely, following this suggestion, in 1951, improving it considerably, I thought.

Quine expressed some interest in the methodological aspect, particularly the problem of constructing a simplicity measure for linguistic theory, and encouraged me to work further on that, as did Nelson Goodman. But that was about all. Among the linguists no one showed any interest in that type of work.

I wasn't particularly disturbed or surprised: I did not think myself that I was doing linguistics. In a sense I was completely schizophrenic at that time. I still thought that the approach of American structural linguistics was essentially right. As I told you, I spend a great deal of time trying to improve and to formalize discovery procedures, in order to overcome their obvious defects. But once they were made precise, they led manifestly to the wrong results. Still, for quite a long time I thought that the mistake was mine, due to wrong formulations. In 1953 I published an article in the *Journal of Symbolic Logic* in which I tried to develop a discovery procedure that I hoped might be the basis for something that would really work. That, for me, was real linguistics. What I was doing otherwise—attempting to construct an explanatory theory of generative grammar—seemed to me a different kind of work, on the side, so to speak.

Among my contemporaries there were a few who found that work interesting.

The only one who had always thought I should pursue this work and drop the whole discovery procedure business was Morris Halle. He was then a graduate student at Harvard, as I was too, and was also teaching at the same time at MIT. We met in 1951, became close friends, and had endless discussions. He thought that these discovery procedures did not make any sense. I don't remember his arguments, but I do remember disagreeing with him at that time. By 1953, I came to the same conclusion: if the discovery procedures did not work, it was not because I had failed to formulate them correctly but because the entire approach was wrong.

In retrospect I cannot understand why it took me so long to reach this conclusion—I remember exactly the moment when I finally felt convinced. On board ship in mid-Atlantic, aided by a bout of seasickness, on a rickety tub that was listing noticeably—it had been sunk by the Germans and now was making its first voyage after having been salvaged. It suddenly seemed that there was a good reason—the obvious reason— why several years of intense effort devoted to improving discovery procedures had come to naught, while the work I had been doing during the same period on generative grammars and explanatory theory, in almost complete isolation, seemed to be consistently yielding interesting results.

Once I had recognized that, progress was very rapid. In the next year and a half I wrote *LSLT,* which was about 1,000 typed pages, and almost all of what was contained in *Syntactic Structures* and the 1958 Texas Conference paper, and so on.

As for the reception accorded to *LSLT,* there is little to say. I've already told you that I did not have the impression the reaction on the part of linguists was surprising. I offered *LSLT* to the MIT Press—who refused it. Quite rightly, I think, because at that time the situation was very unfavorable for a general book on that subject, especially one by an unknown author. I also submitted a technical article on simplicity and explanation to the journal *Word,* at the suggestion of Roman Jakobson, but it was rejected virtually by return mail. So I had little hope of seeing any of this work published, at least in a linguistic journal. But frankly, that did not trouble me greatly. I had a research position at the Research Laboratory of Electronics at MIT, which I obtained thanks to Morris Halle and Roman Jakobson, and I taught Scientific French and Scientific German—though I was barely competent—and also some undergraduate linguistics, philosophy, and logic. I did not have any problem making a living, and was free to do the work that interested me.

I should emphasize that although there was very little interest in the work I was doing, at least among linguists, I had absolutely no cause for complaint as far as working conditions were concerned. On the contrary, I was extremely fortunate and knew it. Studying at Penn with Zellig Harris and Nelson Goodman was a highly stimulating experience, and I was very fortunate to be able to continue discussing the work I was doing with Harris, particularly while I was at Harvard from 1951 to 1955 at the Society of Fellows, where I had no responsibilities and was free to do as I wished with all the facilities of Harvard available, a remarkable opportunity. I spent a good deal of time in courses, seminars, discussions, primarily with philosophers at Harvard—Quine, Austin (who visited Harvard then), White, and others. It was a very lively and stimulating period in the Cambridge area for a student with my particular interests.

The research climate at MIT was close to ideal. I could not possibly have obtained a position in linguistics anywhere—I really was not professionally qualified by the standards of the field. At MIT there were no entrenched academic strongholds in the areas that interested me. Morris Halle and I and a few others were free to pursue our research, and later, to design a program of graduate studies. This absence of established structure, along with a general spirit of encouragement for innovation that seemed promising, made it possible for linguistics to flourish at MIT in way that for us at least would have been virtually out of the question elsewhere.

George Miller, who was then in the Harvard Psychology Department, also became interested, and we did some. work together in the mid-fifties. He went on to develop an entirely new domain of psycholinguistics. With his help I was able to spend a rewarding year at the Institute for Advanced Study in Princeton in 1958–9. I should also mention my close friend Eric Lenneberg, who at that time was beginning his extremely interesting studies in the biology of language, working along rather similar lines.

Later on these topics began to gain some attention among linguists, at first at the Texas Conferences in 1958 and 1959, organized by Archibald Hill, to which I was invited. The discussions were animated and sharp, as you pointed out before. Unfortunately, the proceedings of the 1959 conference were never published. There I presented a paper on the generative phonology of English, in which I approached that subject very much in the manner of my work on Hebrew ten years before, but this time with much more confidence in the approach. In general, I published virtually nothing except in journals that were outside the field of linguistics in those years.

Questions of generative grammar attracted the attention of linguists primarily as a result of the publication of a thorough review by Robert Lees of *Syntactic Structures* in 1957 in *Language*. The monograph, which appeared in Holland, would not have been known, I imagine, had it not been for that review-article. Discussion moved to a more general forum in 1962 at the International Congress of Linguists, which was held that year at MIT. I gave a talk there which was later published as a monograph, in a revised form, *Current Issues in Linguistic Theory.* [11] In that talk I tried to explain, in a fairly comprehensive manner, what seemed to me to be the essential differences between generative grammar and structural linguistics. But it was still somewhat difficult to publish in the United States, although the situation had improved greatly with the publication of very important work by Robert Lees, G. H. Matthews, and Edward Klima.

M.R.:   Did you now begin to teach linguistics?

N.C.:   Yes, at the beginning of the sixties we began a program of graduate studies. As I mentioned, we were able to develop our program at MIT because, in a sense, MIT was outside the American university system. There were no large departments of humanities or the related social sciences at MIT. Consequently, we could build up a linguistics department without coming up against problems of rivalry and academic bureaucracy. Here we were really part of the Research Laboratory of Electronics. That permitted us to develop a program very different from any other and quite independent.

About the same time, a graduate program in psychology was established at MIT under Hans-Lukas Teuber's direction, and a little later a graduate program in philosophy was set up. Both developed in a way that was quite congenial to our work, and there has been a good deal of interaction among students and faculty, including joint appointments and jointly taught courses. That continues, and I expect that there will be even closer integration of these fields, along with related areas in engineering and computer science. It seems to me that there is a rather natural emerging discipline of cognitive psychology in which these various threads come together, and within which linguistics can find an appropriate place.

The First Students

M.R.:   Who were the first students and the first researchers of that new program?

N.C.: Morris Halle was already working on a generative phonology of Russian in the 1950s, and we also worked together on the generative phonology of English, at first jointly with Fred Lukoff. Together with Lees, Matthews, Klima, and Lukoff, I was, at least in principle, part of a research project on machine translation in the Research Laboratory of Electronics, headed by Victor Yngve. But the linguists, with the exception perhaps of Matthews, were not much interested in the applied problems of machine translation, as far as I can remember. At the end of the fifties, Matthews, who was a specialist in American Indian languages and had a good mathematical background as well, produced a very important grammar of Hidatsa.

In the technical sense of the term, Robert Lees was our first student, though in reality a colleague. He presented his Ph.D. thesis, on English nominalizations, in 1960. But actually he received an engineering degree. Klima, who worked with us, received his Ph.D. degree at Harvard on historical syntax. He also published a very important and influential article on negation. When the graduate program began, Jerry Fodor and Jerry Katz were here, as was Paul Postal. John Viertel, who was also on the machine translation program, was beginning his work on Humboldt and related topics at that time, and M.-P. Schützenberger was visiting from France. After that, things went very fast . . .

M.R.: That was the birth of the Standard Theory . . .

N.C.: Yes, it was at that period that what was called the Standard Theory was formulated, with major contributions by Fodor, Katz, and Postal, and many students in the new graduate program, a large number of whom are now among the most productive scholars in the field, which has really changed quite dramatically since the period we have just been discussing.

CHAPTER 6

Semantics

I have said above that Chomsky's first model—the model of
Syntactic Structures—*contained essentially three components:
the rewriting rules, the transformational rules, and the morphophonological rules. In 1965 a significantly different model appeared. The tradition that begins with* Aspects of the Theory of
Syntax *(1965) presents this model in the following manner. The*
base component *consists of two elements: the rewriting rules
which, as before, indicate the structure of sequences of words;
and the lexicon, to which are assigned all the syntactic, semantic,
and phonological properties of the lexical items. The base grammar generates the initial phrase marker, or the* deep *structure.*

The transformational component *transforms this initial
structure into other structures, the last of which is termed the*
surface structure. *The base component and the transformational
component constitute the generative part of the model.*

One of the most important innovations of Aspects *is the introduction of two* interpretive *components, the phonological component and the semantic component. Here the status of the
morphophonology has in some way changed. But the semantic
component, at least in the form that was integrated into Chomsky's model at the suggestion of Fodor, Katz, and Postal, was
something completely new. Fodor, Katz, and Postal sought to*

extend the concept of generative grammar to the domain of meaning. Chomsky wanted to make explicit what the speaker knows of syntactic structure. In the same way, they wanted to make explicit what the speaker knows of the "intrinsic" meaning of words and sentences. Toward that end they proposed a model consisting of two parts: in the one part, each word was assigned a description of the following type: X is + or – animate; + or – female; + or – solid; + or – transparent; etc.—this is part of the lexicon. In the other part, rules called "projection rules" compared the properties of words to indicate whether their combination within a sentence was acceptable or not.

The semantic component was to be integrated with the generative grammar at the level of deep structure: it is this syntactic structure which receives the meaning. The Standard Theory is generally visualized in terms of the following schema:

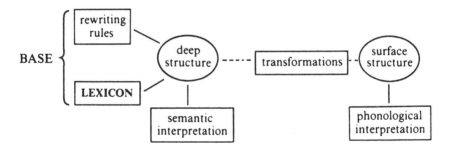

But this model was soon challenged, in particular, as we shall see, because of the exclusive link it postulated between semantics and deep structure.

The Role of Semantics in Grammar

M.R.: With the Standard Theory we enter into the second period in the history of generative grammar, the period in which semantics became the center of discussion.

N.C.: Yes, but it should not be forgotten that the theory which preceded this did explicitly presuppose a general semantic theory, based in part on the work of Goodman and Quine, and in part on Wittgenstein and the Oxford school. I'm speaking now of *LSLT* and *Syntactic Structures.* Contrary to what has been said—there has been a great deal of misunderstanding on this subject—this work accorded a central place to semantics. However, I was skeptical about the general belief that syntax was based on semantic considerations, which is quite a different matter. Many structural linguists and many philosophers—Quine, for example—claimed that grammatical concepts must be defined on the basis of semantic notions. For example, that the concept of phoneme must be defined in terms of synonymy . . .

M.R.:   Which means saying that *r* and *l* are different phonemes because *ramp* and *lamp* don't have the same meaning . . .

N.C.:   Yes, that's one example. Or they also identified the concept of grammaticality with the notion of meaningfulness. But it seemed to me that a grammatical sentence may not have any literal meaning . . .

M.R.:   That was behind the discussion about the sentence which became quite famous, *Colorless green ideas sleep furiously.* For you, this is grammatical, even if it does not rank highest in the degree of grammaticalness. Accordingly, you require that grammatical concepts be defined in terms that are formal and specific, independent of vague semantic notions.

N.C.:   Furthermore, I tried to show that every clear formulation of a hypothesis concerning the alleged necessity to define syntactic notions in semantic terms led to incorrect results. Thinking about these questions led to what was later termed the hypothesis of *autonomy of syntax.*

The more I think about it, the more it seems to me that this thesis is quite natural . . . I also know of no substantive argument that it is incorrect. In the context of language acquisition, the hypothesis implies that one learns the meaning of an expression with a form established on independent grounds. One cannot "pick up" a disembodied meaning that floats about in the air and then construct a form which expresses it. It isn't easy to make much sense of any of this. It seems to me that the elements of syntax are not established on a semantic basis, and that the mechanisms of syntax, once they have been constructed, function independently of the other components of the grammar, which are interpretive components.

M.R.: This hypothesis also explains why speakers arrive at similar phonological and syntactic systems, while the meaning given to words by their experiences may be very different.

N.C.: I think, in fact, that the thesis of the autonomy of syntax, in the form proposed in the fifties and since then, is probably correct. However, I have always explicitly denied and rejected a totally different position which has often been attributed to me: namely, that the study of meaning and reference and of the use of language should be excluded from the field of linguistics. What I said was exactly the opposite. A large part of *Syntactic Structures* and *LSLT* is devoted to the problem of semantic interpretation of formal systems. In fact, these questions were central in both *Syntactic Structures* and *LSLT*. I tried to show that some interesting and moderately subtle aspects of semantic interpretation of sentences can be explained in part in terms of a theory of linguistic levels, developed within the framework of generative transformational grammar. I also argued explicitly that semantic considerations enter in an essential manner into the choice of a correct linguistic theory. Thus the viewpoint of this work was that, given a linguistic theory, the concepts of grammar are constructed (so it seems) on the basis of primitive notions that are not semantic (where the grammar contains the phonology and syntax), but that the linguistic theory itself must be chosen so as to provide the best possible explanation of semantic phenomena, as well as others. Apparently many linguists have failed to make this distinction, and have concluded that I intended to exclude consideration of semantics, when the exact opposite is true: I argued explicitly that semantic considerations are essential for linguistic theory, as I have just said, and devoted a large part of these two books to the defense of that position.

In terms of our preceding discussion, linguistic theory (or "universal grammar") is what we may suppose to be biologically given, a genetically determined property of the species: the child does not learn this theory, but rather applies it in developing knowledge of language. It would be absurd to suppose that this innate linguistic theory, which determines the general form and structure of language, should not be connected in the most intimate manner to the fundamental properties of meaning and language use. Moreover no one, to my knowledge, has ever proposed such an absurd idea, though there has been a great deal of confusion about this subject in the literature.

M.R.: In my opinion, the misunderstanding derives from the fact that the word *semantics* embraces a number of different definitions, and that yours does not correspond to theirs. They remain bound to the definition that is inherent in the traditional logic-derived grammars, which make grammatical concepts dependent on semantic notions. Think of their formulas: *The subject carries out the action, The object suffers the action,* and so on. If you take this semantics away from them, nothing remains. And if, according to them, semantics does not play this primary role, then it does not play any role at all.

N.C.: It seems that two questions are confused: one is the question of the autonomy of syntax; the other is whether the study of meaning and reference belongs to the study of language. There isn't really any problem about that. Everyone has always taken for granted that a central concern of generative grammar is to incorporate linguistic semantics.

The "Fodor-Katz" Hypothesis

M.R.: Very quickly, among those who have accepted the autonomy of syntax, two tendencies can be discerned. Some make the semantic component a representation of the world, while others limit it to very precise and testable problems . . .

N.C.: Personally, in my earliest work *(Syntactic Structures* and *LSLT)* I had in mind a dual theory of meaning, in some sense. On the one hand, I referred to Goodman's attempt to extend the theory of reference to some parts of the theory of meaning, and also to Quine's influential, and I think rather persuasive, critique of a number of standard approaches to the theory of meaning. On the other hand, I had in mind the Oxford theories of language use.

When Fodor and Katz proposed integrating in the Standard Theory rules of semantic interpretation which associated semantic *representations* with syntactic structures, they had in mind something entirely different from what I had proposed. The Standard Theory incorporated their proposals as an innovation. Their rules had an *intensional* character, which did not exist in *Syntactic Structures,* where no linguistic level of *semantic representation* was envisaged. They developed an analogy between phonetics and semantics. Just as the phonetic representation is based on a universal system of phonetic features, so the semantic representation would be based on a universal system of semantic categories, or semantic "distinctive features." The universal system is supposed to be able to represent all possible conceptual thought. Katz takes the view that a semantic theory in his sense should aim to give a complete characterization of the semantic properties of all utterances of all languages, independent of all extralinguistic considerations—an account of whatever can be expressed in any language, whatever can be thought.

It is not at all clear that there exists such a universal semantic system. Perhaps there are semantic properties that are general, universal, of the type proposed by Katz and others. It seems reasonable to suppose that at least traditional notions like "agent of action," "instrument," "goal," "source," and so on, are part of universal semantics; then such notions would be available for semantic representation, perhaps in the sense in which phonological features are available for phonological representation. Julius Moravcsik has discussed the Aristotelian origins of several of these fundamental notions in some very interesting recent work. Furthermore, there seem to be more specific properties which enter into the analysis of the verbal system, for example. To take a case that has been frequently discussed, it seems reasonable to suppose that semantic relations between words like *persuade, intend, believe,* can be expressed in purely linguistic terms (namely: If I persuade you to go, then you intend to go; If I persuade you that today is Tuesday, then you believe that today is Tuesday. These are facts of language and not of the external world). Furthermore, it also seems reasonable to suppose that the fundamental properties of quantifiers (words like *all, any, some,* etc.) and anaphora (the relations between antecedents and pronouns, for example) can be expressed in part on the level of semantic representation, separate from extralinguistic considerations. If so, then these aspects of the theory of meaning can be taken to fall within the "generative grammar," understood as the system of rules that specifies our purely linguistic knowledge of the sound and the meaning of sentences. I might add that apparently divergent approaches tend to be in fairly close agreement, apart from their terminology, about such conclusions.

Why, then, raise a question about the possibility of a universal semantics, which would provide an exact representation of the full meaning of each lexical item, and the meaning of expressions in which these items appear? There are, I believe, good reasons for being skeptical about such a program. It seems that other cognitive systems—in particular, our system of beliefs concerning things in the world and their behavior—play an essential part in our judgments of meaning and reference, in an extremely intricate manner, and it is not at all clear that much will remain if we try to separate the purely linguistic components of what in informal usage or even in technical discussion we call "the meaning of linguistic expression." I doubt that one can separate semantic representation from beliefs and knowledge about the world.

To be sure, someone who believes in a level of representation of the type proposed by Katz can reply: "In doing so, I propose a *legitimate idealization.* I assume, with Frege, that there exist semantic elements common to all languages, independent of everything except language and thought. In rejecting this idealization, you make the same mistake as those who confuse pragmatics with syntax."

Certainly, this objection has some force. But I doubt that it will wholly withstand further reflection. Whenever concepts are examined with care, it seems that they involve beliefs about the real world. This idea is not new: Wittgenstein and Quine, among others, have emphasized that our use of concepts is set within a system of beliefs about lawful behavior of objects; similar ideas have been attributed to Leibniz. Thus, when we use the terms *chair* or *table*, we rely on beliefs concerning the objects to which we refer. We assume that they will not disappear suddenly, that they will fall when they are let go, and so on. These assumptions are not part of the meaning of *chair,* etc., but if the assumptions fail we might conclude that we were not referring to a chair, as we had thought.

In studying semantics one must keep in mind the role of nonlinguistic systems of belief: we have our expectations about three dimensional space, about texture and sensation, about human behavior, inanimate objects, and so on. There are many mental organs in interaction.

To repeat an observation of Wittgenstein's, we would not know how to name an object if at one moment it looked like a chair, and a moment later disappeared, that is to say, if it does not obey the laws of nature. The question: "Is that a chair or not?" would not have an answer according to strictly linguistic criteria. Admittedly it is difficult to establish such conclusions. Too little is understood about cognitive *systems* and their interaction. Still, this approach seems reasonable to me; to give it some real content, it would be necessary to discover something comparable to a generative grammar in the domain of factual knowledge, which is no small task. My own speculation is that only a bare framework of semantic properties, altogether insufficient for characterizing what is ordinarily called "the meaning of a linguistic expression," can be associated correctly with the idealization "language."

The Truth of Sentences

M.R.:   In Katz's semantic component, there is not only the universal semantics, independent of knowledge of the world, but also the *projection rules,* whose role is to exclude sentences devoid of meaning. This mechanism would exclude *Colorless green ideas sleep furiously,* because it cannot be true that ideas are green, and one cannot sleep furiously . . . But does that not mean reintroducing a notion—the "truth" of propositions—which has nothing to do with grammar?

N.C.:   Everybody believes that truth conditions are somehow related to semantic representation. However, the question is far from simple. On this subject, John Austin has given some interesting examples. Take the sentence: *New York is 200 miles from Boston.* Is it true or false? If the statement is made in answer to a question that you ask in order to find out how long it will take you to go by car, four hours or four days, it is true. But if you have just 10 gallons of gas, and I know that your car will do 20 miles per gallon, and you want to know whether you can go from Boston to New York without stopping, then the statement is false if the real distance is 210 miles. And so on.

Thus all sorts of considerations determine the truth conditions of a statement, and these go well beyond the scope of grammar.

Suppose I say: *The temperature is falling.* Nobody knows exactly what that means without extralinguistic presuppositions. Does it mean that the temperature is lower than it was five minutes ago? Perhaps. But if I say: *The temperature is falling,* meaning that we are heading toward an ice age, then my statement may be true even if the temperature is rising locally. Even for the simplest sentences it is impossible to set truth conditions, outside the context of language use. And we must also distinguish fixed beliefs, temporary beliefs, etc.

M.R.:   Can one summarize what you have said by contrasting two conceptions of semantics: the one, "extensional," presented in *Syntactic Structures,* treated the relation between certain elements of language and external objects (for example, anaphora): the other, "intensional," which claims, as Katz does, to account for all meanings of words and sentences without appealing to our knowledge of the world? In this respect, the work of Ray Jackendoff[1] belongs to the conception of *Syntactic Structures.*

N.C.: I'm not quite in agreement with that characterization. Thus I agree with Katz that certain analytic connections exist among linguistic expressions, certain truths hold solely by virtue of linguistic facts: for instance, the relation between *I persuaded him to leave* and *He intends to leave,* which I mentioned a little while ago. In such cases we are dealing with properties of semantic representation that are "intensional" and are strictly part of "grammar," in a natural sense of the term. The same is true of the so-called thematic relations ("agent," "goal," etc.) developed in a very interesting manner in the work of Jackendoff which you have mentioned. One might say that this work of Jackendoff's is quite compatible with the program of *Syntactic Structures,* but he developed a semantic theory in a direction that was not in any fashion proposed or suggested there.

M.R.: This is what is called "interpretive semantics" ... Recently you have replaced *semantic representation* by the expression *logical form.* Can you explain the nature of this change?

N.C.: I used the expression *logical form* really in a manner different from its standard sense, in order to contrast it with *semantic representation.* I used the expression *logical form* to designate a level of linguistic representation incorporating all semantic properties that are strictly determined by linguistic rules. To determine the precise relation between "logical form," so defined, and semantic theory and description, which inextricably involves contributions from other cognitive systems— that stands as an important question. Recent work has some interesting suggestions on this matter.

M.R.: As far as co-reference is concerned—that is, the question of the relation between nouns and pronouns and extralinguistic objects—certain laws are linguistic, others belong to discourse.

N.C.: In the case of co-reference, the matter is reasonably well understood. There exist principles that are completely linguistic. For example, in *John sees him, John* and *him* cannot be taken to refer to the same person, that is to say, they cannot be co-referential (though to be precise, it is intended rather than actual co-reference that is at issue). That is a linguistic rule. Similarly, in *John expected him to leave, John* and *him* cannot be co-referential. Take a more complex case: *I seem to John to like him.* Here *John* and *him* can be co-referential, but in *John seems to me to like him, John* and *him* cannot be co-referential. In this case it seems that we are dealing with rules of sentence grammar, which satisfy the general conditions that govern such rules.

M.R.: In French we find an almost identical difference in *Marie regarde Pierre le coiffer,* where *Pierre* and *le* cannot be co-referential, while in *Pierre regarde Marie le coiffer, Pierre* and *le* can be co-referential.

N.C.: In all these cases there is a network of relations that determines what can be and what cannot be co-referential, and these relations are governed by principles that form part of the grammar. For example, the difference between *Pierre believes he is intelligent* and *He believes Pierre is intelligent* is due to what are called relations of "command": co-reference is impossible if the pronoun is located "higher" in the phrase structure than its nonpronominal antecedent. Now in the second case *Pierre* is found in a subordinated position, thus "lower" than *he,* so that they cannot be co-referential in the relevant sense.

M.R.: In the majority of cases, English and French present analogous facts. In other, more subtle cases they differ. For example, in English one can say: *Harry thought it was impossible to wash himself in such conditions,* where *himself* refers back to *Harry.* In French a word-for-word translation of this sentence would be bizarre. It is necessary to add a pronoun in the subordinate clause: *Henri pensa qu'il LUI était impossible de se laver (lui-même) dans telles conditions.*

N.C.: Why is this so? These are interesting questions. One does not know what these phenomena indicate until one finds the rules that explain them. All this belongs to the first category of anaphoric relations.

In the second category we have the problem of determining the reference of words such as *the others* or even *he* in sentences of the type: *He has arrived, Some reacted well, but the others were angry* . . . It is not grammatical principles (or more precisely, principles of sentence grammar) which govern the relations of these pronouns to their antecedents or intended referents. There are many other conventions in discourse beyond the rules of sentence grammar. If I say, while showing you this photograph, *He is a good kid,* that would be quite correct, because it is perfectly acceptable to present this boy to you in this way in this context: we are looking at a photograph on my desk, and we share certain assumptions about photographs, and specifically photographs that one puts on one's desk; you imagine that this is a photograph of my son because otherwise it wouldn't be there, and so on. Thus, in a much larger context which is not linguistic but rich in beliefs of varied sorts, my statement is perfectly appropriate. But these conventions of reference are not part of grammar. To express them would require a richer theory, integrating a number of cognitive systems, including your assumptions about what one expects to see on my desk. All that plays a role in what some might call the full semantic representation.

To develop the inferences that follow from this statement, we would have to consider the "reference" of pictures and all the assumptions concerning the persons about whom I am likely to talk, their relations to me, etc. The actual reference of linguistic expressions in real life involves the interaction of cognitive systems. And grammar is only one of these. Much the same is true of most of our concepts, which are embedded within systems of belief about the nature of the world; the latter enter into the kind of semantic representation required to account for legitimate reference, truth conditions, speech acts, and so on.

Interpretive Semantics and Generative Semantics

M.R.:   We have just seen that Katz's semantic component, which he formulated in 1963, with its reference to a universal semantic system, has been challenged. However, it is what gave birth, toward the end of the sixties, to a "schismatic" tendency, which is opposed to generative grammar in its "Standard" form: generative semantics. Due to a further misunderstanding, this generative semantics has also been attributed to you. Briefly summarized, this theory rejects the autonomy of syntax with respect to semantics, and claims that the deep structure is to be identified with the semantic representation.

Today generative semantics in its initial form has been virtually abandoned (to the degree that there is no new formulation to replace it by improving it), although all kinds of people doing all kinds of things doubtless continue to call themselves "generative semanticists." In the beginning its principal proponents were Postal, McCawley, Ross, Lakoff . . . also Fillmore.

It was a vogue that still endures in certain European countries like Germany and France.

It seems to me that these theories have recapitulated the weaknesses for which you criticized structuralism, in abandoning the goals of linguistics which you formulated: to explain the acquisition of language. They forget that they were dealing with something real . . .

N.C.:   My feeling is that this work tended to return to a kind of descriptivism. In the case of Fillmore, this is quite explicit. In an article entitled, I believe, "The New Taxonomy," he describes himself as a taxonomist, a descriptivist, and quite rightly. If that is what interests him, I certainly have no criticism; furthermore, he is doing very good work in descriptive semantics. Once again, there's just no argument that one can have about this issue, just as there can't be any argument between someone who does natural history and someone who is looking for biological principles. These are different occupations. Presumably they can learn something from one another.

For the moment Fillmore is not trying to construct a general semantic theory; he does not want to base his work on any comprehensive and explicit theory of language, if I understand him correctly. Rather, he is producing material of greater or lesser interest, which a semantic theory may be able to use some day.

As for "generative semantics," it is difficult to discuss it because nobody, to my knowledge, now advocates an explicit theoretical position under that name. It is now nothing but a rather loose characterization covering the work of a number of people. Insofar as a theory had been clearly formulated, it seems to have generally been abandoned—at least as far as I know—by those who formulated it. Postal is doing quite different things today. I don't know what he currently thinks about generative semantics, but in any case, his recent work—relational grammar—seems to me quite remote from it. In fact, he seems to have put aside the question of the relations between meaning and form, if I understand his most recent work correctly, but perhaps I do not.

John Ross, another important figure in that movement, is working on what he calls non-discrete grammar, that is to say, a theory based on graded concepts rather than discrete categories.

M.R.: That is the theory of "squish," where a word is not defined by its category, but is "a bit of a noun, a lot of a verb, and just a little bit of adjective" ...

N.C.: And so on. He is also interested in the interaction of pragmatics, syntax, and semantics. Therefore, not in generative semantics, at least in the earlier sense of this term. Furthermore, I believe he considers it premature or even wrong to seek an explicit theory.

Lakoff is doing similar work. He is working on "cognitive grammar," which integrates language with nonlinguistic systems. I don't see any theory in prospect there.

In general, I remain skeptical about these latter approaches. They do not distinguish things that seem to me easily distinguishable, for example, grammatical competence from other factors that enter into linguistic behavior. That creates confusion. As for the rest, there is nothing to discuss, because there is now no substantive theory under the heading of "generative semantics."

Where then does the expression "generative semantics" come from? It is a general attitude or point of view which was expressed, for example, by Lakoff in an article entitled "Generative Semantics," or by Postal in his 1969 article "The Best Theory." But nobody—at least not to my knowledge—has accepted this theory, which in the form presented was virtually empty. What the theory asserted was that there exist representations of meaning, representations of form, and relations between the two. Furthermore, these relations between the two representations were virtually arbitrary; Lakoff, in the paper I just cited, proposed arbitrary derivational constraints*—arbitrary rules in effect. If all that is put forward as a theory is that there exist relations between some kind of representation of meaning and of form, then it is difficult to argue about that.

As you said, what was happening in these years has often been misinterpreted. In fact, the Standard Theory, as presented in *Aspects,* for example, was questioned from the very beginning. On the one hand, it was noted in the book itself (which went to press in 1964), that at least some aspects of semantic representation, for example those related to topic and comment, seem to involve surface structure rather than deep struc-

---

*These are constraints on the application of grammatical rules. In the Standard Theory these restrictions apply uniquely to the transition from one structure in a derivation to the next. For Lakoff they apply to any structure at all, which makes them arbitrary and ad hoc. See G. Lakoff, "On Generative Semantics," in D. Steinberg and L. Jacobovits, eds., *Semantics: An Interdisciplinary Reader* (Cambridge, Mass.: MIT Press, 1971).

ture. Subsequent research on the role of surface structure in determining the meaning of a sentence led to what has been called the Extended Standard Theory. On the other hand, in *Aspects* I indicated that there were very different possibilities, for example, some work by Thomas Bever and Peter Rosenbaum, in which a virtual obliteration of the distinction between syntactic and semantic rules was proposed, an idea that led finally to generative semantics. The class of theories that can be developed as alternatives to the theory presented in *Aspects* is vast, and it is indicated there that it would be premature to exclude them with any conviction. The first person who offered a substantial critique of the Standard Theory, and the best, as far as I can recall, was Ray Jackendoff—that must have been in 1964 or 1965. He showed that surface structure played a much more important role in semantic interpretation than had been supposed; if so, then the Standard hypothesis, according to which it was the deep structure that completely determined this interpretation, is false. For example, by studying the interaction of negation and quantification within a sentence, Jackendoff showed that their relative position in the surface structure of the sentence was crucial for interpretation.* Many other such examples were worked out by Ray Dougherty and others.

These observations naturally were of great interest to me. They led a number of linguists to develop what came to be called the Extended Standard Theory. But at the same time that

---

Many arrows didn't hit the target, but many did hit it. Not many arrows hit the target, but many have hit it. Not many demonstrators were arrested by the police. Many of the demonstrators were not arrested by the police.

Another well-known example of a change of meaning depending on the position of quantifiers in the surface structure is presented by the passive-active dichotomy:

Many people are buying the same brands of cigarettes.
The same brands of cigarettes are bought by many people.

The first case can be interpreted as saying that people are faithful to their brand; the second that certain brands are more successful.

Similar but less convincing examples were already noted in *Syntactic Structures* and *LSLT,* even then indicating the role of surface structure in semantic interpretation. But Jackendoff was the first to account for these phenomena in a systematic manner, and thus to integrate them in the theory by proposing interpretive rules.

the Standard Theory was modified to accommodate the role of surface structure, others took a contrary path, relying on a different intuition: they drew the connection between semantic representation and deep structure more closely, to the point where the two became identical. That is of course generative semantics. So described, the basic position is incorrect, because the hypothesis shared with the Standard Theory is false, as I've just pointed out.

Accordingly, to incorporate the role of surface structure in determining semantic representation without abandoning the identification of deep structure and semantic representation, generative semantics introduced the notion of "global rules," that is, rules that relate noncontiguous steps in a derivation; specifically, that relate the underlying abstract semantic representation and those properties of surface structure that enter into the determination of meaning.

Note that these global rules that relate surface structure to the semantic representation, postulated by generative semantics, are quite similar, if not identical, to the interpretive rules proposed by Jackendoff and others. It was quickly proposed that global rules may appear quite generally in the grammar, in phonology as well as in syntax and semantics. A theory that permits global rules has immense descriptive potential. As I've said, to approach an "explanatory" linguistic theory, or—which is the same thing—to account for the possibility of language acquisition, it is necessary to reduce severely the class of accessible grammars. Postulating global rules has just the opposite effect, and therefore constitutes a highly undesirable move, which must be supported by substantial arguments. I do not believe that such arguments have been presented. On the contrary, it does not appear to me that any convincing evidence have been produced in support of global rules.

The situation grew even worse—if that is possible—when generative semanticists began to incorporate nonlinguistic factors into grammar: beliefs, attitudes, etc. That amounts to a rejection of the initial idealization to language, as an object of study. A priori, such a move cannot be ruled out, but it must be empirically motivated. If it proves to be correct, I would conclude that language is a chaos that is not worth studying—but personally I do not believe that any evidence or substantive arguments have been brought forward in favor of such a hypothesis. Note that the question is not whether belief or attitudes, and so on, play a role in linguistic behavior or linguistic judgments. Of course they do, no one has ever doubted that. The question is whether distinct cognitive structures can be identified, which interact in the real use of language and linguistic judgments, the grammatical system being one of these.

Certainly, in the real world everything enters into interaction. But if a physicist had to consider motion pictures of people walking down the street, he would abandon all hope of doing physics. We come back to the question of rationality and idealization.

The people who are working on non-discrete grammars, or on what remains of generative semantics, have not given any substantial reason, as far as I know, for objecting to standard idealizations. It is possible that these idealizations will create problems, and will prove ultimately to be incorrect, in detail or perhaps even in principle. I mentioned some possible examples when we were discussing semantic representation. But I do not have the impression that any significant objection has been presented in the work in generative semantics, on "non-discrete" or "cognitive" grammars. On the contrary, it seems to me that people working in these directions are allowing themselves to be submerged by the phenomena.

M.R.: In the same way, have they not been diverted from what you consider the real goal of linguistics: explaining the acquisition of language?

N.C.: They would not agree, I suppose, but I believe it is true. Nevertheless, we are talking about a straw man: generative semantics does not now exist, in any reasonably well-defined sense of the term. The term *generative semantics* remains, but today its content has become completely obscure.

M.R.:   Still, its brief success seemed brilliant, and I began to ask myself at that time whether the reason for that was not ideological, as in the case of empiricism. It was a way of going back to the dominant structuralism. Often the intellectuals have thought that they could avoid the issue of generative grammar by leaping over a stage: directly from structuralism to Lakoff's semantics . . .

N.C.:   Perhaps. They are in fact rather similar. A number of linguists, particularly you yourself in your article on "Remind," as well as Ray Dougherty and Bever and Katz and some others, have tried to establish a connection between generative semantics and neo-Bloomfieldian descriptivism, quite persuasively, in my opinion.

M.R.:   The case grammars of Fillmore have had a great deal of success in France as a result of the translation of one of his articles in the journal *Langages.*

N.C.:   Here again it seems to me that there is a great deal of misunderstanding about what is going on. Case grammar is based on certain assumptions that are common to all linguistic theory, namely, that between verbs and noun phrases there are such relations as "agent," "instrument," "goal," and so on. Take the Standard Theory, in the form presented, say, by Jerrold Katz. It incorporates a system of "semantic relations" that are very difficult to distinguish from the "cases" of Fillmore, that is, if they are not completely indistinguishable.

Take the Extended Standard Theory: it incorporates thematic relations of the sort studied by Jackendoff, expanding on earlier work by J. Gruber. Every semantic description includes something like a "case grammar," at least insofar as this theory simply proposes that the familiar semantic relations, which are also discussed in the traditional grammars, link verbs to noun phrases. The interesting question is how to integrate this "case grammar" into the theory of language . . .

M.R.:   And not to substitute case grammar for the theory of language . . .

N.C.: Yes, the question of integration remains open; one can disagree about it. In my opinion, quite solid empirical arguments have been advanced against the particular theses of Fillmore's case grammars. In particular, such arguments have been presented by Ray Dougherty and several others, myself included. I do not know what Fillmore thinks about this at present. As I've said, right now he seems to be more interested in descriptive semantics—his "new taxonomy"—than in problems of general linguistic theory, if I understand him correctly. But if one thinks of "case grammar" as nothing other than the theory which incorporates the traditional semantic relations in a certain form, without any more specific hypotheses as to their nature or their integration within generative grammar, then we have a system with which one can work easily, at least in a superficial way. It is sufficient to take any language and to designate in each sentence the agent, the instrument, the goal, etc., and one will have a case grammar in this restricted sense, which is without much interest. That isn't even applied linguistics. Let me emphasize again: this is not Fillmore's "case grammar," which did put forth specific hypotheses, but ones that were, I believe, shown to be incorrect.

M.R.: That is curious, this repugnance for studying syntactic structures.

N.C.: I would say the same about the study of semantic structures. Because any nontrivial research in semantics must go much further than these elementary concepts. Think of phonology: if a phonological theory merely says: "There are vowels and there are consonants," then it isn't a very interesting theory, because all theories are in accord on this point, no matter what differences there may be otherwise. The question becomes interesting when we ask: "How is the category 'vowel' integrated in a serious theory of phonological structure?"

It is the same thing in semantics. It is very important to discover how the categories recognized by everyone (under their different names) are to be integrated into a general theory, and to refine and elaborate these categories. If not, you are just doing taxonomy. In this respect I should mention some recent work by Jackendoff, which moves toward an "explanatory" semantics in quite an interesting way, integrating the "thematic relations" (or "cases") in a more general theory. That seems to be very promising work.

M.R.:   You have mentioned the new "relational grammar" of Postal. This is a grammar which, it is said, formulates its rules in terms of *functions* and not, as generative grammar proposes, in terms of syntactic categories. For example, the passive is expressed by saying: "An object becomes a subject." Generative grammar says: "Such a noun phrase, occurring within the structure *X*, can be placed within the structure *Y.*" Generative grammar presents arguments for not employing functions in the formulation of transformations. Postal seems to be proposing a return to Jespersen in order to reinforce his position.

N.C.:   Before talking about relational grammar and the passive, I want to say a few words about Jespersen. On the one hand, Jespersen was writing more or less as a philosopher, for example, in his *Philosophy of Grammar;* on the other hand as a grammarian, in his work on English grammar. In his philosophical work he is one of the first in this century to have stressed the notion of "free expression," what I have called the "creative" aspect of language. Here he went a good deal further than the structuralists, including Saussure, who had only quite primitive things to say on this subject. It is only due to the tools furnished by modern logic that this notion, discussed in some form by Descartes and Humboldt, for example, can now be studied seriously. Moreover, Jespersen devoted a large part of his *Philosophy of Grammar* to what has more recently been called "the autonomy of syntax." He raised the question of the relation between "notional concepts" and those of formal grammar, and had some quite interesting things to say about this. All that brings him close to contemporary concerns. I've written about this in a paper called "Questions of Form and Interpretation," given at the fiftieth anniversary of the Linguistic Society of America.

The situation is more complex when one turns to his work as a grammarian. Although he introduced a certain number of interesting innovations, I think it is fair to say that for the most part he remained within the framework of traditional grammar which, as I've already pointed out, offers examples and descriptions without giving the explicit principles that account for them. He did not formulate the problem of designing an explicit linguistic theory. But his work remains a mine of perceptive and useful observations and insights.

Now what is the connection between Jespersen and "relational grammar"? In the first place, it is difficult to discuss this precisely, because up to now (January 1976) this grammatical theory has not been presented in a systematic manner. It remains to be seen just exactly how it is related to various other approaches.

Certainly Jespersen, like all traditional grammarians, relies very heavily on the concept of grammatical relation. But what does that concept involve? It is not very clear. The term is used in many ways. For example, there is the notion of "thematic relations"—or the "cases" of "case grammar." One may say that in the two sentences: *The key opens the door* and *John opens the door with the key,* the noun phrase *The key* and the verb *open* enter into the same type of "thematic relation," namely, "instrument." Here we have one notion of grammatical relation—a semantic notion.

There is also a purely formal notion. Take for example the sentence: *I promised John that I would leave.* Formally we have a direct object, because no preposition separates the verb from its complement; but in another sense, this is an indirect object, a dative. The French translation of that sentence, *J'ai promis à Jean de partir,* contains a formal indirect object, as does the nominalized form in English: *My promise to John to leave.* For that sentence one must therefore distinguish two notions of "grammatical relations." Furthermore, insofar as one might also argue that *John* is the goal of the action, according to the thematic relations, there are three different things to distinguish. Perhaps there are others.

On which of these notions does relational grammar base itself? Apparently not on thematic relations; that much seems clear. What about the other two just mentioned? In *I promised John that I would leave,* does relational grammar consider *John* to be a direct object or an indirect object—or perhaps both at different levels? Suppose that we take *John* to be an indirect object. That would mean that at some abstract level of representation we have something analogous to *I promised to John that I would leave,* with a preposition between the verb and the noun.

At some other level *John* must be a direct object in the framework of relational grammar, because the passive can be applied: *John was promised that I would leave.* According to the principles of relational grammar, if I understand them, only a direct object can be "passivized," in other words, raised to subject. It is necessary to add a rule that turns an indirect object into a direct object. But such a rule seems completely ad hoc in this case.

M.R.:   Yes. After that, how can one prevent *Je parle à Jean* from becoming *Je parle Jean?*

N.C.:   I'm not sure. Suppose one takes *John* to be only a direct object in these sentences. In that case the relation is already expressed in terms of phrase markers, the syntactic structures. The direct object, in this sense, is the noun phrase in the configuration:

M.R.:   I heard Postal speak at the colloquium in Chicago in 1973; he sought to prove that the passive transformation is universal ... However, in general, it is not the grammatical rules which are universal, but the conditions imposed on the rules.

N.C.: I remain skeptical about the assumption that there is a rule of "passive," either in a single language or universally, across languages. In English it seems to me that there is good evidence for a transformational passive, a rule that moves a noun phrase to the subject position of the sentence or a noun phrase, giving such structures as *The city was destroyed* and *The city's destruction,* corresponding to *Destroy the city* and *Destruction of the city,* respectively. But this should not, I think, be regarded as a "rule of passive"; rather, it is a special case of a much more general rule of noun phrase (NP) movement that applies as well to derive such sentences as *John seems to be a nice fellow,* corresponding to *It seems that John is a nice fellow,* in which the NP-movement rule did not apply. To say that English has a "passive rule" seems to me insufficiently general. Rather, it has an NP-movement rule that happens to form passives, as a special case.

But "passive" does not seem to me a unitary phenomenon, either in a single language or across languages. Other languages use quite different means to achieve an effect similar to the English passive—which may be regarded, loosely, as a device to shift topic or to allow for subjectless sentences. In a language that uses, say, morphological devices in the construction roughly corresponding to English passive we would expect to find somewhat different properties for this construction.

In English, for example, the displaced noun phrase is not necessarily the direct object of the verb. To be sure, most frequently it is the direct object, as in *John saw Bill—Bill was seen by John.* But it can also be the notional indirect object: recall, *Bill was promised that I would leave.* Or again, this noun phrase may not have any relation to the main verb, as in *Believe (John to be a fool),* which can become *John was believed to be a fool.*

M.R.: In traditional terms, one says that the subject of the subordinate clause becomes the subject of the main clause.

N.C.: In a language with a NP-movement rule we may also find that idiomatic expressions are subject to "passivization": corresponding to *Someone has taken advantage of Bill,* you have *Bill was taken advantage of* and *Advantage was taken of Bill.* Also, *Advantage seems to have been taken of Bill, Bill seems to have been taken advantage of,* and so on.

M.R.: And one must not forget that the passive can be applied to what was formerly an indirect object: *Someone gave a book to John—Someone gave John a book—John was given a book.*

N.C.: All these examples support the hypothesis that there is a rule displacing a noun phrase which follows the verb, independently of its function. One can go further. In his doctoral thesis, Joe Emonds argued plausibly that the rule forming passives is one of a general class of rules that are "structure-preserving" in the sense that the result of the transformation is a structure similar to those generated by the rewriting rules. Thus NP-movement places the displaced noun phrase in the subject position.

M.R.: That is an important limitation. Otherwise it would seem a priori that transformations can generate structures of any kind.

N.C.: Well, we see that the passive structure consists of the copula *be* followed by something like an adjective phrase. *John was seen* has a structure similar to *John was good. The door was closed* is ambiguous: either base-generated, like *The door was open,* or formed by NP-movement like *The door was opened.*

There are other properties of passivization that follow from quite general properties of movement rules. Fiengo has interesting things to say about this in his dissertation. There is a review of the matter in my book *Reflections on Language.*

In general, the passive construction in English exhibits a certain network of properties that follow from the assumption that a rule of NP-movement applies. In contrast, in many languages what corresponds roughly to English passive has different properties. There is a transitive verb construction with direct object, and a transitive verb may also appear with a different morphology with its direct object as subject. Contrary to the case in English, the subject of the passive form must be the direct object of the corresponding active form. It cannot be the subject of an embedded phrase, for example. Idiomatic expressions behave differently. There would be no reason to postulate a passive transformation for these languages: passive morphology is a lexical property of the verb.

In fact, it is not quite correct to say, as I just did, that there are two different types of language in this respect. It would be more accurate to say that there are two (and perhaps more) fundamental processes for forming what we informally call the "passive": one, transformational; the other, lexical. For example, English also has a lexical passive, as in one of the two senses of *The door was closed.* This lexical passive is perhaps clearer in negative structures like *untaught, unread,* etc. In *John was untaught,* or *The book was unread,* we must consider the passive as lexical, for quite general reasons, and not transformational—because in principle transformations may not generate lexical structures (this principle has been disputed, but I think it is correct). Note that in these cases the participles with the prefix *un-* behave exactly as predicted—like a lexical passive. We have *John was taught French* with the passive transformation, but not *John was untaught French,* because the lexical passive can only be formed with the direct object as the passive subject. Similarly we find lexical idiosyncrasies among the lexical passives, but not in the case of transformational passives, as the theory predicts. The meaning of *John was untaught, untutored,* is not predictable by means of a general rule from the meaning of *teach John, tutor John.* In the same way, the idiomatic expression *John was unread* certainly does not correspond to *read John.* But *John was taught French,* for example, has a meaning that is entirely predictable by a general rule as, in principle, in the case of true transformational rules: it has essentially the same meaning as *X taught John French.* These examples illustrate what seems to be a phenomenon of considerable generality. For reasons of principle rooted in the general theory of grammar, there are two quite different constructions called "passive," probably more.

I do not see any reason to suppose that there is a universal rule covering these distinct kinds of construction. To postulate a universal "rule of passive" would tend to obscure all these differences and also the general principles involved in their explication.

M.R.:   French seems to be an intermediate case . . .

N.C.:   French is an interesting case. I think the question requires more extensive study. For the moment it remains open.

CHAPTER 7

The Extended
Standard Theory

M.R.: The theory which you propose at present is the Extended Standard Theory. A short time ago you mentioned that the contribution of Ray Jackendoff played a determining role in the elaboration of the new version of the model.

N.C.: By demonstrating the role of surface structure in semantic interpretation, yes. Contrary to what the Standard Theory of *Aspects* proposed, it seems highly probable that surface structure plays a primary role in semantic interpretation.

In fact, the sole—though essential—contribution of deep structure to determining the meaning of an expression seems to be the representation of so-called thematic relations, such as the relation of *key* to *open* as "instrument" in *John opened the door with a key, The key opened the door,* etc. The Extended Standard Theory assumes that the rewriting rules of the base generate deep structure in which lexical items are inserted. The thematic relations between the verb and the noun phrases which are grammatically related to it are defined at this level. Other semantic properties are determined by rules applying to surface structure. We have spoken of the co-reference of nouns and pronouns, where the relationships between positions in the surface structure appear to be decisive, and also of the interaction of negation and quantifiers. There too surface structure position is critical, a fact recognized in both the Extended

Standard Theory and generative semantics. There are other phenomena that relate to surface structure, for example, focus and presupposition.

M.R.:   Recently the Extended Standard Theory has incorporated a new concept, which seems most promising for syntax, semantics, and phonology: the concept of "trace." You define a trace *t* as a phonological zero element, which marks the position of an element that has been displaced by a transformation. For example:

> *Whom did you see?*—Whom did you see *t*? etc.

Lisa Selkirk, Thomas Wasow, and Robert Fiengo have shown the role of this in both phonology and semantics.

N.C.:   Within the framework of trace theory, one can even go further and say that *all* of semantic representation, including thematic relations, can in a sense be derived from surface structure: to be sure, with a considerably enriched notion of "surface structure," because the new surface structures contain traces, in terms of which thematic relations as specified by the base rules can be reconstructed.

M.R.:   In effect, the thematic relations say, for example, that the indirect object of the verb *teach* is a GOAL. That relation is preserved if the indirect object is displaced by a transformation. For example:

To whom	does	Pierre	teach Latin
GOAL		AGENT	THEME

According to Jackendoff, the relation is displaced together with the noun. With trace theory (the trace being linked "as by an invisible thread" to the element which it replaced) one can attribute the thematic relation of the surface structure, because the order of the deep structure is still represented:

To whom	does	Pierre	teach	Latin	*t*
		AGENT		THEME	GOAL

N.C.: *To whom* receives its thematic relation by the intervention of its trace.

M.R.: The trace is a sort of memory of deep structure recorded in the surface structure.

N.C.: From another point of view the trace in this case can be considered as indicating the position of a variable bound by a kind of quantifier which is introduced into the logical form by rules applying to the surface structure. In this latter version, the theory has roughly the following form: Deep structures are generated by the base component, with their specific properties. Transformations form surface structures enriched by traces. These surface structures are associated by further rules to representations of sound (phonetic representation) and meaning (logical form).

M.R.: That gives the following schema:

N.C.: This is an alternative model of language as a cognitive system. Remember that by the phrase "logical form" I mean that partial representation of meaning that is determined by grammatical structure. Beyond that, we can study the interaction of this cognitive system with others, just as in physiology, once the heart has been identified, we can study its interaction with other organs.

M.R.: It seems to me that you have chosen the expression "logical form" because all the semantic facts that depend on linguistic structure can be expressed in terms of traditional or modern logic.

N.C.: I wouldn't want to imply that. Choice of the term *logical form* may or may not have been a wise terminological decision—the term is used in other ways. But terminology aside, there are interesting directions for research here. It has often been supposed (by me too) that the choice of logic used to express "logical form" is of no importance. For example, for thinking about quantifiers in natural language, any two logics having the same expressive power seemed to be equivalent. This seems reasonable if the relation between syntactic structure and logical form is taken to be expressed by a principle that applies in "one step," as it were. But in the model we are sketching out now, the derivation of logical form proceeds step by step. Logical form is determined by a derivational process analogous to those of syntax and phonology. Then the choice of logical notation becomes crucial. It is possible that certain rules will be stated properly at an intermediate level in terms of one logic and not in terms of another; and this appears to be the case. For example, a logic with variables and a logic without variables have the same expressive power. But if the logical form is derived step by step, it turns out that a logic with variables is required to express certain general principles which explain facts of language. Consequently, it becomes possible to obtain empirical evidence to answer the question: Which is the correct system of logic, the notation actually used in mental representation?

There is interesting evidence suggesting that the right logic is a classical logic with variables. Perhaps we can explain in these terms why classical logic with variables is so intuitive. We can consider it to be, in effect, a simplified version, somewhat schematized, of the logical form determined by surface structure. It can virtually be "read off the mind." In contrast, logical systems without variables, even though they often have the same expressive power, are more counterintuitive, and are generally understood more readily through the mediation of classical logic. It can also be shown, I believe, that they simply do not furnish the types of representation appropriate for formulating rules that relate the surface structure to the logical form in the most general way.

Montague's theory of quantification is one such case. The situation with respect to the choice of a logic is in a certain way comparable to familiar problems in phonology. Thus, two systems of distinctive features can have the same "expressive power" in principle, but one might be preferred to the other—and we can conclude that it is correct for language, and the other false—because one permits the formulation of certain generalizations and explanatory principles while the other doesn't. The situation seems to me to be the same with regard to the relation of surface structure to logical form. As far as I can see, certain significant generalizations require a classical logic containing variables, where at times the variables reflect the presence of a trace in surface structure.

M.R.:   That is what you talked about in your lecture at Vincennes. It seems to me that these recent discoveries also explain the history of the relations between logic and language theory. Before generative grammar, all those who wanted to account for the languages in a somewhat systematic manner turned to logic to furnish them a "generative base." That was true of certain structuralists—here I'm thinking of Šaumjan—and it was true of the grammatical tradition.

The first act of generative grammar was to separate itself from that tradition. You said: Though logic is necessary for the construction of scientific theory, the syntax of natural languages is not reducible to logic. No, deep structure is not the logical structure of propositions; and so on. The theory of syntax elaborates its own concepts.

However, one question remained: If the structure of language does not depend on logical structure, *how is it possible that generations of philosophers could speak of these questions and work on them to such an extent,* and understand each other? How does one explain this "intuition" of which you speak? The hypothesis of a "logical form" as a component interpreting surface structure could answer that question; philosophers and grammarians have never studied the properties of surface structure, even though they thought they saw deep structures there. The Port-Royal *Grammaire Générale* analyzed the sentence, *Dieu invisible a créé le monde visible* into the propositions *Dieu est invisible,* etc. It was thought that the complex of these propositions constituted the deep structure of the sentence. Now it is the opposite that is true: deep structure is a part of syntactic structure, and the complex of propositions is deduced from *interpretive rules* belonging to the semantic component, which give a "content" to the surface structure. It is therefore hardly astonishing that logical form is related to surface structure. But the point of view is altogether different.

N.C.:   Completely. Not long ago I thought that there was no sense to the question whether, say, traditional logic with variables or Montague's theory of quantifiers, for example, is the *right* logic, the logic that is in fact employed in logical form and plays a part in explaining semantic properties of language. But that was incorrect. The fact that it is possible to find empirical arguments bearing on this question in itself constitutes an interesting result.

CHAPTER 8

Deep Structure

M.R.: Perhaps by retracing the history of deep structure we can take up that of generative grammar again, this time from another viewpoint?

N.C.: If you like. Let us begin with that phrase: the term *deep structure* itself was proposed in the context of the Standard Theory. Recall that this theory proposed the existence of a class of structures:

—which were generated by the rules of the base component;

—which received semantic interpretation;

—which were converted by transformations into well-formed surface structures.

M.R.: And which contained the lexical items.

N.C.: Yes. This was the point at which lexical items were inserted. It was thus simply a technical term.

However, the expression had been used in other ways. For example, Wittengenstein had used the distinction *deep grammar-surface grammar.* Hockett adopted similar terminology in his *Course of Modern Linguistics.* What they had in mind was the distinction between things which are not presented directly and those which are.

Whorf made use of the notion "covert categories," that is, categories which have a functional role with no morphological reflection.

The point is that similar expressions had already appeared in the literature. Speaking of generative grammar, however, one must use the term in its technical sense, putting aside loose associations of ideas or more or less vague similarities.

In the earlier version of the theory, say, in *LSLT,* there was no concept of "deep structure." The concept closest to it was the technical notion *T-marker.* This determined the semantic representation. This T-marker represented the transformational history of sentences, just as the P-marker (phrase marker) represented a derivational history of rewriting rules. Remember that first model. It was supposed that rewriting rules generate a finite number of abstract objects, which could be transformed into surface structures by "singulary" transformations operating to form a simple sentence; thus one obtained a finite class of "kernel sentences" such as *John said that, Bill has just come in;* and also simple derived sentences such as *This book has been read by everyone in England,* etc.

"Generalized" transformations embedded certain structures within others: *John said that Bill has just come in,* etc.

The arrangement of these singulary and generalized transformations formed the transformational history represented by the T-marker. This marker consequently showed how sentences are associated with one another, what are the relations among their parts, and so on. It is in this respect that it can be compared to deep structure.

In the version that followed next, the term *deep structure* was in some ways "overdetermined": we have seen that in the Standard Theory it is generated by the base, receives the lexical items and undergoes semantic interpretation, and, finally, is converted to well-formed surface structure. It is important to note that these properties are independent. The structure which undergoes semantic interpretation is not necessarily the one which is the locus of lexical insertion, or which is transformed into surface structure.

In fact, the work which followed *Aspects* distinguished these different properties and showed that they had to be dissociated.

The Extended Standard Theory maintains that it is not the deep structure which undergoes semantic interpretation. We have seen that under trace theory one can say that surface structure is associated directly with semantic representation.

What happened to the concept of "deep structure" is what happens in the development of any theory. Terms are defined within a particular context, and this context changes as people construct different empirical hypotheses. The terms then take on a different meaning.

Take the term *atom:* that term does not signify today what it meant for the Greeks. Concepts change constantly as the theoretical matrix changes. In the natural sciences no one fails to understand that—at least not to too great a degree. But in a field like linguistics it bothers people enormously. The only thing we can do is try to preserve the clarity of ideas.

For some, "deep structure" continues to mean that structure which bears semantic representation.

M.R.:   Following generative semantics . . .

N.C.:   More or less. I have continued to use the term for the structure generated by the base, which is transformed into well-formed surface structure. The source of confusion lies in the fact that we employ the same term in two different senses.

However, the greatest confusion comes from people working at the periphery of the field, for example, some literary critics who use the term in a vaguely Wittgensteinian sense. Many people have attributed the word *deep* to grammar itself, perhaps identifying "deep structure" and "universal grammar."

I have read many criticisms saying how ill-conceived it is to postulate innate deep structures. I never said that, and nothing I have written suggests anything of the sort, though such a view has been maintained by others.

Similarly, I have often read that what I am proposing is that deep structures do not vary from one language to another, that all languages have the same deep structure: people have apparently been misled by the word *deep* and confuse it with *invari-*

ant. Once again, the only thing I claim to be "invariant" is universal grammar.

M.R.:   In *Reflections on Language* you replace the term *deep structure* with *initial phrase marker.*

N.C.:   To try to avoid precisely those confusions we've just mentioned. But if people want to be confused, they will always succeed, no matter what term you use. The expression "initial phrase marker" has the advantage of sounding like a technical term. Yet it can still be misleading: how is one going to interpret "initial"? As earliest in time? That would be senseless.

M.R.:   Furthermore, the fact that semantics has been linked to deep structure . . .

N.C.:   . . . has made people think that everything "deep" must relate to semantics. People think that semantics must be something "deep." Again an association that provokes misunderstandings. We come back to the question of the different ways in which things can be interesting or intellectually "deep."

Semantics seems deep in part because it remains obscure. That does not necessarily mean that it really is a deep subject. Perhaps it is trivial and we don't yet recognize that. Perhaps there is nothing very interesting to understand. To be sure, semantics is interesting in itself. But on the intellectual level it may turn out that phonology requires extremely abstract rules that enter into complex deductions and explain a large number of phenomena. In that sense phonology is deep—as physics is deep. Is semantics "deep" in that sense? For the moment the answer is no. To merit the term *deep,* a subject must provide answers to certain questions that attain a certain level of intellectual depth. But all this has nothing to do with the technical notion "deep structure."

M.R.:   And then too, the work of Joan Bresnan (which shows that the accentuation of English sentences must take into consideration not only surface structure, but also deep and intermediary structures) destroys the idea that the phonological aspect of language only involves the surface . . .

N.C.:   That's true, and that is another aspect of the Standard Theory that has been properly criticized.

M.R.:   In the Standard Theory we have a symmetry of relations: deep structure–semantic interpretation, and surface structure–phonological interpretation.

N.C.:   Today it seems that a different schema may be necessary: surface structure determines semantic representation—that is, in the enriched sense of surface structure in which certain properties of underlying deep structure are captured by means of trace theory.

M.R.:   And deep structure may determine the phonology. That would give:

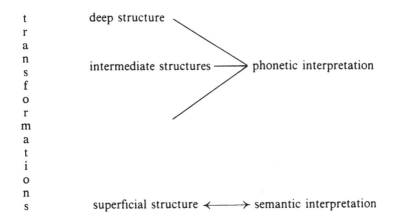

N.C.:   But that's not all. Another property attributed to the deep structure in the Standard Theory has been questioned. That is the idea that it expresses *all* the grammatical relations among lexical items. Take the thesis of Jean-Roger Vergnaud on relative clauses.[1] He puts forward the hypothesis that in a sentence containing a relative clause, the noun phrase which appears in the main clause is in fact "raised" from the relative clause. For example, the sentence *I saw the man who was there* is derived from a deep structure like

I saw (— (the man was there)).
     NP   S

The noun phrase *the man* is taken from the embedded clause
and placed in the NP position left empty to the right of the verb
in the main clause. Under this hypothesis a noun phrase is left
empty in the deep structure and a noun is inserted in this
structure by a transformational rule. That would imply that the
grammatical relation (hence the thematic relation) between *see*
and *man* is not determined in the deep structure. The grammatical relation between the structural positions is determined
by the deep structure, but not the relation between the lexical
elements. So here we have again an interesting idea modifying
the definition of deep structure.

Carlos Otero has advanced an interesting idea that is more
radical. He suggests that lexical insertion takes place altogether
in surface structure. Why? For one thing, because transformations never refer to the phonetic properties of words. If words
enter into the structure at the level of surface structure, this fact
would be explained. This theory predicts that the idiosyncratic*
properties of words do not have any effect on transformations,
which seems to be true.

This hypothesis is particularly interesting for those languages
where inflectional morphology has considerable effect on the
internal structure of words. In English that only happens in the
case of irregular words. But when the regular morphological
forms vary greatly, one might want to say that the word is
generated in the form in which it appears in the surface structure. Other considerations are also relevant. The question remains open, but if the answer is positive, then surface structure
is the locus of lexical insertion.

M.R.:   Sometimes the word *deep* is accorded value for reasons just as bad as those for which it has been criticized. People

---

*A particular property of each word which distinguishes it from other words. See also
p.136.

see the possibility of a new hermeneutics here. This is actually the same mistake . . .

N.C.: Yes, in terms of things that are "hidden," that are to be discovered; but there are many aspects of phonology that are "deep" in this sense of the word.

M.R.: The word *surface** is equally misleading . . .

N.C.: Surface structure is something quite abstract, involving properties that do not appear in the physical form . . . It is by virtue of such properties that language is worth studying.

M.R.: Personally I find quite fascinating an abstraction or depth that is linked to trace theory—that is, *the astonishing study of the structuring effect of silence:* in phonology, the trace changes the intonation; in semantics, it blocks co-reference . . .

N.C.: That is a really interesting property of surface structures.

M.R.: In poetry too, in metrics, these structuring silences are essential . . . But don't you think that by placing so much stress on surface structure, you invite being accused of returning to structuralism? In general, whenever you have refined a concept, you have been accused of abandoning your fundamental hypotheses. I remember reading that your definition of degrees of grammaticalness signifies that you have abandoned the concept of grammaticalness!

N.C.: Well, in fact, the notion of "degree of grammaticalness" was developed at the same time as the notion of "grammaticalness," within the theory of generative grammar, that is, in the early 1950s. A chapter of *LSLT* is devoted to this question, and I also refer to it in *Syntactic Structures.* But what is more important is that the kind of criticism you're referring to reveals once again the difference between the attitude of the natural sciences on the one hand, and one often found in the social sciences and "humanities" on the other. The latter, which lack the intellectual content of the natural sciences, are to a great degree involved with personalities rather than ideas. In science it is self-evident that concepts are going to change; that

---

*"Superficiel" in French, thus even more so—Translator.

is just to say that you hope to learn something. This is not theology, after all. You do not make declarations which you must preserve unchanged for the rest of your life. By contrast, in the social sciences or in humanistic studies, positions are often personalized. Once you have taken a position, you are supposed to defend it no matter what happens. The positions of one or another school are identified with individuals. It becomes a question of honor not to change, that is, to learn nothing. In linguistics that is very striking: you are accused of refuting yourself if you modify your position. I have often read such criticism, and I find it difficult to comprehend.

If you are concerned to discover the truth, whether you work alone or in a group, it is evident that you are going to change your mind often—each time an issue of a serious journal appears. When there is real progress, these changes will be significant. You come to think in a different way. The first approximations have to be changed to other approximations, better ones.

As far as the alleged "return to structuralism" is concerned: first of all, suppose that were true—fine! It often happens that hypotheses in the natural sciences are abandoned at a certain period because they are inadequate, but are then reconstructed later when a higher level of comprehension has been attained. Take the theory of the atom: abandoned, then resurrected in a different form. That does not mean that we have returned to Democritus! Not at all. Things progress, new perspectives open up, reinterpreting what was previously rejected. There is no "personal defeat" in that.

Take the question of Cartesianism. It was entirely correct to abandon the Cartesian doctrine for a long time. I think it is correct to return to something like it today, but in a substantially different form.

M.R.:   It does not seem to me that in the case of surface structure we have a return to whatever it may have been.

N.C.:   The work of the last ten years has shown that surface structure plays a role which was not suspected previously. Can one therefore speak of a return to structuralism? In my opinion, that does not make any sense in this case. The technical concept of surface structure did not really exist in structuralist theories, and recent theories raise a large number of questions concerning surface structure that could not have been posed within the structuralist framework. That concept, in the current sense, appeared only with generative grammar, as an infinite class of structures . . .

M.R.: It is defined by its opposition to *deep structure,* etc.

N.C.: And as I've said, a surface structure which incorporates traces is much more abstract than the earlier notion. Thus we have a concept of surface structure defined in terms of rules that generate an infinite set of objects, standing in opposition to deep structure, and considerably more abstract than before, in that properties of deep structure are captured through trace theory.

On the other hand, suppose one were to discover that the structuralist concept of phoneme plays a very important role, previously unsuspected. Suppose that the arguments that have been advanced against the existence of a phonemic level could be surmounted within another conceptual framework. That would not be a return to an old idea, but an advance to a new idea, giving a new significance to an old concept. That would be progress.

When theories and the concepts that appear in them are personalized, one looks to see "who" is wrong; but that is not the correct way of thinking. That "who" may have been right in the context of his or her own time, wrong in the context of a richer theory, and will perhaps prove right once again. That's fine. Furthermore, there is nothing wrong with being wrong. Progress is based on interesting ideas which generally prove wrong—either incomplete, misconstrued, or completely wrong.

M.R.: In the humanities certain professors spend their time in effect teaching their Ph.D. thesis.

N.C.: Anybody who teaches at age fifty what he was teaching at age twenty-five had better find another profession. If in twenty-five years nothing has happened which proves to you that your ideas were wrong, it means that you are not in a living field, or perhaps are part of a religious sect.

M.R.: In a field where you are only asked to *apply* a theory to a new object, this kind of sclerosis can also appear. Within the framework of structuralist phonology, for example, you are offered a method for finding the phonological system of a language, and when you have found it, the work is completed. In generative phonology, that is where the work begins . . .

N.C.: Structuralist phonology—quite apart from the question of its validity—posed rather limited questions. And as you say, once you have answered these questions, the interesting work can begin.

That aspect of structuralism troubled me when I was a student. I liked linguistics very much, it was intriguing. But it was not too clear what the point was; in a sense the discipline was closed. Suppose one had completed the phonemic analysis of all the languages in the world, as well as the morphological analysis and analysis of constituents, in the sense of structuralist methodology. These are finite systems (with some ambiguity in the latter case), analyzable according to procedures that were taken to be essentially perfected, except for some details, and which were applicable to any language. Such a field is hardly worth the trouble of exploring. Rather like in natural history: imagine that you have described all the butterflies . . .

M.R.: On this point structuralist linguistics is deceptive, just as is the way it is taught. What do the professors ask of students? To apply a ready-made method. One is condemned to repeat what has already been established. Personally, my enthusiasm for linguistics was born largely at the moment when I understood that it offered a means to do intellectual *and* creative work within the "humanities." Instead, in literary studies and in the human and social sciences students were asked to apply methods without any reflection . . .

Certainly, the intellectual creativity inherent in generative grammar is also based on rules, but those are explicit rules which one can challenge or change.

N.C.: Furthermore, if some field is still at the level where procedural methods can be applied, then it is at a very primitive level indeed. A purely descriptive level, say, like Babylonian astronomy, or not even that. There are no "methods" in this sense in a field having real intellectual content. The goal is to find the truth. How to do that, nobody knows. There are no procedures that can be outlined in advance for discovering scientific truth. You cannot train a creative physicist or biologist by telling him: "Here are the methods, apply them to a new organism." That may be the way to train a lab technician, but not a scientist. You do that when you don't know how to find meaningful work for students. It is an admission of failure.

What you expect of a scientist is to discover new principles, new theories, even new modes of verification . . . That won't happen by learning a fixed procedure. The same is true of linguistics today. It is impossible to explain to someone the procedure he must apply in order to find the generative grammar of some language. What one looks forward to is the discovery of new phenomena that will show that the theories which have been proposed are false, that they must be changed—new questions that no one has thought of posing before, at least in a clear manner, new contributions to understanding, achieved perhaps with new "methods." And finally, new ideas and new principles, which will reveal how limited, false, and superficial are the assumptions that we hold to be valid today.

M.R.: At times that may disturb students accustomed to traditional instruction, where it is sufficient to learn passively what you are taught. In generative grammar, in effect, instruction consists in the explication of fundamental concepts, and in the presentation of the history of the discipline in terms of a detailed account of different hypotheses. One can explain the manner in which something is demonstrated, how such a demonstration is constructed. But one cannot tell anyone how to find a new idea, how to invent. Invention is linked to the *desire* to understand one's chosen field better.

CHAPTER 9

Universal Grammar
and Unresolved Questions

M.R.: These last years you have concentrated your linguistic work on the discovery of the *conditions imposed on rules,* that is, hypotheses concerning universal grammar. This is the third epoch of generative grammar which I defined at the beginning.

N.C.: We may think of universal grammar as the system of principles which characterizes the class of possible grammars by specifying how particular grammars are organized (what are the components and their relations), how the different rules of these components are constructed, how they interact, and so on.

M.R.: It is a sort of metatheory.

N.C.: And a set of empirical hypotheses bearing on the biologically determined language faculty. The task of the child learning a language is to choose from among the grammars provided by the principles of universal grammar that grammar which is compatible with the limited and imperfect data presented to him. That is to say, once again, that language acquisition is not a step-by-step process of generalization, association, and abstraction, going from linguistic data to the grammar, and that the subtlety of our understanding transcends by far what is presented in experience.

M.R.: The expression "mental organ" has appeared on occasion in these hypotheses . . .

N.C.: I think that is a correct and useful analogy, for reasons we have already discussed. The problems concerning this "mental organ" are very technical, perhaps too much so to enter into detail here. A particular grammar includes rewriting rules, transformational rules, lexical rules, rules of semantic and phonological interpretation. It seems that there are several components in a grammar, several classes of rules, each having specific properties, linked in a manner determined by the principles of universal grammar. The theory of universal grammar has as its goal to determine precisely the nature of each of these components of the grammar and their interaction. For reasons we have already discussed—having to do with the uniformity of acquisition of a highly complex and articulated structure on the basis of limited data—we can be sure that universal grammar, once we have understood it correctly, imposes severe restrictions on the variety of possible rule systems. But this means that the permissible rules cannot express in detail how they function, and it also means that the rules tend to overgenerate —one cannot include *within the rules themselves* the restrictions placed on their application. What many linguists have tried to do is to abstract from the rules some quite general principles that govern their application. The study of these abstract conditions is a particularly interesting part of universal grammar. I have been working on this topic since the beginning of the 1960s, and more specifically in the past few years. From about 1970, I have been working on and writing about some fairly radical hypotheses on this subject.

These hypotheses restrict very severely the expressive power of transformational rules, thereby limiting the class of possible transformational grammars. To compensate for the fact that the rules, thus restricted, tend to generate far too many structures, several quite general principles have been proposed concerning the manner in which transformational rules must be applied to given structures. These general principles are of a very natural type, in my opinion, associated with quite reasonable constraints on information processing, in ways that are probably related quite closely to the language faculty. What I hope to be able to show is that these principles provide the basic framework for "mental computation," and that in interaction with rules of limited variety and expressive power, they suffice to explain the curious arrangement of phenomena that we discover when we study in detail how sentences are formed, used, and understood. I doubt that they will work entirely, but I believe that they are on the right track. This type of approach has proven very productive, much more so than I expected. In my opinion this is a reasonable way to develop the Extended Standard Theory. Some work has been published, and more is on the way. I feel that the work of the past few years is much more encouraging than has been the case for quite some time. I'm very happy about it . . .

M.R.:   That is obvious, in any case . . .

N.C.:   Yes, I feel that we are getting somewhere. I hope that I'll be able to find the time . . .

M.R.:   However, these recent results, unlike what was done previously in semantics, for example, were not foreseen in the initial program of *LSLT*. These are new kinds of problems.

N.C.:   Considerably different. The theory presented in *LSLT* permitted a great number of rules. I tried at first to provide a system rich enough to express as much as I could imagine. Now, in a sense, I'm trying to do the opposite, to limit the expressive power of the rules. In *LSLT* there is no distinction between rules and conditions on rules. That distinction appeared first in *Current Issues in Linguistic Theory*, with the A/A condition,* the principle of recoverability of deletion, and a certain number of others, proposed as conditions belonging

---

*This condition hypothesizes that a constituent of the category *A* cannot be extracted from within another constituent of the same category *A*. This prevented, for example, the complement of a noun contained within a direct object from being chosen as the NP displaced by the passive transformation:

(a) *John saw ((Mary)'s brother)*
        NP   *NP*

(b) *Mary was seen brother by John*

to universal grammar. Ross developed this approach in an original and very important way in his thesis, as did others. A recent book by Richard Kayne on French syntax is a particularly important contribution in this direction. This line of research has proven very productive.

M.R.:   Many misunderstandings have surrounded your reference to universal grammar. Some have even taken it to be a universal language. In my opinion this is due to the fact that it is very difficult to imagine what a condition imposed on a rule is, without knowing what linguistic structure is . . .

N.C.:   . . . And without knowing what a rule is, yes.

M.R.:   For that a minimum knowledge of linguistics is required. Otherwise one imagines "spontaneously"—that is to say, due to the philosophic tradition internalized through the mediation of the contemporary vocabulary—that universal grammar is like logic. That is why so often one has seen very different kinds of people confuse "universal grammar" with "deep structure," because by "deep structure" they understand the logical subject-predicate proposition, supposed by philosophers as underlying all language. This confusion is impossible in generative grammar. Universal grammar is a sort of metatheory; deep structure, as we have seen, is a technical term pertaining to the particular grammar, and designating a precise stage in the derivation of a sentence.

N.C.:   In the same fashion, some philosophers have objected that human beings do not have "innate grammars"—as they think I have proposed. This is simply to confuse universal grammar with grammar. It is important to keep in mind that universal grammar is not a grammar, but rather a theory of grammars, a kind of metatheory or schematism for grammar. In that sense, the theory presented in *LSLT* or in any general book on linguistic theory is an attempt to formulate the principles of universal grammar, at least in the sense in which I am using the expression "universal grammar." As linguistic work progresses, we can hope that it will lead to a deeper understanding of "universal grammar," that is, linguistic theory, with the constraints this theory imposes on what counts as a possible human language.

As you have remarked, much of the work of the past few years has been concentrated on universal grammar in a more clear-cut and sharper fashion than before. The difference, of course, is "quantitative," insofar as every formulation of linguistic theory is intended as a contribution to universal grammar. But the remark is correct in that there has been, I believe, some real progress toward formulating the principles of universal grammar, at least in the domain of syntax and phonology (much less in semantics, where research has not yet produced principles of any substantial scope or explanatory power). But as you emphasize correctly, universal grammar in the sense in which the term is used in the work on generative grammar must not be confused with deep structure.

Unresolved Questions

M.R.:   Today many linguists are working within the framework of generative grammar, and on all kinds of languages. This theory has already permitted the discovery and explanation of a large number of facts; in general, the results of this work are accessible to anyone who wishes to take the trouble to read them. However, in spite of the number of positive results, I imagine that many questions are still without an answer.

N.C.:   Certainly! But it is useful to distinguish two types of questions: internal questions and external questions. By internal questions I mean those that arise from the moment when you begin to work within a particular version of linguistic theory, for example, the Extended Standard Theory. By external questions I mean those concerning the choice of this general type of theory instead of others based on quite different assumptions, the epistemological status of the theory, the problem of the legitimacy of its idealizations, the interactions with other systems, and so on.

As far as internal questions are concerned, they are innumerable. They arise whenever you attempt to test the theory you have formulated and try to improve it; there is no interesting hypothesis, to my knowledge, which is not confronted by counterexamples that are very serious—for example, the conditions on rules, such as the specified subject condition.* In my opinion, some of these hypotheses are reasonably well substantiated. Nevertheless, when you study complex linguistic material, a large number of phenomena do not seem to obey these conditions, others seem to obey different conditions, and still others do not follow any conditions that have been proposed.

To be concrete, take "reflexivation." That is a process which varies from one language to another. In English reflexivation works rather like bound anaphora, that is, the kind of anaphora that one finds in sentences like *John lost his way,* where *his* must obligatorily refer back to *John.* (By contrast, in *John lost his book* there is no bound anaphora, because here *his* can refer to anyone, including *John.*)

The idea of treating reflexivation as a case of bound anaphora is due to Michael Helke, who developed it in his Ph.D. thesis at MIT several years ago. It seems to me quite correct, for English and for a number of other languages. According to this view, reflexives are a special case of bound anaphora. Therefore, *John hurts himself* is analogous to *John lost his way.* And more generally, the conditions which hold for bound anaphora apply also to reflexivation.

However, even in English, this matter is not at all clear. Thus, many speakers accept such sentences as *The pictures of themselves that I gave them are hanging in the library, They thought that some pictures of themselves would be on exhibit,* and so on. In his book Jackendoff gives many complicated examples of varying degrees of acceptability; a number have been suggested by others too. These facts raise many problems.

---

*See above, p. 61.

Furthermore, in other languages reflexivation has very different properties; this is true in Korean, for example. While in English the antecedent of the reflexive must be found in the same sentence, in Korean the form that seems to correspond most closely to the English reflexive can refer to something not mentioned in the sentence at all. This has been studied by Wha-Chun Kim in a recent MIT dissertation. The phenomenon is obscured by certain rules which tend to choose an antecedent nearer to the reflexive pronoun, but it seems that these are rules of preference, and in fact reflexives can refer back to something given in common knowledge or previous discourse. In such a language the rules of reflexivation do not seem to belong to the sentence grammar in the strict sense: the rule which governs the form that is comparable to the English reflexive seems rather to be a rule of "discourse," or to be more exact, a rule which relates linguistic competence to the other cognitive systems that play a role in performance.

There are also languages where the behavior of what is considered to be the reflexive is different from the case of either English or Korean. For example, Polish, Japanese, perhaps Classical Greek. In these languages the reflexive must be bound to something in the same sentence, it appears, but not under the restrictive conditions governing English reflexive—rather, some very general conditions on anaphora, involving domination, grammatical relation, and perhaps linear precedence apply.*

If you want to ask embarrassing questions, you can ask me what all this means. Does it mean that reflexivation can be simply anything? Certainly not. Do these different classes of reflexives have common properties? Are they governed by other principles of anaphora? Are they similar to reciprocal pronouns? How do they behave with respect to the conditions on rules? In many cases they violate conditions on rules which seem valid otherwise. Is it that we do not know how to formu-

---

*See pp. 181–82.

late the rules governing the reflexive, or is it that the conditions on rules are wrong, or is there some other reason? All these remain open questions.

For virtually everything that has been studied seriously, questions of this nature arise. To answer them, one might undertake investigations of a wide range of languages. I'm not sure that that is likely to be the most productive approach. If the conditions in question are at a certain level of abstraction, then no "phenomenon" will confirm or refute them; only rules can do so. Therefore one must begin by establishing a system of rules to see if they are compatible with the conditions. The phenomena in themselves tell us nothing about the validity of a condition on rules. They bear on the condition only indirectly, to the extent to which the phenomena corroborate a system of rules that can be evaluated with respect to its conformity to the postulated conditions. One cannot verify a condition by referring to a traditional grammar, or by asking an informant. Serious work on particular languages shows how difficult it is to establish a correct rule. Only too often one's early assumptions prove wrong. This does not mean that these abstract conditions on rules cannot be falsified; it means that one must work quite seriously on a language before it is possible to argue that a condition is falsified or verified.

The problem is quite general. A particular language must be studied in depth before facts and arguments emerge which have real theoretical significance. You can always look at a language and make some observations: "Here are the cases, the relations, etc." That does not mean much. Because when we study the problem closely, what seems true on the surface may be quite misleading. These internal questions may not be easy to resolve; they require hard work. One must study a language in considerable depth to find the facts that bear on principles of any significance.

Serious questions arise concerning the attitude one should take toward apparent counterexamples. At what point must they be taken seriously? In the natural sciences apparent counterevidence is often ignored, on the assumption that it will somehow be taken care of later. That is quite a sane attitude. Within reasonable limits, of course, not to excess. Because we must recognize that our comprehension of nontrivial phenomena is always extremely limited. That is true in physics and far more true in linguistics. We understand only fragments of reality, and we can be sure that every interesting and significant theory is at best only partially true. That is not a reason for abandoning theories or abandoning rational research.

At a given moment one has to cut short the questions that arise. One must try to assess the relative importance of the phenomena or rules that contradict one's hypotheses, as compared with the evidence supporting them. Then, one will either put aside counterevidence to be dealt with later, or else decide that the theory is inadequate and must be reconstructed. The choice isn't easy. There is no algorithm. And as this kind of problem arises constantly in the course of research, it is an intuitive judgment whether or not one should persevere within a given framework—because of the positive results and in spite of the apparent counterexamples. In general, there has been considerable progress in linguistics, if one considers the positive results—even if innumerable problems remain at each stage. "Methodologists" sometimes assert that a counterexample serves to refute a theory and shows that it must be abandoned. Such an injunction finds little support in the practice of the advanced sciences, as is well known, virtually a truism, in the history of science. The willingness to put aside the counterexamples to a theory with some degree of explanatory force, a theory that provides a degree of insight, and to take them up again at a higher level of understanding, is quite simply the path of rationality. In fact, it constitutes the precondition for significant progress in any nontrivial field of research.

M.R.:   And the external questions?

N.C.:   With respect to those, there are quite a few that one must keep in mind. For example, there is the question of the autonomy of syntax, which opposes formal grammar to "full" grammar. Is this an appropriate abstraction? Is it correct to say that the concepts of phonology and syntax are defined on the basis of formal primitive notions and not semantic primitives? Or is the distinction a proper one in the first place?

M.R.: We have seen that generative grammar replies "yes" to this question.

N.C.: At least certain tendencies within generative grammar. This answer seems to me to be the correct one, with certain qualifications. But one must not forget that these are important questions. In the same way, one may question the legitimacy of the idealization to language in the first place. Is it legitimate to say that grammar is a mechanism which associates phonetic representation and logical form? Does such a system really exist? Is one saying something correct about the human mind when one postulates that there is a mental organ consisting of a system of rules relating phonetic representation to logical form through the mechanism of syntax? That assumption involves a commitment to the legitimacy of a certain idealization. But of course we don't suppose that there is a box inside the brain. What this idealization means has often been misunderstood.

One can maintain with Ross and Lakoff, for example, that such a system does not exist, that grammatical rules must take into account personal beliefs and attitudes. If they are right, grammar constitutes an illegitimate idealization. I don't feel that there is justification for this position, but the question cannot be brushed aside a priori.

To demonstrate the legitimacy of an abstraction, it must be shown in the first place that it leads to interesting results. Then one must indicate how it is integrated within a more general schema. On this subject, just about everything remains to be done. How can a model of competence be integrated within performance models, models of speaking, and perception? To develop a model of performance, a model of competence must be presupposed; it is difficult to imagine a coherent alternative. It remains to be shown how knowledge of language is put to use. However, if for the moment there are no other plausible approaches, that does not mean they will never exist.

Finally, the physical realization of all these systems, of competence and of performance, remains quite unknown. We can only speak in a very abstract manner about properties of the mind. What are the physical mechanisms that satisfy the abstract conditions that we are now able to study? What corresponds physically to these systems and properties about which we make hypotheses? These are fundamental questions. Very little is known about the physical bases of these systems.

M.R.:   Can one consider as "external" the questions posed by sociolinguistics?

N.C.:   It is conceivable. I'm not sure what these questions are. One can imagine that the definition of a language or a dialect could be one such question. It seems doubtful that these are really linguistic notions.

What is the "Chinese language"? Why is "Chinese" called a language and the Romance languages, different languages? The reasons are political, not linguistic. On purely linguistic grounds, there would be no reason to say that Cantonese and Mandarin are dialects of one language while Italian and French are different languages. Furthermore, what makes French a single language? I suppose fifty years ago neighboring villages could be found which spoke dialects of French sufficiently different so that mutual intelligibility was limited.

So what is a language? There is a standard joke that a language is a dialect with an army and a navy. These are not linguistic concepts. As for other questions of sociolinguistics, it does not seem clear to me that they have been posed in a way that permits serious answers, for reasons that we have already discussed.

M.R.:   The linguistic concept is *grammar*.

N.C.:   Sociolinguistics is presumably concerned not with grammars in the sense of our discussion, but rather with concepts of a different sort, among them, perhaps, "language," if such a notion can become an object of serious study. As I've already said, it seems to me that any such study should be based on the idealization to systems in idealized homogeneous communities. Beyond that, it is not very clear that there are significant principles governing the extent and character of the variability of the system or systems in the heads of speakers or members of a language community.

Questions of language are basically questions of *power,* the kind of exercise of power that created the system of nation-states as in Europe. Plainly, this is not the only system of political organization. For example, in the old Ottoman Empire, regions such as the Levant incorporated numerous local communities, related to each other in various ways, and with a good deal of linguistic variation as well. Nobody spoke the Classical Arabic taught in the schools, but the so-called dialects were considered inferior. The intervention of the Western imperial powers led to a system of states, leaving bitter and unresolved conflicts and antagonisms, a system in which each individual must define himself as belonging to a nation or a *nation-state.* It is a system imposed from the outside on a region ill-adapted to it. Much the same is true in Africa, where the intrusion of the imperial powers has imposed a framework of *national* organization that does not correspond to the earlier nature of these societies. Consolidation of nation-states, as earlier in Europe, interacts in complex ways with the spread of national languages. There are no doubt important questions here, but it doesn't seem obvious that linguistics has much to contribute to the investigation of them.

M.R.:   What you have just said allows me to turn the accusation certain sociolinguists have made against generative grammar back against them. They called linguistics "imperialistic" because it was preoccupied with idealized systems, and in particular with standard systems, the study of which has been facilitated by prior researches. In short, what these critics want is that one studies the *language* of the people. You have just indicated to what extent that notion originated with bourgeois power, and in particular, with imperialism!

N.C.: I can't see that the charge makes any sense, for reasons we've already discussed—that the perfect speaker of an idealized system does not exist in the real world. In the speech of real speakers idealized systems interact; each of us speaks a variety of these systems, intermingling them in a complex fashion. Because the experience of individuals is different, the mixture of systems is different. But I do not believe that outside these systems there exists a reality of *dialect* or *language.*

Perhaps I am wrong. Perhaps there are constraints on the ways in which linguistic systems can or cannot enter into interaction in a single community, or a wider group, or the mind of a single person. Perhaps we shall find that certain combinations are possible and others impossible. If principles emerge which govern the interaction of these systems, then these will belong to a field called sociolinguistics. Perhaps one may also find a way to relate these principles to principles of sociology . . . No doubt, in social interaction all sorts of questions involve language. Perhaps the study of these questions will draw upon and in turn influence linguistic studies in some significant way. It is conceivable. I'm personally skeptical.

The situation is very different as far as the connection between language and cognitive psychology is concerned. Here there are questions with a fairly clear content, and one has at least some idea of how to approach them. One can look forward to significant progress, I think.

M.R.: Do you think that a new type of formalization would enable us to see language from a totally different viewpoint? For the moment we conceive of sentences as sequences of concatenated elements, that is to say, one placed after the other. Suppose that certain facts tend to prove that this perspective (which is expressed in the rewriting rules) is not the right one, and that we must consider sentences as "discontinuous" sequences: that certain elements can be inserted *between* other elements. Concretely that would be the same as saying that the rewriting rules take over a certain number of tasks presently assigned to transformations: permutations, inversions, adjunctions, and so on. Formally, these are models of insertion (intrication) . . .

N.C.: I personally began with something quite close to that, that is, with a much richer system of base rules and no transformations, in the work on Hebrew that we discussed. So naturally I don't regard this proposal as incoherent or out of the question. Such systems are certainly possible. One cannot be dogmatic in this matter. It is necessary to keep an open mind.

There are also other possibilities. It might be argued that a grammar is a bundle of perceptual strategies relating sound to meaning. That's a perspective very different from the one we've been discussing. It is conceivable that we will ultimately discover that this is the right approach—although I think that we have nothing to support such a belief today.

Once again, in the domain of embarrassing questions, I can see one that relates to your question about base grammar. There are languages where no argument has been found to justify one or another ordering of categories at the level of deep structure. These are languages of relatively free word order. The phenomenon is very interesting, although as yet inadequately described. There are languages where word order seems really to be much freer than in those languages usually called languages with a free word order—like Latin or Russian—which one can describe with rules like the "scrambling" rule* . . .

M.R.: Yes. In Russian or Latin, in spite of everything, word order is subjected to precise rules; and moreover, this involves nuances of semantic interpretation and of presupposition.

N.C.: This question has been studied by Ken Hale, who found such freedom of word order in Walbiri that he was obliged to attribute to such languages grammars of a sort that had occasionally been proposed, where the order of the base is free . . .

---

*The "scrambling rule" is a rule proposed by Ross to explain the inversions and permutations of Latin.

M.R.:   Like the applicational grammar of Šaumjan.

N.C.:   Yes, this requires other kinds of rules, perhaps non-linguistic ones, but involving such notions as "new information," etc. The grammar itself would leave word order fairly free. At least one can imagine this. Then one can ask: Are there actually two types of languages, quite different? Or is there a super-system, of which the two types are species? These are crucial questions, which are far from being clearly understood.

M.R.:   In effect, if two types of languages are possible, this casts doubt on the idea of a universal grammar.

In conclusion, you think that linguistics, in spite of all the problems that remain to be resolved, is the only positive element within the whole range of human sciences, except for a psychology of the future. However, there is one domain of which you have not spoken—generative poetics, which was created by Halle and Keyser at the end of the 1960s.[1] This competely new discipline can be considered a "human science": it meets all of your requirements. It has defined its object and its principles, it has provided itself with a theory of interaction between systems (the relation between literature and language), it has defined its concept of poetic competence. Born of generative grammar, it is not so much applied linguistics as structural poetics was. In my view this is also a field which has a rich future.

N.C.:   All this work is very interesting. However, I have contributed nothing to it, and do not feel qualified to discuss it. Here I have no competence at all; it is one of the innumerable subjects about which I have nothing to say . . .

Notes

Part I.   LINGUISTICS AND POLITICS

Chapter 1. *Politics*

1. In *Liberation* (January 1973).
2. See *Ramparts* (April 1973); *Social Policy* (September 1973).
3. This appeared in the last number of that journal, which was not able to find financial support and no longer exists. *Ramparts,* August 1975.
4. See Dave Dellinger, *More Power Than We Know* (New York: Doubleday, 1975); and N. Chomsky, Introduction to N. Blackstock, ed., *Cointelpro* (New York: Vintage Books, 1976), for some examples.
5. *The New Industrial State* (New York: Signet Books, 1967), p. 335.
6. Manuel Uribe, *Le livre noir de l'intervention américaine au Chile* (Paris: Le Seuil, 1974).
7. Jean Pierre Faye, *Le Portugal d'Otelo: La révolution dans le labyrinthe* (Paris: J.-C. Lattès, 1976), contains an analysis of the reporting on the November 1975 coup in Portugal.
8. Morris Halle and S. Jay Keyser, *English Stress, Its Form, Its Growth and Its Role in Verse* (New York: Harper & Row, 1971), and "Chaucer and the Study of Prosody," *College English,* vol. 28 (1966), pp. 187–219.

Chapter 2. *Linguistics and the Human Sciences*

1. William Labov, *Language in the Inner City—Studies in Black English Vernacular* (Philadelphia: University of Pennsylvania Press, 1972); also *The Study of Non-Standard English* (Urbana, Ill.: University of Illinois Press, 1975).
2. See Basil Bernstein, *Langages et classes sociales* (Paris: Editions de Minuit, 1975).

Chapter 3. *A Philosophy of Language?*

1. E. J. Dijksterhuis, *The Mechanization of the World Picture* (London: Oxford University Press, 1961), p. 466.

2. The text appears in Fons Elders, ed., *Reflexive Waters* (London: Souvenir Press, 1974).

Chapter 4. *Empiricism and Rationalism*

1. See especially *Word and Object* (Cambridge, Mass.: MIT Press, 1960).
2. See Chomsky, *Reflections on Language,* for a detailed discussion.

Part II.   GENERATIVE GRAMMAR

Chapter 5. *The Birth of Generative Grammar*

1. (Cambridge, Mass.: MIT Press, 1975) and (Englewood Cliffs, N.J.: Prentice-Hall, 1977), respectively.
2. Otto Jespersen, *A Modern English Grammar on Historical Principles* (Heidelberg: 1909–49).
3. The first collaborator of Chomsky, who played a primary role in developing the generative phonology of Russian and English, and later a generative theory of the structure of poetry.
4. A specialist in the psychology of language and its biological basis.
5. See his *Methods in Structural Linguistics* (Chicago: University of Chicago Press, 1951), available in manuscript in 1947. My own introduction to linguistics was through proof-reading this MS in 1947.
6. Troubetskoy was founder, with Roman Jakobson, of the Prague Circle. See his *Principles of Phonology,* translated by C. A. M. Baltaxe (Berkeley, Calif.: University of California Press, 1969).
7. See especially his "A Set of Postulates for Phonemic Analysis," *Language,* vol. 37 (1948).
8. See his *Anleitung zu phonologischen Beschreibungen* (Göttingen: Vandenhoeck-Ruprecht, 1935).
9. Z. S. Harris, "Transformational Theory," *Language,* vol. 41 (1965).
10. See N. Chomsky, "Formal Properties of Grammar," and G. A. Miller and N. Chomsky, "Finitary Models of Language Users," both in R. D. Luce, R. Bush, and E. Galanter, eds., *Handbook of Mathematical Psychology,* vol. II (New York: Wiley, 1963); N. Chomsky and M. P. Schützenberger, "The Algebraic Theory of Context-Free Languages," in P. Braffort and D. Hirschberg, eds., *Computer Programming and Formal Systems: Studies in Logic* (Amsterdam, North Holland: 1963); S. Ginsberg, *The Mathematical Theory of Context-Free Languages* (New York: McGraw-Hill, 1966); J. Hopcroft and J. D. Ullman, *Formal Languages and Their Relation to Automata* (Cambridge, Mass.: Addison-Wesley Press, 1969); J. Kimball, *The Formal Theory of Grammar* (Englewood Cliffs, N.J.: Prentice-Hall, 1973); and M. Gross and A. Lentin, *Introduction to Formal Grammars* (New York: Springer-Verlag, 1970).
11. (Holland: Mouton, 1964).

Chapter 6. *Semantics*

1. *Semantic Interpretation in Generative Grammar* (Cambridge, Mass.: MIT Press, 1972).

Chapter 8. *Deep Structure*

1. "French Relative Clauses," an unpublished Ph.D. thesis, MIT, Cambridge, Mass., 1974.

Chapter 9. *Universal Grammar and Unresolved Questions*

1. See Halle and Keyser, *English Stress: Its Form, Its Growth and Its Role in Verse* (New York: Harper & Row, 1971); and "Chaucer and the Study of Prosody," *College English* (December 1966).

Index

abduction, 71

academic world: and U.S. foreign policy, 41. *See also* universities

accessibility and accessible theories, 65–67, 76

ACLU, 25, 26

active-passive relationship, 106, 121, 123, 151n; in Harris's framework, 120–1. *See also* passive; transformations and transformational grammar

adolescence, 98

Akmajian, Adrian: *Introduction to the Principles of Transformational Syntax*, 104

All God's Dangers (Rosengarten), 55

Alperovitz, Gar, 16

American foreign policy, 6, 40–41; Cambodia, 24; Chile, 34, 35, 40; Cold War, 15–17; economic bases, 41; Laos, 10, 30; reconstruction of belief in, 35–36. *See also* Vietnam War

American Intellectual Elite, The (Kadushin), 11

American intellectuals, *see* intellectuals and intelligentsia

American mass media, 6, 19; "balance" policy, 8–9; as capitalistic institutions, 9; social and political analysis in, 6, 7–8; subservience of, 9–10; "vaccination" policy, 34–35. *See also* press

Amin, Idi, 34

anaphora and anaphoric relations, 142, 145, 147, 185; bound, 185

anarcho-syndicalists, 74

anthropology, 59–60

aphasia, 53

applicational grammar, 193

artificial intelligence, 128–9

artificial language, 70

artists, 76

Aspects of the Theory of Syntax (Chomsky), 136, 150, 151, 163, 169

Austin, John, 72, 132, 144

Australia, 7; aborigines, 59–60

autocracy, 91

automata theory, 125

autonomy of syntax, 138–9, 140, 148, 188–9; Jespersen on, 156

Baker, C. L.: *Introduction to Generative Transformational Syntax*, 104

Bar-Hillel, Yehoshua, 130

base component, 104–6, 119, 165, 169, 170; in Chomsky's second model, 136. *See also* rewriting rules

REFLECTIONS
ON LANGUAGE

Preface

Part I of this book is an elaboration of the Whidden Lectures, delivered in January 1975 at McMaster University. Part II is a revised version of my contribution to a volume of essays in honor of Yehoshua Bar-Hillel (Kasher, ed., forthcoming), submitted for publication in June 1974. The latter essay considers some critical discussion of the general point of view developed here, as it had been presented in earlier work. To preserve the internal coherence of the discussion in part II, I have retained some material that recapitulates themes that are developed in a somewhat different form in the Whidden Lectures.

I have presented much of this material in lectures at MIT and elsewhere and am indebted to many students, colleagues, and friends for valuable comments and criticism. The work reviewed in chapter 3 of part I, in particular, incorporates suggestions and research to which many people have contributed, as the citations only partially serve to indicate. Among others, Harry Bracken, Donald Hockney, Ray Jackendoff, Justin Leiber, Julius Moravcsik, and Henry Rosemont have made helpful comments on an earlier version of this manuscript. I have also profited greatly from lively and extensive discussions with members of the faculty of McMaster University.

Noam Chomsky

Cambridge, Massachusetts
April 1975

PART I

The Whidden Lectures

CHAPTER 1

On Cognitive Capacity

These reflections on the study of language will be non-technical for the most part, and will have a somewhat speculative and personal character. I am not going to try to summarize the current state of knowledge in the areas of language study that I know something about, or to discuss ongoing research in any depth. I want to consider, rather, the point and purpose of the enterprise, to ask—and I hope explain—why results obtained in technical linguistics might interest someone who is not initially enchanted by the relation between question formation and anaphora, the principles of rule ordering in phonology, the relation of intonation to the scope of negation, and the like. I will sketch what seems to me an appropriate framework within which the study of language may prove to have more general intellectual interest, and will consider the possibilities for constructing a kind of theory of human nature on a model of this sort.

Why study language? There are many possible answers, and by focusing on some I do not, of course, mean to disparage others or question their legitimacy. One may, for example, simply be fascinated by the elements of language in themselves and want to discover their order and arrangement, their origin in history or in the individual, or the ways in which they are used in thought, in science or in art, or in normal social interchange. One reason for studying language—and for me personally the most compelling reason—is that it is tempting to regard language, in the traditional phrase, as "a mirror of mind." I do not mean by this simply that the concepts expressed and distinctions developed in normal language use give us insight into the patterns of thought and the world of "common sense" constructed by the human mind. More intriguing, to me at least, is the possibility that by studying language we may discover abstract principles that govern its structure and use, principles that are universal by biological necessity and not mere historical accident, that derive from mental characteristics of the species. A human language is a system of remarkable complexity. To come to know a human language would be an extraordinary intellectual achievement for a creature not specifically designed to accomplish this task. A normal child acquires this knowledge on relatively slight exposure and without specific training. He can then quite effortlessly make use of an intricate structure of specific rules and guiding principles to convey his thoughts and feelings to others, arousing in them novel ideas and subtle perceptions and judgments. For the conscious mind, not specially designed for the purpose, it remains a distant goal to reconstruct and comprehend what the child has done intuitively and with minimal effort. Thus language is a mirror of mind in a deep and significant sense. It is a product of human intelligence, created anew in each individual by operations that lie far beyond the reach of will or consciousness.

By studying the properties of natural languages, their structure, organization, and use, we may hope to gain some understanding of the specific characteristics of human intelligence. We may hope to learn something about human nature; something significant, if it is true that human cognitive capacity is the truly distinctive and most remarkable characteristic of the species. Furthermore, it is not unreasonable to suppose that the study of this particular human achievement, the ability to speak and understand a human language, may serve as a suggestive model for inquiry into other domains of human competence and action that are not quite so amenable to direct investigation.

The questions that I want to consider are classical ones. In major respects we have not progressed beyond classical antiquity in formulating clear problems in this domain, or in answering questions that immediately arise. From Plato to the present time, serious philosophers have been baffled and intrigued by the question that Bertrand Russell, in one of his later works, formulated in this way: "How comes it that human beings, whose contacts with the world are brief and personal and limited, are nevertheless able to know as much as they do know?" (Russell, 1948, p. 5). How can we gain such rich systems of knowledge, given our fragmentary and impoverished experience? A dogmatic skeptic might respond that we do not have such knowledge. His qualms are irrelevant to the present point. The same question arises, as a question of science, if we ask how comes it that human beings with such limited and personal experience achieve such convergence in rich and highly structured systems of belief, systems which then guide their actions and interchange and their interpretation of experience.

In the classical tradition, several answers were suggested. One might argue, along Aristotelian lines, that the world is structured in a certain way and that the human mind is able to perceive this structure, ascending from particulars to species to genus to further generalization and thus attaining knowledge of universals from perception of particulars. A "basis of pre-existent knowledge" is a prerequisite to learning. We must possess an innate capacity to attain developed states of knowledge, but these are "neither innate in a determinate form, nor developed from other higher states of knowledge, but from sense-perception." Given rich metaphysical assumptions, it is possible to imagine that a mind "so constituted as to be capable of this process" of "induction" might attain a rich system of knowledge.[1]

A more fruitful approach shifts the main burden of explanation from the structure of the world to the structure of the mind. What we can know is determined by "the modes of conception in the understanding";[2] what we do know, then, or what we come to believe, depends on the specific experiences that evoke in us some part of the cognitive system that is latent in the mind. In the modern period, primarily under the influence of Cartesian thought, the question of what we can know became again a central topic of inquiry. To Leibniz and Cudworth, Plato's doctrine that we do not attain new knowledge but recover what was already known seemed plausible, when this doctrine was "purged of the error of preexistence."[3] Cudworth argued at length that the mind has an "innate cognoscitive power" that provides the principles and conceptions that constitute our knowledge, when provoked by sense to do so. "*But sensible things themselves* (as, for example, light and colors) *are not known and understood either by the passion or the fancy of sense, nor by anything merely foreign and adventitious, but by intelligible ideas exerted from the mind itself, that is, by something native and domestic to it....*"[4] Thus knowledge "consisteth in the awakening and exciting of the inward active powers of the mind," which "exercise[s] its own inward activity upon" the objects presented by sense, thus coming "to know or understand, ... actively to comprehend a thing by some abstract, free and universal ratio's, reasonings...." The eye perceives, but the mind can compare, analyze, see cause-

and-effect relations, symmetries, and so on, giving a comprehensive idea of the whole, with its parts, relations, and proportions. The "book of nature," then, is "legible only to an intellectual eye," he suggests, just as a man who reads a book in a language that he knows can learn something from the "inky scrawls." "The primary objects of science and intellection," namely, "the intelligible essences of things," "exist no where but in the mind itself, being its own ideas. . . . And by and through these inward ideas of the mind itself, which are its primary objects, does it know and understand all external individual things, which are the secondary objects of knowledge only."

Among the "innate ideas" or "common notions" discussed in the rich and varied work of seventeenth-century rationalists are, for example, geometrical concepts and the like, but also "*relational* ideas or categories which enter into every presentation of objects and make possible the unity and interconnectedness of rational experience," [5] including such "relative notions" as "Cause, Effect, Whole and Part, Like and Unlike, Proportion and Analogy, Equality and Inequality, Symmetry and Asymmetry," all "*relative* ideas . . . [that are] . . . no material impresses from without upon the soul, but *her own active conception proceeding from herself whilst she takes notice of external objects.*" [6] Tracing the development of such ideas, we arrive at Kant's rather similar concept of the "conformity of objects to our mode of cognition." The mind provides the means for an analysis of data as experience, and provides as well a general schematism that delimits the cognitive structures developed on the basis of experience.

Returning to Russell's query, we can know so much because in a sense we already knew it, though the data of sense were necessary to evoke and elicit this knowledge. Or to put it less paradoxically, our systems of belief are those that the mind, as a biological structure, is designed to construct. We interpret experience as we do because of our special mental design. We attain knowledge when the "inward ideas of the mind itself" and the structures it creates conform to the nature of things.

Certain elements of the rationalist theories must be discarded, but the general outlines seem plausible enough. Work of the past years has shown that much of the detailed structure of the visual system is "wired in," though triggering experience is required to set the system in operation. There is evidence that the same may be true of the auditory structures that analyze at least some phonetic distinctive features. (Cf. Eimas et al., 1971.) As techniques of investigation have improved, Bower argues, "so has the apparent sophistication of the infant perceptual system." He reviews evidence suggesting that "the infant perceptual system seems capable of handling all of the traditional problems of the perception of three-dimensional space"—perception of solidity, distance, size-distance invariants, and size constancy. Thus "contrary to the Berkeleian tradition the world of the infant would seem to be inherently tridimensional" (Bower, 1972). There is evidence that before infants are capable of grasping, they can distinguish graspable from ungraspable objects, using purely visual information (Bruner and Koslowski, 1972).

Gregory observes that "the speed with which babies come to associate the properties of objects and go on to learn how to predict hidden properties and future events would be impossible unless some of the structure of the world were inherited—somehow innately built into the nervous system." [7] He suggests further that there may be a "grammar of vision," rather like the grammar of human language, and possibly related to the latter in the evolution of the species. Employing this "grammar of vision"—largely innate—higher animals are able to "read from retinal images even hidden features of objects, and predict their immediate future states," thus "to classify objects according to an internal grammar, to read reality from their eyes." The neural basis for this system is gradually coming to be understood since the pioneering work of Hubel and Wiesel (1962). More generally, there is every reason to suppose that "learning behavior occurs via modification of an already functional structural organization"; "survival would be improbable if learning in nature required the lengthy repetition characteristic of most conditioning procedures," and it is well known that animals acquire complex systems of behavior in other ways (John, 1972).

Despite the plausibility of many of the leading ideas of the rationalist tradition, and its affinity in crucial respects with the point of view of the natural sciences, it has often been dismissed or disregarded in the study of behavior and cognition. It is a curious fact about the intellectual history of the past few centuries that physical and mental development have been approached in quite different ways. No one would take seriously a proposal that the human organism learns through experience to have arms rather than wings, or that the basic structure of particular organs results from accidental experience. Rather, it is taken for granted that the physical structure of the organism is genetically determined, though of course variation along such dimensions as size, rate of development, and so forth will depend in part on external factors. From embryo to mature organism, a certain pattern of development is predetermined, with certain stages, such as the onset of puberty or the termination of growth, delayed by many years. Variety within these fixed patterns may be of great importance for human life, but the basic questions of scientific interest have to do with the fundamental, genetically determined scheme of growth and development that is a characteristic of the species and that gives rise to structures of marvelous intricacy.

The species characteristics themselves have evolved over long stretches of time, and evidently the environment provides conditions for differential reproduction, hence evolution of the species. But this is an entirely different question, and here too, questions can be raised about the physical laws that govern this evolution. Surely too little is known to justify any far-reaching claims.

The development of personality, behavior patterns, and cognitive structures in higher organisms has often been approached in a very different way. It is generally assumed that in these domains, social environment is the dominant factor. The structures of mind that develop over time are taken to be arbitrary and accidental; there is no "human nature" apart from what develops as a specific historical product. According to this view, typical of empiricist speculation, certain general principles of learning that are common in their essentials to all (or some large class of) organisms suffice to account for the cognitive structures attained by humans, structures which incorporate the principles by which human behavior is planned, organized, and controlled. I dismiss without further comment the exotic though influential view that "internal states" should not be considered in the study of behavior.[8]

But human cognitive systems, when seriously investigated, prove to be no less marvelous and intricate than the physical structures that develop in the life of the organism. Why, then, should we not study the acquisition of a cognitive structure such as language more or less as we study some complex bodily organ?

At first glance, the proposal may seem absurd, if only because of the great variety of human languages. But a closer consideration dispels these doubts. Even knowing very little of substance about linguistic universals, we can be quite sure that the possible variety of languages is sharply limited. Gross observations suffice to establish some qualitative conclusions. Thus, it is clear that the language each person acquires is a rich and complex construction hopelessly underdetermined by the fragmentary evidence available. This is why scientific inquiry into the nature of language is so difficult and so limited in its results. The conscious mind is endowed with no advance knowledge (or, recalling Aristotle, with only insufficiently developed advance knowledge). Thus, it is frustrated by the limitations of available evidence and faced by far too many possible explanatory theories, mutually inconsistent but adequate to the data. Or—as unhappy a state—it can devise no reasonable theory. Nevertheless, individuals in a speech community have developed essentially the same language. This fact can be explained only on the assumption that these individuals employ highly restrictive principles that guide the construction of grammar. Furthermore, humans are, obviously, not designed to learn one human language rather than another; the system of principles must be a species property. Powerful constraints must be operative restricting the variety of languages. It is natural that in our daily life we should concern ourselves only with differences among people, ignoring uniformities of structure. But different intellectual demands arise when we seek to understand what kind of organism a human really is.

The idea of regarding the growth of language as analogous to the development of a bodily organ is thus quite natural and plausible. It is fair to ask why the empiricist belief to the contrary has had such appeal to the modern temper. Why has it been so casually assumed that there exists a "learning theory" that can account for the acquisition of cognitive structures through experience? Is there some body of evidence, established through scientific inquiry, or observation, or introspection, that leads us to regard mental and physical development in such different ways? Surely the answer is that there is not. Science offers no reason to "accept the common maxim that there is nothing in the intellect which was not first in the senses," or to question the denial of this maxim in rationalist philosophy.[9] Investigation of human intellectual achievements, even of the most commonplace sort, gives no support for this thesis.

Empiricist speculation and the "science of behavior" that has developed within its terms have proved rather barren, perhaps because of the peculiar assumptions that have guided and limited such inquiry. The grip of empiricist doctrine in the modern period, outside of the natural sciences, is to be explained on sociological or historical grounds.[10] The position itself has little to recommend it on grounds of empirical evidence or inherent plausibility or explanatory power. I do not think that this doctrine would attract a scientist who is able to discard traditional myth and to approach the problems afresh. Rather, it serves as an impediment, an insurmountable barrier to fruitful inquiry, much as the religious dogmas of an earlier period stood in the way of the natural sciences.

It is sometimes argued that modern empiricism overcomes the limitations of the earlier tradition, but I think that this belief is seriously in error. Hume, for example, presented a substantive theory of "the secret springs and principles, by which the human mind is actuated in its operations." In his investigation of the foundations of knowledge, he suggested specific principles that constitute "a species of natural instincts." Modern empiricists who disparage Hume have simply replaced his theory by vacuous systems that preserve empiricist (or more narrowly, behaviorist) terminology while depriving traditional ideas of their substance. I have discussed this matter elsewhere (cf. chapter 4), and will not pursue it here.

In recent years, many of these issues, long dormant, have been revived, in part in connection with the study of language. There has been much discussion of the so-called "innateness hypothesis," which holds that one of the faculties of the mind, common to the species, is a faculty of language that serves the two basic functions of rationalist theory: it provides a sensory system for the preliminary analysis of linguistic data, and a schematism that determines, quite narrowly, a certain class of grammars. Each grammar is a theory of a particular language, specifying formal and semantic properties of an infinite array of sentences. These sentences, each with its particular structure, constitute the language generated by the grammar. The languages so generated are those that can be "learned" in the normal way. The language faculty, given appropriate stimulation, will construct a grammar; the person knows the language generated by the constructed grammar. This knowledge can then be used to understand what is heard and to produce discourse as an expression of thought within the constraints of the internalized principles, in a manner appropriate to situations as these are conceived by other mental faculties, free of stimulus control.[11] Questions related to the language faculty and its exercise are the ones that, for me at least, give a more general intellectual interest to the technical study of language.

I would now like to consider the so-called "innateness hypothesis," to identify some elements in it that are or should be controversial, and to sketch some of the problems that arise as we try to resolve the controversy. Then, we may try to see what can be said about the nature and exercise of the linguistic competence that has been acquired, along with some related matters.

A preliminary observation is that the term "innateness hypothesis" is generally used by critics rather than advocates of the position to which it refers. I have never used the term, because it can only mislead. Every "theory of learning" that is even worth considering incorporates an innateness hypothesis. Thus, Hume's theory proposes specific innate structures of mind and seeks to account for all of human knowledge on the basis of these structures, even postulating unconscious and innate knowledge. (Cf. chapter 4.) The question is not whether learning presupposes innate structure—of course it does; that has never been in doubt—but rather what these innate structures are in particular domains.

What is a theory of learning? Is there such a theory as *the* theory of learning, waiting to be discovered? Let us try to sharpen and perhaps take some steps towards answering these questions.

Consider first how a neutral scientist—that imaginary ideal—might proceed to investigate the question. The natural first step would be to select an organism, O, and a reasonably well delimited cognitive domain, D, and to attempt to construct a theory that we might call "the learning theory for the organism O in the domain D." This theory—call it LT(O,D)—can be regarded as a system of principles, a mechanism, a function, which has a certain "input" and a certain "output" (its domain and range, respectively). The "input" to the system LT(O,D) will be an analysis of data in D by O; the output" (which is, of course, internally represented, not overt and exhibited) will be a cognitive structure of some sort. This cognitive structure is one element of the cognitive state attained by O.

For example, take O to be humans and D language. Then LT(H,L)—the learning theory for humans in the domain language—will be the system of principles by which humans arrive at knowledge of language, given linguistic experience, that is, given a preliminary analysis that they develop for the data of language. Or, take O to be rats and D to be maze running. Then LT(R,M) is the system of principles used by rats in learning how to run mazes. The input to LT (R,M) is whatever preliminary analysis of data is used by rats to accomplish this feat, and the output is the relevant cognitive structure, however it should properly be characterized as a component of the state achieved by the rat who knows how to run a maze. There is no reason to doubt that the cognitive structure attained and the cognitive state of which it is a constituent will be rather complex.

To facilitate the discussion, let us make two simplifying assumptions. Assume first that individuals of the species O under investigation are essentially identical with respect to their ability to learn over the domain D—for example, that humans do not differ in language-learning capacity. Second, assume that learning can be conceptualized as an instantaneous process in the following sense: assume that LT(O,D) is presented with a cumulative record of all the data available to O up to a particular moment, and that LT(O,D), operating on that data, produces the cognitive structure attained at that moment. Neither of these assumptions is true: there are individual differences, and learning takes place over time, sometimes extended time. I will return later to the question of just "how false" these assumptions are. I think that they give a useful first approximation, helpful for the formulation of certain issues and possibly much more.

To pursue the study of a given LT(O,D) in a rational way, we will proceed through the following stages of inquiry:

1. Set the cognitive domain D.

2. Determine how O characterizes data in D "pretheoretically," thus constructing what we may call "the experience of O in D" (recall the idealization to "instantaneous learning").

3. Determine the nature of the cognitive structure attained; that is, determine, as well as possible, what is learned by O in the domain D.

4. Determine LT(O,D), the system that relates experience to what is learned.

Step 4 relies on the results attained in steps 2 and 3.

To avoid misunderstanding, perhaps I should stress that the ordering of steps is a kind of rational reconstruction of rational inquiry. In practice, there is no strict sequence. Work at level 4, for example, may convince us that our original delimitation of D was faulty, that we have failed to abstract a coherent cognitive domain. Or, it may lead us to conclude that we have misconstrued the character of what is learned, at step 3. It remains true, nevertheless, that we can hope to gain some insight at the level of step 4 only to the extent that we have achieved some understanding at levels 2 and 3 and have selected, wisely or luckily, at level 1. It is senseless to try to relate two systems—in this case, experience and what is learned—without some fairly good idea of what they are.

Parenthetically, we might observe that step 3 is missing in many formulations of psychological theory, much to their detriment. In fact, even the concept "what is learned" is missing in familiar "learning theories." Where it is missing, the basic questions of "learning theory" cannot even be formulated.

How does the study of behavior fit into this framework? Surely a prerequisite to the study of behavior is a grasp of the nature of the organism that is behaving—in the sense of "prerequisite" just explained. An organism has attained a certain state through maturation and experience. It is faced with certain objective conditions. It then does something. In principle, we might want to inquire into the mechanism M that determines what the organism does (perhaps probabilistically) given its past experience and its present stimulus conditions. I say "in principle," because I doubt that there is very much that we will be able to say about this question.

No doubt what the organism does depends in part on its experience, but it seems to me entirely hopeless to investigate directly the relation between experience and action. Rather, if we are interested in the problem of "causation of behavior" as a problem of science, we should at least analyze the relation of experience to behavior into two parts: first, LT, which relates experience to cognitive state,[12] and second, a mechanism, M_{CS}, which relates stimulus conditions to behavior, given the cognitive state CS.

To put it schematically, in place of the hopeless task of

investigating M as in (I), we may more reasonably undertake research into the nature of LT as in (II) and M_{CS} as
in (III).

(I)   M: (experience, stimulus conditions) $\longrightarrow$ behavior

(II) LT: experience $\longrightarrow$ cognitive state CS

(III) M_{CS}: stimulus conditions $\longrightarrow$ behavior (given
CS)

I think that we can make considerable progress towards
understanding LT as in (II); that is, towards understanding
particular LT(O,D)'s, for various choices of D given O, and
the interaction among them. It is this problem that I want
to consider here. I doubt that we can learn very much, as
scientists at least, about the second of these two parts,
M_{CS}.[13] But it seems to me most unlikely that there will be
any scientific progress at all if we do not at least analyze
the problem of "causation of behavior" into the two components LT and M_{CS} and their elements. An attempt along
the lines of (I) to study directly the relation of behavior to
past and current experience is doomed to triviality and scientific insignificance.

Returning to the problem of learning, suppose that we
have determined a number of LT(O,D)'s, for various choices
of organism O and cognitive domain D. We can now turn
to the question: What is "learning theory"? Or better: Is
there such a theory as learning theory? The question might
be put in various ways, for example, the following two:

(1)   Is it the case that however we select O and D,
we find the same LT(O,D)?

(2)   Are there significant features common to all
LT(O,D)'s?

Before considering these questions, let us return to the
first of our simplifying assumptions, namely, with regard to
variability within the species O. I would like to suggest

that the interesting questions of "learning theory," those that might lead to a theory that is illuminating and that will ultimately relate to the body of natural science more generally, will be those for which our first assumption is essentially correct. That is, the interesting questions, those that offer some hope of leading to insight into the nature of organisms, will be those that arise in the investigation of learning in domains where there is a nontrivial structure uniform for members of O (with certain parameters relating to rapidity of learning, scope of learning, rate of forgetting, and other such marginal phenomena for which variability is to be expected). These are the questions that deal with significant characteristics of the species, or perhaps, of organisms generally. Again, I see no reason why cognitive structures should not be investigated rather in the way that physical organs are studied. The natural scientist will be primarily concerned with the basic, genetically determined structure of these organs and their interaction, a structure common to the species in the most interesting case, abstracting away from size, variation in rate of development, and so on.

If we can accept this judgment, then LT(O,D) can be characterized for O taken not as an individual but as a species—hence for individuals apart from gross abnormalities. And we may proceed to qualify question (1), asking whether LT(O,D) is identical with LT(O′,D′) apart from such matters as rapidity, facility, scope, and retention, which may vary across species and, to a lesser extent, among individuals of a given species.

Consider now question (1), so qualified. Surely the answer must still be a firm No. Even the crudest considerations suffice to show that there is no hope of reaching a positive answer to this question. Take O to be humans (H) and O′ rats (R); D to be language (L) and D′ maze running (M). If even some vague approximation to question (1) had a positive answer, we would expect humans to be as much superior to rats in maze-learning ability as they are in language-learning ability. But this is so grossly false that the question cannot be seriously entertained. Humans are roughly comparable to rats in the domain M but incomparable in the domain L. In fact, it seems that "white rats can even best college students in this sort of learning"—namely, maze-learning (Munn, 1971, p. 118). The distinction between the pair (LT(H,L), LT(R,L)) on the one hand and the pair (LT(H,M), LT(R,M)) on the other cannot be attributed to sensory processing systems and the like, as we can see by "transposing" language into some modality accessible to rats. (Cf. chapter 4, note 14.) As far as is now known—and I say this despite suggestions to the contrary—the same is true if we consider other organisms (say, chimpanzees) in place of rats. Putting this interesting but peripheral question to the side, it is surely obvious at once that no version of question (1) is worth pursuing.

Let us turn to the more plausible speculation formulated in question (2). No answer is possible, for the present. The question is hopelessly premature. We lack an interesting conception of LT(O,D) for various choices of O and D. There are, I believe, some substantive steps possible towards LT(H,L), but nothing comparable in other domains of human learning. What is known about other animals, to my knowledge, suggests no interesting answer to (2). Animals learn to care for their young, build nests, orient themselves in space, find their place in a dominance structure, identify the species, and so on, but we should not expect to find significant properties which are common to the various LT(O,D)'s that enter into these achievements. Skepticism about question (2) is very much in order, on the basis of the very little that is known. I should think that for the biologist, the comparative physiologist, or the physiological psychologist, such skepticism would appear quite unremarkable.

Thus, for the present, there seems to be no reason to

suppose that learning theory exists. At least, I see no interesting formulation of the thesis that there is such a theory that has initial plausibility or significant empirical support.

Within the odd variant of empiricism known as "behaviorism," the term "learning theory" has commonly been used, not as the designation of a theory (if it exists) that accounts for the attainment of cognitive structures on the basis of experience (namely, (II) above), but rather as a theory that deals with the relation of experience to behavior (namely, (I) above). Since there is no reason to suppose that learning theory exists, there is certainly no reason to expect that such a "theory of behavior" exists.

We might consider contentions more plausible than those implicit in questions (1) and (2). Suppose that we fix the organism O, and let D range over various cognitive domains. Then we might ask whether there is some interesting set of domains $D_1, \ldots, D_n$ such that:

(3) $LT(O,D_i) = LT(O,D_j)$; or $LT(O,D_i)$ is similar in interesting ways to $LT(O,D_j)$.

There might be some way of delimiting domains that would yield a positive answer to (3). If so, we could say that within this delimitation, the organism learns in similar or identical ways across cognitive domains. It would be interesting, for example, to discover whether there is some cognitive domain D other than language for which $LT(H,L)$ is identical to or similar to $LT(H,D)$. To date, no persuasive suggestion has been made, but conceivably there is such a domain. There is no particular reason to expect that there is such a domain, and one can only be surprised at the dogmatic view, commonly expressed, that language learning proceeds by application of general learning capacities. The most that we can say is that the possibility is not excluded, though there is no evidence for it and little plausibility to the contention. Even at the level of sensory processing there appear to be adaptations directly related to language, as already noted.[14] The proposal that language learning is simply an instance of "generalized learning capacities" makes about as much sense, in the present state of our knowledge, as a claim that the specific neural structures that provide our organization of visual space must be a special case of the class of systems involved also in language use. This is true, so far as we know, only at a level so general as to give no insight into the character or functioning of the various systems.

For any organism O, we can try to discover those cognitive domains D for which the organism O has an interesting LT(O,D)—that is, an LT(O,D) that does not merely have the structure of trial-and-error learning, generalization along physically given dimensions, induction (in any well-defined sense of this notion), and so on. We might define the "cognitive capacity" of O as the system of domains D for which there is an interesting learning theory LT(O,D) in this sense.[15] For D within the cognitive capacity of O, it is reasonable to suppose that a schematism exists delimiting the class of cognitive structures that can be attained. Hence it will be possible, for such D, for a rich, complex, highly articulated cognitive structure to be attained with considerable uniformity among individuals (apart from matters of rate, scope, persistence, etc.) on the basis of scattered and restricted evidence.

Investigating the cognitive capacity of humans, we might consider, say, the ability to recognize and identify faces on exposure to a few presentations, to determine the personality structure of another person on brief contact (thus, to be able to guess, pretty well, how that person will react under a variety of conditions), to recognize a melody under transposition and other modifications, to handle those branches of mathematics that build on numerical or spatial intuition, to create art forms resting on certain principles of structure and organization, and so on. Humans appear to have characteristic and remarkable abilities in these domains, in that they construct a complex and intricate intellectual system, rapidly and uniformly, on the basis of degenerate evidence. And structures created by particularly talented individuals within these constraints are intelligible and appealing, exciting and thought-provoking even to those not endowed with unusual creative abilities. Inquiry, then, might lead to nontrivial LT(H,D)'s, for D so chosen. Such inquiry might involve experimentation or even historical investigation—for example, investigation of developments in forms of artistic composition or in mathematics that seemed "natural" and proved fruitful at particular historical moments, contributing to a "mainstream" of intellectual evolution rather than diverting energy to an unproductive side channel.[16]

Suppose that for a particular organism O, we manage to learn something about its cognitive capacity, developing a system of LT(O,D)'s for various choices of D with the rough properties sketched above. We would then have arrived at a theory of the mind of O, in one sense of this term. We may think of "the mind of O," to adapt a formulation of Anthony Kenny's,[17] as the innate capacity of O to construct cognitive structures, that is, to learn.

I depart here from Kenny's formulation in two respects, which perhaps deserve mention. He defines "mind" as a second-order capacity to acquire "intellectual abilities," such as knowledge of English—the latter "itself a capacity or ability: an ability whose exercise is the speaking, understanding, reading of English." Moreover, "to have a mind is to have the capacity to acquire the ability to operate with symbols in such a way that it is one's own activity that makes them symbols and confers meaning on them," so that automata operating with formal elements that are symbols for us but not for them do not have minds. For the sake of this discussion, I have generalized here beyond first-order capacities involving operations with symbols, and am thus considering second-order capacities broader than "mind" in Kenny's quite natural sense. So far there is no issue beyond terminology. Secondly, I want to consider mind (in the narrower or broader sense) as an innate capacity to form cognitive structures, not first-order capacities to act. The cognitive structures attained enter into our first-order capacities to act, but should not be identified with them. Thus it does not seem to me quite accurate to take "knowledge of English" to be a capacity or ability, though it enters into the capacity or ability exercised in language use. In principle, one might have the cognitive structure that we call "knowledge of English," fully developed, with no capacity to use this structure; [18] and certain capacities to carry out "intellectual activities" may involve no cognitive structures but merely a network of dispositions and habits, something quite different.[19] Knowledge, understanding, or belief is at a level more abstract than capacity.

There has been a tendency in modern analytic philosophy to employ the notion "disposition" or "capacity" where the more abstract concept of "cognitive structure" is, I believe, more appropriate. (Cf. chapter 4; also Chomsky, 1975a.) I think we see here an unfortunate residue of empiricism. The notions "capacity" and "family of dispositions" are more closely related to behavior and "language use"; they do not lead us to inquire into the nature of the "ghost in the machine" through the study of cognitive structures and their organization, as normal scientific practice and intellectual curiosity would demand. The proper way to exorcise the ghost in the machine is to determine the structure of the mind and its products.[20] There is nothing essentially mysterious about the concept of an abstract cognitive structure, created by an innate faculty of mind, represented in some still-unknown way in the brain, and entering into the system of capacities and dispositions to act and interpret. On the contrary, a formulation along these lines, embodying the conceptual competence-performance distinction (cf. Chomsky, 1965, chap. 1) seems a prerequisite for a serious investigation of behavior. Human action can be understood only on the assumption that first-order capacities and families of dispositions to behave involve the use of cognitive structures that express systems of (unconscious) knowledge, belief, expectation, evaluation, judgment, and the like. At least, so it seems to me.

Returning to the main theme, suppose that we now select a problem in a domain D that falls outside of O's cognitive capacity. O will then be at a loss as to how to proceed. O will have no cognitive structure available for dealing with this problem and no LT(O,D) available to enable it to develop such a structure. O will therefore have to proceed by trial and error, association, simple induction, and generalization along certain available dimensions (some questions arise here, which I put aside). Taking O to be humans, we will not expect the person to be able to find or construct a rich and insightful way to deal with the problem, to develop a relevant cognitive structure in the intuitive, unconscious manner characteristic of language learning and other domains in which humans excel.

Humans might be able to construct a conscious scientific theory dealing with problems in the domain in question, but that is a different matter—or better, a partially different matter, since even here there are crucial constraints. An intellectually significant science, an intelligible explanatory theory, can be developed by humans in case something close to the true theory in a certain domain happens to fall within human "science-forming" capacities. The LT(H,D)'s involved in scientific inquiry, whatever they may be, must be special and restrictive, or it would be impossible for scientists to converge in their judgment on particular explanatory theories that go far beyond the evidence at hand, as they customarily do in those few fields where there really is significant progress, while at the same time rejecting much evidence as irrelevant or beside the point, for the moment at least. The same LT(H,D)'s that provide for the vast and impressive scope of scientific understanding must also sharply constrain the class of humanly accessible sciences. There is, surely, no evolutionary pressure that leads humans to have minds capable of discovering significant explanatory theories in specific fields of inquiry. Thinking of humans as biological organisms in the natural world, it is only a lucky accident if their cognitive capacity happens to be well matched to scientific truth in some area. It should come as no surprise, then, that there are so few sciences, and that so much of human inquiry fails to attain any intellectual depth. Investigation of human cognitive capacity might give us some insight into the class of humanly accessible sciences, possibly a small subset of those potential sciences that deal with matters concerning which we hope (vainly) to attain some insight and understanding.

As a case in point, consider our near-total failure to discover a scientific theory that provides an analysis of Mcs of (III) on page 17—that is, our very limited progress in developing a scientific theory of any depth to account for the normal use of language (or other aspects of behavior). Even the relevant concepts seem lacking; certainly, no intellectually satisfying principles have been proposed that have explanatory force, though the questions are very old. It is not excluded that human science-forming capacities simply do not extend to this domain, or any domain involving the exercise of will, so that for humans, these questions will always be shrouded in mystery.

Note, incidentally, how misleading it would be to speak simply of "limitations" in human science-forming capacity. Limits no doubt exist, but they derive from the same source as our ability to construct rich cognitive systems on the basis of limited evidence in the first place. Were it not for the factors that limit scientific knowledge, we could have no such knowledge in any domain.[21]

Suppose that in investigating organisms, we decide, perversely, to restrict ourselves to tasks and problems that lie outside their cognitive capacity. We might then expect to discover simple "laws of learning" of some generality. Suppose further that we define a "good experiment" as one that provides smooth learning curves, regular increments and extinction, and so on. Then there will be "good experiments" only in domains that lie outside of O's cognitive capacity. For example, there will be no "good experiments" in the study of human language learning, though there may be if we concentrate attention on memorization of nonsense syllables, verbal association, and other tasks for which humans have no special abilities.

Suppose now that some branch of inquiry develops, limited in principle to "good experiments" in something like this sense. This discipline may, indeed, develop laws of learning that do not vary too greatly across cognitive domains for a particular organism and that have some cross-species validity. It will, of necessity, avoid those domains in which an organism is specially designed to acquire rich cognitive structures that enter into its life in an intimate fashion. The discipline will be of virtually no intellectual interest, it seems to me, since it is restricting itself in principle to those questions that are guaranteed to tell us little about the nature of organisms. For we can learn something significant about this nature only by inquiry into the organism's cognitive capacity, inquiry that will permit no "good experiments" in the strange sense just specified, though it may lead to the discovery (through experiment and observation) of intricate and no doubt highly specific LT(O,D)'s. The results and achievements of this perversely limited, rather suicidal discipline are largely an artifact. It will be condemned in principle to investigation of peripheral matters such as rate and scope of acquisition of information, the relation between arrangement of reinforcers and response strength, control of behavior, and the like. The discipline in question may continue indefinitely to amass information about these matters, but one may question the point or purpose of these efforts.

A more elaborate study of cognitive capacity raises still further questions. Thus, some intellectual achievements, such as language learning, fall strictly within biologically determined cognitive capacity. For these tasks, we have "special design," so that cognitive structures of great complexity and interest develop fairly rapidly and with little if any conscious effort. There are other tasks, no more "complex" along any absolute scale (assuming that it is possible even to make sense of this notion), which will be utterly baffling because they fall beyond cognitive capacity. Consider problems that lie at the borderline of cognitive capacity. These will provide opportunity for intriguing intellectual play. Chess, for example, is not so remote from cognitive capacity as to be merely a source of insoluble puzzles, but is at the same time sufficiently beyond our natural abilities so that it is challenging and intriguing. Here, we would expect to find that the slight differences between individuals are magnified to striking divergence of aptitude.

The study of challenging intellectual tasks might give some insight into human intelligence, at the borders of cognitive capacity, just as the study of the ability to run a four-minute mile may give useful information about human physiology. But it would be pointless to study the latter feat at a very early stage of our understanding of human locomotion—say, if we knew only that humans walk rather than fly. Correspondingly, in the present state of our understanding of mental abilities, it seems to me that, for example, the study of chess-playing programs

may teach something about the theory of chess, but is unlikely to contribute much to the study of human intelligence. It is good procedure to study major factors before
turning to tenth-order effects, to study the basic character
of an intricate system before exploring its borders, though
of course one can never know in advance just what line of
inquiry will provide sudden illumination.[22]

In the case of human cognition, it is the study of the
basic cognitive structures within cognitive capacity, their
development and use, that should receive priority, I believe, if we are to attain a real understanding of the mind
and its workings.

The preceding discussion is not very precise. I hope
that it is at least suggestive as to how a rational study
of learning might proceed. Let me now turn to the particular questions in the "theory of learning" that concern
language.

Let us take O to be humans (H) and D to be language
(L). What is LT(H,L)? Of the two simplifying assumptions mentioned earlier, the first—invariability across the
species—is, so far as we know, fair enough. It seems to
provide a close approximation to the facts. Let us therefore accept it with no further discussion, while keeping
a cautious and skeptical eye on the second assumption,
that learning is "instantaneous." I will return to the latter
in chapter 3.

LT(H,L) is the system of mechanisms and principles
put to work in acquisition of knowledge of language—acquisition of the specific cognitive structure that we are
calling "grammar"—given data which are a fair and adequate sample of this language.[23] The grammar is a system
of rules and principles that determine the formal and semantic properties of sentences. The grammar is put to use,
interacting with other mechanisms of mind, in speaking
and understanding language. There are empirical assump-

tions and conceptual distinctions embedded in this account, and they might be wrong or misguided, but I think it is not unreasonable, given present understanding, to proceed with them.

To relate these remarks to earlier discussion, note that I am insisting that the relation of experience to action be subdivided into two systems: LT(H,L), which relates experience to cognitive state attained, and M$_{CS}$, which relates current conditions to action, given cognitive state attained (cf. (II)–(III), p. 17). One of the cognitive structures entering into the cognitive state CS attained and put to use by M$_{CS}$ is grammar. Again, I see few present prospects for the scientific study of M$_{CS}$, though the study of LT(H,L), it seems to me, can be profitably pursued.

Let us define "universal grammar" (UG) as the system of principles, conditions, and rules that are elements or properties of all human languages not merely by accident but by necessity—of course, I mean biological, not logical, necessity. Thus UG can be taken as expressing "the essence of human language." UG will be invariant among humans. UG will specify what language learning must achieve, if it takes place successfully. Thus UG will be a significant component of LT(H,L). What is learned, the cognitive structure attained, must have the properties of UG, though it will have other properties as well, accidental properties. Each human language will conform to UG; languages will differ in other, accidental properties. If we were to construct a language violating UG, we would find that it could not be learned by LT(H,L). That is, it would not be learnable under normal conditions of access and exposure to data. Possibly it could be learned by application of other faculties of mind; LT(H,L) does not exhaust the capacities of the human mind. This invented language might be learned as a puzzle, or its grammar might be discovered by scientific inquiry over the course of generations, with the intervention of individual genius, with explicit articulation of principles and careful experimentation. This would be possible if the language happened to fall within the bounds of the "science-forming" component of human cognitive capacity. But discovery of the grammar of this language would not be comparable to language learning, just as inquiry in physics is qualitatively different from language learning.

UG will specify properties of sound, meaning, and structural organization. We may expect that in all of these domains, UG will impose conditions that narrowly restrict the variety of languages. For familiar reasons, we cannot conclude from the highly restrictive character of UG that there is a translation procedure of any generality or significance, even in principle (cf. Chomsky, 1965). And quite obviously, nothing is implied about the possibility of translating actual texts, since a speaker or writer naturally presupposes a vast background of unspecified assumptions, beliefs, attitudes, and conventions. The point is perhaps worth noting, since there has been much confusion about the matter. For some discussion, see Keyser (1975).

We can gain some insight into UG, hence LT(H,L), whenever we find properties of language that can reasonably be supposed not to have been learned. To make the discussion more concrete, consider a familiar example, perhaps the simplest one that is not entirely trivial. Think of the process of forming questions in English. Imagine again our neutral scientist, observing a child learning English. Suppose that he discovers that the child has learned to form such questions as those of (A), corresponding to the associated declaratives:

(A) the man is tall—is the man tall?
     the book is on the table—is the book on the table?
     etc.

Observing these facts, the scientist might arrive at the following tentative hypothesis as to what the child is doing, assuming now that sentences are analyzed into words:

> *Hypothesis 1:* The child processes the declarative sentence from its first word (i.e., from "left to right"), continuing until he reaches the first occurrence of the word "is" (or others like it: "may," "will," etc.); he then preposes this occurrence of "is," producing the corresponding question (with some concomitant modifications of form that need not concern us).

This hypothesis works quite well. It is also extremely simple. The scientist has every right to be satisfied, and will be able to find a great deal of evidence to support his tentative hypothesis. Of course, the hypothesis is false, as we learn from such examples as (B) and (C):

> (B) the man who is tall is in the room—is the man who is tall in the room?
>
> (C) the man who is tall is in the room—is the man who tall is in the room?

Our scientist would discover, surely, that on first presentation with an example such as "the man who is tall is in the room," the child unerringly forms the question (B), not (C) (if he can handle the example at all). Children make many mistakes in language learning, but never mistakes such as exemplified in (C). If the scientist is reasonable, this discovery will surprise him greatly, for it shows that his simple hypothesis 1 is false, and that he must construct a far more complex hypothesis to deal with the facts. The correct hypothesis is the following, ignoring complications that are irrelevant here:

> *Hypothesis 2:* The child analyzes the declarative sentence into abstract phrases; he then locates the first occurrence of "is" (etc.) that follows the first noun

phrase; he then preposes this occurrence of "is," forming the corresponding question.

Hypothesis 1 holds that the child is employing a "structure-independent rule"—that is, a rule that involves only analysis into words and the property "earliest" ("leftmost") defined on word sequences. Hypothesis 2 holds that the child is employing a "structure-dependent rule," a rule that involves analysis into words and phrases, and the property "earliest" defined on sequences of words analyzed into abstract phrases. The phrases are "abstract" in the sense that neither their boundaries nor their categories (noun phrase, verb phrase, etc.) need be physically marked. Sentences do not appear with brackets, intonation boundaries regularly marking phrases, subscripts identifying the type of phrase, or anything of the sort.

By any reasonable standards, hypothesis 2 is far more complex and "unlikely" than hypothesis 1. The scientist would have to be driven by evidence, such as (B), (C), to postulate hypothesis 2 in place of the simpler and more elementary hypothesis 1. Correspondingly, the scientist must ask why it is that the child unerringly makes use of the structure-dependent rule postulated in hypothesis 2, rather than the simpler structure-independent rule of hypothesis 1. There seems to be no explanation in terms of "communicative efficiency" or similar considerations. It is certainly absurd to argue that children are trained to use the structure-dependent rule, in this case. In fact, the problem never arises in language learning. A person may go through a considerable part of his life without ever facing relevant evidence, but he will have no hesitation in using the structure-dependent rule, even if all of his experience is consistent with hypothesis 1. The only reasonable conclusion is that UG contains the principle that all such rules must be structure-dependent. That is, the child's mind (specifically, its component LT(H,L)) contains the instruction: Construct a structure-dependent rule, ignoring all structure-independent rules. The principle of structure-dependence is not learned, but forms part of the conditions for language learning.

To corroborate this conclusion about UG (hence LT(H,L)), the scientist will ask whether other rules of English are invariably structure-dependent. So far as we know, the answer is positive. If a rule is found that is not structure-dependent, the scientist will be faced with a problem. He will have to inquire further into UG, to discover what additional principles differentiate the two categories of rules, so that the child can know without instruction that one is structure-dependent and the other not. Having gotten this far, the scientist will conclude that other languages must have the same property, on the assumption that humans are not specifically designed to learn one rather than another language, say English rather than Japanese. On this reasonable assumption, the principle of structure-dependence (perhaps, if necessary, qualified as indicated above) must hold universally, if it holds for English. Investigating the consequences of his reasoning, the scientist would discover (so far as we know) that the conclusion is correct.

More complex examples can be produced, but this simple one illustrates the general point. Proceeding in this way, the scientist can develop some rich and interesting hypotheses about UG, hence LT(H,L). Thus, learning theory for humans in the domain of language incorporates the principle of structure-dependence along with other more intricate (and, I should add, more controversial) principles like it. I will return to some of these in the third chapter.

Keeping this single example of a principle of UG in mind, let us return now to the "innateness hypothesis." Recall that there is no issue as to the necessity for such a hypothesis, only as to its character.

Assuming still the legitimacy of the simplifying assumption about instantaneous learning, the "innateness hypothesis" will consist of several elements: principles for the preliminary, pretheoretic analysis of data as experience, which serves as input to LT(H,L); properties of UG, which determine the character of what is learned; other principles of a sort not discussed in the foregoing sketch.

We might, quite reasonably, formulate the *theory of language* so as to reflect this way of looking at LT(H,L). A theory is a system of principles expressed in terms of certain concepts. The principles are alleged to be true of the subject matter of the theory. A particular presentation of a theory takes some of the concepts as primitive and some of the principles as axioms. The choice of primitives and axioms must meet the condition that all concepts are defined in terms of the primitives and that all principles derive from the axioms. We might choose to formulate linguistic theory by taking its primitive concepts to be those that enter into the preliminary analysis of data as experience, with the axioms including those principles expressing relations between the primitive concepts that enter into this preliminary analysis (thus, the primitive notions are "epistemologically primitive"; they meet an external empirical condition apart from sufficiency for definition). The defined terms belong to UG, and the principles of UG will be theorems of this theory. Linguistic theory, so construed, is a theory of UG incorporated into LT(H,L) in the manner described.

The "innateness hypothesis," then, can be formulated as follows: Linguistic theory, the theory of UG, construed in the manner just outlined, is an innate property of the human mind. In principle, we should be able to account for it in terms of human biology.

To the extent that our simplifying assumption about instantaneous learning must be revised, along lines to which

I will return, we must accordingly complicate the "innateness hypothesis."

A fuller version of the "innateness hypothesis" for humans will specify the various domains belonging to cognitive capacity, the faculty of mind LT(H,D) for each such domain D, the relations between these faculties, their modes of maturation, and the interactions among them through time. Alongside of the language faculty and interacting with it in the most intimate way is the faculty of mind that constructs what we might call "commonsense understanding," a system of beliefs, expectations, and knowledge concerning the nature and behavior of objects, their place in a system of "natural kinds," the organization of these categories, and the properties that determine the categorization of objects and the analysis of events. A general "innateness hypothesis" will also include principles that bear on the place and role of people in a social world, the nature and conditions of work, the structure of human action, will and choice, and so on. These systems may be unconscious for the most part and even beyond the reach of conscious introspection. One might also want to isolate for special study the faculties involved in problem solving, construction of scientific knowledge, artistic creation and expression, play, or whatever prove to be the appropriate categories for the study of cognitive capacity, and derivatively, human action.

In the next two chapters I want to say something more about a few of these mental faculties and their interaction.

CHAPTER 2

The
Object of Inquiry

I hope it will not be too repetitive if I begin by summarizing briefly what I have said so far, elaborating here and there along the way.

The theory of language is simply that part of human psychology that is concerned with one particular "mental organ," human language. Stimulated by appropriate and continuing experience, the language faculty creates a grammar that generates sentences with formal and semantic properties. We say that a person knows the language generated by this grammar. Employing other related faculties of mind and the structures they produce, he can then proceed to use the language that he now knows.[1]

With the progress of science, we may come to know something of the physical representation of the grammar and the language faculty—correspondingly, the cognitive state attained in language learning and the initial state in which there is a representation of UG (universal grammar) but of no specific grammar conforming to UG. For the present, we can only characterize the properties of grammars and of the language faculty in abstract terms.

It is sometimes argued that this contingency, inescapable for the present, deprives the theory of language of empirical content. The conclusion is incorrect. Thus, the single example I have so far given, the principle of structure-dependence, can easily be falsified if false, and the same is true of other proposals within UG or particular grammars. Similarly, it is possible to imagine discoveries in neurophysiology or in the study of behavior and learning that might lead us to revise or abandon a given theory of language or particular grammar, with its hypotheses about the components of the system and their interaction. The abstract nature of these theories permits some latitude in interpretation of particular results, especially insofar as we do not have a clear picture of how cognitive structures are embedded within the theory of performance. Latitude is not total license, however. The theoretical psychologist (in this case, the linguist), the experimental psychologist, and the neurophysiologist are engaged in a common enterprise, and each should exploit as fully as possible the insights derived from all approaches that seek to determine the initial state of the organism, the cognitive structures attained, and the manner in which these cognitive structures are employed. Care is necessary, however. Not infrequently in the psycholinguistic literature we read that particular conclusions about the nature of grammar, or about UG, or about the role of grammar in language use, must be rejected because they are inconsistent with what is known about the organization of memory, behavior, and so on. But what is actually known or even plausibly surmised about these matters is limited and generally still quite remote from the questions that arise in the theoretical study of language. There are some suggestive relations between sentence complexity and processing difficulty, and some other matters. Such evidence should be seriously considered for its possible bearing on the nature of the cognitive state attained and the mechanisms for attaining it.[2] But the evidence available does not support conclusions that are blandly presented in the literature, without argument, as if they were somehow established fact.[3]

A physical organ, say the heart, may vary from one person to the next in size or strength, but its basic structure and its function within human physiology are common to the species. Analogously, two individuals in the same speech community may acquire grammars that differ somewhat in scale and subtlety.[4] What is more, the products of the language faculty vary depending on triggering experience, ranging over the class of possible human languages (in principle). These variations in structure are limited, no doubt sharply, by UG; and the functions of language in human life are no doubt narrowly constrained as well, though no one has as yet found a way to go much beyond a descriptive taxonomy in dealing with this question.[5]

Restricting ourselves now to humans, suppose that we understand psychology to be the theory of mind, in the sense outlined earlier. Thus psychology is that part of human biology that is concerned at its deepest level with the second-order capacity to construct cognitive structures that enter into first-order capacities to act and to interpret experience. Psychology has as its primary concern the faculties of mind involved in cognitive capacity. Each such faculty of mind is represented as one of the LT(H,D)'s of earlier discussion. These faculties enable a person to attain intricate and uniform cognitive structures that are vastly underdetermined by triggering experience, and that need not relate to such experience in any simple way (say, as generalizations, higher-order generalizations, etc.). Rather, the relation of a cognitive structure to experience may be as remote and intricate as the relation of a nontrivial scientific theory to data; depending on the character of the "innateness hypothesis," the relation might be even more partial and indirect.

Such cognitive structures form part of the cognitive state achieved by the person at a given stage of maturation. This state also incorporates habit structures, dispositions, and capacities to employ cognitive structures. The primary concern of the study of learning is to identify the domains within cognitive capacity and to discover LT(H,D) for each such domain D. Furthermore, this inquiry will seek to map out the full system of cognitive capacity, exploring the relations between various domains, the interaction between LT(H,D)'s in learning, common properties or similarities (if any) between them, the ordering of accessibility of cognitive structures or accessibility relative to attained structures, and so on.

Psychology will also explore the organization of behavior under given situations, as these are analyzed by available cognitive structures (this is the study of M_{CS}; cf. (III), p. 17). We might try to approach the classic problem of accounting for action that is appropriate to situations but uncontrolled by stimuli in these terms. Given a partially structured system that provides an evaluation of outcomes, choices that are random except for maximizing "value" may have the appearance of free, purposeful, and intelligent behavior—but one must remain skeptical about this approach, though it is the only one that seems to fall within any conceptual framework intelligible to us.

Within cognitive capacity, the theory of mind has a distinctly rationalist cast. Learning is primarily a matter of filling in detail within a structure that is innate. We depart from the tradition in several respects, specifically, in taking the "*a priori* system" to be biologically determined.[6] Outside the bounds of cognitive capacity, an empiricist theory of learning applies, by unfortunate necessity. Hence little learning is possible, the scope of discovery is minimal, and uniformities will be found across domains and across species.

The language faculty is a particularly interesting element of cognitive capacity. We might inquire into its nature (specifically, the study of UG), its relation to other domains, and its uniqueness. We may ask whether Cartesian doctrine is correct in contending that this faculty is specific to the human species, the unique thinking creature. Does the inability of other species to develop languages of the human type derive from their lack of a specific quality of intelligence rather than from a mere limitation in a common intelligence, as Descartes thought? The dispute is a traditional one. There were, for example, those dismissed contemptuously by Antoine Le Grand, a leading expositor of Cartesian ideas in seventeenth-century England, who speaks of the opinion of "some certain *People* of the *East Indies*, who think that *Apes* and *Baboons*, which are with them in great numbers, are imbued with *understanding*, and that they can *speak* but will not for fear they should be imployed, and set to work." [7] In some ill-considered popularizations of interesting current research, it is virtually argued that higher apes have the capacity for language but have never put it to use—a remarkable biological miracle, given the enormous selectional advantage of even minimal linguistic skills, rather like discovering that some animal has wings but has never thought to fly.

It is a reasonable surmise, I think, that there is no structure similar to UG in nonhuman organisms and that the capacity for free, appropriate, and creative use of language as an expression of thought, with the means provided by the language faculty, is also a distinctive feature of the human species, having no significant analogue elsewhere. The neural basis for language is pretty much of a mystery, but there can be little doubt that specific neural structures and even gross organization not found in other primates (e.g., lateralization) play a fundamental role.[8]

We might expect that the procedures used to train apes in forms of symbolic behavior will succeed as well for humans with severe damage to the neural structures involved directly in language. There is some evidence that this is true.[9] Efforts to induce symbolic behavior in other species might illuminate the specific properties of human language, just as the study of how birds fly might be advanced, in principle, by an investigation of how people jump or fish swim. Some might argue that more is to be expected in the latter case: after all, flying and jumping are both forms of locomotion; both involve going up and coming down; with diligent effort and special training people can jump higher and farther. Perhaps some hopelessly confused observer might argue, on these grounds, that the distinction between jumping and flying is arbitrary, a matter of degree; people can really fly, just like birds, only less well. Analogous proposals in the case of language seem to me to have no greater force or significance.

Returning to human psychology, consider the question how the language faculty fits into the system of cognitive capacity. I have been assuming that UG suffices to determine particular grammars (where, again, a grammar is a system of rules and principles that generates an infinite class of sentences with their formal and semantic properties). But this might not be the case. It is a coherent and perhaps correct proposal that the language faculty constructs a grammar only in conjunction with other faculties of mind. If so, the language faculty itself provides only an abstract framework, an idealization that does not suffice to determine a grammar.

Suppose that there is no sharp delimitation between those semantic properties that are "linguistic" and those that form part of common-sense understanding, that is, the cognitive system dealing with the nature of things named, described, or discussed. Thus, lexical items might be related by principles that form a kind of central core for a system of common-sense beliefs,[10] with no sharp distinction between analytic and synthetic propositions. Or, imagine that terms for "natural kinds" are in part characterized by "stereotypes" in Hilary Putnam's sense.[11] A tiger, then, is something not too unlike given exemplars, and with the same internal structure (perhaps unknown) as the stereotype. Under this assumption, lexical items are located in a "semantic space" generated by the interaction of the language faculty and other faculties of mind. Few if any of these words will have "senses" in the sense of Frege, strictly speaking. The "criterion in mind" that determines the applicability of the term "tiger" will involve actual exemplars. The essential role of possibly unknown inner structure permits change of presumed reference without a change in the concept itself ("a change of sense"); and the reference of the term will be a function of the place of the associated concept in the nonlinguistic system of common-sense understanding. Only through its association with the latter system will the term "tiger" acquire something on the order of a Fregean "sense," though the linguistic system may provide some more abstract semantic properties (say, some "semantic markers" of the sort that Katz discusses[12]).

Suppose further that the operation of rules of grammar is in part determined by semantic properties of lexical items; to form passive sentences, for example, we must take into account semantic properties of verbs and their "thematic relations" to surrounding noun phrases.

These are by no means implausible ideas. If they are correct, the language faculty does not fix a grammar in isolation, even in principle. The theory of UG remains as a component of the theory of mind, but as an abstraction. Note that this conclusion, if correct, does not imply that the language faculty does not exist as an autonomous component of mental structure. Rather, the position we are now considering postulates that this faculty does exist, with a physical realization yet to be discovered, and places it within the system of mental faculties in a fixed way. Some might regard this picture as overly complex, but the idea that the system of cognitive structures must be far more simple than the little finger does not have very much to recommend it.

The place of the language faculty within cognitive capacity is a matter for discovery, not stipulation. The same is true of the place of grammar within the system of acquired cognitive structures. My own, quite tentative, belief is that there is an autonomous system of formal grammar, determined in principle [13] by the language faculty and its component UG. This formal grammar generates abstract structures that are associated with "logical forms" (in a sense of this term to which I will return) by further principles of grammar. But beyond this, it may well be impossible to distinguish sharply between linguistic and nonlinguistic components of knowledge and belief. Thus an actual language may result only from the interaction of several mental faculties, one being the faculty of language. There may be no concrete specimens of which we can say, These are solely the product of the language faculty; and no specific acts that result solely from the exercise of linguistic functions.[14]

Questions of this nature face us no matter what corner of language we try to investigate. There is no "sublanguage" so primitive as to escape these complexities, a fact that comes as no surprise to someone who is persuaded of the essential correctness of the rationalist framework outlined earlier. For in accordance with this view, a grammar is not a structure of higher-order concepts and principles constructed from simpler elements by "abstraction" or "generalization" or "induction." Rather, it is a rich structure of predetermined form, compatible with triggering experience and more highly valued, by a measure that is itself part of UG, than other cognitive structures meeting the dual conditions of compatibility with the structural principles of UG and with relevant experience.[15] There need be no isolable "simple" or "elementary" components within such a system.

Consider, for example, the category of names and the act of naming, which might be regarded as somehow primitive and isolable. A name, let us suppose, is associated with a thing by an original stipulation, and the association is then conveyed in some manner to others. Consider the original stipulation. The name is drawn from the system of language, and the thing is chosen in terms of the categories of "common-sense understanding." Thus two major faculties of mind, at least, place conditions on the stipulation. There are complex conditions—poorly understood, though illustrative examples are not hard to find—that an entity must satisfy to qualify as a "naturally nameable" thing: these conditions involve spatiotemporal contiguity, *Gestalt* qualities, functions within the space of human actions. (Cf. chapter 4, p. 203.) A collection of leaves on a tree, for example, is not a nameable thing, but it would fall within this category if a new art form of "leaf arrangement" were devised and some artist had composed the collection of leaves as a work of art. He could then stipulate that his creation was to be named "serenity." Thus it seems that there is an essential reference even to willful acts, in determining what is a nameable thing.

Furthermore, in determining that an entity is a nameable thing, we assign it to a "natural kind" that might be designated by a common noun, a "sortal predicate." Otherwise (excluding mass terms), it is not nameable. This assignment involves assumptions about the nature of the thing named, some conceptual and some factual. In our system of common-sense understanding, natural kinds are defined by internal structure, constitution, origin, function (for artifacts), and other properties. This is not to say that we necessarily know the defining structure, and so on, but that we assume that it exists and that new entities are assigned correctly to the "sort" and designated by the sortal predicate just in case they share the "essential properties," whatever they are. We may not know just what internal structure determines that such-and-such is a tiger, but something looking and acting just like a tiger is not properly assigned to this category if it in fact differs from "stereotypic" tigers in internal structure. This is a conceptual requirement, drawn from the structure of common-sense understanding. But factual beliefs and common-sense expectations also play a role in determining that a thing is categorizable and hence nameable. Consider Wittgenstein's disappearing chair. In his terms, we have no "rules saying whether one may use the word 'chair' to include this kind of thing" (Wittgenstein, 1953, p. 38). Or to put it differently, we keep certain factual assumptions about the behavior of objects fixed when we categorize them and thus take them as eligible for naming or description.[16]

At least this much of the system of common-sense understanding seems to be involved in the stipulation that a thing is named so-and-so. Furthermore, the cognitive structure of language imposes its own conditions. Languages do not seem to have a category of pure names, in the logician's sense. Rather there are personal names, place names, color names, and so on. Discussing the Aristotelian theory of language, Julius Moravcsik (1975a) has argued that in it "there are no expressions that perform solely the task of referring. Individuals are given by certain privileged terms that specify domains of discourse." I think this is true of natural language. The domains of discourse must be related to the categories of common-sense understanding, though how closely is a fair question. Needless to say, the structure of the two interacting systems that enter into the act of naming need not be open (or even accessible) to the conscious mind. It is, again, an empirical problem to determine the character of the cognitive structures that are involved in the apparently simple act of naming.

Names are not associated with objects in some arbitrary manner. Nor does it seem very illuminating to regard them as "cluster terms" in the Wittgensteinian sense.[17] Each name belongs to a linguistic category that enters in a determinate way into the system of grammar, and the objects named are placed in a cognitive structure of some complexity. These structures remain operative as names are "transferred" to new users.[18] Noting that an entity is named such-and-such, the hearer brings to bear a system of linguistic structure to place the name, and a system of conceptual relations and conditions, along with factual beliefs, to place the thing named. To understand "naming," we would have to understand these systems and the faculties of mind through which they arise.

I mentioned the notion "essential properties," referring it, however, to the systems of language and common-sense understanding. But it has sometimes been argued that things have "essential properties" apart from such designation and categorization. Consider the sentences:

(1)   Nixon won the 1968 election
(2)   Nixon is an animate object [19]

Surely statement (1) is in no sense a necessary truth. There is a possible state of the world, or a "possible world," in which it is untrue, namely, if Humphrey had won. What about (2)? It is not true *a priori;* that is, we might discover that the entity named "Nixon" is in fact an automaton. But suppose that in fact Nixon is a human being. Then, it might be argued, there is no possible world in which (2) is false; the truth of (2) is a matter of "metaphysical necessity." It is a necessary property of Nixon that he has the property, animacy. Entities can have necessary properties, apart from their designation.

These conclusions seem unnecessarily paradoxical. The sentence (2) is, let us say, a necessary truth (given that in fact Nixon is human). But the term "Nixon" in our language system is not simply a name; rather, it is a personal name. Thus (2) has (approximately) the same meaning as (3):

(3)   the person Nixon is an animate object

The necessity of this statement follows without any attribution of necessary properties to individuals apart from their designation. It is a case of modality *de dicto* rather than *de re*, somewhat like the statement that the man who lives upstairs lives upstairs. The necessary truth of (3) (hence (2), given the linguistic category of the name "Nixon") is a consequence of the necessary truth of the statement that people are animate. This necessary truth may be grounded in a necessary connection between categories of common-sense understanding, or an analytic connection between the linguistic terms "person" and "animate." Under any of these assumptions, we need not suppose that an essential property is assigned to an individual, Nixon, apart from the way he is named or the category of common-sense understanding to which he is assigned.

Suppose, on the other hand, we were to add to natural language a new category of "pure names," including the name "N," for Nixon. Then there would no longer be any intuitive support for a distinction between (1) and (2), with "Nixon" replaced by "N." If we can wrench ourselves from the framework of language and common-sense understanding, within which "Nixon" is a personal name and the thing named is assigned to the natural kind Person (hence Animate), then (1) and (2) are true statements with the same logical status. The argument gives no support to the view that objects as such have essential properties, apart from their designation or the conceptual category in which they are placed. Within this new invented system, divorced from language and common-sense understanding, we have no relevant intuitions to guide us, I believe. Thus we might want to say that there is no way for the thing N to have been anything other than what it is, for then it would have been a different thing; thus, in an uninteresting sense, all its properties are "essential." Or, we might want to say that any of its properties might have been other than what they are. The expository recourse to distinctions between (1) and (2) (for example), between what might have been and what could not have been otherwise, is no longer available to us within the new system we are imagining. For this recourse presupposes the systems of thought and language constructed by the faculties of language and common-sense understanding.[20]

Returning to our familiar cognitive structures of thought and language, suppose that we were to discover that the entity named "Nixon" was in fact an automaton, so that (2) was false. We might then conclude that the personal name "Nixon" had been misused (so we now discover), or we might choose to interpret sentences involving this name within the framework of personification metaphor, one of the natural, if derivative, uses of language. Still, nothing leads us to the notion of essential properties, in this case, to the idea that "some properties of an object may be essential to it, in that it could not have failed to have them" (Kripke, 1972, p. 273).

Similar considerations apply in the case of other examples that have been discussed in connection with the problem of *de re* modality. Kripke (1972) suggests that there could be no situation in which Queen Elizabeth II of England, this very woman, might have had different parents; it is a necessary truth that she had the particular parents she had (though again, we do not know it *a priori*).

His conclusion is that "anything coming from a different origin would not be this object" (p. 314). Having a particular origin, in this case two given parents, is another "essential property" of the object.

My own intuitions differ about the example. Thus, it does not seem to me that a logical problem would arise if Queen Elizabeth II were to write a fictionalized autobiography in which she, this very person, had different parents; we might, I think, take this as a description of the history of this person in a different "possible world," a description of a possible state of this world with the very objects that appear in it.

But suppose that this is not so, and that having a particular origin is an "essential property." Is it, then, an essential property of the thing itself, apart from its designation or categorization in common-sense understanding? I think not. We name the entity with a personal name, "Queen Elizabeth II." We assign it to a category of common-sense understanding, Person. It might be (though as noted, I doubt it) that an object taken to be a person could not be the same person if it had parents other than its own. If so, this is a property of the conceptual system of common-sense understanding, and perhaps also of the related system of language; it is a property of the concept Person. Given the cognitive structures, we can distinguish necessary and contingent properties. We can distinguish between what might have been true of an object categorized and designated within these systems, and what could not have been otherwise. The intuitive force of the argument for essential properties seems to me to derive from the system of language in which the name is placed and the system of common-sense understanding, with its structure, in which the object is located. Dropping this framework, with its *de dicto* modalities and conceptual connections, there seems to remain no intuitive force to the proposal that the object as such has essential properties.

To take another case, Kripke suggests that "(roughly) *being a table* seems to be an essential property of the table" (1972, p. 351), that is, of a particular thing that is a table. Exactly what weight is being carried by the qualification "(roughly)" is unclear. If we drop the qualification, the proposal can hardly stand. Suppose we discover that the designer of this particular object had intended it to be a hard bed and that it is so used. Surely we would then say that the thing is not a table but a hard bed that looks like a table. But the thing is what it is. Neither a gleam in the eye of the inventor nor general custom can determine its essential properties, though intention and function are relevant to determining what we take an artifact to be. Suppose further that the thing in question is a table nailed to the floor. We would be inclined to say that it would have been the same thing had it not been nailed to the floor, but it could not have been other than a table. Thus it is necessarily a table but only accidentally immovable. Consider now another creature with a different language and a different system of common-sense understanding, in which such categories as movable-immovable are fundamental but not function and use. These creatures would say that this immovable object would have been a different thing had it not been nailed to the floor, though it could have been other than a table. To them, immovability would appear to be an essential property of the thing, not "being a table." If this is so, a property may be essential or not, depending on which creature's judgments prevail.

We might discover that humans, operating within cognitive capacity, will not develop "natural" systems of the sort postulated for this hypothetical creature. If true, this would be a discovery about human biology, but I do not see how such biological properties of humans affect the "essence" of things.

Intuitive arguments concerning essential properties must account for the whole range of our intuitions, including the ones just offered if they are indeed correct. An account of the full range of intuitions seems simple enough, if we explain the intuitive force of the argument that such-and-such is an essential property of a thing on the basis of the systems of language and common-sense understanding that we bring to bear in making such judgments. The intuitive differences that Kripke cites are often quite clear, but it seems to me that they have to do with the structure of the systems of common-sense understanding and of language, not with essential properties of things considered in abstraction from our characterization of them in terms of these systems of categorization and representation. A study of human judgments concerning essential and accidental properties may give considerable insight into the cognitive structures that are being employed, and perhaps beyond, into the nature of human cognitive capacity and the range of structures that are naturally constructed by the mind. But such a study can carry us no further than this.

It may well be true that in the case of a natural kind, say tigers, the dictionary definition with its defining properties does not provide criterial conditions for something to be a tiger.[21] Thus, were we to "discover an animal which, though having all external appearances of a tiger as described here, has an internal structure completely different from that of the tiger," we would not conclude that it is a tiger; not because the concept of tiger has changed or because the term "tiger" marks a "cluster concept," but because if "tigers form a certain species or natural kind," then we suppose that some fixed internal structure—even if this is unknown—is required for an object to be a tiger (Kripke, 1972, pp. 317–18). Accepting all of this, it does not follow that if an object is in fact a tiger and tigers are in fact a natural kind, then having this internal structure is an essential property of the object apart from its designation or categorization as a tiger, though it is a necessary truth that a tiger has this internal structure, by virtue of properties of the system of common-sense understanding and the system of language.

In the Aristotelian framework,[22] there are certain "generative factors" that enter into the essential constitution of objects; we gain understanding of the nature of an object insofar as we grasp the generative factors which enable it to be what it is—a person, a tiger, a house, or whatever. Constitution and structure, agent responsible for generation within a system of natural law, distinguishing factors for particular species, are among the generative factors. These generative factors are close, it seems, to Kripke's "essential properties."[23] Under this formulation, there are essential properties of things because of the way the world is in fact constituted, but we may easily drop the metaphysical assumptions and say that x is a generative factor of y under the description D [24] (or, perhaps, when y is categorized as a C within the system of common-sense understanding). It seems to me that this formulation keeps fairly close to what little we can determine, on the basis of introspection and intuition, about our judgments and the logical categories of our statements.

I am raising no objection to the construction of formal theories involving languages with pure names designating entities with individuating essential properties apart from the way they are designated or categorized. One may ask, however, whether the study of such systems, whatever its interest, will provide much insight into the workings of human language and human thought.

What is true of names holds as well of other linguistic categories. There is no simple "point of entry" into the system of language. Color terms have often been taken in empiricist speculation to be particularly simple, learnable in isolation by conditioning, ostension, or association. But in fact, these terms seem to be learned as part of a system of color expressions at a rather advanced stage of language learning.[25] There is no general reason to suppose that a human language has "primitive subsystems" in any interesting sense, and no convincing evidence for such a belief.

Observation of early stages of language acquisition may be quite misleading in this regard. It is possible that at an early stage there is use of languagelike expressions, but outside the framework imposed, at a later stage of intellectual maturation, by the faculty of language—much as a dog can be trained to respond to certain commands, though we would not conclude, from this, that it is using language. The most that we can say with any plausibility is that a relation of "compatibility" holds between the grammar constructed at a given stage of mental growth and linguistic experience, as analyzed at that stage by mechanisms of mind. Given the idealization to instantaneous acquisition, discussed earlier, we may say that the primitives of linguistic theory, selected by the criterion of epistemological priority, provide an analysis of linguistic experience that serves as one term in the relation of compatibility. But beyond this, there is little to say at the moment, and even this much may involve seriously falsifying assumptions, a matter to which I must yet return. But even if legitimate as a first approximation, these assumptions will not carry the burden required by much philosophical speculation about how language is or must be learned. As for the further claim that language is not only learned but taught, and that this "teaching" is essential to establishing the meaning of linguistic expressions, this view receives no support on either empirical or conceptual grounds.[26]

John Searle has urged a distinction between "brute facts" and "institutional facts" (Searle, 1969, pp. 50 f.). Among the former are those described by the so-called observation sentences of the reconstruction of scientific knowledge: "the litmus paper is red," "the pointer reads 23.6," and the like. The existence of "institutional facts," no less objective, "presupposes the existence of certain human institutions." It is an objective fact, say, that Mr. Smith married Miss Jones, but "it is only given the institution of marriage that certain forms of behavior constitute Mr. Smith's marrying Miss Jones." Human institutions are "systems of constitutive rules" of the form "X counts as Y in context C." Searle proposes that "speaking a language is performing acts according to constitutive rules" which determine institutional facts. He argues further that institutional facts cannot be explained in terms of brute facts, but only "in terms of the constitutive rules which underlie them."

In the view we have been considering, the statement of "brute facts" takes place within (at least) a dual framework, involving the interaction of the system of language and the system of common-sense understanding. Likewise, the statement of institutional facts presupposes a theory of human institutions and a related linguistic system. I doubt that the principles entering into the theory of human institutions that persons have developed (largely without awareness) can be reduced simply to the form "X counts as Y in context C," as Searle suggests. An analysis of institutional structure appears to require principles of much more abstract nature. Abandoning empiricist bias, there is little reason to shy away from this conclusion. Again, it is a matter for discovery, not stipulation; discovery, in this case, in the course of investigation of still another faculty of mind and its operation.

In general, cognitive structures of varied sorts are constructed as a person matures, interacting with grammar and providing conditions for language use. An integrated study of cognition should try to make these connections precise, thus leading—we may speculate—to further innate properties of mind.

Note again that there is no inconsistency between this view and the thesis of autonomy of formal grammar, that is, the thesis that the language faculty constructs an abstract formal skeleton invested with meaning by interpretive rules, an integrated structure that fits in a definite manner into a system of language use.

Searle has suggested elsewhere that the latter thesis, while not internally inconsistent, nevertheless derives from an approach to language which "runs counter to quite ordinary, plausible, and common-sense assumptions about language." He takes the "common-sense picture of human language" to be something like this:

> The purpose of language is communication in much the same sense that the purpose of the heart is to pump blood. In both cases it is possible to study the structure independently of function but pointless and perverse to do so, since structure and function so obviously interact. We communicate primarily with other people, but also with ourselves, as when we talk or think in words to ourselves.

Language is the communicative system *par excellence*, and it is "peculiar and eccentric" to insist on studying the structure of language apart from its communicative function.

Searle presents my competing picture in the following terms:

> . . . except for having such general purposes as the expression of human thoughts, language doesn't have any essential purpose, or if it does there is no interesting connection between its purpose and its structure. The syntactical structures of human languages are the products of innate features of the human mind, and they have no significant connection with communication, though, of course, people do use them for, among other purposes, communication. The essential thing about languages, their defining trait, is their structure.

Searle suggests that I have "arbitrarily assumed" that "use and structure . . . [do not] . . . influence each other," and that this rather perverse approach has prevented the construction of a theory of meaning, indeed, that I am fighting "a rearguard action" against "the study of speech acts," which offers the way out of traditional problems in semantics. It is this "failure to see the essential connection between language and communication, between meaning and speech acts," that is the greatest "defect of the Chomskyan theory," he suggests.[27]

Let us examine these objections, and ask whether the picture that Searle rejects is in fact as pointless and perverse as he suggests.

First, I should clarify that I have always rejected some of the positions that Searle attributes to me. Thus, I have never suggested that "there is no interesting connection" between the structure of language and "its purpose," including communicative function, nor have I "arbitrarily assumed" that use and structure do not influence one another, though I have argued—correctly, I think—that particular proposals about this relation are wrong.[28] Surely there are significant connections between structure and function; this is not and has never been in doubt.[29] Furthermore, I do not hold that "the essential thing about languages . . . is their structure." I have frequently described what I have called "the creative use of language" as an essential feature, no less than the distinctive structural properties of language. Study of structure, use, and acquisition may be expected to provide insight into essential features of language.

Consider now Searle's other points. He claims that language has an "essential purpose," communication, and regards my denial of this claim as counter to common sense and implausible. It is difficult to argue about common sense. There is, in fact, a very respectable tradition, which I have reviewed elsewhere,[30] that regards as a vulgar distortion the "instrumental view" of language as "essentially" a means of communication, or a means to achieve given ends. Language, it is argued, is "essentially" a system for expression of thought. I basically agree with this view. But I suspect that little is at stake here, given Searle's concept of "communication" as including communication with oneself, that is, thinking in words. We do, I am sure, think without words too—at least so introspection seems to show. But insofar as we are using language for "self-communication," we are simply expressing our thoughts, and the distinction between Searle's two pictures collapses. Thus I agree with Searle that there is an essential connection between language and communication once we take "communication" in his broader sense—an unfortunate move, I believe, since the notion "communication" is now deprived of its essential and interesting character. But I remain unconvinced by his contention that there is an essential connection of the sort he claims between meaning and speech acts.

Before turning to this point of disagreement—the only one, I think, when the issues are properly stated—consider Searle's contention that it is "pointless and perverse" to study the structure of language "independently of function," bearing in mind the qualifications just noted. Pursuing his analogy, there is no doubt that the physiologist, studying the heart, will pay attention to the fact that it pumps blood. But he will also study the structure of the heart and the origin of this structure in the individual and the species, making no dogmatic assumptions about the possibility of "explaining" this structure in functional terms.

Similarly in the case of language. Consider, again, the principle of structure-dependence discussed earlier. This seems to be a general property of an interesting class of linguistic rules, innate to the mind. Following what I take to be Searle's suggestion, let us try to account for it in terms of communication. I see no way of doing so. Surely this principle enters into the function of language; we might well study the ways in which it does. But a language could function for communication (or otherwise) just as well with structure-independent rules, so it would seem. For a mind differently constituted, structure-independent rules would be far superior, in that they require no abstract analysis of a sentence beyond words. I think that the example is typical. Where it can be shown that structures serve a particular function, that is a valuable discovery. To account for or somehow explain the structure of UG, or of particular grammars, on the basis of functional considerations is a pretty hopeless prospect, I would think; it is, perhaps, even "perverse" to assume otherwise. Perhaps Searle has something else in mind, but I frankly see no issue here, no counterproposal that has any plausibility to the picture Searle rejects.

Searle argues that "it is quite reasonable to suppose that the needs of communication influenced the structure" of language, as it evolved in human prehistory. I agree. The question is: What can we conclude from this fact? The answer is: Very little. The needs of locomotion influenced the fact that humans developed legs and birds wings. This observation is not very helpful to the physiologist concerned with the nature of the human body. Like physical structures, cognitive systems have undoubtedly evolved in certain ways, though in neither case can we seriously claim to understand the factors that entered into a particular course of evolution and determined or even significantly influenced its outcome. True, if genetically based systems had been seriously dysfunctional the evolutionary development might have been aborted, and insofar as they facilitated differential reproduction they contributed to evolution. But observations at this level of generality are not of much interest. Among the systems that humans have developed in the course of evolution are the science-forming capacity and the capacity to deal intuitively with rather deep properties of the number system. As far as we know, these capacities have no selective value, though it is quite possible that they developed as part of other systems that did have such value.[31] We know very little about what happens when 10^{10} neurons are crammed into something the size of a basketball, with further conditions imposed by the specific manner in which this system developed over time. It would be a serious error to suppose that all properties, or the interesting properties of the structures that have evolved, can be "explained" in terms of natural selection. Surely there is no warrant for such an assumption in the case of physical structures.

When Searle says that "in general an understanding of syntactical facts requires an understanding of their function in communication since communication is what language is all about," I agree only in part. If we take communication to include expression of thought, as he does, then the statement becomes at least a half-truth; thus we will have only a partial understanding of syntax if we do not consider its role in the expression of thought, and other uses of language. This much should arouse no controversy. But from this unexceptionable remark, it does not at all follow that the thesis of the autonomy of syntax is "peculiar and eccentric." If language is to be thought of on the analogy of a physical organ such as the heart, then functional explanations are unlikely to carry us very far, and we should concern ourselves with the structure of the organ that serves these functions.[32] It is, again, a question of fact, not a matter for stipulation, whether the organization of language involves an autonomous syntax in the sense that has been proposed. One can have no *a priori* intuitions about this question, any more than one can sensibly argue, on grounds of intuition, that a certain theory of the structure of the heart is "perverse."

Let us turn now to the sole serious point of disagreement, the "essential connection" that Searle claims to exist between language and communication, between meaning and speech acts. Taking these issues to be related, Searle

(1972) argues against the theory that "sentences are abstract objects that are produced and understood independently of their role in communication," on the grounds that "any attempt to account for the meaning of sentences within such assumptions is either circular or inadequate." He claims further that the account offered by philosophers that he cites (Wittgenstein, Austin, Grice, Searle, Strawson) has "provided us with a way out of this dilemma," by explaining "meaning" in terms of *what the speaker intends the audience to believe or to do*. Others too have made this claim, and have argued that there is a gain in an approach that explains the meaning of linguistic expressions in terms of speaker's intentions, in that this approach permits us to escape "the orbit of conceptual space" that includes the concepts "idea," "semantic marker," Fregean sense, and so on.[33] This approach avoids the "circularity" to which Searle objects in his critique of classical semantics, and in particular, my version of it.

The account to which Searle alludes would, if it were correct, avoid the "circularity" that he claims to exist.[34] But this account fails in many respects. In particular, it offers no way to deal with the many cases in which language is not used for communication (in the narrower sense), normal cases, for which the speaker's intention with regard to an audience offers no particular insight into the literal meaning of what he says. Furthermore, an analysis of the proposals that have been put forth shows that "literal meaning" is reintroduced as an unexplained notion. The approach thus remains within the "orbit of conceptual space" from which one had sought an escape.

Consider first the alleged "essential" connection between language and communication. Searle objects to my statement that meaningful use of language "need not involve communication or even the attempt to communicate," as when "I use language to express or clarify my thoughts, with the intent to deceive, to avoid an embarrassing silence, or in a dozen other ways." In these cases, I suggested, "my words have a strict meaning and I can very well mean what I say, but the fullest understanding of what I intend my audience (if any) to believe or to do might give little or no indication of the meaning of my discourse" (Chomsky, 1971, p. 19).

Despite Searle's qualms, all of this seems to me commonplace and obvious. I can be using language in the strictest sense with no intention of communicating. Though my utterances have a definite meaning, their normal meaning, nevertheless my intentions with regard to an audience may shed no light on this meaning. Take some concrete examples. As a graduate student, I spent two years writing a lengthy manuscript, assuming throughout that it would never be published [35] or read by anyone. I meant everything I wrote, intending nothing as to what anyone would believe about my beliefs, in fact taking it for granted that there would be no audience. Once a year, along with many others, I write a letter to the Bureau of Internal Revenue explaining, with as much eloquence as I can muster, why I am not paying part of my income tax. I mean what I say in explaining this. I do not, however, have the intention of communicating to the reader, or getting him to believe or do something, for the simple reason that I know perfectly well that the "reader" (probably some computer) couldn't care less. What my statements in the letter mean, what I mean—in one sense—in making these statements, is not explicable in terms of what I mean, what I intend, in writing the letter, namely to express support for people undertaking resistance to the criminal violence of the state in more meaningful ways. Once, I had the curious experience of making a speech against the Vietnam war to a group of soldiers who were advancing in full combat gear, rifles in hand, to clear the area where I was speaking. I meant what I said—my statements had their strict and literal meaning—but this had little to do with my intentions at that moment.[36]

These examples are misleading because they are, perhaps, out of the ordinary. In fact, the situation they illustrate is commonplace. Under innumerable quite normal circumstances—research, casual conversation, and so on—language is used properly, sentences have their strict meaning, people mean what they say or write, but there is no intent to bring the audience (not assumed to exist, or assumed not to exist, in some cases) to have certain beliefs or to undertake certain actions. Such commonplace examples pose a difficulty for an analysis of meaning in terms of speaker's intention with regard to an audience, even if it were possible, for the case where there is intent to communicate, to account for what a sentence means in these terms—and this too I doubt, for reasons to which I will return.

Searle (forthcoming) asserts that:

> (A) The simplest cases of meaning are those where the speaker utters a sentence and means exactly and literally what he says. In such cases the speaker intends to produce a certain illocutionary effect in the hearer, and he intends to produce this effect by means of getting the hearer to recognize his intention to produce it, and he intends to get the hearer to recognize this intention in virtue of the hearer's knowledge of the rules that govern the utterance of the sentence.

He then proceeds to an interesting discussion of other, less simple "cases of meaning," such as "in hints, insinuations, irony, and metaphor." But the problem remains that (A) is often false even for the simplest cases. The speaker may mean exactly and literally what he says, but with no intention of the sort that Searle claims must exist. The speaker's actual intentions may vary widely even in these "simplest cases," and may shed no light at all on the meaning of what he says.

Searle has not entirely overlooked these problems. Thus, he considers Grice's theory that "To say that a speaker S meant something by X is to say that S intended the utterance of X to produce some effect in a hearer H by means of the recognition of this intention." As Searle notes, the account fails because it "does not show the connection between one's meaning something by what one says, and what that which one says actually means in the language." To overcome this difficulty, Searle revises Grice's definition in several respects. He introduces the notion of rules for using expressions and develops a broader notion of "effects produced in the hearer." For Searle, these effects include "understanding what I said." Thus, in his revised account (1969, p. 48), the meaning of a sentence is determined by rules, and uttering a sentence and meaning it is a matter of intending to get the hearer to know that certain states of affairs specified by the rules obtain, with the corollary intention of getting the hearer to know these things by recognizing the first intention, and intending him to recognize the first intention by virtue of his knowledge of the rules for the sentence uttered—essentially, (A) above.

Later, I will turn to the question whether crucial questions are not begged by this reference to rules and so on; I think they are. But let us ask how these revisions deal with one general problem that Searle raises against Grice's theory, namely: "I may make a statement without caring whether my audience believes it or not but simply because I feel it my duty to make it." Or, the examples that I just mentioned, which are in a sense even worse, since it is assumed that there is no audience (cf. note 36). Unfortunately, the difficulty Searle cites against Grice survives the revisions. In the cases cited, I, the speaker, have no intention of getting the hearer to know anything or to recognize anything, but what I say has its strict meaning, and

I mean what I say. Thus Searle's revision, for this reason alone, fails to capture the intended notion of meaning; as a factual claim, it is false. The same is true of all other attempts that I know of to explain "meaning" in terms of "speaker's intention in communicating."

In elaborating the issue that he raises against Grice, Searle switches without comment from a discussion of meaning to a discussion of communication. The shift is important. The theory of speaker's intention may well be a contribution to a theory of successful communication. Searle has, however, offered no way to escape the problems he raises against alternative approaches. Still other problems arise, as we shall see, when we consider the nature of the rules involved in the Grice-Searle theories.

Other philosophers have argued in a similar vein. Thus P. F. Strawson (1970) speaks of a "Homeric struggle" over a central issue of philosophy between "theorists of communication-intention" and "theorists of formal semantics." Like Grice and Searle, Strawson opts for the theory of communication-intention. Before examining his reasons, let us try to clarify just what is at issue.

It turns out on investigation that there is actually a fair amount of agreement among the parties to this "struggle on what seems to be such a central issue in philosophy." In particular, all agree, Strawson says, that "the meanings of the sentences of a language are largely determined by the semantic and syntactic rules or conventions of that language." Thus there is a common project—and it is this that interests me particularly—namely, to discover these semantic and syntactic rules and conventions, and more specifically, to extract the universal element in them.

When the theorist of communication-intention wants to distinguish a promise to go to the store from a promise to dry the dishes, he will refer to the results of this common enterprise, which finds its place, in his theory, in the principle that "the meaning of a sentence is determined by rules, and those rules specify both conditions of utterance of the sentence and also what the sentence counts as" (Searle, 1969, p. 48); in one case, the utterance counts as a promise to go to the store, in the other, as a promise to dry the dishes. About this part of the theory, theorists of communication-intention have little to say. It is just this part that concerns me—and, I suspect, others whom Strawson calls "theorists of formal semantics" (I am cited as one).

Similarly, suppose that Searle and Strawson can distinguish a promise from a warning or a prediction or a threat. Then their results will be of immediate interest to the most unregenerate exponent of abstract "meanings," who wishes to express somehow the fact that a given linguistic form— say, "drinks will be served at five"—can be used as a promise, a prediction, a warning, a threat, a statement, or an invitation.

This is not to deny that there is an issue between Strawson and his opponents, but it is less clear where the issue lies. According to Strawson, "where [the two views] differ is as to the relations between the meaning-determining rules of the language, on the one hand, and the function of communication on the other: one party insists, and the other (apparently) refuses to allow, that the general nature of those rules can be understood only by reference to this function."

Strawson then proceeds to inquire into the import of this refusal. But from the initial formulation, his discussion is misleading. It would have been more appropriate to shift the implicit burden of proof, and to say that one party claims that the general nature of the meaning-determining rules can be understood by reference to (and only by reference to) the function of communication, while the other party asks for an argument, and is not too impressed by what is forthcoming. Strawson's misleading formulation persists throughout. Thus, he poses the "central issue" in these terms: "It consists in nothing other than the simple-seeming question whether the notion of truth-conditions can itself be explained or understood without reference to the function of communication." To reformulate the issue more properly, it consists in the question whether reference to the function of communication is essential to analysis of meaning or to explaining "the notion of truth-conditions," as Strawson alleges, or indeed whether it gives us any help in dealing with the central problems of meaning. The "theorist of formal semantics" is unconvinced.

Placing the burden of proof where it belongs, consider Strawson's defense of his claims. He suggests that we take as a primitive the notion "audience-directed belief-expression" (ADBE). To illustrate, "an utterer might have, as one of his intentions in executing his utterance, that of bringing his audience to think that he, the utterer, believes some proposition, say the proposition that p; and he might intend this intention to be wholly overt, to be clearly recognized by the audience." So he might—and he might also have the intention of expressing the proposition honestly, perhaps to clarify his thoughts, perhaps out of a sense of personal integrity, caring little whether his audience believes that he believes it, or even whether there is an audience. Surely such cases are commonplace. Or perhaps his intention is to amuse the audience, to keep the conversation going, or innumerable other possibilities.

What the communication theorist must show, somehow, is that ADBE is central and that communication is, as claimed, the "essential function" of language. He must show that reference to ADBE, reference to the speaker's intentions with regard to what the audience will believe or do, explains something—for example, explains why the statement that p is meaningful when produced with no intention other than honest self-expression. This the communication theorist cannot do. But he must do still more, to establish his claims. He must show how reference to ADBE helps in developing an account of what sentences mean. The prospects seem still more dubious. If we can give an account of the notion "the utterer believes the proposition that p," which appears without explanation in Strawson's example cited above, and explain how this differs from "believing the proposition that q," then it would seem that the central problems have been solved and that further reference to ADBE is not very interesting. But the crucial notion, "the utterer believes the proposition that p (not q)," is common to the contestants in Strawson's struggle, and is in no way clarified by reference to ADBE, contrary to what Strawson suggests. Given this notion, we can (uninterestingly) expound "linguistic meaning" along lines that Strawson reviews; without it, it appears that we cannot.

Strawson suggests that an analysis by Paul Grice gives reason to think that "it is possible to expound such a concept of communication-intention or, as he calls it, utterer's meaning, which is proof against objection and which does not presuppose the notion of linguistic meaning," thus avoiding Searle's "circularity." But Grice's analysis fails in the crucial cases. Observing more closely how it fails, we discover that the differences between opponents in this perhaps less-than-Homeric struggle seem to narrow still further.

Grice considers the crucial notion "occasion meaning in the absence of an audience"—for example, the use of an utterance for self-expression, clarification of thought, and so on (Grice, 1969). He argues that to say that the speaker means such-and-such by uttering x is to say that there is a property P such that x is uttered with the intention that anyone who has P would think what an appropriate audience is supposed to think in the "normal" case of communication to an audience (with various refinements that we may ignore here).

But I see no reason to believe that the speaker must have such intentions as are specified in Grice's definiendum. In cases of the sort mentioned, the speaker has no relevant intentions with regard to what a hearer with P, however chosen, would think. In the case of honest self-expression, the speaker doesn't care. In the case of casual conversation, the speaker's intentions with regard to a hypothetical audience need not go beyond his intentions with regard to the actual audience, and plainly there need be no intention that the actual audience believe that the speaker's beliefs are such-and-such. Furthermore, consider the property P that appears in Grice's definition. This property, Grice suggests, might be, for example, the property of being an English speaker. But this won't do. Suppose the speaker believes that there are native English speakers who habitually misunderstand what they read or hear—the reviewers of his books, for example. Then even if this speaker happens to have the intention that Grice assumes to be necessary, it will be necessary to take P to be something like "is a speaker of English who will think that the utterer believes that Q upon hearing x," where Q is the literal meaning of x. It is only for such "hearers" that the speaker intends that the cognitive response correspond to his meaning in the required way. But now all questions are begged. The notion "literal meaning," or some equivalent, again intrudes, and no way has been offered to escape the "orbit of conceptual space" that includes the suspect abstract notions "linguistic meaning" and the like, even if the utterer happens to have the postulated intentions with regard to a hypothetical audience, as is by no means necessary in the normal use of language.[37]

One can imagine modifications of the proposed definition that would not involve incorrect claims about intentions, but not, so far as I can see, without introducing some notion like "linguistic meaning." As we will see directly, Grice's more explicit and comprehensive theory fails on this count as well. The point is, I think, that the "communication theorists" are not analyzing "meaning" but rather something else: perhaps "successful communication." This concept may indeed involve essential reference to Grice's notion of

"M-intending," namely, the intention of a speaker to produce in the listener an effect by means of the listener's recognition of his intentions, with the elaborations suggested by Searle, Grice, and others. But communication is only one function of language, and by no means an essential one. The "instrumental" analysis of language as a device for achieving some end is seriously inadequate, and the "language games" that have been produced to illuminate this function are correspondingly misleading.[38] In contemplation, inquiry, normal social interchange, planning and guiding one's own actions, creative writing, honest self-expression, and numerous other activities with language, expressions are used with their strict linguistic meaning irrespective of the intentions of the "utterer" with regard to an audience; and even in the cases that the communication theorist regards as central, the implicit reference to "rules" and "conventions" in his account seems to beg the major questions, a matter to which I will return directly.

In any event, it seems that there are a host of interesting problems in the common ground shared by the two theories that Strawson counterposes: namely, the problems of analyzing how the meanings of the sentences of a language are determined by the rules of the language, that is, the grammar—possibly in interaction with other cognitive structures, along lines outlined earlier.

Strawson has failed to establish the claims of the "communication theorist," and the sources to which he refers do no better. Consider now his argument against the theorist of formal semantics. Note that this argument might well be correct without advancing his primary claim. Is it correct?

Strawson finds the opposing theory inadequate because it relies on the unanalyzed and unexplicated notion of "expressing a belief." The "meaning-determining rules for a sentence of the language," in this view, "are the rules which determine *what* belief is conventionally articulated by one who, in given contextual conditions, utters the sentence";

"determining what this belief is, is the same thing as determining what assertion is made." But the notion of "an essentially independent concept of belief-expression," with no reference to communicative intention, requires further explanation, Strawson argues. It is wanting, because "we are debarred from making reference to the end or goal of communication an essential part of our story." The description does not tell us what need of the speaker is satisfied by expressing his belief. Furthermore, it appears on this account that it is "a quite contingent truth about language that the rules or conventions which determine the meanings of the sentences of a language are public or social rules or conventions. This will be, as it were, a natural fact, a fact of nature, in no way essential to the concept of a language. . . ." Thus, on this theory, people learn a language in which they can express beliefs,[39] and also "acquire the *secondary* skill of communicating their beliefs," but the latter is "simply something added on, an extra and conceptually uncovenanted benefit, quite incidental to the description of what it is to have mastered the meaning-rules of the language." Listeners may assume that belief-expressions do in fact express beliefs and are intended for this purpose, but that is a mere contingent fact: "As far as the central core is concerned, the function of communication remains secondary, derivative, conceptually inessential."

With no further argument,[40] Strawson dismisses this account as "too perverse and arbitrary to satisfy the requirements of an acceptable theory." Thus the communication theorist "must be allowed to have won [the game]."

Note that the question whether communication *is* "primary" and "conceptually essential" is begged throughout in Strawson's counterargument. Furthermore, the picture that Strawson rejects as perverse and arbitrary seems quite reasonable and probably correct, though not very illuminating. The organism is so constituted that it acquires a system of language that includes "meaning-determining rules" (again, perhaps, in interaction with other faculties of mind). These rules are then used by the speaker to express his beliefs (*inter alia*). The learner has no "reason" for acquiring the language; he does not choose to learn, and cannot fail to learn under normal conditions, any more than he chooses (or can fail) to organize visual space in a certain way—or, for that matter, any more than certain cells in the embryo choose (or can fail) to become an arm or the visual centers of the brain under appropriate environmental conditions. Having acquired the system of language, the person can (in principle) choose to use it or not, as he can choose to keep to or disregard his judgments concerning the position of objects in space. He cannot choose to have sentences mean other than what they do, any more than he can choose to have objects distributed in perceptual space otherwise than the way they are. Communication is one function that the system may serve; as noted several times, it is by no means the only function, and Strawson nowhere offers a plausible argument that it is the "essential function" (unless we trivialize the issue by introducing "self-communication" as an instance of "communication"), nor does he even enlighten us as to what it means for one use of language to be its "essential function." As for "what need of his it satisfies" to express his beliefs, the answers may range widely: perhaps the need to be honest and forthright, or to impress others and advance his career, or to do himself in, or to maintain certain social relations in a group, among many other possibilities.

As for the fact that the rules of language are "public rules," this is, indeed, a contingent fact. It is a fact of nature that the cognitive structures developed by people in similar circumstances, within cognitive capacity, are similar, by virtue of their similar innate constitution. Thus we share rules of language with others as we share an organization of visual space with them. Both shared systems play a role in successful communication. Hearers sometimes assume that the speaker is expressing beliefs that he holds, at other times not, depending on the circumstances. There is nothing surprising about any of this, though we still understand very little about the cognitive structures developed and their basis in faculties of mind; and questions can be raised about problems that are common to both approaches, specifically, the problem of clarifying the notions "use a linguistic rule," "express the belief that p," and so on.

Strawson's belief that this picture is perverse and arbitrary derives, perhaps, from his unargued assumption that language is consciously taught by conditioning and training and is thus quite different from cognitive or physical structures that develop in the organism by virtue of its nature, under appropriate environmental conditions. Surely there are important differences between the growth of language, the construction of perceptual space, the development of organs in the embryo, and other processes of physical and cognitive development. But these differences are not, I think, of anything like the sort that Strawson seems to suppose. With regard to the questions he raises, the processes are similar in important respects. In none of these cases do issues of "choice" or "reason" or "ends and purposes" arise in accounting for the development of the structures in question in the particular person. We are dealing here with systems that develop in a natural way as a species of animal instinct, in Hume's phrase, entirely without conscious choice, without reasons (for the organism), and certainly without any necessity for training and conditioning. The nature of the structures that develop is in large measure predetermined by the biologically given organization of the mind. If what I am suggesting here is generally true, as I believe it is, then it is the questions that Strawson raises that are "perverse," not the answers that the "theorist of formal semantics" might give to them, along the lines just indicated.

I stress again, however, that even if the proposals of the

"theorist of formal semantics" were as "perverse and arbitrary" as Strawson believes, this would in no way vindicate the "communication theorist." Rather, a positive demonstration is required for the claims of the "communication theorist," and this is lacking.

Searle speculates that my reason for (allegedly) fighting a "rearguard action against [the study of speech acts]" is that I see in this theory a reversion to behaviorism (Searle, 1972). The conclusion is incorrect. My objections to the theory of speech acts, as it has so far been developed, are basically those just stated: it may help to analyze successful communication, and it has led to interesting discoveries about the semantic properties of utterances, but it gives us no way to escape the orbit of conceptual space that includes such notions as "linguistic meaning." Without such intrusion, the theory simply expresses false statements about meaning.

As for the reversion to behaviorism, it seems true of the most careful work within the theory. In what is, to my knowledge, the most careful and comprehensive effort to explain the meaning of linguistic expressions within this framework,[41] Grice presents a system of definitions that rest not only on intentions but also on the speaker's "policy," "practice," and "habit," on the idea of a "repertoire of procedures." To have a procedure in one's repertoire is to have "a standing readiness (willingness, preparedness), in some degree to . . . ," where "a readiness (etc.) to do something [is] a member of the same family . . . as an intention to do that thing." Grice recognizes the inadequacy of this analysis, but gives only some "informal remarks" as to how a proper definition might be constructed. He cites "three main cases in which one may legitimately speak of an established procedure in respect of utterance-type X." One, which we may disregard, has to do with a system of communication that has been devised artificially but never put into operation. Analysis of the other two cases reveals very clearly just how the whole approach leads in an entirely wrong though quite familiar direction.

The two relevant cases reduce to "practice," that is, custom and habit. One is the case in which a speaker has the "practice to utter X in such-and-such circumstances," and thus "*will* have a readiness to utter X in such-and-such circumstances." But this is inadequate, since a speaker may not have "*any* degree of readiness to utter the expression in any circumstances whatsoever." The problem, as Grice notes, is that we seem to need "the idea of [the speaker's] being *equipped* to use the expression"; that is, we need the notion of "competence," in the familiar sense of linguistic theory, outlined earlier. This notion Grice takes to be "problematic," though he does not explain why. It would indeed be problematic to a behaviorist, but not, it seems, within an approach that takes humans to be organisms within the natural world. True, there is much that is not well understood, but there seems no problem in principle in investigating the nature, use, and acquisition of cognitive structures, if we dispense with the *a priori* and completely unwarranted strictures on legitimate theory construction that are part of the behaviorist program.

Grice's final case is intended to deal with the problem that a speaker may be "equipped" to use expressions properly but have no readiness to do so. He suggests that a person may have a "procedure for X" in the required sense if "to utter X in such-and-such circumstances is part of the practice of many members of" the group to which the person belongs. That is, other members of the group "*do* have a readiness to utter X in such-and-such circumstances." But for familiar reasons, this analysis is useless. There are no practices, customs, or habits, no readiness, willingness, or preparedness, that carry us very far in accounting for the normal creative use of language, whether we consider the practices of a person or of a group. Thus, any speaker of English is "equipped," in the sense that Grice requires, to speak or understand an arbitrary sentence on this page, but neither a given speaker nor any group has a practice or readiness to utter these sentences under any circumstances. The same is true even of single words, if we take the notions "practice" and "readiness" seriously.

All of these efforts lead in the wrong track, a furrow already plowed by proponents of empiricist myth, and more recently, of the curious deviation from normal scientific practice called "behaviorism."

A related difficulty has to do with the move from unstructured signals to structured utterances. The move is made in terms of a notion of "resultant procedure," which, as Grice remarks, "has been left pretty unilluminated." His attempt to clarify it involves a shift from "procedure" in the sense of "customary practice" to "procedure" in the sense of "rule," a very different notion, belonging to a totally different "conceptual space." The heart of the matter is, as Grice points out, that we in some sense implicitly accept and appear to follow certain linguistic rules—"an as yet unsolved problem," as he puts it, but the central problem, not a marginal one. Grice remarks that "the proper interpretation of the idea that we *do* accept these rules becomes something of a mystery, if the 'acceptance' of the rules is to be distinguished from the existence of the related practices; but it seems like a mystery which, for the time being at least, we have to swallow."

Since the central problems remain unsolved, and since there is, furthermore, not a hint of an idea as to how to proceed to solve them, it seems that Searle, Strawson, and others have gone well beyond what is appropriate in their claims for the theory of communication-intention and speech acts. Following this approach, we are back with the old mysteries: in what sense do we "accept" the rules of language and how do we follow them to express our thoughts, our beliefs, our wishes, and so on? Reference to customs and practices is simply beside the point, completely unhelpful. Furthermore, we now face new problems, such as the problem of accounting for the normal uses of language cited earlier. The theory of communication-intention seems a blind alley.[42]

We must distinguish between the literal meaning of the linguistic expression produced by S and what S meant by producing this expression (or by saying that so-and-so, whatever expressions he used). The first notion is the one to be explained in the theory of language. The second has nothing particular to do with language; I can just as well ask, in the same sense of "meaning," what S meant by slamming the door. Within the theory of successful communication, we can, perhaps, draw a connection between these notions. The theory of meaning, however, seems quite unilluminated by this effort.

The mystery that Grice cites can be slightly reduced by distinguishing two notions of "acceptance" of rules: in the acquisition of language, and in the use of language. In either case, "acceptance" of rules must be "distinguished from the existence of the related practices." In general, there are no related practices. But in the first case, we should abandon the notion of "acceptance" of rules altogether, with the associated idea that rules are "chosen" and that we have reasons for these choices, as in Strawson's discussion. The rules of language are not accepted for certain reasons, but rather are developed by the mind when it is placed under certain objective conditions, much as the organs of the body develop in their predetermined way under appropriate conditions. So far, there is no mystery. A mystery would arise if we were to attempt to account for the development of rules in terms of practices and customs. Similarly, there would be a mystery if we were to attempt to account for the "acceptance" of the principles by which we organize visual space in terms of our practices and customs. Thus far, at least, the mystery can be resolved by abandoning the residue of empiricism and undertaking the analysis of cognitive capacity along lines sketched earlier.

Mysteries do remain, however, when we turn to the "acceptance" of the rules in language use. Once the system of language and other cognitive structures are developed by the mind, the person has a certain range of choices available as to how to use these systems. What does it mean to say that a person "accepts" the rules, in this context? Perhaps, that he chooses to follow the rules that are part of his current cognitive state, that belong to the cognitive structures his mind has produced. I cannot see what else it might mean. Now, however, we face some real mysteries, namely, those relating to the theory of human action (the theory of M_{cs}; cf. p. 17). The rules that a person "accepts" do not tell him what to say. We may ask how or why we put to use the system of rules that the mind has developed. Under what circumstances do we choose to violate these rules? What kinds of sophistication are involved in this choice, and what are its conceptual limitations? And so on. Appeal to customs and practices is notoriously unhelpful, but appeal to other modes of explanation does not carry us very far either.

The study of the development of cognitive structures ("acceptance of rules," in the first sense) poses problems to be solved, but not, it seems, impenetrable mysteries. The study of the capacity to use these structures and the exercise of this capacity, however, still seems to elude our understanding.

CHAPTER 3

Some General Features of Language

The discussion so far has been rather abstract. I have mentioned only one general property that I think can plausibly be attributed to the language faculty, namely, the principle of structure-dependence of grammatical rules; though if the speculations on semantics and on the interaction of the language faculty and common-sense understanding can be given real substance and pressed beyond a few illustrative examples, then this too would count as a proposal concerning the innate organization of the human mind.

Pursuing these reflections further, I would like to take up three topics. First, I want to add some structure to the account of the language faculty. Then, I would like to return to the simplifying assumption that language learning is instantaneous, tentatively adopted earlier. And finally, I will return to some of the questions raised at the outset concerning the possibilities for a broader theory of human nature and its implications.

In discussing various approaches to the semantics of natural language, I noted that there is a project common to all, namely, to discover "the semantic and syntactic rules or conventions [that determine] the meanings of the sentences of a language" (Strawson, 1970), and more important, to discover the principles of universal grammar (UG) that lie beyond particular rules or conventions. Some believe that "the general nature of such rules and conventions can be ultimately understood only by reference to the concept of communication-intention" (Strawson, 1970). For reasons already discussed, I do not believe that the claim has been substantiated and doubt that it can be. It seems to me to misconceive the general character of language use and to ignore an intellectual element that cannot be eliminated from any adequate account of it. But whatever the future holds on that score, we can still turn with profit to the common project. What, then, can plausibly be said about the rules that determine the formal and semantic properties of the sentences of a language, that is, its grammar?

In the past few years, a number of approaches to the question have been developed and fruitfully applied. I will not be able to survey them here, or to give any compelling reasons in support of those that seem to me most promising, or even to deal with objections that have been raised to the point of view I will present.[1] In the present context, these deficiencies are perhaps less serious than they might seem. My primary purpose is to give some idea of the kinds of principles and the degree of complexity of structure that it seems plausible to assign to the language faculty as a species-specific, genetically determined property. Alternative approaches, while differing in a number of respects,[2] are comparable, I believe, in their implications concerning the more general questions that I have in mind.

Let us begin by considering some implications of the principle of structure-dependence. If it is correct, then the rules of grammar apply to strings of words analyzed into abstract phrases, that is, to structures that are called "phrase markers" in the technical literature. For example, the sentence (1) might be assigned a phrase marker giving the structure indicated in the obvious way by the bracketing, along with other structures omitted here:

(1) $[_S[_{NP}[_{DET}$ the$]$ $[_N$ man$]$ $[_S$ who $[_{VP}$ is tall$]]]$ $[_{VP}$ *is* here$]]$

(S = sentence; NP = noun phrase; DET = determiner; N = noun; VP = verb phrase)

The italicized occurrence of "is" is the one following the first noun phrase; it is this occurrence that is preposed to give the corresponding yes-or-no question, with its phrase marker.

The rule that carries out this operation is called a "(grammatical) transformation." Thus, transformations map phrase markers into phrase markers. One component of the syntax of a language consists of such transformations, with whatever structure (say, ordering) is imposed on this set. Call this the "transformational component."

For the transformational component to function in the generation of structured sentences, it is necessary for some class of initial phrase markers to be provided. Suppose, then, that the syntax contains also a "base component" that generates a class of "initial phrase markers." We take this class to be infinite, thus assigning to the base component the recursive property that any grammar must possess.

The base, in turn, consists of two subcomponents: a "categorial component" and a lexicon. The categorial component presents the basic abstract structures by means of "rewriting rules" that state how a syntactic category can be analyzed into a sequence of such categories. One such rule, for example, would state that Sentence consists of Noun Phrase followed by Verb Phrase (in symbols: S $\longrightarrow$ NP VP). Among the categories that figure in the categorial component are the "lexical categories," Noun (N), Verb (V), Adjective (A), and others. It is a simple matter to devise a procedure by which rules of the categorial component can generate phrase markers of the appropriate type, with lexical categories in place of the lexical items that must ultimately appear in these positions.

The lexicon consists of the lexical items that belong to the lexical categories, each with its phonological, semantic, and syntactic properties. It also contains rules of "word formation" that delimit the class of lexical items and express their general properties.[3] "Lexical transformations" insert items from the lexicon into the abstract phrase markers generated by the categorial component, giving the initial phrase markers.[4] The latter are also abstract, in that only through the application of grammatical transformations and other rules do they become sequences of words that count as sentences of the language, phonologically represented.[5]

Thus, the various components of the base interact to generate initial phrase markers, and the transformational component converts an initial phrase marker, step by step, into a phonologically represented sentence with its phrase marker. The latter complex we call a "surface structure." The sequence of phrase markers generated in this way we call a "transformational derivation."

There is a good deal more to say about the structure of the categorial component of the base and the lexicon, but I will not pursue this topic here.[6]

In the so-called "standard theory,"[7] the initial phrase markers were called "deep structures," but I will avoid the term here, for several reasons. In the standard theory, deep structures were characterized in terms of two properties: their role in syntax, initiating transformational derivations; and their role in semantic interpretation. As for the latter, it was postulated that deep structures give all the information required for determining the meaning of sentences.[8] Clearly, these characterizations are independent; it might turn out that the structures that initiate transformational derivations are not those that determine semantic interpretation. I believe that this is the case.[9] The "extended standard theory" postulates that surface structures contribute in a definite way to semantic interpretation. In the version that I will outline here, I will suggest that perhaps all semantic information is determined by a somewhat enriched notion of surface structure. In this theory, then, the syntactic and semantic properties of the former "deep structures" are dissociated. Either class of properties might, then, be taken as defining the technical notion "deep structure." To avoid the issue, with the possible attendant confusion, I will simply drop the term, speaking only of "initial phrase markers" and "surface structures."

There is another reason for this terminological change. The term "deep structure" has, unfortunately, proved to be very misleading. It has led a number of people to suppose that it is the deep structures and their properties that are truly "deep," in the nontechnical sense of the word, while the rest is superficial, unimportant, variable across languages, and so on. This was never intended. Phonological theory includes principles of language that are deep, universal, unexpected, revealing, and so on; and the same, I believe, is true of the theory of surface structures and other elements of grammar. On occasion, the term "deep structure" has even been used to mean "grammar" or "universal grammar" or "abstract properties of rules," or in other confusing ways. No one, I hope, will be misled into believing that the properties of abstract initial phrase markers necessarily exhaust what may be "deep," or that assumptions about such structures constitute the fundamental thesis of transformational grammar, without which it collapses.

In part, the belief that "deep structures" are uniquely important derives from the role assigned to them in semantic interpretation. There is a widespread feeling that semantics is the part of language that is really deep and important, and that the study of language is interesting primarily insofar as it contributes to some understanding of these questions of real profundity. There is some merit to this view. Thus, the questions having to do with what peo-

ple say and why, questions that relate to the "creative aspect of language use," are surely of great intrinsic interest,
and are also invested with some mystery, in a sense in which
the principles of rule ordering in phonology are not. Analogously, we might say that questions of human behavior are
intrinsically interesting to us in ways in which the behavior
of inanimate objects is not—but we would not therefore
conclude that physics is superficial, in that it confines itself
to inanimate matter and abstracts away from human acts
(say, from the fact that the predictions of physical experiments can be falsified by human intervention, a fact that
cannot be accommodated within physical theory, so far as
we know). The significance of physics does not derive from
the intrinsic interest of its subject matter; no one cares what
happens under the exotic conditions of physical experiments, apart from the relation to physical theory. Physics
is significant, applications aside, because of its intellectual
depth, and if it were to turn out that the principles of
phonology are considerably more sophisticated and intricate
than those of semantics, that they enter into nontrivial arguments to explain surprising facts, that they give us much
more insight into the nature of the organism, then phonology will be a far deeper theory than semantics, despite the
more limited intrinsic interest of the phenomena with which
it deals.[10]

Suppose it is a fact, as I now tend to believe, that a
suitably enriched notion of surface structure suffices to
determine the meaning of sentences under interpretive rules
(insofar as grammar is involved in determining semantic
properties; cf. chapter 2). It may still be the case—I think it
is—that initial phrase markers generated by the base have
significant and revealing properties. It also remains true
that they enter, though now indirectly, into determining
the structures that undergo semantic interpretation, and
that they play a role in the theory of performance. The
thesis of surface-structure interpretation, if true, would con-

stitute a significant empirical discovery, which would in no way diminish the general interest of the results of linguistic inquiry. Under this thesis, the structures called "deep structures" in the standard theory do not play the role formerly attributed to them, but we may still agree with Strawson that "the central thesis of the transformational grammarians, the step which conditions the whole character of their theories, is the insistence that any adequate grammatical theory must recognize a distinction between the superficial syntactic structure of a sentence and its basic structure, between its deep grammar and its surface grammar" (Strawson, 1972). But we must now understand the terms "basic structure" and "deep grammar" to refer to nonsuperficial aspects of surface structure, the rules that generate surface structures, the abstract level of initial phrase markers, the principles that govern the organization of grammar and that relate surface structure to semantic representations, and so on.

I have so far briefly discussed the base component of the syntax and the initial phrase markers that it generates, omitting a host of important matters. Consider now the transformational component and the surface structures formed by its operation. I have mentioned, so far, only one transformational rule, namely, the rule that forms yes-or-no questions such as "is the man who is tall here?" from (1). This rule has the interesting property that it does not apply to embedded sentences, but only to the full sentence structure. Following Emonds, we call it a "root transformation," and the structure to which it applies, a "root sentence" (cf. Emonds, forthcoming). Indirect questions appear in embedded constructions: for example, "I wonder *who John is visiting*," and "the question *whether deep structures exist* is much debated." In this case, however, the root transformation does not apply. We do not say "I wonder *who is John visiting*," with inversion of "is."

Nonroot transformations apply at any depth of embedding. Consider, for example, the rule that preposes "*wh*-words," such as "who" or "where." The initial phrase marker underlying "who is John visiting?" is something like "John is visiting *wh*-someone," omitting bracketing.[11] Applying the rule of *wh*-movement, we derive "who John is visiting." [12] If the sentence is embedded, no further rules apply, and we have, for example, "I wonder who John is visiting." If the sentence is not embedded, we apply the additional rule of inversion, deriving the direct question "who is John visiting?"

Root and nonroot transformations have very different properties, a matter explored in depth by Emonds and others (Emonds, forthcoming). The domain of a nonroot transformation may be other than a sentence. Thus, the rule of extraposition that gives (2) applies to the underlying subject noun phrase of (3):

(2) the only one of Tolstoy's novels that I like is out of print
(3) [NP the only one that I like of Tolstoy's novels] is out of print

Let us refer to a category that can serve as the domain of a transformation as a "cyclic category." [13] There is, I think, good evidence that the transformational component applies to an initial phrase marker with more than one cyclic category in a definite and regular manner, namely, cyclically (hence the term). The transformations first apply to the most deeply embedded cyclic categories, then to the cyclic categories that immediately contain these, and so on, until the full structure is reached, at which point root transformations also apply.

Suppose further that transformations meet a condition of "subjacency," which requires that they apply to positions at the same level of the cycle or in adjacent levels (cf. Chomsky, 1973a). Thus a transformation may not, say, move an item within the cyclic category A to a position within the cyclic category C that includes A if there is a cyclic category B including A and included in C. For example, in the structure (4), where A, B, and C are cyclic, a rule may not move an item from the position X to either position Y, where $[_A \ldots X \ldots]$ is distinct from $[_A X]$:

(4) $[_C \ldots Y \ldots [_B \ldots [_A \ldots X \ldots] \ldots] \ldots Y \ldots]$

In the case mentioned earlier, from the underlying structure (3) we may derive (2), but there can be no rule (or rule application) forming (5) from (3):

(5) $[_{NP}[_{NP}$ the only one $t]$ of Tolstoy's novels] is out of print that I like

The reason is that to form (5), it is necessary to move the sentence "that I like" from the position X of (4) (marked by t in (5); thus the NP "the only one that I like" is A of (4)) to the rightmost position Y of (4), where it appears in (5).[14] In the representation (5), I inserted the symbol t (read "trace") to indicate the position from which the extraposed subject was moved (illegitimately, violating subjacency). As we will see later, this is more than a notational device.

There are examples that appear, *prima facie*, to violate the subjacency condition. Thus consider (6):

(6) John seems to be a nice fellow

There is good evidence that (6) derives from the underlying structure (6′):

(6′) Y seems [$_S$ John to be a nice fellow] [15]

The rule in question—call it "NP-preposing"—raises "John" from its position as subject in the embedded sentence to the subject position marked Y in the main clause. The same rule gives (7) from (7′), where the trace t again marks the position in (7) from which "John" was raised.

(7) John is certain [$_S$ t to win]

(7′) [$_S$ Y is certain [$_S$ John to win]]

But now consider sentence (8), deriving from the initial phrase marker (8′):

(8) John seems to be certain to win

(8′) Y_2 seems [$_\mathrm{S}$ Y_1 to be certain [$_\mathrm{S}$ John to win]]

Here it seems that the rule has moved "John" from the position in which it appears in (8′) to the position marked by Y_2 in (8′). Taking the initial position of "John" to be X of (4), and Y_2 to be Y of (4), we have a violation of the subjacency principle. The solution is of course obvious. (8) is not derived from (8′) directly, but from (8″):

(8″) Y_2 seems [$_\mathrm{S}$ John to be certain [$_\mathrm{S}$ t to win]],

where (8″) is derived from (8′) by the rule of NP-preposing just as (7) is derived from (7′). The rule of NP-preposing applies cyclically, first to (8′) giving (8″), then to (8″) giving (8), each application governed by the principle of subjacency. If we were to replace "certain" in (8) by a word that does not permit NP-preposing on the first cycle, say "probable," [16] then we could not derive the sentence analogous to (8), namely, "John seems to be probable to win." Similarly, if we were to replace "seem" by a word that does not permit NP-preposing, no sentence analogous to (8) would be derivable.[17]

The same considerations apply to certain other examples that might appear to violate the subjacency condition. Consider, for example, the slightly awkward sentences (9) and (10), where the trace t marks the position in the initial phrase marker from which *who* was moved: [18]

(9) who do the police think [$_\mathrm{S}$ that the FBI discovered [$_\mathrm{S}$ that Bill shot t]]

(10) who did John believe [$_\mathrm{S}$ that Mary said [$_\mathrm{S}$ that Tom saw t]]

The operation of *wh*-movement appears to violate subjacency in these cases. But, as we already know, the rule of *wh*-movement is a cyclic, not a root transformation. Applying the rule cyclically to the form underlying (9), we derive the intermediate forms (9′), (9″), and finally (9), just as cyclic application of NP-preposing gave (8):

(9′) the police think [s that the FBI discovered [s who Bill shot *t*]]

(9″) the police think [s who the FBI discovered [s *t* that Bill shot *t*]]

In the same way, we derive (10).

We thus have three applications of *wh*-movement in the derivation of (9). The first application gives the grammatical sentence (9′) and the third gives the grammatical sentence (9), but the structure (9″) derived from (9′) is not a grammatical sentence. We could have had a grammatical sentence on the second application if we had chosen the verb "know" instead of "think" in the underlying initial structure; thus, (11):

(11) the police know who the FBI discovered that Bill shot

The distinction between (9″) and (11) lies in the properties of the verbs "think" and "know"; the verb "know" takes an indirect-question complement, but not the verb "think."

Let us now consider a slightly more complex example involving subjacency. In the examples that preceded I have been playing rather fast-and-loose with the item "that," which has vanished and reappeared several times without explanation.[19] Call this word a "complementizer." Thus the sentential structure "that Bill shot someone," which may be taken as the most deeply embedded sentence within the structures underlying (9) and (11), consists of a complementizer followed by a structure containing all the other elements of a sentence. Following Bresnan (1972), let us assume that the initial rule of the categorial component of the base states that the sentence S consists of a complementizer and a "reduced sentence": thus the initial rule is (12):

(12) S ⟶ COMP S_{red}

So far, I have not been distinguishing between S and S$_{red}$, and I will also ignore the distinction, where irrelevant, in later discussion. Let us assume further that *wh*-movement does not simply prepose the *wh*-word but rather places it in the complementizer position. The reasons for this would take us rather far afield, but I think that the proposal is well motivated.[20] There are rules, which I will not discuss here, that introduce "that" into the COMP position under certain conditions when this position is not filled by a *wh*-word. On this theory, it follows that there can be no *wh*-movement within phrases that have no complementizers, for example, noun phrases. Compare the two structures (13) and (14):

(13) COMP John discovered [s COMP Bill had seen who]

(14) COMP John discovered [NP pictures of who]

From (13) we can derive (13') and then (13'') by repeated cyclic *wh*-movement:

(13') COMP John discovered who Bill had seen

(13'') who did John discover that Bill had seen? [21]

But from (14) we can derive only (14''), not (14'):

(14') COMP John discovered who pictures of

(14'') who did John discover pictures of?

In the case of (14''), the acceptability of the sentence depends in part on the main verb; thus some people find it more natural with "find" in place of "discover." [22] But no change in verb will help (14'), which has an entirely different status. It is simply ungrammatical, and remains so under any interchange of lexical items. It is the *structure* that is impossible. The fundamental difference between (13') and (14') results from the fact that noun phrases do not have complementizers. Note that there is no violation of subjacency in the formation of (14'') from (14) by a single application of *wh*-movement. (Cf. note 21.)

Compare now the initial phrase markers (15) and (16):

(15) COMP John believed [$_s$ COMP Mary said [$_s$ COMP Tom saw *wh*-someone]]

(16) COMP John believed [$_{NP}$ the claim [$_s$ COMP Tom saw *wh*-someone]]

From (15) we can derive the sentence (10), repeated here as (15'), by repeated cyclic *wh*-movement, observing the principle of subjacency:

(15') who did John believe that Mary said that Tom saw?

From (16), however, we cannot analogously derive (16'):

(16') who did John believe the claim that Tom saw?

The sentences are analogous in structure except for the fact that (15) has a sentence with a COMP where (16) has an NP without a COMP. As we know, *wh*-movement moves a *wh*-word into a COMP position, so that (15') can be derived step by step just as (9) was derived (cf. (9'), (9'')). But it is impossible to derive (16') cyclically in a parallel way since there is no COMP position to receive the *wh*-word in the intermediate structure NP. Furthermore, by the principle of subjacency, (16') cannot be derived directly from (16). Therefore, it cannot be derived at all. There is no grammatical sentence corresponding to the initial phrase marker (16),[23] though from such structures as (15) we can derive three well-formed surface structures, depending on the choice of lexical items.

Plainly, there is no semantic problem in the case of (16'). If the sentence were syntactically well formed, it would have a definite and unambiguous meaning, and there is no choice of lexical items that will improve matters, as there was in the case of (9)–(11).[24] The principle of subjacency, along with other assumptions that entered into the preceding argument, provides an explanation for the ungrammaticalness of (16'). In turn, such examples as (16') provide empirical support for the principle of subjacency.

In the first chapter, I argued that the principle of structure-dependence must be attributed to universal grammar, since it is used correctly in the cases illustrated there even in the absence of relevant experience. The same is true in this case. It is difficult to imagine that every speaker of English who is capable of the discriminations on which this argument is based has been given instruction, or even relevant evidence, to establish the fact. A far more reasonable assumption is that the general principles that exclude (16′) (among others, the principle of subjacency, if the argument just sketched is correct) are simply innate to the language faculty, as part of the schematism that determines admissible grammars and the ways in which their rules apply, thus determining the class of languages accessible to humans by application of the language faculty.

Against such a conclusion, two arguments might be adduced (and often have been, in comparable cases). First, we know of no genetic mechanisms adequate to account for the innate structures postulated. Second, it is improper (or perhaps "question-begging") to assign such complexity to the mind as an innate property. As for the first argument, it is correct, but irrelevant. The genetic mechanisms are unknown, just like the mechanisms responsible for such learning as takes place or for the development of physical organs. The argument just presented is essentially an argument in theoretical psychology. Studying the use and understanding of language, we reach certain conclusions about the cognitive structure (grammar) that is being put to use, thus setting a certain problem for the neurologist, whose task it is to discover the mechanisms involved in linguistic competence and performance. Noting that the mechanisms appear to function in the absence of relevant experience and quite uniformly for individuals of vastly differing experience, we draw the natural conclusion that they are not learned, but are part of the system that makes learning possible. This conclusion sets a further task for human biology, which will attempt to find the genetic mechanisms that guarantee that the mental organ, language, will have the required character. There is nothing further to say, on this score.

The second argument has even less merit. It is a dogmatic assumption, and not a particularly plausible one, that the principles in question must have been developed in a few years of experience rather than through tens of thousands of years of evolution or perhaps by the operation of physical laws yet unknown. No questions are begged when we reach the natural conclusion that the mind is comparable in complexity to physical organs of the body that are not involved directly in higher mental functions. The argument merely reiterates empiricist prejudice. It is no more interesting than the claim that man must have an immortal soul.

Returning again to the technical discussion, I think that the subjacency principle is reasonably well motivated, and thus can be proposed as a principle of universal grammar, alongside of the other assumptions that we have been considering, subject to further investigation. Applying this and other principles of comparable generality, we can explain quite a number of the phenomena noted by Ross in his very illuminating study of "island constraints." [25]

Ross suggested in his work that rightward-movement rules are "bounded"—in our terms, constrained by the principle of subjacency—while leftward-movement rules need not be. Thus leftward-movement rules fall into two categories, those subject to subjacency and those that are unbounded. The distinction has persisted through subsequent work, with such rules as wh-movement given as examples of unboundedness, but not NP-preposing, which has been taken to be bounded and cyclic. Under the present analysis, wh-movement is also bounded and cyclic. The apparent asymmetry between leftward-movement and rightward-movement rules reduces to an independent left-right asymmetry in the position of complementizer. Several interesting constraints on rules fall out as special cases. If all examples of allegedly unbounded rules are subject to a similar analysis, then we may considerably improve the general theory of transformations, eliminating the category of unbounded rules. While not all problems that arise when this approach is pursued have been solved, my own feeling is that it is probably correct.

In addition to rules governed by subjacency and unbounded rules, it has been generally assumed that there are rules governed by a "clause-mate constraint" that requires that they cannot relate an item in an embedded sentence to anything outside that sentence. In terms of the abstract formula (4), modified here as (4′) to avoid the issue of subjacency, a rule that is governed by the clause-mate condition cannot, say, move an item from position X to position Y or conversely, or modify an item in position X by virtue of its relation to an item in position Y, if B = S:

$$(4') \; [_C \ldots Y \ldots [_B \ldots [_A X] \ldots] \ldots Y \ldots]$$

I have argued elsewhere that there is no evidence for such a constraint. The examples that have been used to motivate it are explained by independently motivated general principles.[26] If this is correct, then there is only one category of transformational rules: all such rules are governed by the subjacency principle. It is an interesting question whether (or to what extent) rules of semantic interpretation are also governed by this or some similar principle.[27]

Instead of pursuing these matters further, let us return to the examples (9″) and (11), repeated here:

(9″) the police think who the FBI discovered that Bill shot

(11) the police know who the FBI discovered that Bill shot

We may think of the *wh*-word in a question (direct or indirect) as a kind of quantifier. Thus, the "logical form" of (9″) and (11) can be taken to be (17) and (18), respectively:

(17) the police think for which person x, the FBI
       discovered that Bill shot x

(18) the police know for which person x, the FBI
       discovered that Bill shot x

In these logical forms, there is a variable x and a quantifier, "for which x," binding it. Suppose that we were to identify the variable x with the trace t left by the movement rule. Recall that the surface structure of (11), under the present theory, is something like (19):

(19) [$_S$ the police know [$_S$ who the FBI discovered [$_S$ that
       Bill shot t]]

To convert (19) to its logical form, all that is required is the information that "who" is a quantifier binding t and meaning "for which person t." [28] With only notational modifications of the theory of transformations we can guarantee that the item "who" is identified in surface structure as the item that binds t. With a further principle that interprets "who" as "for which person x," we derive the logical form (18) from the surface structure (19).

We have not yet settled the question of the basis for the distinction in grammaticalness between (9″) and (11). Is it a difference of syntax or semantics? Is it determined at the level of base structure or surface structure? One possibility is that questions, direct or indirect, have a complementizer distinct from the one that appears with declarative structures, and that verbs are marked in the lexicon as to whether they may or may not appear with sentential complements containing this complementizer. Semantic interpretation will involve the position of this complementizer relative to other items in surface structure. I have elaborated a version of this position elsewhere, and shown how some fairly complex examples can be handled from this point of view in what seems a rather natural way. (See Chomsky, 1973a, for some discussion.)

This proposal still leaves open the status of the distinction: syntactic or semantic? I am not persuaded that the question makes very much sense, or that any reasonably clear criteria exist to settle it. Suppose that someone claims to have a very refined sort of "grammatical intuition" that tells him whether the deviance of (9″) is "syntactic" or "semantic." Such a person, then, will have an answer to the question left open here. Personally, I have no such intuitions. I can make the judgment that certain sentences are fine and others deviant (say, (11) and (9″), respectively), but have no further intuitions that provide me, in such cases as these, with the basis for these judgments. I am therefore skeptical that others have such intuitions. I suspect that they are adhering to certain traditional explanations, which may or may not be correct. (See Chomsky, 1965, chap. 4.) It remains, I think, an open and perhaps interesting question to establish sharper criteria that will help to make the question "syntactic or semantic?" more precise in such cases as these.

However these questions are resolved, we do have a simple way to derive the "logical form" of the sentences in question from surface structures in which trace appears. Let us now stipulate explicitly what we have been tacitly assuming: when a transformation moves a phrase P from position X to position Y it leaves in position X a trace bound by P. As we will see directly, this "trace theory of movement rules" has considerable justification from several independent points of view.

Notice that what we have been developing is a theory of semantic interpretation of surface structures. The position of the "quantifier" in surface structure relative to verbs determines whether the sentence has a meaning and what this meaning is. But a problem arises. Thus, to understand the sentences we have been discussing we must surely also know the position in the initial phrase marker of the phrase that has been moved. Thus consider again (6), derived by NP-preposing from (6'):

(6) John seems [$_s$ t to be a nice fellow]

(6') Y seems [$_s$ John to be a nice fellow]

To understand the sentence (6) we must know that "John" is the subject of the embedded sentence. The initial phrase marker provides this information, but the surface structure (it appears) does not. The same is true of the other examples we have been discussing. In fact, it was precisely such considerations as these that motivated the principle of the standard theory that deep structures (our "initial phrase markers") determine semantic interpretation.

But notice that under the trace theory of movement rules, the motivation disappears. The position of the bound trace in surface structure allows us to determine the grammatical relation of "John" in (6) as subject of the embedded sentence. Similarly, in the other cases. Thus, such examples as these do not choose between the standard theory and the theory that interpretation is determined by surface structure, given the trace theory of movement rules. We have, however, found some reason to suppose that surface structure does play a role in semantic interpretation; namely, the position of the quantifier "who" in surface structure is relevant to the interpretation of such sentences as (9)–(11). There is a great deal more evidence that surface-structure information contributes to the determination of meaning. Thus, it seems reasonable to postulate that *only* surface structures undergo semantic interpretation, though our "surface structures" are no longer those of the standard theory, by virtue of the trace theory of movement rules.

Objections come to mind, and I will return to some of them a little later. Let us put them aside for the moment and continue to explore the possibility that with the trace theory of movement rules, it is possible to unify the theory of semantic interpretation, restricting it to surface structures.

The original motivation for the trace theory was in part that it facilitated semantic interpretation along the lines just indicated. But there were also independent considerations that led to the same theory. (Cf. Chomsky, 1973a.) Before turning to these, let us consider some further applications of the trace theory in semantic interpretation.

Consider active-passive pairs such as (20)–(21):

(20) beavers build dams

(21) dams are built by beavers

There are various problems as to how the passive construction should be analyzed, but all approaches within the framework of transformational grammar agree that one component of the passive is a rule that moves the noun phrase "dams" from its underlying position as the object, as in (20), to the subject position, where it appears in (21). Thus, under the trace theory, the surface structure of (21) will be something like (22):

(22) dams are [$_{VP}$ built *t* by beavers]

Sentences (20) and (21) plainly differ in range of meaning. Sentence (21), in its most natural interpretation, states that it is a property of dams that they are built by beavers. Under this interpretation, the sentence is false, since some dams are not built by beavers. But there is no interpretation of sentence (20), under normal intonation at least, in which it asserts that dams have the property that they are built by beavers; (20) cannot be understood as referring to all dams. Sentence (20) states that beavers have a certain property, namely, that they are dam builders, but does not imply (under any interpretation) that their activities in dam building account for all dams; in fact, (20) might be true if beavers never exhibit their species characteristic, say, if all beavers are in zoos.

Thus the position of the word "dams" in surface structure plays a role in determining the meaning of the sentences (20) and (21). In particular, to understand (21), it is important to know that the noun phrase "dams" is the subject of the sentence.

However, to understand (21) it is also important to know that the noun phrase "dams" bears the grammatical relation of direct object to the verb "build," as in the initial phrase marker. Thus, we must know that "dams" is the subject of (21) in one sense, but is the object of the verb of (21), and hence not the subject, in another sense. The necessary information is conveyed in the surface structure (22). We may assume that the subject-predicate relation is defined on surface structures, so that "dams" is the subject of (21). But the position of the trace bound by "dams" serves to indicate that it bears the appropriate semantic relation to the verb "build." We return to some further discussion. For the present, I simply want to note that two kinds of "grammatical relation" seem to be involved in the interpretation of sentences such as (20) and (21): one, the relation verb-object of the initial phrase marker, accounting for the similarity in meaning between these sentences; and another, the relation subject-predicate of the surface structure, accounting for the difference in meaning. Both relations are represented appropriately in surface structure.

Note that in these examples a question of quantification seems to be involved. We have already observed that in some cases, a kind of "quantification" of an unconventional sort is determined by surface structure. There is considerable evidence that this is true quite generally, and that the same is true of the scope of logical particles, and other aspects of what might be called "logical form." [29]

Consider now some relations between the rule of *wh-*

movement and interpretation of pronouns noted originally by Paul Postal (1971). I adapt here a reanalysis of this and related material by Thomas Wasow (forthcoming). Compare the sentences (23) and (24):

> (23) *who* said Mary kissed *him*?
>
> (24) *who* did *he* say Mary kissed?

In the case of sentence (23), we may understand the pronoun ("him") to refer to the person whose name answers the query "who?" But in the case of (24) this interpretation is inappropriate. To put it very misleadingly, there can be a relation of anaphora or coreference between the italicized expressions of (23) but not those of (24). But the structure of (24) is a possible anaphora structure; compare (25), which is analogous in categorial structure to (24), though the pronoun "he" in (25) can be taken as referring to John:

> (25) *John* said *he* thought Mary left

What is the explanation for this curious fact?

With trace introduced into the surface structures, we have (23′) and (24′) corresponding to (23) and (24), respectively: [30]

> (23′) who [$_{S_{red}}$ *t* said Mary kissed him]
>
> (24′) who [$_{S_{red}}$ he said Mary kissed *t*]

In both cases, the *wh*-movement rule has raised the *wh*-word "who" to the complementizer position, leaving trace in the position in which the *wh*-word appeared in the initial phrase marker. Applying the method of semantic interpretation outlined earlier, we have the "logical forms" (23″) and (24″):

> (23″) for which person *x*, *x* said Mary kissed him?
>
> (24″) for which person *x*, he said Mary kissed *x*?

The bound variable *x* functions roughly as a name. Thus

we would expect (23″) and (24″) to have interpretations
analogous to (26) and (27), respectively:

> (26) *John* said Mary kissed *him*
> (27) *he* said Mary kissed *John*

In sentence (26), the pronoun can refer to John, but in (27)
it cannot. The relevant principle again involves surface
structure. (Cf. Wasow, 1972, forthcoming; Lasnik, 1974.)
We may assume it without further discussion here. Applying the principle governing (26) and (27) to the analogous
examples (23″) and (24″), we see that in (23″) the pronoun "him" can bear an anaphoric relation to the bound
variable *x* (as in (26)), whereas in (24″) the pronoun "he"
cannot bear an anaphoric relation to *x* (as in (27)). Thus
we can understand (23″) as having essentially the meaning
represented in (28):

> (28) for which person *x*, *x* said Mary kissed *x*?

In the case of (24″), no such interpretation is possible, any
more than it is in the analogous construction (27). The
pronoun "he" must therefore be taken to be referring to
someone whose identity is fixed elsewhere in the discourse
or context of utterance.

Thus the distinction between (23) and (24) is readily
explained by available mechanisms, given the trace theory
and the principles of semantic interpretation of surface
structure suggested earlier. Furthermore, we can now dispense with such notions as "coreference between *he* and
who" or "anaphoric relations" between these terms—notions which are, strictly speaking, without sense, since
"who" is not a referential expression but rather a kind of
quantifier in these cases, and therefore cannot enter into
relations of anaphora.

Certain qualifications must be added to extend this account to a broader class of cases, and, as in the cases discussed earlier, some problems remain unsolved. But this
does, I think, capture the essence of the matter. Pursuing

this approach, we will develop the theory of anaphora so as to apply to "logical forms" derived from surface structure, making essential use of trace as analogous to a bound variable.[31]

Let us now turn to some independent lines of argument that lead, again, to the trace theory of movement rules. Consider the sentences (29)–(32):

(29) it seems to us that Bill likes each other

(30) we expected Bill to like each other

(31) we were shocked by Bill's hatred of each other

(32) Tom seems to us to like each other

None of these are grammatical. They have something of the character of such violations of the subjacency condition as (16'). That is, the sentences are not senseless. There is no semantic reason why they should not have the same meanings as (29')–(32'), respectively, just as (33) and (33') are close to synonymous:

(29') it seems to each of us that Bill likes the other(s)

(30') each of us expected Bill to like the other(s)

(31') each of us was shocked by Bill's hatred of the other(s)

(32') Tom seems to each of us to like the other(s)

(33) we seem to like each other

(33') each of us seems to like the other(s)

In general, the structures *each of us . . . the other(s)*, *we each . . . the other(s)*, and *we . . . each other* have very similar if not the same meanings. Thus, there is no warrant for ruling out sentences (29)–(32) on grounds of senselessness.

These and many other examples exemplify the "specified-subject condition," still another general condition on rules. The condition, which I will not attempt to state precisely here,[32] implies that no rule can relate X and Y in a structure such as (34), where α is a cyclic category subjacent to X and Z is its subject:

$$(34) \ldots X \ldots [_a Z - \ldots Y \ldots]$$

Consider now the reciprocal rule that relates the phrase "each other" to its noun-phrase antecedent; we may put aside the interesting question whether there is a rule that moves "each" from the antecedent noun phrase to form the phrase "each other" in addition to the interpretive rule relating the antecedent and the reciprocal phrase. Taking X of (34) to be "we" (or "us"), Z to be "Bill," and Y to be "each other," the reciprocal rule is blocked in (29) and (30) (with α = S),[33] and in (31) (with α = NP),[34] by virtue of the specified subject condition.

Still unexplained, however, is the example (32). Here, there is no embedded subject Z, as in the other three cases. There is no phrase corresponding to the subject noun phrase "Bill" of (29)–(31). The last comment must be qualified. There is no subject noun phrase *physically present* in the position corresponding to that of "Bill" in (29)–(31), namely, before "to like each other." But there is a subject noun phrase "mentally present" in this position, namely, "Tom," which we understand to be the subject of "like," just as the (physically present) "Bill" is the subject of "like" in (30). Evidently, in interpreting these sentences we are concerned not with the physical position of subjects in sentences, but with their "mental position," that is, their position in the abstract structures that we are postulating in the subpart of theoretical psychology (called "linguistics") that we are developing. Our theory must account for the fact that a person who knows English operates appropriately with abstract mental structures, whatever the physical form of the sentence may be. And at a deeper level, our general theory must account for the fact that the speaker comes to know that it is abstract rather than physical structures that are relevant in interpreting (29)–(32).

Note again that, as in the case of the principle of structure-dependence, it is difficult to believe that the person

developing knowledge of English as a "mental organ"
is *taught* the relevant principles. People are not trained or
conditioned to treat (32) "on the analogy" of (29)–(31).
Rather, they just know that they are to do so, quite without training or even presentation of relevant experience
that might determine this conclusion. Our theoretical psychology must account for these facts.

Recall that (32) is derived from an abstract structure
(35) by NP-preposing, just as (6) was formed from (6'):

(35) Y seems to us [s Tom to like each other]

The surface structure corresponding to (32), under the
trace theory, is therefore (36):

(36)   Tom seems to us [s t to like each other]

Thus under the trace theory, there *is* a subject Z in the
embedded sentence in the surface structure in exactly the
position filled by "Bill" in the embedded cyclic categories
of (29)–(31). Assuming as before that the specified-subject
condition applies to surface structures, determining the
relation of the reciprocal phrase "each other" to its antecedent, we have an explanation for the ungrammatical
status of (32). Namely, the specified-subject condition rules
it ungrammatical, exactly as in the case of (29)–(31). A
speaker who is forming and interpreting sentences by the
postulated means (specifically, making use of the specified-
subject condition and the trace theory) will regard (32) as
analogous, in the relevant respects, to (29)–(31). If, furthermore, the specified-subject condition and the trace theory
are part of universal grammar, part of the biologically
necessary schematism that determines the "essence of human language," the speaker will know all of this without
instruction or even relevant evidence, as appears to be the
case.

Thus, we have an entirely independent motivation for the
trace theory.

Summarizing these remarks, we seem to have the following general structure for grammar. The rules of the categorial component and the lexicon provide initial phrase markers. Applying transformations to these, we derive surface structures (including traces), which undergo semantic interpretation. The rules of semantic interpretation assign the scope of logical operators ("not," "each," "who," etc.) and fix their meaning, assign antecedents to such anaphoric expressions as reciprocals ("each other") and necessarily bound anaphors (e.g., "his" in "John lost his way," where "his" must refer to John, as contrasted with the unbound anaphor "his" in "John found his book," where "his" may refer to any male, including John).[35] The result of application of these rules we may call a "logical form."

It would be reasonable to say that the theory of grammar—or more precisely, "sentence grammar"—ends at this point. The conditions on grammar so far discussed—the specified-subject condition, subjacency, and so on—apply to the rules of sentence grammar. Sentence grammar involves such rules as NP-preposing, *wh*-movement, scope assignment, assignment of antecedents to bound anaphors, and also rules determining thematic relations and other aspects of semantic structure that may be properly assigned to the abstract system of language, depending on how the questions raised in the preceding chapter are answered.

What we have been calling "grammar" in the preceding discussion is actually sentence grammar, in this sense. Given the logical forms generated by sentence grammar, further rules may apply. Pronouns not yet assigned antecedents may be taken to refer to entities designated elsewhere in the sentence, though this is never necessary and is not permitted under certain conditions, for example, in (27). These further rules of reference determination may involve discourse properties as well, in some manner; and they interact with considerations relating to situation, communicative intention, and the like. Similarly, though the reciprocal "each other" in (29)–(31) must be assigned an antecedent by a rule of sentence grammar, the correspond-ing phrase "the others" in (29')–(31') need not be taken to refer to members of a class designated (namely, by "each of us") elsewhere within the same sentence. As noted be-fore, the rules of sentence grammar obey quite different conditions from those that apply beyond. The former, for example, are governed by the specified-subject condition; the latter are not (see also note 27). Other semantic rules apply, interacting with rules belonging to other cognitive structures, to form fuller representations of "meaning" (in some sense).

Schematically, this seems to me a reasonable picture of the general nature of grammar and its place within the system of cognitive structures. To recapitulate in a dia-gram, we may have a system of roughly the following structure:

$$(37) \quad \text{Sentence grammar:} \xrightarrow{\quad B \quad} \text{IPM} \xrightarrow{\quad T \quad} \text{SS} \xrightarrow{\quad SR-1 \quad} \text{LF}$$

$$\left\{ \begin{array}{c} SR-2 \\ \text{other systems} \end{array} \right\} : \quad \text{LF} \longrightarrow \text{``meaning''}$$

Thus, the rules of the base (B), including the rules of the categorial component and the lexicon, form initial phrase markers (IPM). The rules of the transformational component (T) convert these to surface structures (SS), which are converted to logical forms (LF) by certain rules of semantic interpretation (SR–1; namely, the rules involv-ing bound anaphora, scope, thematic relations, etc.). This much constitutes sentence grammar; certain general con-ditions on rules appear to apply throughout this system. The logical forms so generated are subject to further in-terpretation by other semantic rules (SR–2) interacting with other cognitive structures, giving fuller representa-tions of meaning.

Examples of the sort just discussed provide empirical support for the trace theory on grounds of the functioning of grammatical rules, syntactic and semantic. There is another independent line of argument of a more abstract sort. Consider the effect of the rule of NP-preposing on phrase markers. In the case of such examples as (6) and (36), this rule takes the subject of an embedded sentence and raises it to the subject position in a "higher clause." The effect, then, is as illustrated in (38):

$$(38) \ Y \ldots [_\text{s} \text{NP} \ldots] \longrightarrow \text{NP} \ldots [_\text{s} t \ldots]$$

In contrast, there are no rules that "lower" a noun phrase to the subject position (or, I believe, any position) in the embedded sentence. We might stipulate this asymmetry as a new condition on transformations.

Let us return now to the passive construction, and in particular, the rule that moves the noun phrase following the verb to the subject position, to give such forms as (22):

$$(22) \ \text{dams are} \ [_\text{VP} \ \text{built} \ t \ \text{by beavers}]$$

This too is a rule of NP-preposing. In fact, though this is debatable, I think it is the same rule of NP-preposing as the subject-to-subject rule of (38). The effect of NP-preposing, in the case of (22) and many other passives, is as indicated in (39):

$$(39) \ Y \ [_\text{VP} \ \text{V NP}] \longrightarrow \text{NP} \ [_\text{VP} \ \text{V} \ t]$$

Again, there is an asymmetry. There are rules that raise objects to subject position, but none, it appears, that move subjects to object position. Again we might stipulate this asymmetry as still another condition on rules.

Clearly, there is something similar about these two asymmetries involving the rule of NP-preposing. How can we capture it? We might stipulate that there is a hierarchy of positions, with subjects having precedence over objects [36] and subjects of higher clauses having precedence over subjects of embedded clauses. Rules are permitted to move elements only to positions that precede in the hierarchy. But this is no real improvement. It is only a notational convention, and we might ask why we set up this hierarchy, rather than some other one, say, in which subjects precede objects and there is no relation (or the converse relation) between elements that are not in the same clause. There is no logical connection between the principles illustrated in (38) and (39) that determines the structure of the hierarchy.

A considerably better approach would be to exploit the fact that in both cases the permissible rules are rules of "upgrading" which move a noun phrase closer to the "root of the sentence," that is, to a less embedded position; the impermissible rules are rules of "downgrading," which increase the embeddedness of the noun phrase. We might stipulate, then, that upgrading rules are permitted, but not downgrading rules. Thus the two principles fall together.

This is an improvement, but there are two problems. First, there are counterexamples to the proposal, as it stands. Second, we might still want to find an explanation for the upgrading principle to the extent that it is true. That is, we might hope to account for it in terms of some independent principle.

To illustrate the falsity of the upgrading conjecture, consider the sentences (40)–(42):

    (40) there is a book on the table

    (41) the city was destroyed by the enemy

    (42) the candidates have each indicated their
            willingness to debate

There are familiar analyses—not without competitors, but at least quite plausible—that postulate that in these cases a rule of downgrading applies. In the case of (40), we might argue that the source is (43), and that a transformational rule forms (43'), which in turn becomes (40) by a rule of *there*-insertion, which erases (replaces) the trace:

(43) a book [$_\text{VP}$ is on the table]

(43') t [$_\text{VP}$ is a book on the table]

In the case of (41), we might assume the derivation (44):

(44) (i) the enemy [$_\text{VP}$ destroyed the city]
            (initial phrase marker)

  (ii) t [$_\text{VP}$ destroyed the city by the enemy]
            (by NP-postposing)

  (iii) the city [$_\text{VP}$ was destroyed t by the enemy]
            (by NP-preposing)

We omit here some interesting questions about the status of the agent *by*-phrase, the auxiliary and the verbal inflection; see page 114 and note 46. The rule of NP-preposing erases the trace left by NP-postposing.

The sentence (42) might be formed by a rule of *each*-movement from (45):

(45) the candidates each [$_\text{VP}$ have indicated their willingness to debate]

These are all plausible analyses. In each case, a rule of downgrading applies.

Robert Fiengo has observed that the trace theory of movement rules permits us to formulate our conjecture with regard to the two asymmetries (38) and (39) in such a way as to avoid the counterexamples and at the same time to reduce the conjecture to an independent principle, thus overcoming both of the problems that arise.[37] Consider again the permissible rule of NP-preposing as in (38) and (39) and the impermissible rule of downgrading NP, which reverses the direction of the arrows in (38) and (39). The permissible rule gives the structures (46), and the impermissible rule gives the structures (47):

(46) (i) NP ... [$_\text{S}$ t ...] (right-hand side of (38))

  (ii) NP [$_\text{VP}$ V t]   (right-hand side of (39))

$$(47) \quad (i) \quad t \ldots [_s \text{NP} \ldots]$$
$$(ii) \quad t \, [_{\text{VP}} \text{V NP}]$$

Taking *t*, as before, to be a variable bound by NP as antecedent, notice that the permissible cases are instances of permissible relations between an antecedent noun phrase and an "anaphoric" element that it controls, whereas the impermissible cases are instances of impermissible anaphoric relations.[38] Thus, the examples (46′) are of the form (46) and are grammatical, whereas the examples (47′) are of the form (47) and are ungrammatical:

(46′) (i) *the candidates* expected [$_s$ *each other* to win] [39]

     (ii) *the candidates* [$_{\text{VP}}$ hated *each other*]

(47′) (i) *each other* expected [$_s$ *the candidates* to win]

     (ii) *each other* [$_{\text{VP}}$ hated *the candidates*]

An antecedent must be "superior" in the phrase marker to the anaphor it controls, in such cases as these. Assuming the relation between noun phrase and trace to be analogous to that between antecedent and anaphor, as is entirely natural, we can reduce the upgrading principle to an independently motivated condition on the antecedent-anaphor relation.

This is a substantial step forward. We have now provided an explanation for the upgrading convention, insofar as it holds. Given the trace theory, it follows as a consequence of an independent principle of language. Under this analysis, the problem with the impermissible examples of the type (47) is that, in effect, they have a free variable not within the scope of a binding quantifier or noun phrase in their semantic interpretation, and thus are not sentences.

But the same analysis also overcomes the difficulty that the upgrading principle was falsified by the counterexamples (40)–(42). In cases (40) and (41), the offending trace has been erased by a later rule; thus the surface structure does not violate the antecedent-anaphor principle. In case

(42) there is no antecedent-anaphor relation between the phrase moved and its trace; it is senseless, in this case, to regard the trace as a bound variable, though it makes good sense to do so when the phrase moved is a noun phrase. Thus, we can interpret (6) along the lines indicated earlier, as having the logical form (48):

(6) John seems [$_s$ t to be a nice fellow]

(48) for x = John, x seems [$_s$ x to be a nice fellow]

But no such analysis is possible in the case of *each*-movement, since "each" is not a referential expression, nor does it bind a variable as a quantifier except in association with a noun phrase that gives the type of the variable, as in "the candidates each," which can be interpreted as "for each x, x a candidate." But in the latter case, it is the full noun phrase "the candidates each" and not the word "each" which binds the variable, which is thus crucially distinct from the trace left by *each*-movement.

The upgrading principle would have had to be stated in the form (49) to avoid the counterexamples noted:

(49) Movement rules may upgrade, but they cannot downgrade unless the position that they vacate is filled by a later rule, or unless the item downgraded is not a noun phrase.

So formulated, the convention overcomes the counterexamples, but is too *ad hoc* to have any real credibility; and it is, furthermore, without explanation or significant analogue elsewhere in the theory. But under the trace theory, (49) follows as an immediate consequence of independent principles of anaphora.

The general principle that emerges from this discussion, once again, is that since the trace is being interpreted as in effect a variable, surface structures with traces must meet the general conditions on expressions with variable-like expressions such as the reciprocal phrase "each other." Nothing further need be said, in these cases at least, to distinguish permissible from impermissible rule applications.

These considerations again make essential use of the trace theory, and thus provide an independent motivation for this theory at an entirely different and more abstract level of discussion.

Principles of the sort that we have just been discussing are of considerable importance. They restrict the class of possible rules, and also, the possible application of established rules. Therefore, they contribute to solving the fundamental problem of linguistic theory, hence of "learning theory" as this was construed in the first chapter, namely: to constrain the class of "learnable systems" so that it becomes possible to explain the rapidity, uniformity, and richness of learning within cognitive capacity. The same is true of the argument, given earlier, that we can eliminate the notions "unbounded" and "clause-mate" from the theory of transformations. In general, the same is true of all the conditions on organization of grammar and application of rules that we have been describing. These are all steps towards what has been called "explanatory adequacy." [40] From one point of view, we can properly say that these principles provide explanations for the fact that the data are such-and-such, and thus go well beyond the descriptions of such facts in particular grammars. From another point of view, the same principles serve to account for an important aspect of human learning, that is, for the construction of certain cognitive structures that play an essential role in thought and its expression (and derivatively, in communication).

If these principles can be substantiated or improved, the class of potential grammars is vastly reduced. Many potential rules are eliminated outright. Furthermore, by limiting the possible application of rules, principles of the sort discussed make it unnecessary to make available in the theory of transformations as rich an apparatus as would otherwise be needed to delimit the application of particular rules. Thus, the principles constrain the variety of grammars by reducing the "expressive power" of grammatical rules.

We might even set ourselves the goal, still distant but perhaps attainable, of so restricting the apparatus of the theory of transformations that rules can only be given in the form "move NP," with other conditions on their application expressed either as general conditions on rules, or as properties of initial phrase markers, or as properties of surface structures. In all three cases, we will try, of course, to abstract properties of universal grammar from particular conditions on rules, initial phrase markers, and surface structures. As a case in point, recall the conditions on anaphora in surface structures, to which appeal was made in the analysis of the upgrading convention.

If this goal can be reached, not only will the various cases of NP-preposing fall together, but further, these will fall together with the rule of NP-postposing that gave (44ii). Restrictions on the "expressive power" of rules, even if not as dramatic as these speculations suggest, contribute to the dual goal of attaining explanatory adequacy and accounting for the acquisition of cognitive structures, that is, for human learning.

Principles such as subjacency, the trace theory, and the specified-subject condition contribute to this end, along with other principles, among them the principle of structure-dependence and the conditions on the organization of grammar and the various types of rules that can appear in the several components of grammar. Insofar as these proposals are correct, they are contributions to universal grammar, hence to the characterization of the language faculty that is one essential component of innate mental structure.

Pursuing the discussion of possible rules a step further, consider again the derivation (44) suggested for passives.

An analogous derivation might be proposed for "passives" of nominal constructions. Thus, (50):

(50) (i) the enemy—destruction of the city
          (initial phrase marker)

(ii) t—destruction of the city by the enemy
      (by NP-postposing)

(iii) the city's—destruction t by the enemy
      (by NP-preposing)

There is, however, a striking difference between the derivations (44) and (50).[41] Namely, in the case of the passive of the sentence, (44), the rule of NP-preposing must apply if the rule of NP-postposing has applied. There is no such sentence as (51), corresponding to (44ii):

(51) t destroyed the city by the enemy

But in the case of the "passive" of the nominal, (50), NP-postposing may apply without a subsequent application of NP-preposing, giving such sentences as (52), corresponding to (50ii):

(52) the destruction of the city by the enemy

The distinction is explicable in our terms. In the case of (51), there is an offending trace, violating anaphora conditions, standing as a free variable in the logical form derived from surface structure. But in (52) the trace has been erased by a rule spelling out the determiner.[42] It may be, then, that the same rules are involved, with differences in applicability that are reducible to other properties of the constructions involved.

We have noted a number of cases that seem to fall together under a rule of NP-preposing, without, however, going into a number of difficulties that arise when these phenomena are unified or the possible solutions to these difficulties. We have discussed such cases as these:

(53) John seems [$_s$ t to be a nice fellow]

(54) John is certain [$_s$ t to win the election]

> (55) the city [vp was destroyed *t* by the enemy]
>
> (56) the city's [np destruction *t* by the enemy]

Other examples fall within the same rubric, e.g.:

> (57) John [vp was believed [s *t* to be a suitable candidate]]
>
> (58) the bed [vp was slept in *t*] [43]

Others of quite different types also come to mind as possible candidates for a similar analysis.[44] The rule of NP-preposing applies over quite an array of possible constructions; as we would expect, if the speculations of the preceding discussion prove to be justified.

Notice that if there were no passives such as (57), (58), and those of note 43, we might be hesitant to postulate a rule of passive formation in the first place. Many languages lack such constructions, restricting the "passive" to reduced passives such as (59), with no agent phrase and with the subject serving as the direct object in related transitive constructions, where "pass" indicates some passive inflection:

> (59) John kill-pass   (analogous to "John was killed")

In such cases, there is no motivation for postulating a rule to form passives from actives; the facts can be described with no less (I think greater) facility within the lexicon, under rules of word formation.[45]

The theory of grammar makes a variety of devices available, and languages may differ as to their choice among them. We would expect these choices to have certain consequences both in the syntax and the semantics. Thus, it can hardly be accidental that the English passive makes use of the copula and that the verb morphology is so clearly analogous to certain adjectival constructions, so that the rules forming passives map initial phrase markers into independently existing structures of the subject-predicate form.[46] This fact may well find its place within a theory of surface-structure semantic interpretation, making essential use of the subject-predicate construction in surface structure, the theory of traces, and other related ideas. Further discussion would carry us too far afield, into areas that have so far barely been explored in a systematic way within the theory of generative grammar.

We have been operating so far on the assumption that surface structures alone undergo semantic interpretation. But there are some obvious objections to this conjecture. Thus, we have come across several rules that erase the trace left by earlier movement rules. In such cases, the position of a phrase in initial phrase markers will no longer be marked in surface structure. But in some cases at least, this initial position seemed essential for semantic interpretation. Thus, consider the passives (44iii) and (50iii):

(44) (iii) the city was destroyed *t* by the enemy

(50) (iii) the city's destruction *t* by the enemy

The surface forms contain no trace for the phrase "the enemy." But to understand the sentences, we must know that this phrase bears the semantic relation of "agent" to the verb "destroy," as is indicated in the initial phrase markers (44i) and (50i). Thus it seems that contrary to our conjecture, initial phrase markers must enter into semantic interpretation. It was for such reasons as these that formulations of the extended standard theory have in the past postulated that semantic interpretation applies to paired deep and surface structures (initial and surface phrase markers).

John Goldsmith has observed that in the derived forms (44iii) and (50iii) there is a formal structure that indicates the semantic relation of the phrase "the enemy" to the verb, namely, the *by*-phrase. Similarly, in the "there is" constructions (cf. (40)), though the trace is erased, the surface structure suffices to determine the relations of the moved noun phrase to the verb. He proposes, then, that a rule may erase a trace only if the element binding the trace appears in surface structure in a position that identifies the semantic relation it bears. Thus, the rule of NP-preposing may apply to give the passives, erasing a trace, but there could be no rule, for example, that erases the trace in (53) (= "John seems t to be a nice fellow"), and no derivation such as (60), giving (62) from the initial phrase marker (61):

(60) (i) NP_1 V NP_2 [$_s$ X VP] (initial phrase marker)

    (ii) t V NP_2 [$_s$ NP_1 VP]   (by NP-postposing)

    (iii) NP_2 V t [$_s$ NP_1 VP]   (by NP-preposing)

(61) John persuaded Bill [$_s$ X to stay awhile]

(62) Bill persuaded t [$_s$ John to stay awhile]

The structure (60iii) does not violate anaphora conditions, so that the derivation (60) cannot be ruled out along the lines of our earlier discussion of downgrading. But the derivation violates Goldsmith's principle.

In many well-known cases, this principle seems to suffice. It also, again, has the important property that it substantially restricts possible rule applications, an important desideratum, for reasons already explained.

Accepting Goldsmith's principle of recoverability of semantic relations, it seems that we can tentatively postulate that only surface structures undergo semantic interpretation. With this step, we can unify a considerable amount of quite fruitful research of the past few years that has shown that many aspects of semantic interpretation are best expressed in terms of properties of surface structure. In general, this is true of what might be called "logical properties" of sentences, properties involving scope of quantifiers and logical particles, anaphora, presupposition, and the like. In earlier versions of the extended standard theory, it was proposed that surface structure determines all semantic properties apart from "thematic relations" such as agency, goal, and instrument, these being determined by the interaction of lexical properties and the grammatical relations of initial phrase markers (deep structures).[47] If the argument presented here is correct, we can improve this picture, taking surface structures (now enriched by the trace theory) to be the sole elements that enter into semantic interpretation.

The trace theory permits us, in effect, to carry over to surface structures certain properties of phrase markers that initiate derivations or that appear at an intermediate stage of derivation.[48] It might be argued that this is a rather far-reaching and undesirable modification of earlier theory, rather like the introduction of "global rules": rules that apply, not to the last phrase marker of a derivation so far constructed, but to a set of phrase markers already derived, including the last of these. But this would be a misunderstanding. There is, indeed, a serious objection to global rules. This device enormously increases the class of admissible grammars and thus moves us a long step away from our goal of attaining explanatory adequacy in linguistic theory and accounting for the possibility of language learning.[49] Thus one would accept global rules only under the pressure of powerful evidence, which, I believe, has so far not been forthcoming. But the trace theory does not extend the class of admissible grammars. Nor does it restrict this class. Rather, it changes the class and is thus immune to the methodological objections that are rightly raised against the introduction of global rules. The structures generated are enriched, but the class of grammars is not.

It is quite true that the trace theory allows properties of earlier stages of derivation to appear in surface structure, but this in itself is nothing new. One might imagine a theory of transformations postulating operations that disregard the categories of the initial phrase markers (the labels on the brackets, in the notation we have been using here). In comparison, the conventional theory carries categorial information over to derived structure. One would not therefore argue that the conventional theory already contains global rules, since properties of initial phrase markers (namely, the categories that appear within them) are carried over to surface structures. The conventional theory generates richer surface structures than an alternative that disregards categories in transformational derivations, and in much the same sense, the trace theory enriches the class of derived structures as compared with the conventional theory, requiring that additional properties of earlier stages of derivation appear at later stages (including surface structures) with all the consequences that follow for rule application. The issue of globality does not arise.

This discussion by no means exhausts the arguments pro and con, and avoids serious questions that arise under more careful formulation and more extensive application. I hope that the discussion is, nevertheless, sufficient to give some indication of the kinds of principles that it seems reasonable to postulate as general properties of human language.

This discussion has been restricted to English, a serious limitation. Nevertheless, I have not hesitated to suggest that the principles that appear to have explanatory power for English are principles of universal grammar. On the assumption that the language faculty is a common human possession, the inference is plausible (though, obviously, nondemonstrative). The logic of the argument has already been outlined. On the assumption of uniformity of language capacity across the species, if a general principle is confirmed empirically for a given language and if, furthermore, there is reason to believe that it is not learned (and surely not taught), then it is proper to postulate that the principle belongs to universal grammar, as part of the system of "pre-existent knowledge" that makes learning possible.

Under the simplifying assumptions of chapter 1, then, it it reasonable to propose that principles of the sort outlined here find their place in the component of the innate language faculty that determines what kind of system can be learned. Recall that there were two major simplifying assumptions: first, that individual differences can be ignored; and second, that learning is "instantaneous." As noted before, the first assumption is true to a very good approximation, so far as is known. Apart from gross abnormalities, there is no known reason to suppose that individuals differ in ways relevant to the present discussion, though there are no doubt differences in fluency, talent, and knowledge that would appear at a finer level of detail.

But the assumption that learning is instantaneous is obviously false. We might, more realistically, say that children proceed through a sequence of cognitive states S_0, $S_1, \ldots, S_f$, where S_0 is the "initial state," prior to any language learning, and S_f is the "final state," a "steady state" attained fairly early in life and not changing in significant respects from that point on. When the child has attained this steady state, we say that he has learned the language. Attainment of a steady state at some not-too-delayed stage of intellectual development is presumably characteristic of "learning" within the range of cognitive capacity.

Consider now the transition from one state to the next, say, from state S_5 to state S_6.

We may ask various questions about this transition. First, what is the input to the learning theory available to the child at this stage, call it LT_5? To be realistic, it is surely not at all the data available up to stage S_5, considered as a cumulative record. No one remembers which sentences he has heard in the past. Rather, the input to LT_5 consists of two parts: (i) the grammar attained at state S_5; and (ii) new data available at S_5. Thus, LT_5 will operate on the tentative theory constructed so far by the child, the theory that organizes past experience, not on a list of all data so far utilized.[50] We may ask, then, whether we would seriously falsify the account of learning (and if so, in what respects) by assuming that the input to LT_5 is the data so far utilized rather than the grammar that represents the child's theory at this point (along with other new data).

We may also ask a slightly more subtle question. The grammar generates a system of "potential experience," including the actual experience that led to the construction of the grammar (and excluding parts of actual experience that have been ruled out as wrong or irrelevant in the course of learning), but also including far more, in fact, infinitely more. Furthermore, as already noted, no one can recall which sentences he has heard (with insignificant exceptions). The notion of "familiarity" does not apply in any relevant way to sentences of a language. Ideas expressed may be unfamiliar, and so may turns of phrase. But over a vast range sentences are "familiar" to us if they are part of the language generated by our grammar, subject to qualifications relating to length, complexity, absurdity, insight, and so on, which are not to the point in the present context. We may now ask whether we falsify the account of learning by assuming that the input to LT_5 is the language generated by the grammar available at stage S_5 rather than the grammar itself; the two possibilities differ, since different grammars may generate the same language.

Without pursuing such complications any further, let us distinguish two approaches to the question of the input to LT_5: an *extensional* approach, which takes the input to be "experience" (say, sentences with formal and semantic properties), either the finite record of experience so far or the infinite set generated by the grammar available at state S_5; and an *intensional* approach, which assumes the input to LT_5 to be the grammar itself. In either case, a second input is the new data available.

We might ask some further questions. Is LT_5 different

from LT_6? More generally, is LT_i different from LT_j, for i distinct from j? Are the child's learning capacities different at different stages of development? Does he handle evidence differently at these various stages? Are there well-defined stages, marked by different modes of learning, or do "learning strategies" mature more or less continuously, or do they remain constant (with changes only in other systems, such as memory or attention span), or do they decay? Are there "critical periods" for various phases of language learning? Does LT_i depend in part on theories already constructed, or is it fixed in some maturational sequence? These are all serious questions, the kinds of questions that arise in developmental psychology.[51] To my knowledge, there are no answers that are very informative at the level required to pursue the investigation into language learning beyond the earliest stages, which involve very little of the specific structure of language.

If there were answers to such questions as these, we might develop a more realistic theory of language learning. It might reveal that our simplifying assumption, namely, that the mechanism for language learning is extensional and instantaneous, was far off the mark. It would follow, then, that the conclusions suggested with regard to universal grammar would also have to be modified.

Frankly, I doubt that the simplifying assumption, though obviously false, significantly affects the validity of the analysis based on it. If our initial assumption does indeed seriously falsify the situation, if there are substantially different stages with fundamentally different LT_i's, if these are in an important way intensional, and if furthermore the character of LT_i depends significantly on grammars (or other cognitive structures) already attained, then we would expect to find substantial differences in the result of language learning depending on such factors as order of presentation of data, time of presentation, and so on. But we do not find this, at least at the level of precision of currently available analytic tools. Nor does ordinary experience suggest that this is so. Despite considerable variety in learning experience, people can communicate readily (at the level of communication relevant to this discussion), with no indication that they are speaking fundamentally different languages. It seems that the cognitive structure attained—the grammar—does not vary much, if at all significantly, on the basis of the factors that should lead to enormous differences, were the possibilities just sketched in fact realized. This seems true within rather broad limits. Such principles of universal grammar as structure-dependence and others more intricate seem immune to variability in these factors.

There are, it appears, striking uniformities in steady state attained, through wide variation in conditions of learning. These facts suggest that the initial idealization, with its falsifying assumption about instantaneous extensional learning, was nevertheless a legitimate one and provides a proper basis for pursuing a serious inquiry into human cognitive capacity. At some stage in the progress of inquiry it will no doubt have to be qualified, but one may seriously question whether this stage has been reached in the study of linguistic competence and universal grammar.

These are imprecise and qualitative conclusions, based on evidence that is hardly compelling. They surely might be called into question. To me, these conclusions seem nevertheless quite reasonable, given what is now known. To the extent that the simplifying assumption about instantaneous extensional learning must be revised, we must accordingly complicate the "innateness hypothesis" formulated earlier, namely, that the theory of universal grammar is an innate property of the mind. I will drop the matter with these inconclusive remarks. Further substantive proposals are unfortunately rather limited, though not entirely lacking (see note 50).

I have been attempting to locate language, conceptually at least, within a general system of cognitive capacity that is determined by the innate faculties of mind, and to show how one particular line of empirical inquiry might lead towards a better understanding of the innate faculty of language. Whether or not the proposals outlined here, under more precise formulation, stand the test of time and further research, it seems to me that the questions raised point to the more serious issues in the field that is sometimes labeled, misleadingly, "the theory of learning."

The study of language falls naturally within human biology. The language faculty, which somehow evolved in human prehistory, makes possible the amazing feat of language learning, while inevitably setting limits on the kinds of language that can be acquired in the normal way. Interacting with other faculties of mind, it makes possible the coherent and creative use of language in ways that we can sometimes describe, but hardly even begin to understand.

If we undertake the study of humans as organisms in the natural world, the approach I have outlined seems entirely reasonable. Given the role of language in human life and probably human evolution, and given its intimate relations to what I have been calling "common-sense understanding," it would not be very surprising to discover that other systems within cognitive capacity have something of the character of the language faculty and its products. We should anticipate that these other cognitive systems too set limits on human intellectual achievement, by virtue of the very structure that makes it possible to acquire rich and comprehensive systems of belief and knowledge, insight and understanding. I have already discussed this matter briefly in connection with the "science-forming capacity" (whatever it may be).

I would like to stress again that these conjectures should not seem in any way surprising to the natural scientist.

Rather, they conform reasonably well to what is known about how the brain works in other domains, say, the construction of visual space, or more generally, our concept of physical space and the objects in it. Furthermore, as a number of biologists have pointed out, something of the sort is to be expected on simple evolutionary grounds. Citing Lorenz,[52] Gunther Stent points out that Darwinian considerations offer a "biological underpinning" to a kind of Kantian epistemology, but in addition, these considerations concerning the evolutionary origin of the brain explain "not only why our innate concepts match the world but also why these concepts no longer work so well when we attempt to fathom the world in its deepest scientific aspects," thus perhaps posing a "barrier to unlimited scientific progress." [53] The reason, simply, is that there is no reason to suppose that the capacities acquired through evolution fit us to "fathom the world in its deepest scientific aspects." He also warns that "it is important to give due recognition to this fundamental epistemological limitation to the human sciences, if only as a safeguard against the psychological or sociological prescriptions put forward by those who allege that they have already managed to gain a scientifically validated understanding of man." A warning that we might well bear in mind in a period when pseudoscientific pretense serves so well the needs of dominant coercive ideologies.[54]

Notice that these quite natural views on the scope and limits of knowledge set no finite limits on human progress. The integers form an infinite set, but they do not exhaust the real numbers. Similarly, humans may develop their capacities without limit, but never escaping certain objective bounds set by their biological nature. I suspect that there is no cognitive domain to which such observations are not appropriate.

Suppose that the social and material conditions that prevent free intellectual development were relieved, at least for some substantial number of people. Then, science, mathematics, and art would flourish, pressing on towards the limits of cognitive capacity. At these limits, as noted earlier, we find various forms of intellectual play, and significant differentiation among individuals who vary little within the domain of cognitive capacity. As creative minds approach the limits of cognitive capacity, not only will the act of creation be limited to a talented few, but even the appreciation or comprehension of what has been created. If cognitive domains are roughly comparable in complexity and potential scope, such limits might be approached at more or less the same time in various domains, giving rise to a "crisis of modernism," marked by a sharp decline in the general accessibility of the products of creative minds, a blurring of the distinction between art and puzzle, and a sharp increase in "professionalism" in intellectual life, affecting not only those who produce creative work but also its potential audience. Mockery of conventions that are, ultimately, grounded in human cognitive capacity might be expected to become virtually an art form in itself, at this stage of cultural evolution. It may be that something of the sort has been happening in recent history. Even if correct, such speculations would not lead us to deny that there is surely a vast creative potential as yet unexplored, or to overlook the fact that for most of the human race, material deprivation and oppressive social structures make these questions academic, if not obscene. As Marx wrote in his early manuscripts, echoing Humboldt, animals "produce only under the compulsion of direct physical needs, while man produces when he is free from physical needs and only truly produces in freedom from such need." By this criterion, human history has barely begun for the majority of mankind.

If the approach to the study of cognitive capacity outlined earlier is a proper one, then we can hope to develop a theory of human nature in its psychological aspects. The possibility of such a theory has often been denied. This denial is implicit in the scholastic doctrine that the mind contains nothing beyond what the senses convey. One might read a similar conclusion into the various efforts in the modern period to relate human reason and the scope of human intelligence to the weakness of instinct, an idea that can be traced at least to Herder. (Cf. Chomsky, 1966, pp. 13ff.) Empiricist and later behaviorist psychology are firmly grounded in the doctrine that there is no nontrivial theory of human nature. Or more accurately, that such a theory is limited to the physical organs of the body, with the sole exception of those parts of the brain involved in higher mental functions. I will return directly to some of the ramifications of this doctrine.

I think it is fair to say that these empiricist views are most plausible where we are most ignorant. The more we learn about some aspect of human cognition, the less reasonable these views seem to be. No one would seriously argue today, for example, that our construction of perceptual space is guided by empiricist maxims. The same, I think, is true of the language faculty, which relates more closely to the essential nature of the human species. I suspect that the empiricist position with regard to higher mental functions will crumble as science advances towards an understanding of cognitive capacity and its relations to physical structures.[55]

The claims of empiricism have often been put forth, not as speculation, but as established fact, as if they must be true or have been demonstrated. Such claims must be evaluated on their merits, but if they are found to be without support, plain wrong, or seriously exaggerated, as I believe invariably proves to be the case, then it is appropriate to search elsewhere for an explanation for their appeal and power.

In part, the commitment to empiricist doctrine in the human sciences is a reaction to the speculative character of earlier work, its lack of firm empirical foundation. Surely this has been true of the study of language. There is, however, an obvious gap in reasoning. We can agree that classical rationalist and empiricist doctrines should be recast (or perhaps replaced) so as to be more directly susceptible to empirical test, and that empirical evidence should be brought to bear, as far as possible, in determining their validity. Those who fashioned the traditional doctrines would not have quarreled with this principle. Descartes and Hume and Kant were grappling with problems at the borders of scientific knowledge, problems that a e both conceptual and empirical, and sought such evidence as they could muster to justify their theoretical speculations. (Cf. chapter 4, pp. 224–7.) But from a justifiable concern for empirical confirmation, we cannot argue to a commitment to empiricist doctrine. Rather, empiricist and rationalist theories alike must be cast in a form in which they are subject to confirmation, and this task seems no more difficult in one case than in the other. I have tried to suggest how these theories can be so reformulated, without doing violence to certain basic leading ideas (though others must be discarded), and have argued further that where we have any glimmerings of understanding, we are led to theories with a distinctively rationalist character.

But the conflict between rationalist and empiricist doctrines, and the grip of the latter on the modern temper, cannot be explained solely on the "intrinsic" grounds just mentioned. As Harry Bracken (1973a) has emphasized:

> The empiricist/rationalist debates of the seventeenth century *and* of today are debates between different value systems or ideologies. Hence the heat which characterizes these discussions.

The issues have changed from the seventeenth century to today, though there may well be some common threads. Complicating the matter further, the issues and conflicts can be perceived along many dimensions and in quite different ways. But the social and ideological context has always been critical, a fact often noted. Locke's epistemology, as John Yolton shows, was developed primarily for application to religious and moral debates of the period; "the vital issue between Locke and his critics [on the doctrine of innateness] was the grounds and foundations of morality and religion" (Yolton, 1956, p. 68). Throughout the modern period, not to speak of earlier eras, such questions lie in the background of seemingly arcane philosophical controversies and often help explain their issue.

Classical British empiricism arose in often healthy opposition to religious obscurantism and reactionary ideology. Its appeal, perhaps, resides in part in the belief that it offers a vision of limitless progress in contrast to the pessimistic doctrine that humans are enslaved by an unchangeable nature that condemns them to intellectual servitude, material deficit, and eternally fixed oppressive institutions. Thus, it might be understood as a doctrine of progress and enlightenment.

This may also be the reason for the appeal of empiricist ideology in Marxist thought, a commitment that has often been expressed in the most extreme forms. Gramsci went so far as to argue that "the fundamental innovation introduced by Marxism into the science of politics and history is the proof that there does not exist an abstract, fixed and immutable 'human nature' . . . but that human nature is the totality of historically determined social relations" (Gramsci, 1957, p. 140)—a statement that is surely false, in that there is no such proof, and a questionable reading of Marx. In his introduction to Jean Itard's study of the Wild Boy of Aveyron, Lucien Malson asserts categorically that "the idea that man has no nature is now beyond dispute"; the thesis that man "has or rather is a history," nothing more, "is now the explicit assumption of all the main currents of contemporary thought," not only Marxism, but also existentialism, behaviorism, and psychoanalysis. Malson too believes that it has been "proven" that the term "human nature" is "completely devoid of sense." His own critique of "psychological heredity" aims to "destroy . . . the notion of human nature" by demonstrating that there are no "mental predispositions [present in the embryo] which are common to the species or to man in general." To be sure, there are inherited biological characteristics, but not in the area in which man "displays his peculiarly human qualities." "The natural in man is due to inborn heredity, the cultural to his acquired heritage," with no contribution from "psychological heredity" (Malson, 1972, pp. 9–12, 35).

Such claims are not untypical of left-wing opinion, a fact that demands explanation, since plainly there is no compelling empirical argument to buttress them. The explanation, I think, is the one just given: it has been assumed that empiricist doctrine is fundamentally "progressive," as in certain respects it was in an earlier period.

There are quite independent issues that must be clearly distinguished in considering a doctrine put forth as a theory of human nature, or of the lack of any such distinctive nature. Is it correct, or at least plausible? What were its social and political implications at certain historical periods in fact? How were these implications perceived? To what extent (if at all) did these implications, as perceived, contribute to the reception of the doctrine? What (if anything) does this tell us about the commitments of those who defend it? All these questions arise in the case of the advocacy by the revolutionary left of empiricist principles, in particular the doctrine that human nature is nothing but a historical product and thus imposes no limits and suggests no preferred directions for social change.

I have been discussing, so far, only the question of truth and plausibility; there is, I believe, little of either. As a problem of intellectual and social history, the matter is complex. Empiricism has indeed served as a doctrine of progress and enlightenment. It is closely associated with classical liberal thought, which has been unable to survive the age of industrial capitalism.[56] What remains of value in classical liberal doctrine is, in my opinion, to be found today in its most meaningful form in libertarian socialist concepts of human rights and social organization. Empiricism rose to ascendancy in association with a doctrine of "possesive individualism" that was integral to early capitalism,[57] in an age of empire, with the concomitant growth (one might almost say "creation") of racist ideology. Bracken has argued that

> racism is easily and readily stateable if one thinks of the person in accordance with empiricist teaching because the essence of the person may be deemed to be his colour, language, religion, etc., while the Cartesian dualist model provided . . . a modest conceptual brake to the articulation of racial degradation and slavery. [1973b] . . . Empiricism provides a model of the person in which colour, sex, language, religion, etc. can be counted as essential without the logical embarrassments such suggestions as coloured minds create within Cartesianism. [1974, p. 158]

He has argued that "the relation between empiricism and racism is historical," not in that there is a logical connection, but in that empiricism facilitated the expression of the racist ideology that came naturally enough to philosophers who were involved in their professional lives in the creation of the colonial system (Bracken, 1973b). He has also developed the theme that

> the anti-abstractionism and anti-empiricism of Cartesianism are connected with concern for human freedom. More generally, the rationalist model of man is taken to support an active and creative mind which is neither impressed from "outside" to "inside" nor considered to be malleable. . . . Cartesian thought constitutes a vigorous effort to assert the dignity of the

person. . . . [In contrast] the empiricist blank tablet
account of learning is a manipulative model. . . .
[1974, pp. 16, 156; 1973b]

I think that this is an accurate perception, on both conceptual and historical grounds. As for the latter, I have
commented elsewhere on the roots in Cartesian thought of
Rousseau's opposition to tyranny, oppression, and established authority; and at a greater remove, Kant's defense
of freedom, Humboldt's precapitalist liberalism with its
emphasis on the basic human need for free creation under
conditions of voluntary association, and Marx's critique of
alienated fragmented labor that turns men into machines,
depriving them of their "species character" of "free conscious activity" and "productive life," in association with
their fellows (Chomsky, 1973b, chaps. 8, 9).

A similar line of argument has been developed by Ellen
Wood. She suggests that Kant's attack on certain aspects of
empiricist doctrine "is not simply an epistemological quib-
ble, but a far-reaching argument about the nature of human
freedom," and that Marx's work can be understood in part
as an attempt "to give concrete expression to Kant's notion
of freedom as self-activity." "The controversy over the nature of mind," she correctly observes, "has a great deal to
do with the question of man's place in the natural order."
The question whether "the human mind [is] to be regarded
simply as a responsive cog in the mechanism of nature," as
in empiricist doctrine, or as "a creative, determinative
force" is a crucial one, which arises in many forms in the
context of the debate over various models of mind (Wood,
1972, pp. 29, 28, 174).

Kant described "man's inclination and duty to *think
freely*" as "the germ on which nature has lavished most
care."[58] A concern for this "species character" lies at the
core of Cartesian thought and animates an intellectual tradition (not the only one) that derives in part from it, not
limiting itself, however, to the inclination and duty to think

freely, but also affirming the need to produce freely and creatively, to realize one's full potentialities, to revolt against oppression, and to take control of the institutions of economic, political, and social life.

The doctrine that the human mind is initially unstructured and plastic and that human nature is entirely a social product has often been associated with progressive and even revolutionary social thinking, while speculations with regard to human instinct have often had a conservative and pessimistic cast. One can easily see why reformers and revolutionaries should become radical environmentalists, and there is no doubt that concepts of immutable human nature can be and have been employed to erect barriers against social change and to defend established privilege.

But a deeper look will show that the concept of the "empty organism," plastic and unstructured, apart from being false, also serves naturally as the support for the most reactionary social doctrines. If people are, in fact, malleable and plastic beings with no essential psychological nature, then why should they not be controlled and coerced by those who claim authority, special knowledge, and a unique insight into what is best for those less enlightened? Empiricist doctrine can easily be molded into an ideology for the vanguard party that claims authority to lead the masses to a society that will be governed by the "red bureaucracy" of which Bakunin warned. And just as easily for the liberal technocrats or corporate managers who monopolize "vital decision-making" in the institutions of state capitalist democracy, beating the people with the people's stick, in Bakunin's trenchant phrase.

The principle that human nature, in its psychological aspects, is nothing more than a product of history and given social relations removes all barriers to coercion and manipulation by the powerful. This too, I think, may be a reason for its appeal to intellectual ideologists, of whatever political persuasion. I have discussed elsewhere [59] the strik-

ing similarity in the doctrines evolved by authoritarian so-
cialists and ideologists of state capitalism, those who
constitute "a secular priesthood claiming absolute authority, both spiritual and lay, in the name of unique scientific
knowledge of the nature of men and things" (Berlin, 1972),
the "new class" of technical intelligentsia, who hope to
bring about "the reign of *scientific intelligence,* the most
aristocratic, despotic, arrogant and elitist of all regimes." [60]
The "empty organism" doctrine is a most natural one for
them to adopt.

Creativity is predicated on a system of rules and forms,
in part determined by intrinsic human capacities. Without
such constraints, we have arbitrary and random behavior,
not creative acts. The constructions of common sense and
scientific inquiry derive no less from principles grounded
in the structure of the human mind. Correspondingly, it
would be an error to think of human freedom solely in
terms of absence of constraint. Bakunin once remarked that
"the laws of our own nature . . . constitute the very basis
of our being" and provide "the real condition and the effective cause of our liberty." A libertarian social theory will
try to determine these laws and to found upon them a
concept of social change and its immediate and distant
goals. If, indeed, human nature is governed by Bakunin's
"instinct for revolt" or the "species character" on which
Marx based his critique of alienated labor, then there must
be continual struggle against authoritarian social forms
that impose restrictions beyond those set by "the laws of
our own nature," as has long been advocated by authentic
revolutionary thinkers and activists.

It is reasonable to suppose that just as intrinsic structures of mind underlie the development of cognitive structures, so a "species character" provides the framework for
the growth of moral consciousness, cultural achievement,
and even participation in a free and just community. It
is, to be sure, a great intellectual leap from observations

on the basis for cognitive development to particular conclusions on the laws of our nature and the conditions for their fulfillment; say, to the conclusion that human needs and capacities will find their fullest expression in a society of free and creative producers, working in a system of free association in which "social bonds" will replace "all fetters in human society." [61] There is an important intellectual tradition that stakes out some interesting claims in this regard. While this tradition draws from the empiricist commitment to progress and enlightenment, I think it finds still deeper roots in rationalist efforts to establish a theory of human freedom. To investigate, deepen, and if possible substantiate the ideas developed in this tradition by the methods of science is a fundamental task for libertarian social theory. Whether further investigation will reveal problems that can be addressed or mysteries that will confound us, only the future can tell.

If this endeavor succeeds, it will refute Bertrand Russell's pessimistic speculation that man's "passions and instincts" render him incapable of enjoying the benefits of the "scientific civilization" that reason can create (Russell, 1924), at least if we understand "passions and instincts" (as Russell sometimes did) to include the "instincts" that provide the basis for the achievements of the creative intellect, as well as the "instinct of revolt" against imposed authority—in some measure, a common human attribute. Rather, success in this endeavor might reveal that these passions and instincts may yet succeed in bringing to a close what Marx called the "prehistory of human society." No longer repressed and distorted by competitive and authoritarian social structures, these passions and instincts may set the stage for a new scientific civilization in which "animal nature" is transcended and human nature can truly flourish.

PART II

CHAPTER 4

Problems and Mysteries in the Study of Human Language

I would like to distinguish roughly between two kinds of issues that arise in the study of language and mind: those that appear to be within the reach of approaches and concepts that are moderately well understood—what I will call "problems"; and others that remain as obscure to us today as when they were originally formulated—what I will call "mysteries." The distinction reflects in part a subjective evaluation of what has been achieved or might be achieved in terms of ideas now available. Others see mysteries, incoherence, and confusion where to me the issues seem rather clear and straightforward, and conversely.

Among the problems are these: What kinds of cognitive structures are developed by humans on the basis of their experience, specifically, in the case of acquisition of language? What is the basis for the acquisition of such structures and how do they develop? Without prejudicing the outcome of this investigation, we may say that humans are innately endowed with a system of intellectual organization, call it the "initial state" of the mind. Through interaction with the environment and maturational processes, the mind passes through a sequence of states in which cognitive structures are represented. In the case of language, it is fairly obvious that rapid and extensive changes take place during an early period of life, and a "steady state" is achieved which then undergoes only minor modification. Abstracting away from the latter, we can refer to this steady state as the "final state" of the mind, in which knowledge of language is somehow represented. We can construct hypotheses concerning the initial and final states, and can proceed to validate, or reject, or sharpen these hypotheses by methods of inquiry that are familiar. We might proceed, in principle, to explore the physical realizations of the initial and final states and the processes involved in the changes of state that take place.

In these domains, much is unknown. In this sense there are many mysteries here. But we have a certain grasp of the problem, and can make progress by posing and sometimes answering questions that arise along the way, with at least some degree of confidence that we know what we are doing.

On the other hand, when we turn to such matters as causation of behavior, it seems to me that no progress has been made, that we are as much in the dark as to how to proceed as in the past, and that some fundamental insights are lacking.

Roughly, where we deal with cognitive structures, either in a mature state of knowledge and belief or in the initial state, we face problems, but not mysteries. When we ask how humans make use of these cognitive structures, how and why they make choices and behave as they do, although there is much that we can say as human beings with intuition and insight, there is little, I believe, that we can say as scientists. What I have called elsewhere "the creative aspect of language use" remains as much a mystery to us as it was to the Cartesians who discussed it, in part, in the context of the problem of "other minds." Some would reject this evaluation of the state of our understanding. I do not propose to argue the point here, but rather to turn to the problems that do seem to me amenable to inquiry.

Imagine a scientist, henceforth S, who is unencumbered by the ideological baggage that forms part of our intellectual tradition and is thus prepared to study humans as organisms in the natural world. Let us consider a course of inquiry that S might undertake, sketching conclusions that he might tentatively reach along the way, and then confront S with some of the questions of methodology and principle that have been raised by a number of philosophers who have discussed the nature and goals of linguistic theory.

S might begin with the observation that people seem to act in systematic ways with respect to the objects around them and that they use and respond to expressions in organized ways. He might also conclude that humans, rather early in their lives, seem to arrive at steady states of development in these respects, states which are then modified only in detail and which provide a basis for human actions and responses. Investigation of these matters requires idealization and abstraction, but S should not be put off by this familiar contingency of rational inquiry. S might now proceed to characterize these steady states, attributing to the organism two cognitive structures: (i) a system of beliefs and expectations about the nature and behavior of objects, and (ii) a system of language. Suppose that he calls the first system "common sense" and the second "grammar." S might then proceed to try to account for what people do, perhaps in experimentally contrived situations, on the basis of these two postulated structures and further assumptions about information-processing capacities.

S might study, for example, the ability of his subjects to recognize and identify complex physical objects and predict their behavior under various circumstances. He might find that there are qualitative differences in their ability to recognize human faces and other objects of comparable complexity. This investigation might lead S to attribute to his subjects, as an element of their common sense, an abstract theory of possible faces and a system of projection which (abstracting away from the effects of memory restrictions and the like) enables the subject to predict how a face will appear under a range of empirical conditions, given a few presentations.

S might also discover that his subjects react quite differently to the expressions (1)–(4):

(1) John's friends appeared to their wives to hate one another

(2) John's friends appeared to Mary to hate one another

(3) John's friends appealed to their wives to hate one another

(4) John's friends appealed to Mary to hate one another

Asked to verify (1) and (2), the subjects might inquire whether the wives (respectively, Mary) think that each friend hates the other friends. Asked to verify (3), they might seek to determine whether each friend directed his wife to hate the other wives. The subjects would assign (4) an entirely different status, though if pressed, they could impose an interpretation—presumably, that each friend appealed to Mary to hate the other friends. In the case of (1)–(3) the problem of "imposing an interpretation" in this sense does not arise. S might contrive various experimental techniques to sharpen and clarify these results, and with luck and diligence he might arrive at a plausible theory: namely, the grammar attained by his subjects as part of their final state incorporates a system of rules that characterize (1)–(3) but not (4) as well formed, that assigns "John's friends" as the subject of "hate" in (1) and (2) but not (3) (rather "their wives" is the subject of "hate" in this case), that assigns a 1–1 correspondence to John's friends and the wives in (3), and so on.

S's conclusions about these matters would be stated in a theoretical language that he would devise, including such notions as "well formed," "subject," and others, and again it would be necessary to construct various idealizations. He would discover that when expressions become too complex in specific ways (for example, with too much "self-embedding," an abstract property of structures that S might discover if he proceeded properly), subjects respond in ways that are not predictable in terms of grammar alone, though given time and computation space under contrived experimental conditions their responses converge on those predicted in terms of the grammar. On the basis of such discoveries, S would be led to distinguish between the grammar and a system of information processing perhaps not specific to language, and to account for actual behavior in terms of the interaction of these systems.

Similarly, S might discover that grammar interacts with other systems of knowledge and belief to determine how sentences are interpreted. Thus he might conclude that the 1–1 correspondence assigned to John's friends and the wives in (3) is in part a matter of grammar and in part the result of factual knowledge. Suppose "their wives" is replaced by "their children" in (3). Then interpretations multiply; one is that each friend appealed to his children to hate one another (but not to hate the children of other friends). There is still a 1–1 correlation between John's friends and a set of sets of children, but not between the friends and the union of these sets. The 1–1 correlation between friends and wives derives in part from factual assumptions about monogamy, which also eliminate interpretations of "one another" of the sort that are possible (indeed, I believe, favored) when "their wives" is replaced by "their children."

Proceeding in this way, S might develop a general theory of cognitive structures in which grammar appears as a specific component. While S would remain properly cautious about such conclusions, he would not, if rational, shy away from them on grounds of their complexity and abstractness.

Examples such as (1)–(4) would reveal to S that such notions as "analogy" and "generalization" do not carry him very far in understanding human cognitive capacities, at least in the domain of language. Thus, although (1) and (3) are very similar—they differ only in one phonological feature, hence minimally—nevertheless, speakers of the language understand them in very different ways, ignoring the obvious analogies. Similarly, (4) can be interpreted "on the analogy" of (1), (2), or (3), and subjects, if pressed, might well impose such an interpretation. Nevertheless the status of (4) is entirely different from that of its "analogues," and the obvious generalizations are not employed by S's subjects to incorporate (4) within their grammatical system. These are typical examples that would lead S to reject the idea that an account of language can be based on notions of analogy and generalization as these have often been employed in the intellectual tradition of his subjects. Noting further the persistence of the contrary belief in the face of disconfirming evidence [1] that is quite easy to come by, S might try to discover ideological or social factors that lead his subjects to reject theories that seem to offer some hope of success, while clinging to beliefs that appear to be inconsistent with even the most elementary observations.

Putting the sociological investigation to the side, S might continue to investigate the hypothesis that the final state of his subjects incorporates a generative grammar embedded among and interacting with other cognitive structures. He might take the grammar to be a system of rules and principles that assigns to each of an infinite set of expressions a semantic, phonetic, and syntactic representation, each of these being a representation in some universal system. There are, of course, alternative hypotheses to be considered; in other words, S is engaged in empirical science. Given the suggested approach, various qualifications are possible, and many questions arise about the nature of these rules and representations. These are the questions that S would pursue in attempting to refine and elaborate his theory of the final state.

Thus S's analyses would proceed at two levels of abstraction. He would be concerned with relations between particular stimuli and particular percepts—the relation, for example, between (1) and an abstract characterization of it that serves as a basis for S's explanation of how his subjects deal with it. S's analysis would proceed to a still higher level of abstraction, at which he would consider the general system of rules (grammar) that determines these particular relationships. This grammar is an explanatory theory, going far beyond the evidence at hand, and easily falsifiable by new investigations. S might conclude that his subjects attribute "knowledge of a language" to their fellows when he, S, is attributing a corresponding grammar to these subjects as part of their final state (again, under appropriate idealizations).

Pursuing his efforts to map out the cognitive structures of his subjects, S might conclude that each of them possesses an unconscious theory of humans in accordance with which they attribute knowledge of language to other humans. S might also proceed to investigate the physical representation of grammars, theories of humans, common sense, information-processing systems, other systems of factual knowledge and belief, and other cognitive structures that appear to be components of the attained steady states. In this way, he would develop a science of human cognitive structures and, perhaps, their physical basis. His inquiry might take various turns and face innumerable problems, but again, there seems no reason to expect that in this domain he would run up against impenetrable mysteries.

Suppose that among the people that S is investigating

some happen to be physicists. Observing their behavior in prediction, inquiry, exposition, and so forth, S might attribute to these individuals still another cognitive structure, call it "knowledge of physics." S would now be postulating, *inter alia*, three cognitive systems, each somehow represented in the human mind: grammar, common sense, and knowledge of physics. He might notice that there are striking differences between these systems. Knowledge of physics is conscious knowledge; the physicist can expound and articulate it and convey it to others. In contrast, the other two systems are quite unconscious for the most part and beyond the bounds of introspective report. Furthermore, knowledge of physics is qualitatively distinct from the other two cognitive structures in the manner of its acquisition and development. Grammar and common sense are acquired by virtually everyone, effortlessly, rapidly, in a uniform manner, merely by living in a community under minimal conditions of interaction, exposure, and care. There need be no explicit teaching or training, and when the latter does take place, it has only marginal effects on the final state achieved. To a very good first approximation, individuals are indistinguishable (apart from gross deficits and abnormalities) in their ability to acquire grammar and common sense. Individuals of a given community each acquire a cognitive structure that is rich and comprehensive and essentially the same as the systems acquired by others. Knowledge of physics, on the other hand, is acquired selectively and often painfully, through generations of labor and careful experiment, with the intervention of individual genius and generally through careful instruction. It is not quickly and uniformly attained as a steady state, but is transmitted and modified continually on the basis of controlled inquiry and an explicit record that provides the basis for the next stage of construction.

Having discovered this much, S should realize that humans are somehow specifically adapted to acquire grammar and common sense, as they are adapted to walk and not to fly. Proceeding to a still higher level of abstraction in his inquiries, S would attempt to characterize this specific adaptation. Thus returning to the postulated theory of faces, he might ask how this theory, with a characterization of possible faces and a system of projection, arises in the organism. Why is it, specifically, that there is no comparable theory, as part of common sense, for certain other objects of comparable complexity? What assumptions about the initial state of the organism and its biologically determined maturational processes might account for the construction of this aspect of common sense within empirically given conditions of time and access to data? Investigation of this problem might lead S to the hypothesis that basic elements of the theory of human faces are represented in the initial state, as a biologically determined innate property. Knowing something about the evolution of organisms, S would not regard this as a strange or unexpected conclusion. Notice, incidentally, that biologically determined systems might begin to function only at a particular level of maturation, or after appropriate triggering experience. Thus the theory of faces (like language) might be innate, though fully functional only at a particular stage of development.

To test these hypotheses and other related ones, S might try to vary conditions of exposure and to study the variety of systems of common sense that result. To the extent that there is concomitant and systematic variation, S would adjust his postulates concerning innate structure. In this way, he would develop a theory of learning of common sense in the only rational way, namely, by characterizing as closely as possible the states achieved by the organism—steady states, in the case of common sense—and then specifying a function that assigns the attained steady state as a value given a characterization of the data available. The resulting theory of learning of common sense might involve complex assumptions as to the interaction of maturation and experience, with regular succession of states of determinate kinds (in the sense, say, of Piagetian theory). Whatever the complexity of the problem, it seems to pose no special mysteries, and we can see how it would be investigated.

There are various approaches that S might explore in attempting to construct a theory of learning of common sense. To mention two, he might postulate a schematism, innate to the mind, that is refined and further articulated by experience. Thus he might conclude that the visual system contains analyzing mechanisms that interpret sensory presentations in terms of line, angle, and motion, and that these mechanisms are simply put into operation on exposure to appropriate experience, so that, as Descartes and Cudworth proposed, we see a presented figure as a (perhaps distorted) regular geometrical figure because of the mind's initial adaptation to produce such figures as "exemplars" for the interpretation of experience. Similar ideas might be developed to explain recognition of faces, and much else.

Alternatively, S might suppose that the mind is a blank tablet, equipped only with the ability to record impressions and retain faded impressions, to construct associations among presented impressions, to match impressions (perhaps along certain innately given dimensions), to generalize along dimensions that are innate or constructed, to modify the probability of response in terms of contingencies of reinforcement defined in terms of the stimulus space, and so on. Let us call these two quite different approaches R and E, respectively. I mean to suggest, by this terminology, that they reflect leading ideas of rationalism and empiricism. I have discussed the historical question elsewhere, and will return to it below; for the moment, I will only restate my belief that these formulations, as presented,[2] were quite appropriate, and that they offer an illuminating framework for the investigation of problems of learning. As just noted, S is not bound to a strict version of R or E, but might develop a more complex approach, with successive stages based on the interplay of maturation and experience, and so on.

In the case of grammar, similar remarks apply. S would discover that there is considerable variety in attained grammars, but that individuals are not specifically adapted to acquiring one or another of these systems. Rather they will, with essentially equal facility, acquire knowledge of the language of the community in which they live, given minimal conditions of exposure and care.[3] Investigating this problem, S might make another quite appropriate idealization to a hypothetical uniform and homogeneous speech community, now abstracting away from the observed variety within given societies. He would try to discover the property of the mind P that enables a child endowed with P to acquire the grammar of the language spoken under this idealization. As in the case of any empirical hypothesis, the legitimacy of the idealization might be challenged, but in this case S would do well to proceed with the idealization, attempting to explain the complex real-life situation in terms of P and other human capacities. S would not thereby be ignoring the intriguing problems of variation of dialect and individual style, as sometimes alleged. Rather, he would be approaching these questions in terms of a specific theory, devised for the idealization. If indeed there is such a property P, and if, as seems likely, it is a fundamental factor in acquisition of language in the complex situations of real life, then S would now be in a position to undertake a serious investigation of the more complex problems with some hope of success.

Having gotten this far, S would now proceed to investigate the property P. Again, he might proceed in the manner of R, formulating a general schematism (call it "universal grammar") and an evaluation procedure which, he would postulate, jointly constitute P, or an essential element in it. Endowed with these systems in its initial state,[4] the child develops a grammar by employing the evaluation procedure to select among grammars that conform to universal grammar. If the latter is sufficiently restrictive, a small amount of evidence might lead quickly to the selection of a grammar that is very rich and complex and that goes well beyond this evidence; in particular, a grammar that provides representations for sentences that are not related by any useful notion of "analogy" or "generalization"[5] to the evidence available. Another approach, along the lines of E, would be to formulate certain analytic procedures, again attributed to the organism as an innate property, which can be applied to the data of sense to produce a grammar. If we interpret the methods of structural linguistics based on segmentation and classification as a "learning theory" (contrary to the intentions of those who developed these methods, so far as I know), then it would be reasonable to regard these as an instance of E, perhaps the most complex version that has yet been developed.

Adopting an approach of the character of R or E, or some combination of the two, S would now be trying to develop a theory of language learning, again in the only rational way. Namely, he would first characterize as closely as he could the states achieved, and then, having made certain assumptions about what is learned, he would attempt to specify a function that assigns appropriate constituents of the achieved final state as a value given the characterization of the data available to the learner. This function would constitute his theory of language learning.

To make the discussion a bit more concrete, consider again examples (1)–(4). Let us suppose that S has moved from the study of the relation between particular stimuli and particular percepts to a study of the grammar that determines an infinite class of such relations by assigning a structural description to each expression, in particular, a representation in terms of phonetic, semantic, and syntactic properties. In the case of (1)–(4), let us say that the grammar he postulates is a familiar transformational grammar of the sort described in chapter 3, which derives the surface structures of (1)–(4) from the initial phrase markers ("deep structures") (1')–(4') respectively (omitting details):

(1') $[_S [_{NP} X] [_{VP}$ appeared $[$ to their wives $]$
 $[_S [_{NP}$ John's friends$] [_{VP}$ to hate one another$]]]]$
(2') Same as (1'), with "Mary" in place of "their wives"
(3') $[_S [_{NP}$ John's friends $] [_{VP}$ appealed $[$ to their wives $]$
 $[_S [_{NP} X] [_{VP}$ to hate one another$]]]]$
(4') Same as (3'), with "Mary" in place of "their wives"

We may take X to be an initial phrase marker variable (an abstract *proform*) which is either replaced in a derivation or placed by an interpretive rule within the scope of a controlling NP. (1) (respectively, (2)) is derived from (1') (respectively, (2')) by the rule of NP-preposing which replaces the matrix subject X by the embedded NP "John's friends." We might think of this operation as leaving a "trace," t, interpreted (by convention) as controlled by the NP that has been moved from this position. In the case of (3), an interpretive rule assigns X to the control of the NP "their wives." The mode of application of this rule is a property of the verb "appeal"; compare (5), where "they" refers to the wives, and (6), where it refers to John's friends:

(5) John's friends made an appeal to their wives that they (should) hate one another
(6) John's friends made a promise to their wives that they would hate one another

Suppose we now assume that "thematic relations" such as agent, instrument, and so on are assigned in a general way in terms of relations expressed in initial phrase mark-

ers and lexical properties, and that other aspects of semantic representation (scope, anaphora, etc.) are determined by
surface structure.[6] Suppose we also have a *reciprocal rule*
that gives the meaning of structures of the form . . . *NP
. . . one another . . .* , when the two phrases in question
are "anaphorically related." This rule is not without its
complications. Thus, compare "John's parents hate one another," "John's grandparents hate one another." [7] In the
case of (3) and (4) the anaphoric relation cannot hold between "John's friends" and "one another," though it can
hold between "their wives" and "one another," and between "Mary" and "one another." (In the latter case, the
reciprocal rule gives gibberish, accounting for the status of
(4).) The condition that determines how this anaphoric
relation may apply is of considerable generality. One might
propose various formulations. I will call it the "specified-
subject condition" (henceforth SSC) and formulate it as
follows:

(7) In a structure of the form [. . . X . . . [Z − WYV] . . .],
     no rule can relate X and Y if Z is the subject of WYV
     and is not controlled by X.

For discussion of the condition and related matters, see
Chomsky (1971, 1973a); also chapter 3, pages 101–3. This
condition prevents an anaphoric relation from holding in
the unwanted cases discussed above. It also applies in many
other cases. Consider the following:

(8) Mary appeared to John's friends to hate one another

(9) (a) John's friends appeared to me to hate us
    (b) John's friends appealed to me to kill us
    (c) I appeared to John's friends to hate us
    (d) I appealed to John's friends to kill us

(10) (a) John's friends saw pictures of one another (themselves)
     (b) John's friends saw Mary's pictures of one another
         (themselves)

(11) (a) who did you see pictures of?

(b) who did you see Mary's pictures of?

(12) (a) I didn't see pictures of many of the children

(b) I didn't see John's pictures of many of the children

(13) (a) Latin is a waste of time for us—to study

(b) Latin is a waste of time for us—for them to teach us

(c) it is a waste of time for us—to study Latin

(d) it is a waste of time for us—for them to teach us Latin

(8) has no interpretation. "John's friends" cannot be related anaphorically to "one another" because of SSC, since the trace left by NP-preposing is controlled by "Mary"; and the reciprocal rule cannot assign an interpretation to the pair *Mary, one another.* (9a) and (9d) are fully grammatical, but (9b) and (9c) have the same oddity as do "I hate us" and "I'll kill us." A rule called by Postal the "unlike-person constraint" (UP) requires that a pair (NP, pronoun) have disjoint reference.[8] UP does not apply in cases (9a) and (9d), being blocked by SSC. If we replace "us" by "them" in (9a–d), grammaticality is reversed throughout for the same reasons, if "them" is interpreted as anaphoric. In the case of (10b), but not (10a), SSC blocks the reciprocal and reflexive rule (under an appropriate definition of "subject," discussed in Chomsky [1972b, 1973a]); thus (10a) is grammatical, but not (10b). The same is true of (11a,b). (12a) may be interpreted as meaning that I saw pictures of few (=not many) of the children, but (12b) cannot be interpreted analogously as meaning that I saw John's pictures of few (not many) of the children. The reason is that SSC blocks the rule assigning the meaning *few* to *not . . . many.* Thus, if (12b) is interpretable at all, it can only be understood as meaning that John's pictures of many of the children are such that I didn't see them. (13a) is a paraphrase of (13c), but (13b) is not well formed, and in particular, is not a paraphrase of the well-

formed (13d). Again SSC explains the difference, if we take the abstract phrase structure to be as indicated by "—" in (13), a conclusion for which there is independent evidence. Thus once again, analogies are blocked by the general condition SSC.

It is worth emphasizing that each of these examples adds further support to the conclusion that approaches of the character of E, which assigns a fundamental role to segmentation, classification, analogy, and generalization, are mistaken in principle. Furthermore, in these examples at least, "semantic explanations" seem beside the point. Thus there is no semantic consideration that blocks the interpretation (13d) for (13b), or that prevents (8) from having the perfectly sensible interpretation "it appears to each of John's friends that Mary hates the other(s)," just as (2) has the interpretation "it appeared to Mary that each of John's friends hates the other(s)." In such cases, we might trivialize the notion "analogy" by building into it some condition equivalent to SSC, but this is clearly beside the point. (Cf. note 5.) Notice that SSC itself might well have a functional or semantic explanation, but this is a different matter. (Cf. Chomsky [1973a] for some discussion.)

Such examples might lead our scientist S to postulate a grammar containing such rules as NP-preposing, reciprocal interpretation, UP, a rule giving the meaning of *not . . . many,* and so on. The rules would be governed by such principles as SSC, and by the general principles of interpretation of initial phrase markers and surface structure mentioned earlier (cf. note 6, and chapter 3, pp. 94–117). If S is inclined to believe that the theory of language learning is of the character of E, he will attempt to design procedures of association, habit formation, induction, or analysis by segmentation and classification that will give this grammar as "output" on the basis of a record of data. A system of procedures will be tested for adequacy in terms of its success in this task. As just noted, an analysis of properties of the grammar suggests that no such approach is feasible and that a theory of the character of R is much more likely to be successful.

Following this line of thinking, S might ask what elements of the grammar might be candidates for universal grammar, the schematism that constitutes an element of the initial state (the property P). The empirical conditions of his problem are plain enough. The variety of languages provides an upper bound on the richness and specificity of the properties that he may assign to universal grammar. The necessity of accounting for acquisition of particular grammars provides a lower bound. Between these bounds lies the theory of language learning, what we have called "LT(H,L)" in chapter 1.

S might propose, for example, that SSC, some of the principles of interpretation of initial phrase markers and surface structures (cf. note 6), the conditions on permissible grammatical rules, and so on are elements of universal grammar, whereas such rules as NP-preposing are specific to English or have properties specific to English. Thus he might conclude that a child must learn the rule of NP-preposing or some of its properties, but need not learn SSC, or the general properties of grammar. Rather, he would have this information available as an element of P, a property of his initial state (though, as noted earlier, this genetically determined property may, as in other familiar cases, function only at a certain maturational stage or under appropriate triggering conditions). The child will thus select a grammar meeting these conditions and containing the rule of NP-preposing with its particular properties. Evidence for the latter rule is considerable, as noted in chapter 3 and references cited there.

Since there has been much confusion about these matters, perhaps it may be useful to recall a still simpler case that illustrates the general point. Consider again the discussion of the principle of structure-dependence of rules discussed in chapter 1, pp. 30–3. For reasons explained there, S would naturally conclude that some feature of the child's initial state leads him to reject the structure-independent hypothesis 1 to account for question formation, selecting instead the more abstract and complex structure-dependent hypothesis 2, on the basis of evidence compatible with both.[9] S might conclude that universal grammar provides a notation for rules that simply does not permit the formulation of structure-independent rules, despite the advantages that they would have for some different organism or device. This conclusion would constitute one part of S's theory of language learning. The example again supports the more general conclusion that a theory of language learning is of the character of R rather than E.

If we sufficiently enrich the system of universal grammar, postulated as an element of the innate property P, it may be possible to account for acquisition of grammar on the basis of the limited evidence available. At least, this seems a feasible prospect (but see note 4).

Suppose that S succeeds in developing a tentative theory of learning for common sense and for language. If my guess is right, these would be of the character of R; that is, they would involve fixed and highly restrictive schemata which come into operation under limited conditions of exposure to data, determine the interpretation of these data as experience, and lead to the selection of systems of rules (grammar, common sense) which are put to use in human action and interaction. It is not excluded that the schematisms for grammar and for common sense have nontrivial common elements, and S will naturally search for these.[10] There may be "generalized learning strategies" that form part of both of these empirical theories. On the other hand, it seems likely that these schematisms will have unique elements as well, just as common sense may well have special devices to distinguish faces from other geometrical objects. There is no reason to expect to find in the property P significant analogues to the analyzing mechanisms for identification of faces or determination of line, angle, and motion.[11] There is no reason to expect that the principle of structure-dependence or SSC will appear in the theory of common sense. At some sufficiently abstract level, one may find analogies; S might ask whether the system for identifying faces involves an abstract representation or model and a "transformational system" of projection. But as a scientist, S would have no dogmatic beliefs as to the character of the various systems of learning and their interrelation. Rather, this would be an empirical problem that he would hope to solve.

To the extent that S succeeds in characterizing the innate properties of mind that make possible the learning of grammar and common sense, he would be able to explain why these systems are qualitatively so different from the third cognitive structure mentioned earlier, knowledge of physics. That is, he would now regard the properties of mind that underlie the acquisition of language and common sense as biological properties of the organism, on a par in this respect with those that enable a bird to build a nest or reproduce a characteristic song; or, for that matter, comparable to the properties that account for the development of particular organs of the body. (Cf. chapter 1.) Humans are not specially adapted, in the same way, to the learning of physics.

Parenthetically, S might conclude that something similar is true of physics as well. The human mind is a biologically given system with certain powers and limits. As Charles Sanders Peirce argued, "Man's mind has a natural adaptation to imagining correct theories of some kinds. . . . If man had not the gift of a mind adapted to his requirements, he could not have acquired any knowledge" (ed. Tomas, 1957). The fact that "admissible hypotheses" are available to this specific biological system accounts for its ability to construct rich and complex explanatory theories. But the same properties of mind that provide admissible hypotheses may well exclude other successful theories as unintelligible to humans. Some theories might simply not be among the admissible hypotheses determined by the specific properties of mind that adapt us "to imagining correct theories of some kinds," though these theories might be accessible to a differently organized intelligence. Or these theories might be so remote in an accessibility ordering of admissible hypotheses that they cannot be constructed under actual empirical conditions, though for a differently structured mind they might be easily accessible.

If S regards humans as part of the natural world, such speculations will seem by no means strange or incomprehensible to him, and he might in fact attempt to investigate them and establish specific conclusions about these matters through scientific inquiry. In pursuing this effort, he would note that while man's mind is no doubt adapted to his requirements, there is no reason to suppose that discovery of scientific theories in particular domains is among the requirements met through natural selection. S might go on to develop a theory of problems and mysteries for the human organism. There would be problems in domains where admissible (or readily accessible) hypotheses are close to correct, and mysteries elsewhere—for this organism. To take a specific case, consider the question of causation of behavior discussed briefly in chapter 1. It might be that our inability to deal with this question reflects a temporary condition of ignorance, a defect that can be overcome, in principle, as science progresses. But S might discover that this optimistic view is incorrect and that the human mind is inherently incapable of developing scientific understanding of the processes by which it itself functions in certain domains. Kant suggested that the "schematism of our understanding, in its application to appearances and their mere form, is an art concealed in the depths of the human soul, whose real modes of activity nature is hardly likely ever to allow us to discover, and to have open to our gaze" (trans. Kemp,

1958). Perhaps this is true, in some respects at least. There is nothing contradictory in the belief that investigation of the inherent intellectual capacities of a specific biological organism, humans, might lead S—even if S is human himself—to a scientific demonstration that some possible sciences lie beyond human grasp, perhaps the science of causation of behavior among them. I am not urging this conclusion, but merely noting that it is not ruled out *a priori.*

Returning to the more comfortable matter of problems that do not seem to be mysteries, let us suppose that S has now established the basis for the fundamental distinction between grammar and common sense, on the one hand, and knowledge of physics, on the other. Though the latter, too, is derived on the basis of specific properties of mind, it does not reflect these properties in the same way as language and common sense do. Hence the vast qualitative difference in relative accessibility.

S could not, I believe, determine that common sense and grammar are qualitatively different in this respect from physics merely by inspecting the three cognitive structures that he has been led to attribute to humans within his comprehensive theory of their attained intellectual organization. If our present beliefs are near correct, the grammar of language is a highly intricate system of rules and principles. There is no absolute sense of the notion "simplicity" in terms of which grammar is "simpler" than, say, atomic physics, and although common sense has not been investigated in a comparable way, much the same may well be true in this case. The qualitative differences that S would discover in his investigation of humans doubtless reflect the structure of the mind as a contingent biological system. This is the only rational conclusion, I believe.

This Peircean view of acquisition of cognitive structures should not be strange to physiological psychologists, at least. (Cf. chapter 1, pp. 8–9.) It might be suggested that much of learning theory has been investigating an artifact— "unnatural" learning under experimental conditions devised so as to be outside the organism's inherent capacities, conditions which thus provide smooth learning curves and the like, but perhaps tell us very little about the organisms studied.[12]

When a learning theory is formulated with sufficient precision, it becomes possible to ask whether it is capable in principle of accounting for the attainment of a state of intellectual organization or a cognitive structure that we have reason to postulate for the mature organism. Suppose, for example, that a specific learning theory can be demonstrated to have the following property: an otherwise unstructured system that can be modified in accordance with the mechanisms of this theory can approach, in the limit, any finite-state device that produces strings left to right as it shifts from state to state, but nothing other than such a device. Since it is well known that even the syntax of extremely simple systems (e.g., propositional calculus) cannot be represented by such a device and that the syntax of language surely cannot, we can conclude at once that the learning theory is inadequate as a theory of language learning.[13] Thus a theory which predicts convergence towards demonstrably inadequate systems must obviously be rejected as a theory of the actual attainment of systems that are far richer. In this case, then, S could go beyond the conclusion that general learning theories of known sorts are completely implausible.

In fact, the scientist S, if indeed unencumbered by our intellectual tradition, would, I think, be unlikely ever to have considered the notion that there is a "theory of learning" in any interesting sense. Thus, suppose that there is a general theory of learning that applies to rats as well as humans, and that humans differ from rats simply in that they make use of its mechanisms more rapidly, fully, and effectively, and can thus attain more complex states by means of the devices postulated in this theory. We would then conclude that humans must be as far superior to rats in maze-running ability as they are in ability to acquire language. But this is grossly false. Similar observations would lead a rational scientist to conclude at once that the human ability to learn language involves a special faculty or cognitive system of some sort, distinct from the cognitive system that underlies the ability to learn how to run a maze, and unavailable to rats or, as far as we know, any other organism.[14] For if language were simply acquired by a "generalized learning strategy" that applies as well in other domains (say, maze running), we would expect other organisms that are comparable to humans in these other domains (and thus, by assumption, use strategies similar to those employed by humans in these domains) to have comparable language-acquisition ability as well. (Cf. pp. 18, 19.)

The properties of common sense that are involved in the special human ability (if such exists) to deal with faces as compared with other geometrical figures, the properties of universal grammar, the properties that distinguish grammar and common sense from knowledge of physics, would also lead S to reject the hypothesis that there is a general learning theory, common to all organisms, undifferentiated in a single organism with respect to cognitive domain. These observations would lead S to the natural conclusion that the intellectual organization of a mature human is a complex integrated system that includes cognitive structures that are acquired on the basis of rather specific initial adaptations. The nontrivial content of the "theory of learning" would be given by specifying these initial adaptations and the ways in which they change through maturation and experience. The steady states that are attained uniformly and rapidly should give particular insight into the nature of the organism. These steady states might well reflect quite different physiological properties and structures. There is little reason to suppose that there are "laws of learning" of any substance and generality that account for the acquisition of these complex and specific steady states, or for the integration of cognitive structures that constitute the mature mind.

Problems of acquisition of knowledge and belief have generally been investigated in a way that to a natural scientist might seem rather perverse. There has been little attention to the problem of characterizing "what is learned." Rather, certain *a priori* assumptions have been presented as to how learning takes place: principles of association, habit formation, and the like. These *a priori* assumptions have been pursued with speculative and experimental studies of the systems that might be acquired by these methods, with virtually no effort to establish that the systems that can be acquired are those that are acquired. A more natural approach, it seems to me, is the one sketched above: analysis of the states attained, followed by attempts to determine the nature of systems capable of attaining these states under given conditions of time and access to data, and investigation of the physical basis for these achievements, whatever it may be.

Psychologists sometimes go so far as to define their discipline so as to exclude consideration of the states attained. Thus it is common to distinguish "linguistics," taken as the study of grammar, from "psychology," which is concerned with behavior and learning.[15] To a scientist following the course outlined for S, this would seem a senseless distinction. Linguistics is simply that part of psychology that is concerned with one specific class of steady states, the cognitive structures that are employed in speaking and understanding. The study of language learning is concerned with the acquisition of such cognitive structures, and the study of behavior is concerned with the ways in which they are put to use. It is self-defeating to construct a discipline that is concerned with use and attainment of some cognitive structure, but that excludes consideration of the structure itself.

Equally misleading, I think, is the tendency in philosophical discussion to speculate on the ways in which language and its use might be taught. Language is not really taught, for the most part. Rather, it is learned, by mere exposure to the data. No one has been taught the principle of structure-dependence of rules, or SSC, or language-specific properties of such rules as NP-preposing. Nor is there any reason to suppose that people are taught the meaning of words. It may be true that "teaching someone how to use an expression is the native soil from which talk about meaning has grown," [16] but this historical comment gives little reason to suppose that explanations of meaning are exhausted, or even advanced, by an account of teaching. The study of how a system is learned cannot be identified with the study of how it is taught; nor can we assume that what is learned has been taught.

To consider an analogy that is perhaps not too remote, consider what happens when I turn on the ignition in my automobile. A change of state takes place. We might investigate the characteristics of the new state by examining fumes from the exhaust, the vibration level, the motion of the car when I press the accelerator, and so on. A careful study of the interaction between me and the car that led to the attainment of this new state would not be very illuminating. Similarly, certain interactions between me and my child result in his learning (hence knowing) English. We can learn something about this new state in ways outlined earlier.[17] But a careful study of the interactions between me and my child that result in his attaining this new state might give little insight into what it is that he has learned or what kind of an organism he is.

No doubt John Austin (1940) is correct in saying that when we are asked, "What is the meaning of (the word)

rat?" we can reply in words or get the questioner to imagine an experience or situation in which the word would
or would not be used. But from this observation we cannot
go on to conclude, as he does, that this description tells us
all that we might reasonably want to know about the meaning of the word. It seems that he is relying on the implicit
assumption that when we have described how we might
teach, we need no longer ask what is learned. Austin is thus
limiting himself to a description of turning on the ignition,
whereas the model of language that he is condemning in
these remarks is concerned rather to give an account of the
state of the system that is activated by these manipulations.

Let us ask finally how S might go about describing the
results of his inquiries. Specifically, consider the much-de-
bated question whether the cognitive structures S is attributing to the organism constitute some kind of belief or
knowledge.

Consider first the case of common sense. S is attributing
to his subject a system of rules and principles concerning
the organization and behavior of objects. S claims that his
subject differs from a rock or a bird in that this cognitive
structure is an element of his final state. Since the subject
is a physical organism, the system attributed to him must
have a finite representation. Evidently, there are many
conceivable finite representations of the system, however
much we know about it, but S will not therefore conclude
that there is no way to choose among these on empirical
grounds. The empirical evidence is never exhausted. Furthermore, discoveries now unanticipated may reveal the
relevance of certain types of evidence that seem now to
have no bearing on the issue. S might arrive at a general
principle of organization that excludes some finite representations but not others, and he might show that acquisition of cognitive structures in this and other cases can be
explained on the assumption that this general principle is

operative as an innate schematism. Such a demonstration would provide evidence in support of a finite representation that observes the principle, and against another finite representation that violates it. In this and innumerable other ways S might try to determine which of the various imaginable finite representations of the cognitive system are plausible candidates for a theory of the final state of his subject. On the basis of a postulated representation of a cognitive system, and other assumptions about information processing, S will try to explain many phenomena, such as why it is that his subject takes two presentations to be the same face but not two others. S will thus try to account for the fact that his subject believes he is seeing the same face twice. One might imagine various direct or indirect ways in which such specific beliefs and expectations could be tested.

S might refer to the postulated cognitive structure as a "system of beliefs." The finite representation postulated as the subject's characterization of his system of beliefs and many beliefs that are implied by it will be unconscious, no doubt, and inaccessible to introspection. In many instances, the subject does express beliefs. S will explain this fact by showing how these expressed beliefs follow from the finite representation. Suppose that the subject expresses beliefs that do not follow, or rejects beliefs that do, or neither accepts nor rejects beliefs that are assigned a definite status under this characterization, or acts in such a way that S must attribute to him beliefs that are inconsistent with the characterization. Then S will try to explain this result in terms of the interaction of other systems with the cognitive system of belief; failing in this effort, he will have to revise the finite representation.[18]

It may be expected that conscious beliefs will form a scattered and probably uninteresting subpart of the full cognitive structure. At least, if this is so, there should be no reason for surprise. Nor do I see any objection to S's practice in referring to the cognitive structure attributed to the subject as a system of beliefs.

Consider now the case of grammar. If S speaks English, he will say that some of his subjects have "learned French" and now "know French." Furthermore, in many specific instances, they can articulate their knowledge, as knowledge that so-and-so. Again, the set of such cases is unlikely to be of much interest in itself. S will attempt to explain these instances by showing how they follow from the grammar of French, interacting with other cognitive structures. In this way, he will try to account for facts analogous (for French) to those mentioned earlier (cf. (1)–(13)). The problems of confirmation and choice of theories are analogous to those that arise in the case of investigation of common sense.

Obviously, the grammar is not in itself a theory of performance (behavior). It is, however, proper for S to propose that the grammar is a component of such a theory and to proceed at this point to construct a theory of interaction of structures that would serve as a theory of performance for his subjects.[19] S might refer to the grammar attributed to the speaker as a representation (or model) of his knowledge of his language. S might also want to say that the subject who knows the language knows the grammar, and that in his initial state he knew universal grammar. Thus S's subject differs from an English speaker, a rock, or a bird in that he knows the grammar of French (to use the suggested terminology). He is like an English speaker, and different from a rock or a bird, in that in his initial state he knew universal grammar.

Since some might object to this terminology, S might prefer to invent some technical terms. Let us say that if a speaker knows the language L then he *cognizes* L. Furthermore, he cognizes the linguistic facts that he knows (in any uncontroversial sense of "know") and he cognizes the principles and rules of his internalized grammar, both those that might be brought to awareness and those that are forever hidden from consciousness. Furthermore, he cognizes the principles that underlie the acquisition of language in the first place, the principles of universal grammar (assuming that the approach outlined earlier is correct). Thus a person who knows English cognizes certain facts, for example, that necessarily bachelors are unmarried and that "is" goes with singular subjects. He also cognizes that specific rules are ordered in a certain way relative to one another. Furthermore, the person cognizes that transformations apply in a cyclic ordering and obey SSC, that initial phrase markers and surface structures contribute to semantic interpretation in ways described earlier, and that transformations are structure-dependent. The latter examples constitute part of "innate cognization" (assuming that the theory suggested earlier is correct).

If we decide to use the word "know" in a narrow sense, restricting it to conscious "knowledge of" or to "knowing how" ("why, who . . . ," and so on) as this notion is often construed, then "knowledge of" as in "knowledge of language" will have to be explicated in terms of the new technical vocabulary, so it appears.[20] In this usage, what is "known" will be a rather ill-defined and, perhaps, a scattered and chaotic subpart of the coherent and important systems and structures that are cognized. For psychology, the important notion will be "cognize," not "know."

Or, we might make the decision to sharpen and perhaps extend the term "know" so that it has just the properties of "cognize," thus eliminating the new terminology. Then we will be able to explain explicit knowledge of certain facts by showing how these cases are related to the system of "tacit knowledge." [21]

I doubt that this question can be settled by consideration of "ordinary usage," which seems to me vague and inexplicit at just the crucial points. The philosophical tradition is varied. Leibniz, for one, spoke of unconscious knowledge, though he seems to have regarded all knowledge as accessible to consciousness. Hume described instincts as those parts of an animal's "knowledge" that it "derive[s] from the original hand of nature," in contrast to the "parts of knowledge" that it learns from observation.

It seems to me that the principles that determine our systems of knowledge and belief interact so completely and inseparably with "our knowledge," in anyone's sense of this term, that it would be difficult to develop a coherent account that would isolate "true knowledge." However, it is unclear that more than terminology is at stake here. Thus S might choose to abandon the terms "knowledge" and even "knowledge of language" (if some find that offensive), while noting that there is little warrant in ordinary usage for these decisions. If so, he will speak of acquiring, cognizing, and competence, instead of learning, knowing, and knowledge.

As long as we are clear about what we are doing, either approach seems to me quite all right. "Provided we agree about the thing, it is needless to dispute about the terms" (Hume).

Consider now some of the objections that have been raised to the approach sketched above. I cannot survey the literature here, but will mention a few cases that I think are typical. I will not consider further the question that some philosophers seem to feel is crucial, namely, whether the term "knowledge" is properly used in these accounts.

Robert Schwartz argues that "the fact that we can specify [a subject's] competence in terms of a formal system of generative rules does not in itself imply that [he] has represented a *corresponding* system in him." [22] This observation is surely correct. No nontrivial theory is ever "implied" by the evidence available. But Schwartz apparently wants to say something beyond this truism. He suggests the following example to illustrate the "messy issue" that he thinks arises. Suppose a certain device, D, labels spheres "+" if their density is greater than 1 and "−" if their density is less. Suppose that a system of equations E is proposed, involving relations between volume, density, weight, and so on, which describes the output of D. But, Schwartz notes, D "might not employ a set of principles anything like [E]." Thus it might never consider weight, volume, and so on, but might contain a liquid of density 1 and label "+" any sphere that sinks, and "−" any sphere that floats. "Would it be reasonable to claim that our equations [E] are internally represented in this machine?" His answer is that it would not, even though "in some sense the liquid in the machine could be held to 'stand for' the equations [E]."

Suppose that S, observing D, concluded that its "cognitive state" involves calculations of the sort expressed in E. Further investigation might convince S that this conclusion is wrong and that a very different principle is employed, namely, the one Schwartz suggests. It would not, of course, be "reasonable" to persist in maintaining that D "employ[s] a set of principles anything like [E]," since this conclusion has been refuted. The fact that E continues to describe input-output relations correctly is uninteresting to S, once he has discovered the actual principles employed. There is no "messy issue" here.

Of course, if S were simply satisfied to say that E describes input-output relations, he would not have proceeded with further investigation to determine whether D actually employs principles like E. But as a scientist, S would have been interested to discover what it is about D that makes E an accurate description. To determine this, he might put forth the working hypothesis that D actually calculates in accordance with E, or that E enters in some important way into the actual performance of D. And he would then seek evidence bearing on this hypothesis. He would be interested to discover that this hypothesis is false. No such inquiry would occur to someone who was so lacking in curiosity as to leave the matter with the statement that E correctly describes regularities in D's behavior. But there seems no problem of principle here.

Schwartz observes that in the case of a person riding a bicycle, any specific proposal as to the organization of the system of habits and skills involved "is subject to doubt, and as long as such doubt remains, care must be taken in interpreting the assertion that the laws of physics [internally represented in some specific fashion] model [the subject's] bicycle skills." Again, the observation is correct. Since nontrivial theories are not "implied" by data, care must always be taken when they are proposed. I see absolutely no interest in this observation, nor should S pay the least attention to it. He already knew that he was engaged in empirical research. Schwartz seems to feel that something more is at stake, but he gives no indication of what it may be, and gives no reference to any work to which these strictures seem at all relevant.

The preceding example has to do with S's theory of common sense, but Schwartz applies the argument as well to his theory of grammar. He notes that "any true description of regularities of or within the set of grammatical sentences will tautologically be true of the output of [the subject's] competence." If we find a specific regularity in the subject's language, then he "might be said to 'know' this regularity but only in the sense that he will consider strings that violate this rule ungrammatical." "These regularities then are regularities true of what [the subject] knows (the class of grammatical sentences) and not regularities he knows." Insofar as Schwartz is simply proposing a usage for the term "know," I see no interest in pursuing the discussion, except to point out that it seems curious to accept "X knows the class of grammatical sentences" (and, I suppose, "X has learned rules that specify this class," i.e., "X has learned a grammar") but not "X knows the rules of his grammar."

Let us replace "know" by "cognize" in the preceding discussion, to avoid the terminological issue. Should we say, then, that the subject cognizes the rules and regularities only in the sense that he considers strings that violate them ungrammatical? Only if we are so lacking in curiosity as to be unwilling to try to determine whether a particular theory about the subject is in fact correct. If S were satisfied to say only that some theory describes regularities true of the class of sentences that the subject cognizes, he would not conduct further investigation to choose between this theory and some other theory describing the class of sentences in terms of some different system of rules. But, there surely are ways of investigating alternative theories. Thus consider the theory of English sketched earlier. S might propose that the reciprocal rule is a transformational rule moving "each" and "one" to give "each other" and "one another" from initial phrase markers of the form *each of NP . . . the other, one of NP . . . the other.* His colleague S′ might propose rather that "each other" and "one another" are base-derived and interpreted by a semantic rule. S″ might propose that the underlying structures are conjunctions.[23] If S, S′, and S″ are satisfied to observe that their theories describe correctly certain regularities, then further investigation stops. If they proceed, in the manner of any scientist, to attribute cognitive structures differing in these respects to their subjects, they will then proceed to seek other data to choose among these hypotheses.

The evidence might be quite varied. For example, it might derive from other languages. Thus suppose that postulating a transformational rule violates a certain principle U, and that by taking U (which, say, is otherwise confirmed) to be part of universal grammar, we can explain certain facts in other languages just as SSC serves to explain certain facts in English. On the empirical assumption of uniformity among humans with respect to language acquisition, this evidence would serve to counter S's assumption that the English-speaking subjects are, in fact, making use of a cognitive structure that involves a transformational movement rule. Thus the contrary theories of S' and perhaps S'' receive some indirect, but valuable, empirical confirmation. Many other kinds of evidence can be sought.

S, S', and S'' have every reason to take their hypotheses to be working hypotheses concerning the steady state attained by their subject and thus subject to further confirmation or disconfirmation. Surely there can be no general objection to the normal "realist" assumptions of any scientist in this case (though, obviously, care must be taken, etc.).

Perhaps what Schwartz has in mind is something different. Perhaps he has in mind a case in which two theories are compatible with all the evidence that might in principle be obtained. If so, S should simply dismiss this consideration, as any working scientist would. The notion "all the evidence that might in principle be obtained" surely requires some explanation. I doubt that any sense can be made of it. Furthermore, even if we accept it as meaningful, nothing follows with regard to S's enterprise. In the real world, he will never have exhausted the evidence, and with diligence and imagination can seek new evidence to select between empirically distinguishable theories.

Suppose that S comes up with several theories as the best ones he can devise without examination of the internal structure of his subjects. Then he will say, regretfully, that he cannot determine on the basis of the evidence available to him which (if any) of these theories correctly characterizes the actual internal structure. In Schwartz's sphere example, S will not be able to determine whether E or rather the account in terms of a liquid of density 1 is the correct theory. As in the case of the spheres, so in the case of language: S will not be perplexed about the nature of the theories he is proposing and their relation to fact; rather, he will be annoyed that he cannot (by hypothesis) proceed to choose among theories that seem plausible. In any event, there seems no reason for S to abandon the standard procedure of any scientist, with its conventional realist assumptions, in such cases as these.

Schwartz then proceeds to raise certain objections to the study of language learning as pursued by S. He feels that "the psychologically interesting question is whether the factors that shape the learning of language are specific to language or whether they are general features of the learning apparatus." He argues that "the child develops many skills and competences, acquires knowledge of relationships and regularities in his environment, learns games and complex patterns of social behavior, etc., in essentially the same 'untaught' manner he learns language," and in these cases too standard behavioral theories seem inadequate. Yet it would, he believes, "seem implausible to claim distinct innate schemata responsible for each." He further suspects that there will be "no *interesting* version" of the claim that children "would encounter enormous . . . difficulty learning a language not of the predestined form," since children acquire complex symbol systems that "do not fit the natural language mold." It would, he argues, be "circular" to claim simply that "any symbol system that violates the Chomskian canons is not a language and thus outside the scope of the claim."

These remarks are offered in criticism of "Chomsky's approach to language-learning," namely, the one sketched earlier. Taking his comments in turn, it would surely be interesting to determine whether the factors that shape language learning are specific or general, though it is curious to insist that this is "*the* psychologically interesting question." Thus suppose the question to be resolved by elementary observations such as those noted earlier (cf. pp. 18–19, 158–9), which suggest that the factors that shape language learning are specific. Are there no psychologically interesting questions left? Perhaps this is true for someone wedded to traditional dogma, but surely many questions remain for a scientist, who would be interested to discover the detailed character of the factors that are involved in acquiring various cognitive structures.

The failure of familiar learning theories to account for cognitive structures apart from language is repeatedly emphasized in the work that Schwartz is criticizing. Noting that other systems are learned "untaught" and have complex properties, uniform among learners, one would naturally proceed as outlined earlier in each such domain: determine the character of the system acquired, the evidence on the basis of which it was acquired, and the innate factors that make possible the acquisition of this system on the basis of the available evidence. Thus, if the principles of structure-dependence, SSC, and so on appear to be properties of the acquired system of language, we will attempt to account for this fact by postulating an innate mechanism capable of determining these principles on the basis of the available data; for reasons already discussed, it seems plausible to regard these principles as comparable to those that determine the nature and function of organs. In other domains, we find quite different properties and will proceed in a comparable way, postulating whatever innate structures are required to explain the facts. Schwartz believes that it is "implausible" to postulate distinct innate schemata for different "skills and competences," but since he offers no arguments, we may disregard the judgment. It has no more weight than the unargued belief that embryos learn to have eyes or that people learn to organize perceptual space by the mechanisms involved in word association. There is no place for such dogmatic claims. Schwartz never considers any of the obvious reasons for doubting that there is an undifferentiated learning theory, nor does he give any argument for his beliefs apart from the observation that many skills and competences are learned untaught, from which we can conclude only that a theory that presupposes teaching is wrong.

Schwartz's claim of "circularity" is obviously in error. When S proposes that universal grammar has certain properties, he is advancing an empirical hypothesis. We may test it by studying the facts of language. In principle, we might test the proposal by asking whether a child will use language in accordance with the principles put forth even in the absence of evidence that these principles apply, as in the cases discussed earlier. Thus, observing that no child ever makes the mistake of producing (14) instead of (15), corresponding to the declarative (16), S might postulate that a property of the child's initial state excludes the structure-independent hypothesis 1 of chapter 1 (p. 31) as unformulable.

> (14) is the man who tall is in the room?
>
> (15) is the man who is tall is in the room?
>
> (16) the man who is tall is in the room

S might then proceed to ask whether other phenomena obey the principle advanced, or he might proceed in principle to construct an appropriate experimental situation in which such examples as (14) and (15) are never presented, and ask whether subjects invariably use the structure-dependent rule that gives (15) rather than (14). If so, he will have gained confirming evidence for the empirical hypothesis that the principle of structure-dependence is part of universal grammar, since that assumption provides an explanation for the facts. Similar remarks apply in the case of the more complex examples discussed earlier. In practice, because of conditions of time and feasibility, more indirect tests must be sought, but the logic of the situation is clear enough, and even the existence of tests that could be used in principle suffices to refute the charge of circularity.

There is good reason to anticipate that further research will support the conclusion that principles of the sort discussed earlier do constitute part of the innate schematism for language acquisition. Thus it is surely implausible to suppose that in the cases in question (e.g., (14) and (15)), every child has had sufficient relevant experience with appropriate examples. On the contrary, it is often a difficult problem even to discover examples that bear on the hypotheses in question (cf. SSC.) Yet if we find that people observe these principles, we must seek an explanation for this fact. The only explanation that has been proposed, to my knowledge, is the one suggested before: the principles belong to universal grammar, which is an element of the "initial state." But whether this proposal is right or wrong, there can be no doubt that the project outlined is an empirical one, at every step. Hence the charge of circularity is surely false. If it were justified, there would be no point in testing specific proposals, say, that SSC or the principle of structure-dependence belongs to universal grammar. Being tautological, the proposals could not be false.

For similar reasons, we can readily see why there might be—and indeed, already is—an "interesting version" of the hypothesis that children would encounter considerable difficulty in learning languages that violated postulated universals, contrary to Schwartz's contention. At least this is true if we take an "interesting version" of the hypothesis to be one that has far-reaching empirical consequences and considerable explanatory value.

It is easy to see where Schwartz's argument goes astray. In the first place, he is overlooking the fact that we have certain antecedently clear cases of language, as distinct from maze running, basket weaving, topographical orientation, recognition of faces or melodies, use of maps, and so on. We cannot arbitrarily decide that "language" is whatever meets some canons we propose. Thus we cannot simply stipulate that rules are structure-independent, then concluding that examples such as (14) and (15) are not relevant to "language" as determined by this stipulation. Of course, there are unclear cases as well, and there is the constant problem of determining when a theory must be abandoned in the face of apparent counterevidence (see note 18), or when cognitive domains have been improperly delimited in the first place. But these are hardly new problems unique to this enterprise. On the contrary, they arise constantly in any rational inquiry.

Furthermore, quite apart from the matter of antecedently clear cases, recall that S is attempting to map out the full system of cognitive structures for his subject, determining their character and interaction, at each step making certain idealizations and advancing empirical hypotheses, hence taking steps that are not "implied" by his data, naturally. If he finds that other symbol systems "do not fit the natural language mold," he will try to determine what mold they do fit. He will study their character and the basis for their acquisition, proceeding in the same manner as in his study of language, untroubled by dogmatic beliefs about the "uniformity" of learning.

Ultimately, S will hope to find that symbol systems that fit different molds also have different neural representations, and that the various innate factors postulated to account for the facts will also, where distinct, have different physical representations. Little is known as yet, but there is at least evidence that essential linguistic structures and functions are normally represented in the left hemisphere, and that some of the other "symbol systems" that Schwartz (following Goodman) irrelevantly introduces into the discussion are primarily controlled by the right hemisphere, perhaps in areas homologous to the language centers (nonspeech sounds, speech sounds not used in the context of speech, melodies, etc.); cf. chapter 2, note 8. There also appear to be some differences in the stage of maturation at which various centers are established in their function (recent work on face recognition reported by Susan Carey is suggestive in this regard). Whether or not these tentative proposals prove correct on further investigation, clearly they are of the sort that a scientist concerned with symbol systems, their character, interaction, and acquisition, should explore. Schwartz seems to believe that any departure from the "natural language mold" in the case of other symbol systems must be accidental—that is that any innate schematism for language learning must simply be a general schematism for learning. But he has offered no argument whatsoever for this contention, and he simply ignores the many obvious problems it faces, some mentioned earlier.

The concerns about theory and evidence that Schwartz expresses and his objections to the program outlined earlier are typical of much recent discussion. But the objections have no foundation and the concerns, where justified at all, have no bearing on the issues, so far as I can see, in that they apply in a comparable way to any variety of empirical inquiry. They are worth considering in detail only because of the insight they provide into empiricist assumptions.

If Schwartz's claims on these matters had any merit, they should apply as well to the study of physical organs. Suppose that S develops a theory T dealing with the structure and function of the human eye, and postulates the innate factors F to account for the growth of an organ satisfying T. Suppose now that he turns his attention to the liver. Paraphrasing Schwartz, we might argue that it is "implausible" to postulate distinct innate factors F' (which, along with F and others, constitute the genetic coding that determines the nature of the organism) to account for the growth of the liver. After all, the eye and the liver are both organs, and it would be "circular" to claim that any organ not satisfying T is not an eye "and thus outside the scope of the claim" embodied in F. Or, suppose that S decides to study the eyes of mammals and insects, postulating different genetic mechanisms to account for the striking differences in the final states attained and the pattern of development. Following Schwartz, we counter that he has committed a logical error, since the insect eye is also an eye and it would be circular to claim that an organ that violates the theory of the mammalian eye is not a mammalian eye "and thus outside the scope of the claim" concerning the basis for its development. Plainly, none of this can be taken seriously.

It is a question of fact whether map reading and language use involve the same or similar mechanisms (e.g., SSC, the principle of the transformational cycle, etc.), and whether the cognitive structures involved develop on the basis of the same or similar innate factors. The observation that we call both language and maps "symbol systems" contributes no more to an inquiry into their nature, function, and origin than the observation that the mammalian and the insect eye are called "eyes" or that the eye and the liver are called "organs." Similarly, the observation that both symbol systems are learned is as informative as the observation that both organs develop. No conceptual argument can establish that a scientist is wrong to postulate fundamentally different cognitive or physical structures, or to attempt to explain these differences on the basis of distinct innate factors. An empirical argument must be brought to bear. This Schwartz entirely fails to do. Consequently, his discussion is simply beside the point.

Similar arguments are developed in Atherton and Schwartz (1974). Much of their discussion is devoted to refutation of positions on "innateness" that have never appeared in the literature, to my knowledge. At the very end, they point out that the psychologist "must postulate

the existence of whatever capacities can be shown necessary for language mastery." But, they assert, "to argue
that the features responsible for natural language are so
highly task-specific that they can be separated from cognitive life in general would be to strip the claim that natural language is innately *species*-specific of most of its
metaphysical as well as its theoretical and philosophical
interest." This remark, which ends the paper, is the only
observation they make which has any real bearing on S's
program (or familiar variants of it in earlier discussion),
apart from points already discussed.

But there is a crucial logical slip in their formulation.
They assume without argument that if the features responsible for natural language are "highly task-specific"
then these features "can be separated from cognitive life
in general." But this does not follow. Correspondingly, the
assumption that the eye involves highly specific mechanisms does not imply that "the features responsible for
[the eye]" can be separated from the general (physical or
cognitive) functioning of the organism. Given empiricist
prejudice, the argument is perhaps comprehensible. Thus,
on these assumptions, "cognitive life in general" is a system developed incrementally by means of association, conditioning, habit formation, generalization, induction, abstraction of certain specific kinds that have been proposed
(I omit, again, vacuous formulations of empiricist theory).
Any highly specific system developed on the basis of other
principles will therefore be "separated from cognitive life
in general." Abandoning empiricist prejudice, we will explore various cognitive domains, attempting to map out
their structures, interaction, and function and to determine the "features responsible" for the cognitive structures that develop. As in the case of the physical structure
of an organism, so in the case of its cognitive organization,
the discovery that some cognitive structure develops on
the basis of highly specific features implies nothing about

its relations, however intimate, to other structures that enter into the organism's cognitive state.

As for the notion of metaphysical, theoretical, or philosophical interest, since Atherton and Schwartz do not explain what they mean, I will drop the matter.

W. V. O. Quine argues along somewhat similar lines in his discussion of methodological problems of linguistics in Quine (1972). In a familiar terminology, grammars are said to be "weakly equivalent" if they generate the same set of sentences and "strongly equivalent" if they generate as well the same set of structural descriptions. Quine asks us to consider the following situation. Suppose that two grammars are "extensionally equivalent" over the class of sentences, that is, weakly equivalent. Suppose further that "both systems *fit* the behavior . . . of all us native speakers of English." Plainly these systems do not "guide" behavior in the sense that "the behaver knows the rule and can state it" and this knowledge "causes" the behavior ("guiding is a matter of cause and effect").[24] But it would be wrong, Quine holds, to suggest that English speech might be "rule-guided" in some other sense, that is, unconsciously. In his view, it is senseless to say that "two extensionally equivalent [weakly equivalent] systems of grammatical rules need not be equally correct" and that "the right rules are the rules that the native speakers themselves have somehow implicitly in mind." What he rejects is the doctrine that "imputes to the natives an unconscious preference for one system of rules over another, equally unconscious, which is extensionally equivalent to it." Quine accepts the notion of

> implicit and unconscious conformity to a rule, when this is merely a question of fitting. Bodies obey, in this sense, the law of falling bodies, and English speakers obey, in this sense, any and all of the extensionally equivalent systems of grammar that demarcate the right totality of well-formed English sentences. These

are acceptably clear dispositions on the part of bodies and English speakers.

What Quine questions is my "intermediate notion of rules as heeded inarticulately."

The same considerations, Quine argues, bear on the doctrine of linguistic universals. "Timely reflection on method and evidence should tend to stifle much of the talk of linguistic universals," he suggests, since such reflection will reveal that there are distinct but extensionally equivalent grammars and it may be impossible to determine unequivocally when apparent uniformities are simply an artifact of the translation process.

Quine believes that there is considerable "folly" in the proposals he criticizes, though it can be cured in time by "conscientious reflection on method and evidence." He is willing to concede that some course of inquiry might "convince us that there is indeed an unarticulated system of grammatical rules which is somehow implicit in the native mind in a way that an extensionally equivalent system is not." But he feels that "clarification of criteria" has not been given sufficiently for this "enigmatic doctrine."

One can certainly sympathize with Quine's "plea against absolutism" and his desire for clarification of criteria. But nothing in his account suggests that there is any problem here that has so far gone unrecognized, or that there is any folly to be cured. Specifically, I find no argument against S's procedure (which, of course, is familiar from earlier accounts), or, for that matter, against any account that appears in the literature.

Consider one of the few relevant concrete cases that Quine discusses, namely, the problem of choosing between two extensionally equivalent grammars, one of which assigns to the sentence *ABC* the immediate constituents *AB–C* and the other, *A–BC*. Is there some "enigma" here? I think not, though there are surely problems. Proposals for resolving the problems have been advanced in the literature of generative grammar since the outset, and I think that they are right in principle, though sometimes difficult to apply in practice.

Suppose that S faces this problem, and does not think much of Quine's "unimaginative suggestion": Ask the natives. Suppose that S has evidence to suggest that intonation patterns are determined by grammatical structure.[25] The evidence might come from the language in question or from other languages, which are relevant for reasons already discussed. Such evidence might bear on the choice between the two proposed grammars; thus we might discover that the rules needed for other cases give the correct intonation if we take the constituents to be *A—BC* but not *AB—C*. Or suppose that S has reason to postulate that transformations are structure-dependent in this sense: a transformation applies to a string partitioned into a sequence of strings each of which is either arbitrary or is a string of a single constant category. Suppose that specific transformations—say, coordination—observe constituent structure in this sense. These principles, which might be supported by all sorts of evidence, might lead to a choice between the two grammars in this case (say, if we found that where *ABC* and *ADE* are well formed, then so is *A—BC and DE*; though where *ABC* and *FGC* are well formed, still *AB and FG—C* is not). Other evidence might be derived by application of the principle that contextual features of lexical items are internal to constituents, or from semantic considerations of varied sorts. Given a rich general theory of universal grammar, S might bring many kinds of evidence to bear on the question. Examples abound in the literature.

Is there anything enigmatic in all of this, apart from the inescapable problems of empirical uncertainty? I think not. At least, Quine suggests nothing, here or elsewhere.

Quine's sole point reduces to the observation that there will always be distinct theories that are compatible with

all the evidence at hand. That is true if we restrict ourselves, as he sometimes unreasonably suggests, to consideration of weak generation of sentences; and it will remain
true if we consider as well a variety of other evidence.
But this observation is without interest. Again, S already
knew that his nontrivial theories were underdetermined
by evidence. Quine has offered no reason to suppose that S's
investigation of language is subject to some problem that
does not arise in his investigation of common sense, or in
any scientific investigation of any subject matter. Hence
his strictures on method and on linguistic universals, and
his general charge of "folly," are entirely without force.

Though Quine does not explicitly invoke his principle
of "indeterminacy of translation" in this connection, it
seems that his discussion here is related to that principle.
I have argued elsewhere [26] that this principle amounts to
nothing more than the observation that empirical theories
are underdetermined by evidence. Quine gives a counterargument in Quine (1969a). He asserts that "the indeterminacy of translation is not just inherited as a special case
of the under-determination of our theory of nature. It is
parallel but additional." His argument is as follows:

> (17) Consider from this realistic point of view, the
> totality of truths of nature, known and unknown,
> observable and unobservable, past and future.
> The point about indeterminacy of translation is
> that it withstands even all this truth, the whole
> truth about nature. This is what I mean by say-
> ing that, where indeterminacy of translation ap-
> plies, there is no real question of right choice;
> there is no fact of the matter even to *within* the
> acknowledged under-determination of a theory
> of nature.

The remarks of (17) constitute Quine's full answer to my
query: In what respect does the problem of determining

truth in the study of language differ from the problem of determining truth in the study of physics?

Quine's "realistic point of view" takes theory in physics as "an ultimate parameter"; that is, "we go on reasoning and affirming as best we can within our ever under-determined and evolving theory of nature," which includes "ourselves as natural objects." With this, our scientist S of .course agrees, and he studies language exactly as he studies physics, taking humans to be "natural objects." Quine's formulation (17) merely reiterates his belief that somehow indeterminacy of "translation" (actually, what is at stake, on Quine's grounds, is the status of all propositions about language that face more than his "ordinary inductive uncertainty," hence virtually all of the nontrivial study of language) withstands all of the truth about nature. The remark (17) is false if the study of "translation" is part of the theory of nature, and true otherwise. But Quine's assertion (17) gives no reason to doubt that the theory of "translation" is part of the theory of nature, hence underdetermined by evidence only as physics is. And this was the only point at issue.

Similarly, when Quine asserts that there is no fact of the matter, no question of right choice, he is once again merely reiterating an unargued claim which does not become more persuasive on repetition. If the underdetermination of physical theory by evidence does not lead us to abandon the "realistic point of view" with regard to physical theory, then the comparable underdetermination of grammatical theory by evidence does not support Quine's claim that there is no fact of the matter in this domain to be right or wrong about: for example, in the case of the constituent analysis of the sentence *ABC*, the rule of NP-preposing, SSC, the principles of semantic interpretation discussed in chapter 3, a theory of the meaning of a word, or whatever. Neither here nor elsewhere has Quine given any argument whatsoever to justify his assertion that statements about language that go beyond his notion of "ordinary induction" (with its uncertainties) are subject to some methodological doubts that do not hold (in principle) in any nontrivial empirical study. His thesis of "indeterminacy" thus has no support beyond the truism that theory is underdetermined by evidence in empirical research.

A consistent skepticism will lead one to challenge any empirical assertion about the natural world. Thus noting the underdetermination of a theory of nature, we can pointlessly observe that given any proposed nontrivial physical theory, there are alternatives compatible with all available evidence. If we are willing to follow Quine in granting some sense to the notion "totality of evidence," the same statement can be made about a theory compatible with the totality of evidence. Correspondingly, in the case of propositions of the theory of language that are not derived by "ordinary induction," we can observe, equally pointlessly, that there are alternatives compatible with the evidence.

Quine urges "a change in prevalent attitudes toward meaning, idea, proposition." We must abandon the "conviction . . . that our sentences express ideas, and express these ideas rather than those, even when behavioral criteria can never say which." Depending on how we interpret "behavioral criteria," Quine's assertion is either indefensible, in that it imposes conditions on the study of language that cannot generally be met in empirical inquiry, or it is correct, but simply goes to show that the study of language and translation is in principle on a par with physics. Consider two theoretical propositions of the theory of language, P, which asserts that sentence s "expresses these ideas," and P', which asserts that s "expresses those ideas." Suppose we interpret the phrase "behavioral criteria" in Quine's dictum as meaning "necessary and sufficient conditions couched in terms of observation." Then we cannot expect that P and P' will be differentiated by behavioral criteria. But Quine's proposal, so understood, is unreasonable, in that theoretical concepts and propositions employing them can rarely be provided with "criteria" in this sense, and there is no justification for imposing such a requirement on this branch of empirical inquiry alone. Suppose we interpret the phrase "behavioral criteria" as meaning simply "relevant evidence." Thus what is proposed is that we abandon the conviction that P differs empirically from P' where there is no relevant evidence bearing on the choice between them. But with this proposal the scientist will readily agree. In this respect, the study of language (specifically, translation) is on a par with other branches of empirical science. To choose between P and P', we will seek relevant evidence, which might be indirect and will in general be inconclusive, that is, not logically compelling though perhaps compelling. As we will see directly, Quine vacillates between these two senses of "behavioral criteria" (see below, p. 199 and note 35). Whichever interpretation we pick, the proper conclusions are unsurprising and do not differentiate the study of language (or translation) from physics, in principle.

One might argue that such concepts as "meaning, idea, proposition" have no place in the study of language. Thus one might argue that relevant evidence will never exist for theoretical statements employing these concepts, or that there is a better theory that avoids them entirely but accounts for the relevant evidence. But this kind of critique, justified or not, rests on no novel notion of "indeterminacy." Rather, the issue is in principle just like those that arise in other branches of empirical inquiry.

Quine pursues a similar line of argument in Quine (1968). He points out correctly that whatever problems bedevil translation also appear in the case of our own language: that is, if there is some problem of principle affecting the hypothesis that the native's *gavagai* translates our term "rabbit," then the same problem arises in asking whether "our terms 'rabbit,' 'rabbit part,' 'number,' etc., really refer respectively to rabbits, rabbit parts, numbers, etc., rather than to some ingeniously permuted denotations." The question, Quine holds, is "meaningless," except "relative to some background language." Quine's solution to the dilemma is that "in practice we end the regress of background languages, in discussions of reference, by acquiescing in our mother tongue and taking its words at face value." But this is no help at all, since every question that he has raised can be raised about the "mother tongue" and the "face value" of its words. In fact, there was no interesting problem in the first place, apart from the underdetermination of theory by evidence. Quine has yet to pose any problem that should trouble a natural scientist taking the course suggested for S, a scientist who regards people as "natural objects" and their use of language a part of nature, to be studied in a familiar way.

In the same article, Quine argues that "semantics is vitiated by a pernicious mentalism as long as we regard a man's semantics as somehow determinate in his mind beyond what might be implicit in his dispositions to overt behavior." Is the problem here the reference to "mind," or is it the gap between what is regarded as determinate and what is implicit in dispositions? Suppose that we replace "mind" by "brain" in Quine's formulation. Is there something "pernicious" now? Or suppose we reformulate Quine's thesis as follows: "Science is vitiated by a pernicious physicalism so long as we regard an object's state (structure) as somehow determinate in its physical constitution (body) beyond what might be implicit in its dispositions." Is the latter thesis to be taken seriously? Surely not. But then, neither is the former, at least on any grounds that Quine suggests.

As far as I can see, Quine's thesis of indeterminacy of translation and its several variants (e.g., Quine, 1972) amount to no more than an unargued claim that the study of language faces some problem over and above the familiar underdetermination of nontrivial theory by evidence. But I think that Quine's position on this matter is not only unargued but also of doubtful consistency. Thus consider the following formulation (Quine, 1969b):

> Learning by ostension is learning by simple induction, and the mechanism of such learning is conditioning. But this method is notoriously incapable of carrying us far in language. This is why, on the translational side, we are soon driven to what I have called analytical hypotheses. The as yet unknown innate structures, additional to mere quality space, that are needed in language-learning, are needed specifically to get the child over this great hump that lies beyond ostension, or induction. If Chomsky's antiempiricism or antibehaviorism says merely that conditioning is insufficient to explain language-learning, then the doctrine is of a piece with my doctrine of the indeterminacy of translation.

Consider the "as yet unknown innate structures" mentioned in this passage. Since they are "as yet unknown," presumably they are "knowable," or to put it more properly, hypotheses concerning these innate structures have exactly the status of propositions of natural science, and in fact are simply a part of biology. Consider, then, a set of hypotheses H_1 concerning these innate structures needed in language learning to get the child past the limitations of ostension or induction. Examining these hypotheses, the scientist S might derive a new set of hypotheses H_2 concerning the class of systems that can be attained by an organism equipped with the innate structures characterized by H_1 (he might sharpen these hypotheses H_2 by considering the nature of the available evidence, but for simplicity, let us put this consideration aside). The hypotheses H_2 also fall strictly within natural science, in principle, and raise no new questions of "indeterminacy."

Clearly we can make no *a priori* assumptions about the hypotheses H_1 and H_2; they are to be discovered, tested, refined, by the methods of the natural sciences. It is, in particular, surely possible that H_2 will have bearing on the choice of alternative phrase-structure analyses (e.g., $A—BC$ versus $AB—C$), on the principle SSC, on the theory of surface-structure semantic interpretation, on the trace theory of movement rules, or on the nature and properties of "nameable" objects (e.g., rabbits and rabbit-stages) and all sorts of other matters.

The hypotheses H_2 express properties of language that cannot be determined (by the child, by the linguist) by the methods of "ostension, or induction." But looking back at Quine's earlier account, it was precisely the hypotheses of this character that were allegedly subject to "indeterminacy of translation," [27] a new problem that does not arise in the natural sciences. Presumably it is for this reason that Quine notes that the doctrine under dicusssion is "of a piece with my [Quine's] doctrine of the indeterminacy of translation." Recall, however, that "where indeterminacy of translation applies, there is no real question of right choice; there is no fact of the matter even to *within* the acknowledged under-determination of a theory of nature." Apparently then, the hypotheses H_1 and H_2 have nothing to be right or wrong about and cannot be selected, confirmed, refined, or rejected in the manner of the natural sciences, although they are, as we have seen, perfectly ordinary hypotheses of human biology dealing with "as yet unknown" (hence knowable) innate biological structures and the restrictions and scope they entail with regard to what is learned. In short, it appears that Quine is committed to the belief that this specific part of biology is subject to some new problem of principle that does not arise elsewhere in the natural sciences, despite his earlier claim that "the whole truth about nature" was immune to this strange "indeterminacy." It is difficult to see how one might reconcile these various contentions. I return to other apparent internal contradictions in Quine's doctrines on these matters in a moment.

Consider finally Quine's claim that English speakers obey any and all extensionally equivalent systems of grammar in just the sense that bodies obey the law of falling bodies (see p. 179 above).[28] This is a singularly misleading analogy. The rules of English grammar do not determine what speakers will do in anything remotely like the sense in which the law of falling bodies determines that if people jump from a building, they will hit the ground in a specifiable time.[29] All that the rules of grammar tell us is that a person will (ideally) understand and analyze a sentence in certain ways, not others—a very different matter. But even putting this fundamental difference aside, to be consistent Quine should, I believe, reformulate his claim: English speakers obey any and all of the extensionally equivalent English grammars (whether we consider weak or strong equivalence, or some still stronger notion involving even richer empirical conditions) in just the sense in which bodies obey the law of falling bodies or the laws of some other system of physics that is extensionally equivalent (with respect to some given class of evidence). Put this way, the claim is quite uninteresting, for just the reasons already discussed. Physicists do not need to be cured of the "folly" of assuming that the laws they postulate are true, and of seeking evidence to choose among alternative systems that are (so far) compatible with evidence. Nor does S have to be cured of the analogous "folly" when he is studying a particular organism as part of the natural world.

Part of the interest of the study of language, if conducted in the manner outlined for S, is that it shows the inadequacy of Quine's notions "fitting" and "guiding" for the study of human behavior. A person's behavior is not in general consciously guided by rules in Quine's sense of the term, and we can go well beyond the assertion that it simply "fits" rules in Quine's sense. Rather, the scientist can proceed, in the normal way, to postulate that his theory of humans in fact is true, that humans have the characteristics, the mental organization, the cognitive systems attributed to them under the best theory he can devise. And on this standard "realist" assumption, just the assumption that Quine's physicist adopts, S will proceed to seek evidence that will confirm or disconfirm his theories of human nature and competence. He will try to choose among alternative theories that are compatible with the evidence so far available. Ultimately, we hope, the investigator will go on to ask whether his theory is confirmed by the study of the central nervous system, again, unperturbed by the inevitable underdetermination of theory by evidence.

Pursuing Quine's methodological discussion a step further, consider again Quine (1972). Here Quine objects to what he terms my "nihilistic attitude toward dispositions" and "rejection of dispositions." This seems to him so odd that he adds: "I'd like to think that I am missing something." Indeed he is. A look at the statements of mine that he partially cites makes it quite clear what he is missing. His belief that I "reject dispositions" is based on my criticism of his definition of language as a "complex of present dispositions to verbal behavior, in which speakers of the same language have perforce come to resemble one another" (1960, p. 27). I pointed out (Chomsky, 1969a):

> Presumably, a complex of dispositions is a structure that can be represented as a set of probabilities for utterances in certain definable "circumstances" or "situations." But it must be recognized that the notion "probability of a sentence" is an entirely useless one, under any known interpretation of this term. On em-

pirical grounds, the probability of my producing some given sentence of English . . . is indistinguishable from the probability of my producing a given sentence of Japanese. *Introduction of the notion of "probability relative to a situation" changes nothing, at least if "situations" are characterized on any known objective grounds.* . . .

Quine quotes these remarks, omitting the phrases here italicized. He then says that he is "puzzled by how quickly he [Chomsky] turns his back on the crucial phrase 'in certain definable "circumstances,"' " and he adds that verbal dispositions would be idle if not defined in terms of specific circumstances. His puzzlement derives from his omission of the final sentence of the quoted section, which notes that introduction of "circumstances" helps his case not at all.

Quine further adds that he has "talked mainly of verbal dispositions in a very specific circumstance: a questionnaire circumstance, the circumstance of being offered a sentence for assent or dissent or indecision or bizarreness reaction." But as noted in Chomsky (1969a), this simply makes matters worse. Plainly, a language is not a complex of dispositions to respond under the particular set of *Gedankenexperiments* that Quine considers, nor did Quine make this patently false claim in the work I was discussing (viz., Quine, 1960).

Since Quine insists on the same point elsewhere (Quine, 1974, pp. 14 ff.), perhaps a further word is in order. Quine is concerned here to allay a "curious criticism," namely, my criticism of his characterization of a language as a complex of dispositions to verbal behavior. He cites the same comment from Chomsky (1969a), again omitting the final sentence which notes that his case is in no way improved if we consider "probability relative to a situation," and the further discussion of this point. He then makes the following comment:

> Let us not forget that dispositions have their conditions. The probability that a given lump of salt will dissolve at time *t* is as may be, but the probability that it will dissolve if immersed in water is high. Chomsky's worry may have been a more specific difficulty: that of setting conditions for the triggering of verbal dispositions. This is an important problem, and happily it has an easy solution—a solution, indeed, that was prominent in the book that Chomsky was commenting on. It is the procedure of query and assent, which I shall take up in §12.

Section 12 is an elaboration of the procedure of query and assent of Quine (1960). In this section, Quine discusses "the continuing enterprise of ostensive learning," what he calls "statement learning." He is concerned with "the learning of assent," for example, the way that a child learns "to say 'yes' in the presence of the color red and the sound 'red.'"

Unfortunately, this procedure—even if we grant that it has the role in language learning that Quine proposes—has no bearing whatsoever on the questions that I raised. A language, Quine held, is a "complex of present dispositions to verbal behavior." If we suppose that a complex of dispositions can be represented as a set of probabilities for utterances in certain specifiable circumstances—a supposition that Quine apparently accepts—we face a series of problems that I pointed out. No way of assigning probabilities to utterances on empirical grounds relative to situations seems to offer any hope of salvaging Quine's characterization of language as a complex of dispositions to verbal behavior. I noted further that "clearly, however, a person's total 'disposition to verbal response' under arbitrary stimulus conditions is not the same as his 'dispositions to be prompted to assent or to dissent from the sentence' under the particular conditions" of Quine's query-and-assent procedure. Quine's assertion that the problem of "setting the conditions for the triggering of verbal dispositions" is solved by the query-and-assent procedure can only mean that he is failing to make this crucial distinction. Taking his proposal literally, we must conclude that a language is a complex of dispositions to assent or dissent under the conditions of the query-and-assent procedure. But this is plainly not the case. I see no other interpretation of his claim that the problems of characterizing utterance probability in situations and thus salvaging his definition of "language" as a complex of dispositions to respond (recall that this is what is at issue) "has an easy solution" in terms of his procedure of query and assent.

I suspect that Quine's failure to deal with the numerous and fundamental problems that stand in the way of his proposals derives from his continuing belief that "the child learns most of language by hearing the adults and emulating them" (Quine, 1974). If a child learns most of language by hearing and emulation, and—as Quine elsewhere insists— learning a language is a matter of learning sentences, then the child must learn most of his sentences by hearing and emulation. But this is so grossly false that one can only wonder what Quine may have in mind, particularly since elsewhere he observes correctly that a language is an infinite system characterized by a generative grammar, and further, that conditioning, induction, and ostension do not suffice for language learning. The problem of interpretation is analogous to those mentioned in note 30 below.

Perhaps what Quine means is nothing more than the truism that speakers (adults) provide the child with the data for language learning. But on this interpretation, the child learns all (not most) of language by hearing the adults (or other speakers). And the comment, so understood, loses any relevance to the discussion in which it appears.

The comments in Chomsky (1969a) apply, without modification, to Quine's more recent formulations. I also went on there to make the obvious point that "if a language is a complex of dispositions to respond under a normal set of circumstances, it would be not only finite (unless it included all languages) but also extremely small," for reasons there explained. I also pointed out that Quine avoids the multitude of problems that arise if his account is taken seriously by shifting his ground from "totality of speech dispositions" to "dispositions to be prompted to assent to or to dissent from the sentence," a set of dispositions which, he claims, constitutes all of the evidence available in principle to the linguist. Now in my remarks there is no "rejection of dispositions," but rather, of false or empty statements about dispositions, for example, the statement that a language is a complex of present dispositions to verbal behavior. Quine's response (Quine, 1969a, and elsewhere) deals with none of the issues raised. He responds that dispositions to assent or dissent are surely within the totality of speech dispositions (true, but irrelevant) and that resort to this subset does not avoid the problems but solves them (surely false); and he notes that the problem of distinguishing Japanese from English on empirical grounds does not bear on his experiments concerning dispositions to assent and dissent (true, but irrelevant). Obviously, these remarks, where accurate, have no relation to any of the points raised in my comments.[30]

In Chomsky (1969a) I pointed out that in earlier work Quine had also misused the notion "disposition," namely, in his proposal that synonymy "roughly consists in approximate likeness in the situations which evoke two forms and approximate likeness in the effect on the hearer" (Quine, 1953). This proposal is untenable. Compare the statements "watch out, you'll fall down the stairs" and "watch out, you'll fall down the sequence of steps arranged one behind and above the other, in such a way as to permit ascent or descent from one level to another." Consider the situations which evoke these two synonymous utterances and their effects on hearers. Quine is not alone in this kind of misformulation. William Alston (1963) suggests that a statement of the form " 'x' means 'y' . . . is justified to the extent that when 'x' is substituted for 'y' in a wide variety of sentences, and *vice versa,* the dispositions of members of the linguistic community with respect to employing sentences for the performance of linguistic actions is, in each case, roughly the same for the sentence produced by the alternation as for the sentence which was altered." Again, the example just cited and innumerable others like it show at once that this statement is far from the mark. It is all very well to try to relate comments about meaning, speech acts, and so on to behavior, but not at the expense of factual accuracy. In fact, to deal with these matters I believe one must pursue the course outlined earlier for the scientist S, abstracting to the competence that underlies language use. In the theory of competence, it may be possible to make sense of some notion of "synonymy," but direct analyses in terms of dispositions, so far as I can see, are quite hopeless.

Again, I stress that these remarks do not imply a "rejection of dispositions." On the contrary, I suggest that we take the notion "disposition to respond" seriously, thus concluding that Quine's proposed formulations are quite wrong, I believe irremediably so.

My remarks (Chomsky, 1969a) on efforts to define "language" in terms of dispositions to respond and on probability of utterances in definable circumstances are also discussed in Suppes (1973). He objects that these remarks are "written without familiarity with the way in which probability concepts are actually used in science." His reason is that in considering even the "simplest probabilistic phenomenon," say, coin flipping, we may be dealing with probability of outcome approaching zero, but "it in no sense follows that the concept of probability cannot be applied in a meaningful way to the flipping of a coin." Similarly, "there are many probabilistic predictions about verbal behavior that can be made, ranging from trivial predictions about whether a given speaker will utter an English or

Japanese sentence to detailed predictions about grammatical or semantic structure." Thus, "our inability to predict the unique flow of discourse no more invalidates a definition of language as a 'complex of dispositions to verbal behavior' than our inability to predict the trajectory of a single free electron for some short period of time invalidates quantum mechanics. . . ."

These remarks are completely beside the point. Suppes has failed entirely to understand the questions that were at issue in the discussion to which he refers. It is correct that given a grammar, we can develop "sophisticated applications of probability theory" untroubled by the fact that "the basic objects of investigation have either extremely small probabilities or strictly zero probabilities." Given a characterization of English and Japanese by a grammar, we can make predictions as to whether a given speaker will utter a sentence of English or Japanese, so characterized. But it is equally correct that lacking a characterization of the language by a generative system (or some approximation thereto) we can make little sense of empirical observations of the probability of utterances (whether in empirically definable circumstances, or in some corpus of utterances). In particular, we can make no sensible predictions as to whether the next utterance will be English or something else.

The analogy to quantum mechanics is quite false. Physicists do not characterize the theory of quantum mechanics as a complex of dispositions of electrons to move here or there as experimentally observed. Rather, they develop a theory of such movements and relate it to experimental observation, a totally different matter.

If a language is defined as a "complex of dispositions to verbal behavior," determined simply in terms of probability of response in given situations without reference to any postulated theory of competence, we will be faced with the mass of problems I mentioned. If, on the other hand, the "complex of dispositions" is expressed in terms of a postulated theory of competence, all of the questions at issue are begged.

In the same connection, Suppes objects to the "imperialistic ambitions . . . that many linguists seem to have for a theory of competence" *vis-à-vis* the theory of performance and claims "that the two can proceed independently." He does not explain what he has in mind in referring to these "imperialistic ambitions," but presumably he is thinking of the contention that the study of performance—use of language—can progress only to the extent that we have some understanding of the system that is used. The latter contention, however, is hardly "imperialistic." Rather, it is close to truism. Thus, if all we know about language is that it consists of words, we can study the use of words and construct probabilistic models for word sequences. On the other hand, if we know something about "grammatical or semantic structure," then we can proceed, as Suppes proposes we do, to construct probabilistic models that provide detailed predictions about these postulated structures. The probabilistic grammar that Suppes discusses makes use of a classification of questions on syntactic and semantic grounds; that is, it presupposes a partial theory of competence that provides such a classification. His own examples illustrate the truism that the theory of language use cannot sensibly proceed independently of the theory of competence. No "imperialistic ambitions" have been expressed beyond this truism.

As for Suppes's contention that neither of these theories "need precede" the other, if by "precede" he means "temporally precede," of course there can be no objection. The study of language is concerned with the system and its use. The linguist is thus concerned with the competence acquired and performance models that incorporate this competence and are concerned with its use. It is impossible to lay down *a priori* conditions as to the points in this complex system at which new insights will arise. I fail to see any issue here. (Cf. note 19.) Suppes properly endorses Quine's "plea against absolutism," but he seems to have some misconception as to the nature of the work to which he alludes.

Since Quine has been perhaps the leading critic of the project suggested earlier for the scientist S, it may be helpful to consider further his remarks on the study of language. As I read Quine, we must distinguish two different and, I believe, inconsistent doctrines. The first is that of Quine (1960). Here a theory, and also a language,[31] is "a fabric of sentences variously associated to one another and to nonverbal stimuli by the mechanism of conditioned response," and Quine goes on to specify three mechanisms by which "sentences can be learned": association of sentences with sentences, association of sentences with stimuli, and "analogic synthesis," a notion left obscure apart from a single example, namely, a case of substitution of one word for another in a given context.[32] He also defines a language here as a "complex of present dispositions to verbal behavior, in which speakers of the same language have perforce come to resemble one another," a formulation which, as already noted, is either empty or wrong, depending on how we introduce "situations."

Learning also involves a "quality space" with dimensions and a distance measure to be determined experimentally.

> In fact, the denizens of the quality space are expressly stimulations . . . , any and all, with no prior imposition of dimensions. Any irrelevant features of the stimulations will in principle disappear of themselves in the course of the experimental determination of the quality space . . . [which can be] . . . explored and plotted by behavioral tests in the differential conditioning and extinction of his responses.

"The final dimensionality of someone's quality space, if wanted, would be settled only after all the simply ordinal comparisons of distance had been got by the differential conditioning and extinction tests," by "considerations of neatest accommodation," along the lines of Goodman (1951).[33]

Now consider the proposals of Quine in the late 1960s (1969a,b). He states that the method of conditioning "is notoriously incapable of carrying us far in language" and takes his "doctrine of the indeterminacy of translation" to be "of a piece" with the doctrine that "conditioning is insufficient to explain language learning." He insists that "generative grammar is what mainly distinguishes language from subhuman communication systems," and he speaks of "the as yet unknown innate structures, additional to mere quality space, that are needed in language-learning . . . to get the child over this great hump that lies beyond ostension, or induction." He also adds "an explicit word of welcome toward any innate mechanisms of language aptitude, however elaborate," that can be made intelligible and plausible. While in 1960 Quine was following the Skinnerian pattern, as he repeatedly states, in the later work he defines "behaviorism" merely as the view that all "criteria" must be couched in observation terms and that conjectures must "eventually be made sense of in terms of external observation"—so that "behaviorism" is just another name for weak verificationism.

I see no way to reconcile the earlier and later views. If conditioning is insufficient to explain language learning (1969) then a language is not a fabric of sentences and stimuli associated by conditioned response (1960), and sentences are not "learned" by the three mechanisms of 1960. If generative grammar is the essential defining characteristic of human language, then, again, the earlier account can be dismissed, since a generative grammar can be described neither as a fabric of sentences and stimuli associated by conditioning nor as a complex of dispositions to respond. If innate mechanisms of arbitrary complexity are permissible, so long as conjectures are eventually made sense of in terms of external observations, then there is no reason to assign any special place to dimensional structures such as a "quality space," nor to structures determined by differential conditioning and extinction tests (as distinct, say, from recall or recognition tests).[34]

Quine's later views seem to me an almost complete abandonment of behaviorism and all of its trappings—in my opinion, a welcome move. I say "almost complete" because in the more recent version the notion "conditioned response" still plays a role, one that seems to me highly dubious (cf. below). But it seems to me more interesting that Quine's later views do not fall within the class of systems E (cf. pp. 146f. above), though the earlier version does insofar as it is clear. Thus, if we are prepared to welcome any innate mechanism, however elaborate, we are not bound to procedures of the character of E, but can explore richer and, I believe, more adequate theories.

Quine's discussion of this important matter obscures the central issues. Quine suggests (1969b) that by "rationalism" I mean simply the principle that innate structures must be rich enough to account for language acquisition while not so rich as to be incompatible with data, and he expresses his agreement with this "indisputable point about language." He then adds that "innate biases and dispositions are the cornerstone of behaviorism" and that beyond "qualitative spacing of stimulations," "unquestionably much additional innate structure is needed, too, to account for language learning." His "empiricism" or "behaviorism" will apparently welcome any account of these innate endowments so long as conjectures "can eventually be made sense of in terms of external observation."[35] Thus his "behaviorism" or "externalized empiricism" can certainly accommodate my "rationalist" alternative.

But I nowhere suggested that "rationalism" was to be construed in the way Quine proposes. Rather, I suggested that there are two general approaches R and E (cf. above, pp. 146f.), each of which postulates innate mechanisms, but mechanisms of very different sorts, as explained at some length. Obviously, R and E (or any rational inquiry) should satisfy the "indisputable point about language" which he cites. I suggested further that this requirement cannot be satisfied by any approach of the character of E, in particular, by the approach of Quine (1960), which, I argued (Chomsky, 1965, 1969a) can be subsumed within E insofar as it is not vacuous. Quine's response that behaviorism also postulates innate mechanisms is plainly irrelevant to any issue that was under discussion.

Consider now the roles still assigned to conditioning in Quine's more recent suggestions. These are two:

(18) A quality space is to be determined by conditioning experiments (1969a).

(19) "Conditioned response does retain a key role in language-learning. It is the entering wedge to any particular lexicon, for it is how we learn observation terms (or, better, simple observation sentences) by ostension. Learning by ostension is learning by simple induction, and the mechanism of such learning is conditioning," which is "notoriously incapable of carrying us far in language" (1969b).

As for (18), it is doubtful that a "quality space" can be determined in any sensible way in isolation from other innate cognitive structures. Conditioning experiments can be devised to show that people can associate geometrical objects by shape, by area, by position in visual space, and for all I know, by time of day when presented. Experiments can probably be devised to show that people generalize from one presentation of a face to another that does not "match" it in the sense of Goodman (1951)—for example, a right and left profile—or that they generalize in terms of dimensions determined by a notion of matching (of faces) in Goodman's sense. Furthermore, contrary to Quine's contention (cf. note 33), there is no justification for the belief that Goodman's methods, whatever their interest in their own right, have any privileged position for the investigation of a quality space.

A scientist investigating human cognitive structures might construct an abstract quality space as part of the full integrated system, but I see no reason to suppose that it has a more primitive character than other components of the system, or that it can be determined in isolation, or that a reasonable hypothesis about a quality space is less infected by theoretical considerations with their "indeterminacies" than other components of innate cognitive structure, or that relevant experiments for determining dimensionality can be selected in isolation from the general theory of innate cognitive structure. Thus both the commitment to a particular class of experiments (conditioning and extinction) and the commitment to an isolable quality space with some privileged character seem to me highly questionable.

Consider (19). In the first place, I see no way to make sense of the statement that the mechanism of learning by simple induction is conditioning. But there are more serious issues. Recall that according to the 1960 theory, induction leads to "genuine hypotheses" with "normal inductive" uncertainty, as distinct from the analytical hypotheses that "exceed anything implicit in any native's disposition to speech behavior"; and further, in using such analytical hypotheses—say, in proposing that they constitute part of a generative grammar—we "impute our sense of linguistic analogy unverifiably to the native mind." (Recall that virtually all of syntax, as well as most semantics, consists of analytical hypotheses; 1960, pp. 68ff.) The imputation is unverifiable because of the alleged problems of indeterminacy.

As already noted, Quine seems to have now implicitly rejected all or part of this doctrine. But it seems that in Quine's present view, the mechanisms (namely, conditioning) that account for learning of observation terms are still qualitatively different from those involved in other aspects of language learning. However, I see no reason to suppose that there is any fundamental difference in this regard. Putting to the side now Quine's concerns over "indeterminacy," consider what is perhaps the most "elementary" notion we have, the notion "physical object," which, I suppose, plays a role in the most elementary processes of learning through ostension, induction, or conditioning. But the notion "physical object" seems to be quite complex. At the very least, some notion of spatiotemporal contiguity seems to be involved. We do not regard a herd of cattle as a physical object, but rather as a collection, though there would be no logical incoherence in the notion of a scattered object, as Quine, Goodman, and others have made clear. But even spatiotemporal contiguity does not suffice as a general condition. One wing of an airplane is an object, but its left half, though equally continuous, is not. Clearly some *Gestalt* property or some notion of function is playing a role. Furthermore, scattered entities can be taken to be single physical objects under some conditions: consider a picket fence with breaks, or a Calder mobile. The latter is a "thing," whereas a collection of leaves on a tree is not. The reason, apparently, is that the mobile is created by an act of human will. If this is correct, then beliefs about human will and action and intention play a crucial role in determining even the most simple and elementary of concepts. Whether such factors are involved at early levels of maturation, I do not know, but it is clearly an empirical issue and dogmatic assumptions are out of place. It may be that a schematism of considerable complexity and abstractness is brought to bear in learning processes that might be regarded as very "elementary," whatever sense can be made of this notion; very little sense, I am suggesting. We are, I think, led back again to the Peircean view mentioned earlier. And I think that even Quine's newer doctrine involves empirical claims of a most dubious sort. (Cf. also chapter 2, pp. 43ff.)

I have dwelt on these matters at such length because I believe that the problem of choosing between systems of the general character of R and E, or some combined doctrine, is a very significant one. I've argued elsewhere (e.g., Chomsky, 1965), that these two approaches express leading ideas of rationalist and empiricist speculation. Quine believes that little is at stake, but for the reasons just explained, I think he is mistaken.

Others have taken a similar view. Jonathan Cohen suggests that the arguments I gave against E show only that "techniques of simple enumeration" are inadequate for language learning (or construction of scientific theories, etc.), but that these arguments do not bear on "the techniques of eliminative induction." The latter "are adequate for scientific discovery" and "may also be adequate for language learning." Thus we need not "indulge in the relatively extravagant assumption of innate linguistic universals." [36]

The problem with Cohen's proposal is that there do not exist "techniques of eliminative induction" in any relevant sense. For "eliminative induction" to proceed, we need some specification of the class of admissible hypotheses, in Peirce's sense, or at least some ordering of admissibility, perhaps partial. The theory of universal grammar, as sketched here and in the references cited, is one such specification, of the character of R. But the systems that fall within E as I outlined it fail to provide a specification of admissible hypotheses that offers any hope of accounting for the facts.[37] If the method of "eliminative induction" is supplemented with an initial schematism that limits the class of "humanly possible grammars," it will fall within R; if it is not so supplemented, it is empty. If it is supplemented in this way, it will express the "assumption of innate linguistic universals," which is not only not "extravagant" but, so far as I know, unavoidable.

Cohen presents a number of arguments against assuming innate universals. He points out analogies between language acquisition and scientific discovery, concluding that by parity of reasoning, if the assumption of innate linguistic universals is required for the first, then some analogous assumption is required for the second. This conclusion he takes to be more or less a *reductio ad absurdum*. To account for scientific discovery, he argues, it suffices to postulate the "general capacity for eliminative induction." Why not, then, assume that this capacity suffices for language learning as well?

But Cohen's argument fails for reasons already discussed. The scientist S, casting a finer net than Cohen, notes the analogies between language acquisition and scientific discovery, and also notes fundamental qualitative differences, already discussed. These would lead him, I have argued, to postulate a system of innate linguistic universals. But as S proceeds to map out the full cognitive system of his subjects, he will also try to develop principles that account for scientific discovery. Recognizing that a "general capacity for eliminative induction" is entirely vacuous and leads nowhere unless there is a specification of a class of admissible hypotheses or some ordering of admissibility, he will try to determine this specification. For reasons already noted, it is likely to be very different from the system of linguistic universals that characterizes admissible grammars; were the systems one and the same, the fundamental differences between acquisition of language and common sense on the one hand and knowledge of physics on the other would be inexplicable. It is quite possible that S would postulate a theory of the character of R, with innate universals, to account for the ability to gain scientific knowledge. In fact, I know of no coherent alternative.

Basically, Cohen's arguments fail because of their vagueness. The substantive content of a learning theory is largely determined by the specification of admissible hypotheses, if my proposal is correct. Since we know nothing about the basis for scientific discovery, we can only speculate. But insofar as "parity of reasoning" has any force, it would lead us to suspect that in this domain as well the substantive content of any adequate theory will be given by a characterization of admissible hypotheses, as Peirce argued. Surely nothing is gained by invoking the vacuous concept "eliminative induction." The emptiness of this proposal can be seen at once if we ask the simplest question: How, in principle, could we program a computer to carry out "eliminative induction," in the case of language acquisition or scientific discovery, in the absence of constraints on admissible hypotheses? Cohen's discussion of "eliminative induction" tacitly concedes this point, by presupposing, as an element of this method, "a conception of what is to count as a hypothesis," *inter alia* (p. 51).

Cohen then suggests a further line of argument. He claims that "postulating an innate ability to do *x* in order to explain how it is that children are able to do *x* allegedly without learning from experience" is a "tautological pretence," and that to avoid this "triviality" it is necessary to discover "consequences that are testable independently of the language-learning facts it purports to explain—e.g., some consequences for brain physiology or for the treatment of speech disorders" (alternatively, we must abandon the hypothesis that there are language-specific mechanisms). "But since the Chomskyan theory does lack independently testable consequences [of this kind], it seems that theoretical progress in the explanation of language-learning should not be sought in the direction of richer and richer theories of innate universals, as Chomsky suggests, but in the direction of less and less specific theories of innate endowment that will account for such linguistic universals as there appear to be."

No one doubts the importance of searching for consequences of linguistic theory beyond "the language-learning facts." But consider Cohen's argument, which rests on the assumption that postulating an innate ability to do x to explain how it is that children are able to do x is a tautological pretense. Is Cohen's assumption correct? Suppose that the scientist S postulates the structure-dependent property of rules (SDP) or the principle SSC as an element of universal grammar; thus he postulates that children do not learn these principles, but rather construct a linguistic system observing these principles. Thus S is postulating an "innate ability to observe these principles" in order to explain how it is that children observe those principles "without learning from experience." By Cohen's assumption, S's hypothesis is a tautological pretense and therefore cannot be falsified. But in fact it can be falsified all too easily, say, by further investigation that shows that SDP or SSC is violated elsewhere in the language or in some other language. In fact, proposals concerning universal grammar —hence, on the interpretation suggested earlier, proposals concerning innate capacity—have repeatedly been revised on just such grounds. Thus Cohen's initial assumption is false, and his argument collapses.[38]

The theories of universal grammar so far proposed, though not a tautological pretense as Cohen falsely alleges, are still far from sufficiently rich and restrictive to explain acquisition of language; they do not sufficiently limit the class of admissible hypotheses. Thus, contrary to what Cohen asserts, it seems that theoretical progress in the explanation of language learning should be sought in the direction of richer theories of innate universals, at least, until some other approach is suggested that has some degree of plausibility. Cohen's suggestion that we seek less and less specific theories of innate endowment that subsume linguistic universals merely expresses, once again, the conventional belief that the language faculty has no special properties, that there is simply a generalized learning capacity. But like others who are committed to this belief, he gives no plausible argument for it and does not face the obvious problems that arise in maintaining this view.

It would be necessary, rather than simply desirable, to search for evidence in some other domain (say, neurophysiology) only if we had reached the point of constructing adequate theories [39] that could not be distinguished empirically without such further evidence. This remark is indeed a "triviality," but one that has no bearing on the nontautological character of explanatory hypotheses formulated in the terms outlined earlier, that is, in terms of a postulated schematism of universal grammar.

Notice that if experiments with humans were possible, S could obtain evidence relevant to theories of universal grammar in many other ways. Thus he could test his assumption that SDP and SSC form part of universal grammar by exposing children to invented systems violating the proposed conditions and determining how or whether they manage to acquire these systems. If acquisition of such systems is possible but qualitatively different from acquisition of natural language—if, say, it has the properties of scientific discovery—then S will take this as confirmatory evidence for his theory that SDP and SSC form part of the language faculty, which is one of the several faculties of mind. The fact that such experimental procedures are possible in principle again demonstrates the nontautological character of the explanatory theories in question.

In this connection, Cohen argues that if a Martian's language violated a proposed theory of universal grammar but were learnable by humans, this result would show that universal grammar does not mirror human linguistic capacities. Therefore, he concludes, if we adopt the assumption that there are innate linguistic universals, we must "scour the whole universe, not just the earth, in pursuit of intelligible exotic languages." Thus the project is unfeasible.[40]

This argument fails for two reasons. First, it is based on a fundamental misunderstanding of the nature of scientific inquiry, and second, the formulation is, once again, too imprecise to have any bearing on the issues. Consider the first failing. We note at once that there is no distinction between a "Martian language" and any invented language. Thus we need not "scour the universe" to discover possible counterexamples to a proposed theory, to be presented to human subjects in a learning test. Rather, we can freely invent such counterinstances. Given a proposed theory of universal grammar that provides a system of innate linguistic universals, we can at once construct languages that violate the postulated principles and seek to determine, in one or another way, whether they are accessible to humans in the manner of natural language. We can continue this search for disconfirming evidence indefinitely, and in many ways. If this makes the original project unfeasible, as Cohen claims (eliminating now his irrelevant reference to "scouring the universe"), then any empirical inquiry is unfeasible on exactly the same grounds. Once again, Cohen's discussion of "Martian languages" merely underscores the obvious: nontrivial empirical theory is underdetermined by evidence.

Furthermore, Cohen's discussion is crucially imprecise on the matter of "learnability." Suppose that we have a theory UG of universal grammar. Suppose that we have a system L (Martian or invented, a distinction of no account) violating the innate linguistic universals postulated in UG. Suppose we find that L is learnable by humans exactly in the manner of attested human languages, that is, under comparable conditions of time and exposure to data, with comparable success, and so on. Then we reject UG, just as we would reject it if we found evidence from attested human languages contradicting its assumptions. Suppose, however, that we find that L is "learnable" only as physics is learnable. This discovery does not refute UG, just as UG is not refuted by the observation that college students can learn theoretical physics, a theory that no doubt violates the principles of UG. Obviously, the mind has capacities beyond the language faculty, and the fact that physics (or Martian) is learnable in itself proves nothing about the language capacity.

Finally, Cohen argues that simpler approaches suffice to account for language acquisition, and he sketches a few possibilities. Unfortunately, the latter do not begin to deal with even the most elementary properties of language that have been discussed in the literature, for example, the property of structure-dependence. Consequently, his proposals cannot be taken seriously as they stand. As for the further possibility that ability to use transformations may simply be a special case of "some generic skill," this proposal is entirely empty until the "generic skill" in question is specified; and the proposal is not particularly plausible, for reasons already mentioned.

Cohen's discussion is one of the best and most accurate that I have found, but I think he has given no serious argument for any of his conclusions.[41] Cohen points out that if the approach he is criticizing is a reasonable one and if its specific conclusions do receive some confirmation, then "the case for a *de jure* approach to the semantics of natural languages is considerably strengthened," in a sense of "*de jure* approach" that he develops and rejects. Since his arguments against the general approach lack any force and since there is at least some confirmation for it, it follows that the "*de jure* approach to semantics of natural languages is considerably strengthened," contrary to his intentions, if his reasoning in this regard is correct.

Cohen's failure to confront the only interesting questions

that arise in the case of language learning is revealed still more clearly in his more elaborate discussion of the question in Cohen (1970). Here he suggests again that with a proper concept of eliminative induction, one can overcome the arguments that a language-learning system should have the character of R, as argued in Chomsky (1965) and elsewhere; and he argues further, on the same grounds, that a "general learning strategy" should be able to "do the job." His proposed method of induction presupposes "first of all a certain set of materially similar universal hypotheses, where material similarity is defined over a subject matter . . . and secondly, a set of natural variables . . . that are inductively relevant to such hypotheses" (and, further, it presupposes some method for modifying hypotheses, for moving to higher-order hypotheses, and for idealizing and rejecting certain data; these methods remain unspecified). But unfortunately for his argument, the question at issue was the nature and source of the initial set of universal hypotheses and the "natural variables," and about this question Cohen has nothing to say.[42] In Chomsky (1965) and elsewhere it was argued that the delimitation of these hypotheses must be in terms of principles of the character of R rather than E, and many specific proposals were put forth. Cohen's approach is so vague and inexplicit that we cannot tell whether it falls within R or E; nor can we discover any of its relevant properties from his account. He merely stipulates that his "general learning strategy" is based on an unspecified initial set of hypotheses, a technique (unspecified) for modifying hypotheses, a choice (unspecified) of relevant variables, an initial limitation to "relatively few concepts" (which are unspecified), and so on.

There can be no objection to "an inductive language-learning device" which is "a formulater and tester of hypotheses," with a "nisus toward generalization [that] will lead it to formulate hypotheses about relationships between [the relevant] variables which will subsume and explain, as it were, the more elementary hypotheses that have already been established." None of the questions that concern us are clarified by these remarks, or by references to "the continuity of inductive methodology from first-order, elementary generalizations, through second-order, correlational generalizations, to third-order, theoretical generalizations," or by assuming a "device [that] always hypothesizes as boldly as it can about its initially noticed data. . . ." Contrary to what Cohen asserts, no "light seems to be shed by the proposed account of inductive reasoning," for the simple reason that the proposed account reduces to hand-waving at every crucial point.

Cohen believes that "in syntax the number of relevant variables is vastly fewer, and their size vastly smaller, and hypotheses are much more easily tested, than in most fields of natural science." This, he claims, is the reason why children learn language more quickly than we solve problems in natural science. I doubt that he would maintain this thesis if he were to attempt to formulate the principles that govern language and its use. He also suggests that "the more abstract the concepts that are invoked [in linguistic theory], the more plausible it is to suppose that, if innate at all, these concepts represent certain general abilities that have indefinitely many applications," but he gives no credible argument for this thesis,[43] beyond such claims as the following: "It is certainly not obvious . . . that the structure-dependence of, say, an interrogative transformation is substantially different from the structure-dependence of an individual jump in the children's game of hopscotch." But it seems obvious that the two are "substantially different," since even the notion of "abstract phrase structure" does not appear in the children's game, so that the notion of "structure-dependence" has no nontrivial application in this case.

Cohen also observes that "one has yet to read—in the

psychological literature—of an English speaker for whom there is adequately attested evidence both that he knows some such syntactic feature and that he has never experienced any evidence for it." This is true, for quite uninteresting reasons. No one has ever collected the entire linguistic experience of any speaker; consequently, we do not know for sure that particular speakers who observe the principle of structure-dependence, for example, have not explicitly been taught that they are to produce (15) rather than (14) (see p. 173), though the belief that in every case relevant instruction or evidence has been provided surely strains credulity. Again, the issue is plainly an empirical one, and if one wished to undertake the tedious task of demonstrating that speakers observe the principle without having been instructed that (14) and similar cases are improper, he would know how to proceed.

In short, Cohen's belief that he has shown "the importance of inductive logic for an adequate theory of language" or that he has given some argument against learning theories of the form of R, or some argument in support of general learning strategies, is entirely without foundation. He has simply avoided all of the questions that have been under discussion. The arguments bearing on the choice of an approach of the character of R or E and the arguments in support of the theory that universal grammar specifies innate linguistic universals of the sort that have been extensively discussed are untouched by his discussion. We can, no doubt, define "empiricism" as an approach which includes theories of all imaginable types, in particular theories of the character of both R and E. But this terminological suggestion is of no interest. It remains true that the substantive theories discussed within the empiricist framework are of the form of E and are inadequate, for the reasons that have been discussed at length in the literature and again in earlier discussion here. Incidentally, Cohen's explicit disparagement of Hume's approach amounts to nothing more than a preference for vacuous suggestions over fairly concrete (but wrong) proposals.

Cohen argues that "the real issue" is not the issue between "Humeianism, on the one hand, and Rationalism on the other" (i.e., between E and R, in the sense outlined earlier); rather, "the real issue is about the scope and nature of general learning strategies as against specific ones." But if the latter is "the real issue," then we can only conclude that the real issue has yet to be formulated in any meaningful terms. No "general learning strategies" have been formulated that have even a remote relation to the actual problems that arise when one attempts to account for human learning in such domains as language acquisition, though there are a few "specific ones" that have been proposed that appear to have some plausibility and empirical support. For reasons already discussed, it seems doubtful that there exist general learning strategies of much interest or significance, though of course one must keep an open mind on this. Cohen's contention that the real issue is about the scope and nature of general learning strategies reflects again the dogmatic beliefs about the structure of human cognitive capacities that are enshrined in the empiricist tradition. I see nothing in his discussion to suggest that there is any cogency or plausibility in this traditional doctrine.

John Searle has also suggested that nothing much is at stake in the R-E opposition that I have suggested as a kind of "rational reconstruction" of certain traditional and modern views (Searle, 1972). Referring to a passage from Leibniz which I cited, he comments that if this is the "correct model" for innate structure, as I imply, "then at least some of the dispute between Chomsky and the empiricist learning theorists will dissolve like so much mist on a hot morning [since] many of the fiercest partisans of empiricist and behaviorist learning theories are willing to concede that the child has innate learning capacities in the sense that he has innate dispositions, inclinations, and natural potentialities."

It should be clear from preceding discussion that Searle has also missed the central point. In proposing two conflicting approaches, I explicitly stated that each postulates innate dispositions, inclinations, and natural potentialities. The two approaches differ in what they take these to be: in the case of E, the dispositions are the mechanisms of data processing I outlined, which give something akin to Quine's "genuine hypotheses"; in the case of R, the "dispositions" (et al.) specify the form of the resulting systems of knowledge and belief—roughly, they relate to "analytical hypotheses" in what seems to be Quine's sense.

The basic point seems to me fairly clear in the passages from Leibniz that I cited. As Alan Gewirth pointed out in response to Searle, "Leibniz draws two distinctions where the empiricists draw only one" (Gewirth, 1973). Namely, Leibniz distinguishes "powers," which are "passive, indeterminate, and remote," from "dispositions," which are "active, determinate, and proximate."

> Powers as such require the stimulation of external objects both in order to be activated and in order to receive their perceptual or ideational contents; hence, they have no specific contents of their own. Dispositions, on the other hand, already have determinate contents which the mind can itself activate, given appropriate external occasions. Both powers and dispositions may be called "capacities," but then they are capacities of two quite different sorts. . . . According to this [Leibnizian] model, then, for ideas to be innate as dispositions means that the mind has quite determinate contents of its own which it is itself able to activate and perceive; whereas for ideas to be innate merely as powers would mean that the mind has only diffuse mechanisms whose contents are exhaustively derived from the impact of external stimuli. As Leibniz frequently emphasizes, the latter model, un-

like the former, is unable to explain how the mind can attain the sorts of necessary and universal truths found in logic, mathematics, and other disciplines. And a comparable [44] sort of necessity and universality are attributed by Chomsky to the basic rules of grammar. . . . Far from being compatible with empiricist and behaviorist learning theories, as Searle and Quine hold that it is, Leibniz's doctrine shows how the mind can itself be the exhaustive source of its linguistic competence, for which external stimuli serve only as occasions for activating what is already dispositionally contained in the mind's own structure. Leibniz's doctrine therefore explains, as the behaviorist theory cannot, the necessity and universality of the linguistic rules for forming and interpreting sentences. . . .

Gewirth's comments are exactly to the point. The crucial question is not whether there are innate potentialities or innate structure. No rational person denies this, nor has the question been at issue. The crucial question is whether this structure is of the character of E or R; whether it is of the character of "powers" or "dispositions"; whether it is a "passive" system of incremental data processing, habit formation, and induction, or an "active" system which is the "source of linguistic competence" as well as other systems of knowledge and belief.[45]

A similar distinction is made by Descartes, in passages which I quoted (Chomsky, 1966, p. 78). He takes the "cognitive power" to be a faculty that is not purely passive and that is "properly called mind when it either forms new ideas in the fancy or attends to those already formed," acting in a way that is not completely under the control of sense or imagination or memory. There is in humans, he argues, a "passive faculty of perception" and an "active faculty capable of forming and producing . . . ideas." [46]

Searle argues that both my "historical claim that [my] views on language were prefigured by the seventeenth-century rationalists, especially Descartes" and my "theoretical claim that empiricist learning theory cannot account for the acquisition of language" are "more tenuous than [I] suggest." The theoretical claim is more tenuous because empiricist learning theorists also accept innate dispositions; he cites in particular Quine (1969a), already discussed. I hope it is now clear why Searle's argument with respect to my theoretical claim is beside the point.

As for the historical claim, Searle gives two reasons for his conclusion. First, Descartes did not suggest that "the syntax of natural languages was innate," but rather "appears to have thought that language was arbitrary." Second, "Descartes does not allow for the possibility of *unconscious* knowledge, a notion that is crucial to Chomsky's system."

But Searle has mistaken the historical claim. I nowhere suggested that Descartes's views on language "prefigured" mine in any of the respects Searle mentions.[47] Rather, I opened my discussion of Descartes by noting that he "makes only scant reference to language in his writings." My point was that Descartes's investigation of "the creative aspect of language use" prefigures current ideas (Searle agrees) and that certain Cartesian ideas were developed in the subsequent study of language by others. Furthermore, Cartesian "psychology" contributes to a coherent doctrine that can be drawn from work that I reviewed.

As for the second objection, the notion "unconscious cognization" is crucial to my system (and I am prepared to use "unconscious knowledge" in this sense; see above, pp. 162–6), but I am not at all sure that Descartes would disallow this notion, though I recall taking no stand on the matter. True, Descartes seems to insist that knowledge is accessible to consciousness, but on this entirely different point I have explained repeatedly that I think we must depart from the classical traditions. Thus Searle's objections to my "historical claim" are without any force.

Objections to these historical claims have been made by

others (cf. note 2). I will discuss only one last example, namely Barnes (1972), since it raises questions that relate to the foregoing discussion. Unfortunately, Barnes is rather careless in his references. Thus he asserts that "Chomsky frequently and emphatically maintains that his adoption of the innate hypothesis endorses the rationalism of Descartes and Leibniz and casts out the empiricism of Locke," citing sections of Chomsky (1965, 1966). My references to Descartes, Leibniz, and others are adequately qualified, so far as I know (Barnes cites no counterexample, nor have others, to my knowledge), and there is no discussion at all in the cited references of "the empiricism of Locke." In Chomsky (1966) Locke is not mentioned, and in Chomsky (1965) there are only two references to Locke, one stating that he did not refute the doctrine of innate ideas in the form in which Descartes presented it, and the other, that Locke's remarks on the origin of ideas seem similar in respects noted to Cudworth's. In fact, I have never even discussed—let alone "cast out"—"the empiricism of Locke."

The only further evidence that Barnes cites in support of his contention that I give frequent and emphatic endorsement to the rationalism of Descartes and Leibniz is my statement (Chomsky, 1968a) that "contemporary research supports a theory of psychological *a priori* principles that bears a striking resemblance to the classical doctrine of innate ideas." Barnes neglects to add that in elaborating this statement I noted explicitly that my conclusions seem to me "fully in accord" only with certain specific aspects of this doctrine, namely, Descartes's theory of perception of regular figures, and Leibniz's remarks on innate and unconscious principles and ideas and truths that are innate as inclinations, and so on. And this adequately qualified assertion is, so far as I know, accurate enough. Barnes also refers in this connection to Chomsky (1969c, p. 59), where the only comment even marginally relevant is this: "I think that a case can be made that certain well-founded conclusions about the nature of language do bear on traditional philosophical questions," specifically, "these conclusions are relevant to the problem of how knowledge is acquired and how the character of human knowledge is determined by certain general properties of the mind." Again, I find no emphatic endorsement of the sort he suggests.

Barnes also claims that I use terms "promiscuously"; thus he agrees with the conclusion that my theory is "essentially and irreparably vague." His examples of "promiscuous" use of terms are the following: Chomsky (1965, p. 25), "which glosses 'innate *grammar*' as 'innate *predisposition* to learn a language'"; Chomsky (1969c, p. 88), "which explicates 'innate *grammar*' as 'innate schematism.'" However, neither citation exists. Rather, in the first case I state that an "innate linguistic theory . . . provides the basis for language learning" and that we can use the term "theory of language" with systematic ambiguity to refer to "the child's innate predisposition to learn a language of a certain type and to the linguist's account of this." The linguistic theory "specifies the form of the grammar of a possible human language," but is not a "grammar," let alone an "innate grammar." The second reference that Barnes cites states that "the child makes use of an innate schematism that restricts the choice of grammars." Furthermore, "there is no reason why we should not suppose that the child is born with a perfect knowledge of universal grammar, that is, with a fixed schematism that he uses, in the ways described earlier, in acquiring language." Nowhere do I use the term "innate grammar."

Note that "universal grammar" is not one of the set of grammars made available by linguistic theory (cf. Chomsky, 1965, chap. 1, and elsewhere). Rather, it is a schematism that determines the form and character of grammars and the principles by which grammars operate. Barnes's references suggest that he may be confused about this point. However, when his misreading is corrected, there is—so far

as I can see—no "promiscuous use" of terms, and no vagueness or confusion that arises from the thesis that an innate
schematism of the sort discussed determines an innate predisposition to learn a language of a certain type.

Barnes asserts that "on occasion" I speak "the language
of crude innatism, embracing innate principles and even innate grammars. . . ." But I never embrace "innate grammars"
(except in the quite appropriate sense just mentioned,
namely, innate universal grammar), and my use of "innate
principles" and "universal grammar" as an innate schematism is, so far as I can see, subject to no criticism that Barnes
develops in his discussion of "crude innatism."

Barnes then notes three alleged "major divergencies between Chomsky and his classical forebears." The first is that
neither "Leibniz or any other classical innatist" had any
"particular interest in declaring the principles of grammar
to be innate." As for Leibniz, the remark is irrelevant since
I cited him only in reference to other aspects of the general
set of doctrines that I was surveying. But if Cordemoy,
Arnauld, and others whom I discussed are "classical innatists," then I think a good case can be made that they did
regard as innate certain principles that we would regard as
principles of grammar, though I developed this view, again,
in a manner which seems to me sufficiently and properly
qualified. Barnes also adds that, as distinct from my "classical forebears," I am "not concerned to establish the foundations of science, religion and morality." That too is incorrect.
I am much interested in establishing the foundations of
science and morality, at least, though I regret that I have
little of interest to say about these questions.[48]

The second of the "major divergencies" is that Leibniz
uses arguments that are quite different from mine. This
observation is irrelevant to the extent that it is true. I cited
Leibniz where relevant to my concerns, and also cited a
wide range of arguments that differ from Leibniz's though
they fall within the classical rationalist traditions that I

surveyed under the rubric of "Cartesian linguistics," as this is defined in Chomsky (1966, n. 3).

Barnes's third "divergence" is that the "classical innatists" take P to be "innate in x's mind if x has an innate disposition to know that P," whereas my view is that "P is innate in x's mind if x has an innate disposition to φ, and being disposed to φ is, or entails, knowing that P." He does not explain why I am committed to the latter view and reject the former. In fact, under any sensible notion of "disposition," and any nontrivial choice of φ (i.e., unless φ is taken to be something like "learn a language," with "entails" properly qualified, in his formulation), I see no reason to take either of these formulations seriously. Barnes seems impelled to offer some quasi-operationalist characterization of the concept of "innate in x's mind," but I see no reason to expect such an approach to be more successful in this domain than it is elsewhere in scientific inquiry. Furthermore, Barnes's formulation does not comprehend the range of cases discussed by "classical innatists." In particular, it does not apply to the cases I cited as particularly interesting, such as Cudworth's theory of perception. But even if there is some point buried here, I do not see its bearing on anything that I have discussed or proposed. I have repeatedly emphasized far more striking and significant departures from the views of the "classical innatists" in the reconstruction that I have suggested.

Barnes then raises the question "whether the existence of these innate mechanisms requires the ascription of innate *knowledge* to potential language learners." I have already explained why I think that his qualms in this regard are unwarranted. But he adds some new errors that perhaps merit a word of clarification. He interprets the claim that some principle (say, the principle of cyclic rules or SDP or SSC) is innate as the claim "that the child has an *innate disposition* to speak as the principle requires," and he argues that from the fact that an organism has an innate disposition to act in accordance with some rule or principle, we cannot infer that it has knowledge of the rule or principle. It is wrong, he argues, to identify "items of knowledge, or belief, with dispositions." My "dispositions," he points out, are neither "dispositions toward certain fairly elementary types of behaviour" nor "dispositions to assent to a proposition"— the only two cases in which one might conceivably identify items of knowledge or belief with dispositions, so he maintains.

Barnes's discussion of this point is vitiated by his failure throughout to distinguish competence from performance. A principle such as the one he cites (cyclic application of rules), taken as part of universal grammar, is not a disposition to speak as the principle requires, but rather a "disposition" (if one insists on this term) to acquire a certain competence (i.e., a certain cognitive structure, a grammar, knowledge of language). Having acquired this cognitive structure, a person may be disposed to speak in certain ways, although as I have indicated, there is little of substance that we can say about this matter.

It is perfectly true, as Barnes points out, that if a bird is disposed to fly in accordance with the laws of aerodynamics we need not attribute to it knowledge of these laws, for such reasons as the following: (i) we have (or believe that we can construct) an explanation for its behavior in terms of reflex structures and the like; and (ii) the structural organization that we so attribute to a bird plays no role in accounting for its knowledge of any particular things. In the case of "linguistic dispositions," neither (i) nor (ii) holds. We might regard universal grammar as a "disposition" to acquire certain competence, but not as a disposition to behave in certain ways. And universal grammar, I have argued, is intricately and inseparably interwoven in the mature system of knowledge of language; on the basis of the system of universal grammar, the organism comes to know the language and to know particular linguistic facts. Assuming the existence of this innate system, we can account for such knowledge. Barnes asks, "What, then, is there about innate *linguistic* dispositions that might exalt their status to the rank of knowledge?" Recognizing that these are dispositions to acquire a system of knowledge (knowledge of language, which underlies knowledge of particular linguistic facts), the answer seems evident, although, as I have already observed, there is vagueness and imprecision in the normal usage of "know" that might lead us to replace "know" by the technical term "cognize" throughout this discussion, a matter of little moment, so far as I can see.

Barnes is quite right in observing that my "dispositions" do not fall under either of the categories he suggests, but this fact simply illustrates once again the inadequacy of such an analysis of dispositions, with its failure to distinguish competence from performance, to recognize the intellectual component in nontrivial instances of "knowing how" (cf. Chomsky, 1975a), its limitation to the inadequate framework of "fitting" and "guiding," and related matters already discussed. When we consider "dispositions" that fall beyond Barnes's impoverished framework, for example, the "disposition" to acquire knowledge of language, then I believe reasons can be advanced for speaking of elements of these "dispositions" as "items of knowledge, or belief" (the difference being irrelevant in the case of language, for familiar reasons).

In proposing that R and E represent two fundamentally different ways of approaching the problems of learning (and correspondingly, the origin and nature of knowledge), I have always insisted that I regard the question as an empirical one: it is the problem of determining what are, in fact, the specific properties of the human mind, in particular, the properties of what may be called "the language faculty." A number of critics have argued that by formulating the issue as an empirical hypothesis, I am eliminating any "philosophical interest" and removing the whole matter from the concerns of the classical traditions that I have discussed in this effort at rational reconstruction. As for the matter of "philosophical interest," I take no stand. The term is too vague, and attitudes among those who call themselves "philosophers" are too varied. What I have argued is that the empirical hypotheses I have been investigating do have bearing on what philosophers have said, both in the past (e.g., Hume) and the present (e.g., Quine, who would surely reject any sharp distinction between "philosophical" and "scientific" issues).

What of the more interesting question, whether by formulating the matter explicitly in terms of conflicting empirical hypotheses I am removing the discussion, beyond recognition, from the concerns of traditional debate? I can only comment briefly on this, but I think that the criticism is quite mistaken. It is a mistake to read Descartes, the minor Cartesians, Hume, and others as if they accepted some modern distinction between "scientific" and "philosophical" concerns, or as if they made a distinction between "necessary" and "contingent" along the lines of much current discussion.

Consider Hume.[49] He understood "moral philosophy" to be "the science of human nature" (p. 5). His concern was to discover "the secret springs and principles, by which the human mind is actuated in its operations," and he likened this task to that of the "philosopher" who "determined the laws and forces, by which the revolutions of the planets are governed and directed" (p. 14). He wished to undertake "an accurate scrutiny into the powers and faculties of human nature" and to discover "the operations of the mind," this being "no inconsiderable part of science" (p. 13). "It cannot be doubted," Hume insisted, "that the mind is endowed with several powers and faculties, that these powers are distinct from each other, that what is really distinct to the immediate perception may be distinguished by reflexion; and consequently, that there is a truth and falsehood in all propositions on this subject, and a truth and falsehood, which lie not beyond the compass of human understanding" (pp. 13–14). He makes interesting and substantive claims concerning these empirical issues—for example, that the "creative power of the mind amounts to no more than the faculty of compounding, transposing, augmenting, or diminishing the materials afforded us by the senses and experience" (p. 19), and that the "only three principles of connexion among ideas" are "*Resemblance, Contiguity* in time or place, and *Cause* or *Effect*" (p. 24). The "reasonings from experience . . . on which almost all knowledge depends" involve a "step taken by the mind" on the basis of custom or habit, "a principle of human nature" (pp. 41–3). These operations of the mind "are a species of natural instincts," an "instinct or mechanical tendency"; thus they are "unavoidable" when the mind is placed in certain circumstances (pp. 46–7, 55).

Throughout, Hume takes himself to be studying the relation of knowledge to experience and the empirical principles that determine this relation. He observes that "though animals learn many parts of their knowledge from observation, there are also many parts of it, which they derive from the original hand of nature. . . . These we denominate Instincts."[50] Similarly, "the experimental reasoning itself, which we possess in common with beasts, and on which the whole conduct of life depends, is nothing but a species of instinct or mechanical power, that acts in us unknown to ourselves," undirected by our "intellectual faculties" (p. 108). By virtue of these instincts, experience "is the foundation of moral reasoning [which concerns "matter of fact and existence" (p. 35)], which forms the greater part of human knowledge" (p. 164).

Throughout, Hume is offering substantive proposals about questions that we surely regard as "scientific questions" (as he did too, it seems clear). He is discussing the instinctive foundations of knowledge (including unconscious and even innate knowledge), surely an empirical matter, as he correctly understood the question.

Similarly Descartes could not have answered the question
whether he was a "scientist" or a "philosopher" in the sense
of these terms used by many contemporaries who restrict
philosophy to some kind of conceptual analysis. He was,
surely, both. His approach to innate ideas and mind is a
case in point. As a scientist, he thought he could explain
much of human behavior, and everything else, in terms of
mechanical principles. But he felt compelled to postulate
a second substance whose essence is thought to account for
observations about humans (himself and others). It is not
at all correct to assert, as many do, that his doctrine of innate ideas is an effort solely to account for "necessary
truths" as this notion is understood in contemporary discussion. Within the framework of a theory of innate ideas,
Descartes developed a theory of perception, for example,
but obviously his theory of perception or Cudworth's theory
of the "innate cognoscitive power," with its *Gestalt* properties and related structure, goes well beyond the domain
of necessary truths as understood at present—though it was
a different matter for the man who believed that he had
proved the existence of a God who is no deceiver and who
thus believed that he could show the necessity of all laws of
nature. Plainly Descartes's concept of "necessity" was quite
different, at least in presumed extension, from our own.

It is quite wrong to claim that the tradition was "paradigmatically philosophical" in its concerns,[51] at least if
"paradigmatically philosophical" is to be opposed to "scientific." Correspondingly, it seems to me entirely appropriate
to suggest the rational reconstructions R and E, as I have,
as expressions of some of the leading ideas of rationalist and
empiricist speculation on "the science of human nature,"
on acquisition of knowledge, on those parts of knowledge
derived from the original hand of nature, and so on. I have
repeatedly emphasized that R and E, as I have discussed

them, depart from some of the central ideas of the tradition (e.g., the belief that the contents of the mind are open to introspection); furthermore, these leading ideas often inter-penetrate in the work of one person in complex ways, and we are under no compulsion to adhere strictly to one or the other framework (cf. Chomsky, 1965, 1966). But I do think that by sharpening these opposed conceptions and explor-ing them in the light of empirical research, we can move towards a solution to problems that can now sensibly be posed with regard to the nature and acquisition of cognitive structures. And at the same time, we can gain much insight into the reasons why earlier efforts have often gone astray.

Notes

Part I   THE WHIDDEN LECTURES

Chapter 1. ON COGNITIVE CAPACITY

1. Aristotle, *Posterior Analytics* 2. 19 (ed. McKeon, 1941), pp. 184–6.
2. Cudworth (1838), p. 75. Except for those otherwise identified, quotations that follow in this paragraph are from the same source: respectively, pp. 65, 51, 49, 87, 122–3.
3. Leibniz, *Discourse on Metaphysics* (trans. Montgomery, 1902), p. 45. For a similar view, see Cudworth (1838), p. 64. For quotations and further discussion, see Chomsky (1966), § 4.
4. Cudworth, *True Intellectual System of the Universe*, cited by Lovejoy (1908).
5. Lovejoy (1908).
6. Henry More, "Antidote Against Atheism," cited by Lovejoy (1908).
7. Gregory (1970). Gregory suggests further that the grammar of language "has its roots in the brain's rules for ordering retinal patterns in terms of objects," that is, "in a take-over operation, in which man cashed in on" the development of the visual system in higher animals. This seems questionable. The structure, use, and acquisition of language seem to involve special properties that are, so far as is known, not found elsewhere. Language is based on properties of the dominant hemisphere that may also be quite specialized. There seems to be no obvious relationship to the structure of the visual cortex in relevant respects, though so little is known that one can only speculate. It is not clear why one should expect to find an evolutionary explanation of the sort that Gregory suggests. For more on these matters, see the chapters by R. W. Sperry, A. M. Liberman, H.-L. Teuber, and B. Milner in Schmitt and Worden (1974).
8. This view, popularized in recent years by B. F. Skinner, is foreign to science or any rational inquiry. The reasons for its popularity must be explained on extrascientific grounds. For

further discussion, see my "Psychology and Ideology," reprinted in Chomsky (1973b); also Chomsky (1973c); and the discussion of liberalism and empiricism in Bracken (1972, 1973a).

9. Antoine Arnauld (1964), p. 36. On the importance of considering "language as a biological phenomenon [comparable] to other biological phenomena" and some implications for epistemology and the philosophy of language and mind, see Moravcsik (1975b).

10. See, for example, the references of note 8. I return to the question in chapter 3.

11. Appropriateness is not to be confused with control, nor can the properties of language use noted here (what I have elsewhere called "the creative aspect of language use") be identified with the recursive property of grammars. Failure to keep these very different concepts separate has led to much confusion. For discussion of the creative aspect of language use in rationalist theory, see Chomsky (1966) and (1972a).

12. By LT I mean here the system of LT(O,D)'s, O fixed, D an arbitrary domain. In the terminology suggested, each LT(O,D) constructs a cognitive structure. Operating in concert and interaction, the LT(O,D)'s for given O form a cognitive state.

13. Hence I will not even raise the further question whether there is anything to say about M_2(CS, stimulus conditions), namely, a possible general mechanism ranging over cognitive states that might be called a "general theory of behavior."

14. See Eimas et al. (1971) and the references of note 7 above.

15. Thus we take cognitive capacity to be the set of such domains with whatever further structure this complex may have.

16. Consider the argument of Bourbaki that "as a matter of empirical fact, the bulk of mathematically significant notions can be analyzed profitably in terms of a *few* basic structures such as groups or topological spaces. They regard this fact as a discovery about our thinking . . ." (Kreisel, 1974).

17. Anthony Kenny, "The Origin of the Soul," in Kenny et al. (1973).

18. Imagine some hypothetical form of aphasia in which knowledge is unimpaired but all systems involving performance, i.e., putting knowledge to use, are destroyed. For discussion of this matter, see Stich (1972) and Chomsky and Katz (1974).

19. Thus my use of the term "cognitive capacity" (p. 21) might be misleading, though I have not found a term less likely to mislead.

20. I have discussed elsewhere why I think that modern criticisms of "Descartes's myth" by Ryle and others simply miss the point. Cf. Chomsky (1966), p. 12; (1972a), p. 13; (1975a).

21. On this matter, see chapter 4. Also, Chomsky (1972a), pp. 90ff.; (1971), pp. 20ff.

22. To avoid misunderstanding, I am not making the absurd suggestion that science should study what is familiar and commonplace rather than search for perhaps exotic data that shed light on deeper principles. In the study of language no less than physics, this would be a self-defeating program. Gross coverage of familiar phenomena can be achieved by very different theories; it is generally necessary to seek unusual data to distinguish them. To cite an example, idioms in natural language are (by definition) abnormal, but the capacity of various linguistic theories to deal with their character and peculiarities has often proved quite relevant for distinguishing empirically among these theories.

23. Note that the notions "fair" and "adequate" are yet to be made precise, as biological properties of humans, though it is no great problem to place some reasonable bounds.

Chapter 2. THE OBJECT OF INQUIRY

1. Interesting questions can be raised about just what kinds of knowledge are involved in knowledge of language. For some discussion, see chapter 4, pp. 162–6, and references cited there.

2. There is a valuable critical review of available evidence in Fodor, Bever, and Garrett (1974). See also Fodor, Fodor, and Garrett (forthcoming) for a discussion of the possible bearing of such evidence on lexical decomposition.

   This is not the place to pursue the matter in detail, but some of the argument in the former book relating to issues discussed here is less than compelling. Thus, the authors consider an approach to LT(H,L) stipulating that the grammar acquired must meet (at least) two conditions: conformity to UG and conformity to a data base consisting of phonetically represented sentences. They argue (i) that the condition is not sufficient and (ii) that a "paradox" prevents enrichment of the data base to sufficiency. But (i), while perhaps true, follows only from unexpressed assumptions about the range of permitted grammars; there is no difficulty in formulating constraints on UG sufficient to rule out the alleged counterexamples cited, and they give no general argument from which (i) follows. As for (ii), there is a problem, but no paradox. Furthermore, the problem arises in exactly the same form for any other theory of language learning. Hence I see no force to their strictures, apart from the observation, which is surely correct, that the theory they discuss is far too weak as it stands.

3. Cf., e.g., Braine (1974). Braine asserts that theories of abstract

phonological representation require "assumptions about human memory and learning which are almost certainly wrong," and takes it to be "self-evident" that they impose an "extraordinary burden" on any acquisition theory. But the only thing that is certain, in this regard, is that little is known about human memory and learning that bears even remotely on the issue. Plainly, one can draw no conclusions from the lack of any substantive theory of memory or learning. As for the "extraordinary burden" imposed on a theory of acquisition, nothing can be said in the absence of significant psychological or neurological evidence on representation and acquisition of cognitive structures (apart from the abstract explanatory theories that have been offered and some suggestive experimental work of the sort discussed in Fodor, Bever, and Garrett [1974]). Braine's certainty about what is unknown reflects, once again, the dogmatism that has so impeded psychological theory in the past.

4. Cf. Kramer, Koff, and Luria (1972) for some interesting and relevant data. Furthermore, the knowledge of language attained by an individual in a real speech community is far more complex than under the idealization that we are considering, involving many styles of speech and possibly a range of interacting grammars. The real-world complexity deserves study, and it is reasonable to assume that such study will make essential use of the results obtained under the idealization. Evidently, the real-world complexity gives no reason to doubt the legitimacy of the idealization.

5. Such taxonomies can be of considerable interest, despite their limitations. See, e.g., Austin (1962), Vendler (1967), Fraser (1974), Searle (1975).

6. On some similar notions in comparative ethology, see Chomsky (1972a), pp. 95ff.; chapter 3 below, pp. 123–4.

7. Antoine Le Grand, *An Entire Body of Philosophy, According to the Principles of the Famous Renate Des Cartes*, cited in Watson (1968).

8. See the references of note 7, chapter 1. Also Wood et al. (1971), where it is reported that "different neural events occur in the left hemisphere during analysis of linguistic versus nonlinguistic parameters of the same acoustic signal," and the further work reported in Wood (1973). For more on these matters, see Lenneberg (1967), Millikan and Darley (1967), and Whitaker (1971).

9. Cf. chapter 4, note 14. See also the report of experiments by E. H. Lenneberg on training of normal humans by techniques used with chimpanzees, in Ettlinger et al. (1975). Cf. Fodor, Bever, and Garrett (1974), pp. 440–62, for a review of the whole issue.

10. Assuming now that Quine's suggestive metaphor ("Two Dogmas of Empiricism," reprinted in Quine [1953]) can be developed into a substantive theory. His own efforts in this direction seem to me to raise more problems than they solve. See chapter 4 and references cited there.

11. See Putnam (1962, 1975). Also Kripke (1972). For critical analysis of some of these notions, see Dummett, (1973), chap. 5, appendix; also Katz (1975). For criticism of the notion "semantic representation" from still other points of view, see Fodor, Fodor, and Garrett (forthcoming) and Harman (1973).

12. Katz (1972) and earlier work cited there.

13. That is, under idealizations that seem to me legitimate, if not essential, for serious study of the real-world problems.

14. Even if the semantic content of a lexical item is not fully specified by the grammar, there might still be some analytic connections. Thus, it has been plausibly suggested that such lexical properties as abstract "cause," "becoming," "agency," and "goal" are drawn from a universal set of semantic markers, available for semantic representation in the lexicon. If so, then even if such words as, say, "persuade" and "intend" are not fully characterized by the grammar in isolation from other cognitive structures, it might still be true that the connection between "I persuaded him to leave" and "he intends to leave" (with appropriate temporal qualifications) is analytic, by virtue of the substructure of lexical features and their general properties.

   · One might compare the lexical properties that have been utilized in semantic description with Leibniz's "simpler terms," by which other terms can be defined. For some discussion, cf. Ishiguro (1972), pp. 44ff.

15. Cf. Chomsky (1965), chap. 1. As noted there, an evaluation procedure is required in what we have been calling LT(H,L) if the compatibility conditions are insufficient to narrow the class of grammars considered to be the one (or ones) learned. If further devices for grammar selection can be devised, an evaluation procedure will be an essential part of LT(H,L) or not, depending, again, on the variability in the class of grammars meeting other conditions in this theory. Some have argued that more is at stake here, but I fail to see any issue.

16. A view of this sort is attributed to Leibniz by Ishiguro (1972), pp. 65ff. She argues that in Leibniz's theory, "the individuation of objects and the understanding of satisfaction-conditions for predicates already involve a great number of assumptions about laws of nature. . . ."

17. On this matter, see Kripke (1972).

18. Cf. Dummett (1973), p. 76: "in order to understand a proper name, we must know what sort or category of object it is to

be used as the name of." Cf. Kripke (1972), n. 58, for comments on a similar notion of Geach's.

19. Examples from Kripke (1972), pp. 268ff. As Kripke points out, "the question of essential properties so-called . . . is equivalent . . . to the question of identity across possible worlds," and thus enters into the question of applicability of model-theoretic semantics to the study of semantics of natural language. Kripke argues that the idea "that a property can be held to be essential or accidental to an object independently of its description" is not a philosopher's invention, but an idea that has "intuitive content" to "the ordinary man." While his examples and discussion do, surely, have intuitive force, it is less clear that they pertain to the question of properties essential to an object independently of its description or categorization. It seems to me that they do not suffice to establish the plausibility of this idea.

20. On this matter, see Quine (1969c), p. 343.

21. See the references of note 11.

22. I follow here the exposition in Moravcsik (1975a).

23. Kripke cites substance, origin, function ("being a table"—compare Aristotle's characterization of the "essence of a house" in terms of "purpose or end," as contrasted with the physicist's description in material terms; *De Anima* 403^b). Cf. note 14.

24. Moravcsik argues that this is the proper generalization for the Aristotelian notion "x is the aitia (cause) of y."

25. Cf. Miller (1974). Miller contrasts some of Quine's empiricist speculations on the learning of color terms by conditioning with the actual "conceptual development," which appears to follow a very different course, involving, not conditioning at some "primitive stage," but rather the abstraction of the domain of color, the employment of an innate system of "focal colors," and the location of other colors relative to these in the linguistically determined system. There are, Miller suggests, two "lines of development": "One involves learning to abstract the appropriate attribute and to anchor color perceptions to some internal frame of reference, the other involves discovering which words are relevant to that frame and learning which location in the frame goes with which term." Miller's analysis seems quite compatible with the general account we have been considering.

26. The belief that cognitive structures must be taught as well as learned is so widespread that citation is hardly necessary. To mention only the most recent example that I happen to have seen, D. D. Weiss (1975) argues that "we are so equipped that we can *inherit* [the complex skills and achievements which constitute the entire edifice of civilization], but only by means of *communication*—through teaching, instruction." For some fur-

ther examples on teaching of language, see notes 38 and 39 below, and chapter 4, pp. 161–2.

27. Searle (1972). While I disagree with some of Searle's conclusions, as indicated below, the bulk of his account seems to me accurate and compelling, including many of the critical comments. D. M. Armstrong (1971) suggests that the theory that communication provides *"the* clue to an analysis of the notion of linguistic meaning" can be traced to Locke.

28. Cf., e.g., Chomsky (1957), chap. 9; Chomsky (1975b).

29. Cf. references of preceding note. Also Miller and Chomsky (1963); Chomsky (1965), chaps. 1, 4; and many other references. I am sure that the same observation holds of others who have sought "essential properties" of language in its structural features. Thus A. M. Liberman (1974) suggests "that the distinctive characteristic of language is not meaning, thought, communication, or vocalization, but, more specifically, a grammatical recoding that reshapes linguistic information so as to fit it to the several originally nonlinguistic components of the system." But he would no doubt agree that there are intimate connections between structure and function. How could this fail to be true? Who has ever doubted it?

30. Chomsky (1966); also Chomsky (1964), chap. 1.

31. Cf. chapter 1, note 7, for a possible example.

32. Moravcsik (1975a) argues that "for Aristotle functional differences can never be ultimate; they must be shown to be dependent on constitutive or structural differences." He suggests further that the Aristotelian principle that functional explanation is derivative in this sense "has crucial bearings on explanations" in the social sciences. "Ultimately linguistic dispositions need be explained in terms of the structure of mind and brain. This is already clear in biology. Nobody would try to account for the details of human anatomy in terms of adaptation-value or survival-value. . . ." This seems quite correct.

33. Stampe (1968). Stampe offers a general argument against "the search for the nature of meanings." He holds that a person who believes that meanings are entities of some sort is committed to the view that in the sentence "the meaning of x is obscure," the phrase "the meaning of x" is a referring expression, so that the sentence means "the y which is the meaning of x is obscure." He argues that this conclusion leads to absurdity; there is no entity y which is obscure. But the argument is not very compelling. Someone might take the phrase "the source of the earth's light" to be a referring expression, but not in the sentence "the source of the earth's light is obscure" (the sun is not obscure). Similarly, one might argue that there is a y such that y is the number of the planets, but deny that "the number of the planets" is a referring expression in "the number of the

planets is unknown" (9 is not unknown). It might be argued that such expressions as "the number of the planets" are not referring expressions in any context; for some interesting observations on this matter, see Higgins (1973), chap. 5. It would be rash to argue, on these grounds, that it is incoherent to postulate the existence of numbers. Philosophers who have postulated the existence of meanings do so in the belief that they can construct a successful explanatory theory in these terms. This belief, right or wrong, seems immune to the kinds of argument that Stampe develops.

34. Whether there is indeed a "circularity," as alleged, is another question. Searle's criticisms are really directed against Katz's semantic theory, though Katz is barely mentioned. But Katz has argued that there is no circularity (Katz 1972, 1975). Searle does not explain why he thinks that Katz's argument fails. See now Katz's critique of Searle, and his attempt to incorporate a theory of speech acts within a "semantic theory" of the sort he has developed. (Katz, forthcoming.)

35. The expectation was only partially correct. Twenty years after completion, parts of that manuscript are now in press (Chomsky, 1955–6).

36. Note that all of these are cases in which the "utterer" assumes that there is no audience. Armstrong (1971) states that an analysis of meaning in terms of communication need not require that the speaker definitely believes there is an audience (or even cares), but "clearly he cannot believe that there definitely is no audience," as in these and indefinitely many other cases. If he is correct, then the analysis of meaning in terms of communication that he outlines is impossible for this reason alone.

37. The question is taken up again by Schiffer (1972), pp. 76ff. He considers the case of someone writing with no thought of a potential audience and argues that it seems "essential" to such examples that the "utterer" has the intention "to *provide himself* with various arguments, explanations, etc." Thus, "in each case where it is both the case that we are inclined to say that S meant that p by uttering x and that S apparently had no audience-directed intention, S's utterance x will be part of some activity directed towards securing some cognitive response in himself, and that it is in virtue of this significant resemblance to the standard case that we class these cases as instances of S-meaning." But in the standard case, the "cognitive response" in the hearer is that he is to believe something about the beliefs of the speaker. Thus if we are to assimilate the present case to the standard case, as Schiffer suggests, it would seem that we would be taking "S meant that p by uttering x" to mean that S uttered x with the intention of bringing himself to believe that he believes that p. But this is surely far from

the mark. Furthermore, in perfectly normal cases, S may have no thought of his own possible later use of what he writes (and certainly need not when he speaks or thinks in words). It seems that all of this gets us nowhere.

38. For discussion of certain notions developed in the later work of Wittgenstein, which Strawson takes to be one source for the theory of communication-intention, see Chomsky (1964), p. 24, and (1969b), pp. 275ff. The latter discussion contains some explicit and important qualifications that have been ignored by several critics who argue that it gives an inaccurate account of Wittgenstein's general picture. As it stands, dealing with the particular questions it does, the discussion seems to me entirely accurate. On this matter, see also Moravcsik (1967), pp. 227–9 (which also contains some relevant remarks on speech-act theory).

39. Strawson adopts without comment the common assumption, mentioned earlier, that language must be not only learned but also taught. He writes that "it is a fact about human beings that they simply would not acquire mastery [of a language] unless they were exposed, as children, to conditioning or training by adult members of a community." He assumes that the "procedure of training" is guided by a concern for the ends and purposes of language. For the learners, it is "a matter of responding vocally to situations in a way which will earn them reward or avoid punishment rather than a matter of *expressing their beliefs.*" There is no reason to believe that these factual claims are true.

40. Actually, some other arguments are offered, but they are unconvincing. Thus Strawson asks why, on the semantic theorist's grounds, a person should observe his own rules, or any rules: "Why shouldn't he express any belief he likes in any way he happens to fancy when he happens to have the urge to express it?" Suppose, Strawson argues, that the semantic theorist were to respond that the person wishes to record his beliefs for later reference. Strawson argues that "the theorist is debarred from giving this answer because it introduces, though in an attenuated form, the concept of communication-intention: the earlier man communicates with his later self." But the whole discussion is beside the point. There are two questions: (i) What is the nature of the "meaning-determining rules"? (ii) Why does a person follow the rules that he has (somehow) acquired? Conceivably the answer to (ii) involves reference to communication-intention, but it would not follow that "communication-intention" enters in any way into the explanation of meaning and how it is determined by rule (question (i)). Furthermore, it would suffice for the semantic theorist to respond to (ii) by asserting that it is simply a natural law that a person tends to follow the

rules he has learned. The answer is uninteresting, but not incorrect, for this reason.

41. Grice (1968). This is the only article by Grice that Strawson specifically cites, and it presumably is (at least a part of) what he has in mind in referring to Grice's work as giving reason to believe that a theory of communication-intention can be developed "which is proof against objection and which does not presuppose the notion of linguistic meaning."

42. For a criticism of Grice's theory along partly similar lines, see Ziff (1967).

Chapter 3. SOME GENERAL FEATURES OF LANGUAGE

1. See Chomsky (1972b), chap. 3; also several chapters in Parret (1974). Much of what I will describe here recapitulates or is an outgrowth of ideas presented in Chomsky (1973a). See Postal (1974a) for a critique of the latter, and Lightfoot (forthcoming) for an argument, which I think is correct, that the critique is beside the point, quite apart from questions of truth and falsity. The debate, of course, continues, and there is more that I would like to say about it, but this is not the place.

2. Less so than generally believed, I think. Several positions have emerged, but their proponents differ not only on some substantive issues but also on what the issues are. Consider just three positions: the "standard theory" (ST), the "extended standard theory" (EST), and "generative semantics" (GS). Proponents of GS generally take the major bifurcation to be between ST-EST and GS, and argue that a great deal is at stake. But many proponents of ST and EST, myself included, have argued that the central substantive issue of theory is the one that divides ST from EST-GS (namely, the role of surface structures in semantic interpretation), and that GS differs from EST primarily in that it relaxes some of the conditions on grammars imposed by EST. Part of the confusion of recent debate perhaps results from quite different perceptions as to what the issues are. For further discussion, see the references of the preceding note.

3. On this matter, see Aronoff (forthcoming).

4. Cf. Chomsky (1965), and for a summary, Chomsky (1972a), chap. 5. The rules that insert lexical items are "transformations" in the technical sense that they take into account global properties of the phrase markers to which they apply. But these lexical transformations have distinct properties not shared by operations of the transformational component of the grammar.

5. On the rules and principles that assign phonetic representa-

tions to syntactic structures and the phonological elements that appear in them, see Chomsky and Halle (1968), Bresnan (1973b), and many other sources.

6. Cf. Aronoff (forthcoming). On the structure of the categorial component, see Chomsky (1972), chap. 1, and further work by Dougherty, Bresnan, Jackendoff, Selkirk, Milner, Vergnaud, Halitsky, Siegel, and others.

7. Essentially, the theory outlined in Katz and Postal (1964) and Chomsky (1965). Cf. Katz (1972) for a recent version.

8. My own version of the standard theory was qualified in that I suggested that some aspects of meaning are determined by surface structure. By the time that Chomsky (1965) appeared, I had become convinced that this was true to a significant extent, in part, on the basis of work by Jackendoff.

9. On this matter, cf. Jackendoff (1972), Chomsky (1972a,b), and many other sources.

10. For some further discussion of this question, see Chomsky (1969c), reprinted in Chomsky (1972a).

11. On reasons for supposing that indefinites underlie such questions, see Chomsky (1964), Postal (1965). Note that the present discussion is misleading in that it overlooks the fact that the phrase markers in question are abstract structures ultimately mapped into sentences, and not sentences themselves.

12. Here and in subsequent discussion, I overlook distinctions between "who"–"whom," and other questions of morphology.

13. A transformation may in fact apply nonvacuously to only a subpart of a cyclic category. Williams (1974) suggests that transformations with smaller domains, in this sense, apply prior to those with larger domains, thus generalizing the notion of cyclic application. If this theory is correct, then the significance of what we are designating here "cyclic categories" lies in their role in determining conditions on application of rules (i.e., with regard to subjacency, "command" in anaphora, etc.).

14. Ross (1967) hypothesizes that rightward-movement rules are "bounded" in this sense. I will assume, with Ross, that this is correct. An apparent counterexample in Navajo is presented in Kaufman (1975). Her analysis, which deals with movement of an enclitic to what she assumes to be a complementizer position, suggests that Ross's principle and the more general condition of subjacency discussed here must be qualified somehow. One can think of various possibilities, but pending further study, I will simply leave the question open.

15. This analysis derives from Rosenbaum (1967). I follow here a reanalysis by Bresnan (1972).

16. Following Bresnan (1972), we assume that there are underlying structures corresponding to (i) "it is certain (probable) that John will win," and (ii) "*Y* is certain [John to win]," but not (iii)

"*Y* is probable [John to win]." The examples (i) do not undergo NP-preposing for quite general reasons.

17. I omit an illustrative example, since more complex issues arise that I do not want to pursue here.

18. Examples of this sort were originally discussed in Baker (1970), in a somewhat different system.

19. For one possible explanation, see Chomsky (1973a). For others, see references cited there.

20. On this matter, see Emonds (forthcoming), Bresnan (1972), Chomsky (1973a), and Vergnaud (1974).

21. We might ask why (13″) cannot be derived directly from (13), since there would be no violation of subjacency. There are, I think, good reasons, based on other conditions on transformations. Cf. Chomsky (1973a), and also the discussion below of the specified subject condition, which guarantees that the operation will always be performed on the "minimal domain," in an appropriate sense.

22. On this matter, see Erteschik (1973).

23. Suppose that in (16) we replace "believe" by "consider" and "claim" by "question." Then we can derive "John considered the question who Tom saw." Cf. Chomsky (1973a). We omit here consideration of "echo questions" such as "John believed that Mary said that Tom saw *who*?" or "John believed the claim that Tom saw *who*?"

24. Suppose that in (16) we replace "believe" by "make." Then in place of (16′) we would have "who did John make the claim that Tom saw?" Many speakers find this much more acceptable than (16′). A plausible explanation is that "make the claim" is reanalyzed by a rule of idiom formation as a complex verb meaning, essentially, "claim," so that—after the reanalysis—subjacency is not violated by application of *wh*-movement. On the other hand, there is no such reanalysis possible in the case of "believe the claim."

25. Cf. Ross (1967). For discussion, see Chomsky (1973a). The latter assumed that subjacency is applicable only to extraction rules and does not apply to rules lowering elements into embedded cyclic categories, deletion rules, or interpretive rules. A problem in the proposed explanation for certain island constraints is that these also appear to hold, in some cases at least, for rules that might be taken to be deletion or interpretive rules. On this matter, see the discussion of "comparative deletion" in Chomsky (1973a), Vergnaud (1974), and Bresnan (1975). Also, Postal (1974b), M. Liberman (1974), Liberman and Prince (forthcoming). My own belief is that the explanation offered in Chomsky (1973a) and here will prove to be a subcase of something more general. On subjacency, see also Akmajian (1975).

26. Cf. Chomsky (1973a). See also references of note 1.

27. As noted in Chomsky (1973a), pronominal anaphora violates these principles. The violation was taken there to pose a problem, but further reflection shows that it does not. Pronominal anaphora belongs to an entirely different system of rules involving quite different conditions (e.g., command), not statable in the theory of transformations at all, and not even restricted to sentence grammar. There is, in fact, a rather natural analysis of rules into several categories in terms of their position in the system of linguistic rules and the conditions that apply to them. For some discussion, see below, pp. 104–5.

28. It remains to explain just what this phrase means, how it functions in inference, etc. This poses an interesting problem of descriptive semantics, which I will not explore further here.

29. On this matter, see Jackendoff (1972), Chomsky (1972b), and references cited there.

30. Recall that we are taking sentence to be analyzed as COMP S_{red}; cf. p. 88, above. I have eliminated from consideration the root transformation of subject-auxiliary inversion, for ease of exposition.

31. There is, I think, independent motivation for the assumption that the general principles of anaphora apply to logical forms rather than to surface structures directly, but I will not pursue this interesting question here.

32. Cf. Chomsky (1973a). Also chapter 4, p. 150, (7).

33. In (29), the rule is blocked not only by the specified-subject condition, but also (independently) by what is called the "tensed-sentence condition" in Chomsky (1973a).

34. I assume here an abstract notion of "subject" in accordance with which "Bill" is the subject of the embedded sentences of (29)–(30) and also of the noun phrase "Bill's hatred of each other" in (31). Cf. Chomsky (1972b), chaps. 1, 3.

35. A special case of bound anaphora is reflexivization, as persuasively argued by Helke (1970). For a theory of anaphora of the sort discussed imprecisely here, cf. Lasnik (1974) and Reinhart (1974). For general discussion of related problems, see Fauconnier (1974) and Wasow (1972, forthcoming), and references cited in these works, particularly Dougherty (1969).

36. Cf. Keenan and Comrie (1973), for discussion of a general notion of "precedence" of grammatical relations and its role in determining the domain of syntactic rules. Ross has discussed a related notion of "primacy" in unpublished papers.

37. Cf. Fiengo (1974), where there is also a more detailed discussion of other topics touched on here.

38. On the general notion "anaphora," see the references of note 35.

39. To forestall an irrelevancy, there is no "clause-mate condition" on the rule that relates reciprocals to their antecedents. Cf. Chomsky (1973a). Thus the alleged existence of a rule raising

embedded subjects to the object position in the matrix sentence is beside the point. Cf. references of note 1.

40. Cf. Chomsky (1965), chap. 1, and earlier references cited there.

41. Emonds has argued that a different rule of NP-preposing is involved (cf. Emonds, forthcoming), noting that there are differences in the domain of the rule. Thus NP-preposing applies to the noun phrase "the lecture yesterday," giving "yesterday's lecture," but not to the sentence "he lectured yesterday," giving "yesterday was lectured by him." I think that in many cases, perhaps all, the discrepancies can be attributed to other factors. Thus, as noted before, the subject-predicate relation is defined on surface structures of sentences (but not noun phrases), and it might be plausibly argued that "was lectured (by NP)" is not a possible predicate of "yesterday," accounting for the ungrammaticalness. On the question whether the deviance of the sentence in question is "semantic" or "syntactic" in origin, cf. p. 95 above and the reference cited there. Note that we have not accounted for the possessive in (50iii); on this matter, see Siegel (1974).

42. I deal here only with the simplest case. For a more general discussion, see Fiengo (1974).

43. There are many similar examples in which NP-preposing applies to structures reanalyzed by idiom-formation rules, which assign phrases to the category Verb: e.g., "the argument was taken exception to," "John was taken advantage of," etc. Naturally, these vary in acceptability. See also note 24.

   In ordinary passives such as (55), the rule of NP-preposing disregards the grammatical relation between the verb and the NP following it, at least if we use the term "grammatical relation" in something like its traditional sense. Thus in (55), the rule moves the direct object, but in such cases as "John was told to leave" or "John was promised that he would get the job," it is the indirect object that is preposed (cf. "John was told a story," "a story was told to John"; "our promise to John . . . ," not "our promise of John . . ."; compare also "John was told about the accident," or simply, "John was told."). Thus, it comes as no surprise that in (57), for example, the rule of NP-preposing applies to an NP that bears no grammatical relation to the preceding verb at all. For discussion, cf. Chomsky (1973a) and references of note 1 above. Some of the discussion of this matter in recent literature is misleading in that it fails to make clear that there is general agreement that the rule in question is not limited to direct objects, where the notion "direct object" is understood in the conventional way.

44. Examples that come to mind are the (possible) rules that relate causatives to corresponding intransitives (e.g., "X broke the glass," "the glass broke"; "X melted the wax," "the wax melted";

cf. Fiengo [1974] for discussion) and the so-called rule of "tough-movement" relating "John was easy to please" and "X was easy to please John" (it is argued in Lasnik and Fiengo [1974] that the rule of "tough-movement" in fact deletes, rather than moves, the embedded object, but their arguments apply only to an analysis within the standard theory; cf. Jackendoff [forthcoming]).

45. Cf. Aronoff (forthcoming). Another significant phenomenon motivating a passive rule in English but not in many other languages—e.g., those of the type discussed here—is the application of NP-preposing to "idiom chunks," as in "tabs were kept on them" (for some discussion of cases where this is and is not possible, see Fiengo [1974]), and to noun phrases that do not ordinarily appear in comparable subject positions, e.g., "a man was found to do the job."

46. This fact, surely crucial in the analysis of passives, is discussed extensively in the earliest work on transformational generative grammar; cf. Chomsky (1955). See now Fiengo (1974).

47. Cf. Chomsky (1972b), chap. 3. Cf. also Katz (1972) and references cited there for discussion of thematic relations within the framework of the standard theory. On the issue in general, see Jackendoff (1969, 1972, 1974a).

48. Cf. the discussion of indirect questions in Chomsky (1973a); also Jackendoff (1975). In work within the extended standard theory in which relative clauses are derived by raising of an embedded NP to the antecedent position (eg., Vergnaud, 1974), it was necessary to assume that some grammatical relations that enter into determination of thematic relations are defined, not in deep structure, but at the point of first appearance of lexical items in the relevant position in the cycle. This and some other problems involving cyclic determination of thematic relations are overcome under the trace theory.

49. See my comments in Parret (1974). It is occasionally noted in the literature that theories that do not use global rules employ instead certain syntactic features to deal with such phenomena as agreement, and it is further argued that use of "arbitrary syntactic features" also gives an undesired extension of descriptive power, perhaps even more so than global rules. It is unclear what the relevance of these observations may be, since no one has proposed the use of "arbitrary syntactic features," but rather of narrowly restricted and quite well-motivated ones.

50. For discussion, see Wexler, Culicover, and Hamburger (1974) and work surveyed there.

51. For example, in Piaget's theory of developmental stages. The empirical status of Piaget's theories is controversial. For varying assessments, see Bergling (1974) and Bryant (1974).

52. On Lorenz's views in this connection, see Chomsky (1972a), p.

95. For some discussion of similar conclusions of Monod's, see Chomsky (1971), pp. 13ff.

53. Stent (1975). His argument is not unlike the conjecture in chapter 1, p. 25, that the study of M_{CS} might not fall within the science-forming capacity.

54. On this matter, see Chomsky (1969d) and Chomsky (1973b), chap. 7.

55. For some remarks on these relations, see Chomsky (1972a), pp. 97–8. Cf. Wang (1974), pp. 324ff., for some discussion of Gödel's views on the limitations on mechanistic explanations in biology. It is worth noting that his speculations on this matter, as Wang reports them, do not derive from his mathematical work, which has sometimes been invoked by others in an effort to establish similar conclusions.

56. On the collapse of liberal doctrine in the nineteenth century, cf. Polanyi (1957) and Rocker (1938). For a fuller discussion of my own views on the matters discussed here, cf. Chomsky (1969d), chap. 1; Chomsky (1973b), chaps. 8, 9.

57. On this matter, see Macpherson (1962).

58. Kant, "An Answer to the Question 'What is Enlightenment?' " in Reiss (1970), p. 59. Once "this germ . . . has developed within this hard shell, it gradually reacts upon the mentality of the people, who thus gradually become increasingly able to *act freely*."

59. Cf. references of note 56 and elsewhere.

60. Bakunin, "The International and Karl Marx." Dolgoff (1972), p. 319. The other remarks of Bakunin cited will also be found here. For further discussion of such views and the various forms they have taken, and the realization of some of these prophetic insights, see Chomsky (1973b, c).

61. The terms are Humboldt's. Cf. Chomsky (1973b), chap. 9.

Part II

Chapter 4. PROBLEMS AND MYSTERIES IN THE STUDY OF HUMAN LANGUAGE

1. To be more precise, advocates of these notions often do not formulate them with sufficient clarity so that there could be disconfirming evidence, and in the face of examples such as (1)–(4) simply reiterate their hypothesis that some adequate theory can be developed along the lines they advocate. Such a "hypothesis" is not to be confused with explanatory hypotheses such as S might propose to account for certain facts; the term "prayer" might be more fitting than "hypothesis." Note that suspension

of judgment with respect to apparently intractable evidence is a reasonable, in fact necessary, stance in rational inquiry, but there comes a point when it becomes irrational, particularly when alternative and more adequate theories are available. It seems to me that in this case the point was reached long ago.

2. I emphasize, *as presented.* There are many articles in the literature discussing beliefs attributed to me that I do not hold, have never expressed, and have repeatedly rejected. For discussion of a few recent examples, see Chomsky and Katz (1974, 1975); Chomsky (1974, 1975a).

3. Care should be distinguished from training. Thus certain kinds of human interaction are no doubt necessary for innate mechanisms to operate, but it does not follow that this interaction constitutes teaching or training, or that it determines the character of the systems acquired. Cf. Chomsky (1965), chap. 1, §8, for discussion of this and related problems, and discussion of the alternatives I am referring to here as R and E.

4. Again, more complex versions are possible. S might be led to conclude that there are stages of maturation through which P develops, and perhaps that experience is necessary for this succession to take place, or perhaps even that variety of experience may affect the stages achieved. I will put aside these quite realistic possibilities and consider here the case of learning as an "instantaneous process." As contrasted with the earlier idealizations suggested, this one is distorting and illegitimate—there might be no answer to the questions raised. But at the present stage of our understanding, I think we can still continue profitably to accept it as a basis for investigation. Cf. chapter 3, pp. 119–22.

Peters (1972a) discusses this idealization, arguing that it is not illegitimate. But his discussion fails to distinguish two notions of "input data" for a "language-acquisition device." He takes these data to be structured and organized by earlier analysis—thus his "projection problem" is concerned with the moment of attainment of grammar, all preliminary hypotheses and stages being incorporated into the input data. In this formulation the idealization is not illegitimate. But in the work he is discussing, the input data were taken as an unstructured set (for reasons which I will not discuss here). Thus the idealization is illegitimate, as observed by those who proposed the idealization and those who criticized it.

5. We can, of course, trivialize the learning theory that takes these notions to be fundamental by defining "analogy" and "generalization" in terms of the postulated schematism and evaluation procedure. But I will here take this alternative theory to be a substantive one, which specifies these notions in some nontrivial way, say, in terms of similarity along certain presupposed di-

mensions or replacement in a given substitution class. There are many interesting problems here that would take the discussion too far afield, but that might be pursued with profit.

6. Cf. Jackendoff (1969, 1972) and Chomsky (1972b). Jackendoff (1972) contains a particularly interesting discussion of how control is determined by thematic relations. For a modification of this view in terms of the trace theory of movement rules, see chapter 3.

7. Recall also the effect of replacing "their wives" by "their children" in (3). Cf. Dougherty (1968, 1970, 1971, 1974) and Fiengo and Lasnik (1973) for discussion of the syntax and semantics of these constructions.

8. On the functioning of this rule, first noted by Postal, see Chomsky (1973a). It is immaterial here whether we interpret the rule as requiring disjoint reference or as assigning a preference to it. The disjoint-reference property is actually more general, as noted in Chomsky (1973a).

9. This conclusion is rejected by Beloff (1973, p. 185), on the following grounds: "No doubt one could easily think up dozens of bizarre rules about which one could confidently say that they would not be found in any known language, just as one could easily think up dozens of bizarre customs that would never be found in any known society, but does this mean that we are forced to postulate inborn universals?" Taking the answer to the latter question to be no, Beloff concludes that nothing much follows from the absence of such "bizarre rules" as the structure-independent hypothesis 1 of chapter 1, in natural languages. Analysis of his argument reveals a number of confusions that are, as will be seen below, typical of much discussion. Consider first the conclusion: We are not "forced" to postulate inborn universals. This is true, but irrelevant. Data never force us to a specific nontrivial explanatory theory. The question is whether rational inquiry leads us (not forces us) to postulate inborn universals to explain the facts in question. Second, consider his assumption that hypothesis 1 is "bizarre" as compared with the structure-dependent hypothesis 2. By what standards? Surely not any general considerations of simplicity or naturalness. As noted in chapter 1, such considerations would lead to choice of the structure-independent hypothesis 1. To say that this rule is "bizarre" for humans is simply to rephrase the observation that humans select structure-dependent rules. It is at this point that rational inquiry begins, seeking to discover what properties of the organism or its experience explain particular observations. The same would be true in the case of "bizarre" customs. Contrary to what Beloff seems to be saying, systematic absence of "bizarre" customs or rules always requires explanation. Sometimes uninteresting properties of organisms

may suffice to explain the phenomenon, in which case it will be dismissed as unimportant. The example in question cannot be dismissed in this way. To say that rules or customs are "bizarre" (even if correct, as it is not in this case) is simply to stop short of the only interesting questions. An explanation is required, if not in terms of inborn universals, then in some other way. I should add that Beloff's treatment of these questions is one of the best I know in a text of this sort.

10. Cf. Greenfield, Nelson, and Saltzman (1972) for an attempt to pursue this possibility.

11. There presumably are elements of P relating to identification of distinctive features, rhythmic and intonational features, and so on. Possibly these are analogous in their function to analyzing mechanisms of other perceptual and learning systems.

12. It is not obvious that the results of conditioning experiments in humans really do establish what they claim. In an extensive analysis of the literature, William Brewer (forthcoming) suggests that in fact they do not. Rather, where the experimental paradigm permits investigation of the question, it seems that the conditioning procedures generally amount to no more than a complicated device for providing the human subject with information that he uses, consciously, in responding to the instructions—which explains why a simple instruction may suffice for "extinction." See also Estes (1972) for rather similar suggestions, based on experiments designed to examine this question.

13. A demonstration of this sort is given, in effect, by Patrick Suppes for his theory of stimulus sampling. Cf. Suppes (1969). Suppes takes this result to be evidence in support of his theory. This curious conclusion can perhaps be traced to a serious misunderstanding of the issues that are at stake in the study of learning, discussed by Pylyshyn (1973).

14. We cannot attribute the differences between rat and human in this respect simply to sensory processing abilities; thus rats have sensory modalities that could be used, in principle, for language. Recent attempts to teach symbolic systems to apes might give insights into the differential abilities of apes and humans with respect to the language faculty. One suggestive study indicates that global aphasics with left-hemisphere damage and severely impaired language ability are trainable by the methods used in the experiments with apes (Glass, Gazzaniga, and Premack, 1973). Further work along such lines might be revealing in determining the specific properties of neural structures (e.g., lateralization) that presumably explain the qualitative differences between humans and other organisms in ability to attain cognitive structures. It is perhaps of some interest that the only known example of lateralization outside of humans is a case

of control of a song in one species of songbird (Nottebohm, 1970).

15. For an unusually sophisticated account, which nevertheless seems to me to suffer from a qualified version of this misleading formulation, see Reber (1973).

16. Alston (1963). Alston seems to accept at least this part of an argument for "use-analysis" that he discusses.

17. At this point, the analogy should not be pressed too far. Thus the relation between my pressing the accelerator and the car's moving is explicable in terms of known physical laws, and there seems no reason to doubt that attainment of knowledge of language is within the potential range of that part of natural science that is well understood. But it is an open question whether the same is true of language use.

18. Ultimately. It is never easy to tell when apparent counterevidence should lead to abandonment of a theory. S might attribute to his subject several systems of belief, which may lead to inconsistent beliefs. This raises problems that I will not attempt to explore here.

19. Again, familiar and inescapable contingencies of empirical inquiry should be noted. There is no guarantee that the best theory constructed on the basis of such data as (1)–(13) will be correct; consideration of broader data (in this case, data of performance) might indicate that what appeared to be genuine explanatory principles are spurious and that generalizations discovered are accidental. Investigation of the theory of performance might thus lead to different theories of competence. No problems of principle arise here, though the matter has sometimes been discussed as though they do. I return to examples below. For an account that seems to me generally accurate and perceptive, see Pylyshyn (1973).

20. On the possibility of an explication in terms of "knowing how," see Chomsky (1975a).

21. For argument in support of this decision, see Graves, Katz, et al. (1973).

22. Schwartz (1969). Cf. also Goodman (1969) for some similar remarks, and my comments in Chomsky (1975a). Compare Schwartz's correct but wholly irrelevant observation with Beloff's remark that the data do not "force" us to a specific conclusion (see note 9).

23. For debate over these issues, see the references of note 7. For another example, see Jackendoff (1974b).

24. Quine seems to be assuming that some existing systems of grammar might "guide" Danish speakers of English who have learned English from these rules. But Quine's statement that actual grammars "really fall short ... at some points" is a vast understatement. Furthermore, there is no reason to believe that a

person could consciously master a grammar as a guide to behavior, in Quine's sense. Rather, people learn language from pedagogic grammars by the use of their unconscious universal grammar (and for all we know, this may be unavoidable in principle). Thus no speaker of Danish has to learn from a book that (14) is not the question associated with (16), or that English sentences such as (1)–(13) have the properties determined by SSC. And were they to be made conscious of principles that lead to these results, there is little doubt that these principles could not be consciously applied, in real time, to "guide" performance.

25. For discussion, see Chomsky, Halle, Lukoff (1956); Chomsky and Halle (1968); Bresnan (1973b).
26. Chomsky (1964, 1969a). See note 30.
27. Recall again the scope of Quine's "translation model," which is to be understood as encompassing the problem of understanding another speaker of the same language, learning a first language, the linguist's study of a new language.
28. For a similar proposal, see Hiż (1973).
29. In the latter case too there are familiar idealizations. Thus no physicist is concerned because the law of falling bodies may "fail" if someone reaches out to catch the falling person before he hits the ground, an act which physics, so far as we know, cannot predict or explain. On Schwartz's grounds, we must therefore conclude that physics is empty, since any fact that violates its principles is placed outside the scope of its predictions (paraphrasing Schwartz's remarks on language, discussed above).
30. Quine's responses to other criticisms and queries that I raised in the same article simply avoid or misrepresent the issues. Thus I pointed out that his characterization of language and language learning, if taken literally, conflicts with truisms that he accepts, e.g., that a language is infinite. In response, Quine simply reiterates what I stated explicitly, namely, that he of course accepts the truism. But this does not deal with the criticism, which is that the position he develops is inconsistent with the truism that he accepts. He also claims falsely that I attributed to him the theory that "learning sentences" involves "sentences only as unstructured wholes," but in fact my discussion included all of the devices he suggests for language learning, including the one he cites in response. I will not undertake to review the matter case by case here, but a careful comparison of his response with my criticisms and requests for clarification will show, I believe, that in each case he simply misunderstood the point or misrepresented what I said. The problems in Quine (1960) remain exactly as I stated them, so far as I can see.
31. In Chomsky (1969a) I pointed out tentatively that Quine ap-

pears to be using "theory" and "language" interchangeably in such contexts as these. In his response (Quine, 1969a, p. 310), he makes it explicit that this is so. Thus, he states, "language or theory [is] a fabric or 'network of sentences associated to one another and to external stimuli by the mechanism of conditioned response.'" It is quite impossible to characterize a theory in these terms, over and above the problems involved in the analysis of language.

32. If a language is a fabric of associated sentences and stimuli, and substitution of "hand" for "foot" in the context "my —— hurts" by "analogic synthesis" constitutes a mode of "learning of sentences" (Quine's example), then this case of analogic synthesis must involve a mode of "association." But this conclusion deprives the notion "association" of any meaning.

33. These remarks are in response to my query as to what kind of quality space Quine had in mind. I noted that his examples suggested that he was restricting himself to certain dimensions with simple physical correlates, though he seemed willing to accept a strong version of the theory of innate ideas within this framework. Or, if these examples were not representative, we are left with no idea what the basis for learning is, since one might imagine a quality space with dimensions so abstract that, say, the concept "sentence in English" could be "learned" from one instance by "generalization." The reference to Goodman (1951) is indirect, but, I take it, intended.

34. Even if there is a coherent notion of "quality space" in the sense intended. I return to this question directly.

35. A few lines later he imposes the much narrower requirement that "talk of ideas comes to count as unsatisfactory except insofar as it can be *paraphrased into terms of dispositions to observable behavior*" (my emphasis). This latter requirement seems to me quite unreasonable, in psychology as in any other branch of science. Elsewhere Quine insists that "to make proper sense of the hypothesis that the subject-predicate construction is a linguistic universal, we need an unequivocal behavioral criterion of subject and predicate" (Quine, 1972). Again, this is an entirely unreasonable demand to impose on a theoretical concept such as "subject" or "predicate." To "make proper sense of the hypothesis" it would surely suffice to meet the requirement of Quine (1969b).

36. Cohen (1966), pp. 47–56, for these and following quotations.

37. In Chomsky (1965), I suggested that E, as outlined there, includes such approaches as Hume's theory of learning, Quine (1960), most "behavioral" theories that have been made at all clear, and theories of structural linguistics (apart from some elements of distinctive-feature theory), if interpreted as theories of learning.

38. Recall that the same false claim was advanced by Schwartz. One finds similar arguments rather commonly. Consider, e.g., the following statement by an anonymous reviewer in the *Times Literary Supplement*, October 12, 1973: "What evidence do we have that speakers have developed rules for Chomskyan deep structures? Undoubtedly the transformationalists have not provided it. Nor do they seem to seek it; to justify their grammars they regularly turn to logical criteria of simplicity and generality." (I assume that by "deep structures" the reviewer means something like "grammars.") "Transformationalists" have argued that speakers have developed specific systems of grammatical rules, and have sought to explain, on this basis, innumerable facts about the form and interpretation of utterances. They have thus provided substantial evidence for (and often against) specific hypotheses about the rules that speakers have developed. The reviewer feels that this is no evidence; something else is required. Suppose that a scientist investigating some device were to conclude that its structure is such-and-such, appealing to criteria of simplicity and generality along with the evidence he has accumulated about its behavior. By the reviewer's standards, no matter how much evidence the scientist provides, he has still produced no evidence for his hypotheses concerning the structure of the device; something else is needed. As in the case of Cohen, Quine, and Schwartz, we see here a reflection of the curious unwillingness to deal with human beings as part of the natural world, in accordance with the standards and methods of scientific inquiry. It is noteworthy that in each case, the author feels himself to be defending a scientific approach to the study of human behavior.

39. That is, theories that fall between the upper and lower bounds imposed by empirical requirements, discussed earlier; namely, those that satisfy the "indisputable point about language" that Quine quotes. Cf. pp. 200–201.

40. Notice that if the project Cohen is criticizing were merely unfeasible in that it would be necessary to "scour the universe" for relevant evidence, this would demonstrate that postulating linguistic universals is no "tautological pretence," contrary to Cohen's earlier claim, since on this assumption relevant evidence does not exist in principle.

41. Cohen asserts that my historical allusions to Descartes and Leibniz are inaccurate in that Descartes and Leibniz denied that innate ideas explain linguistic competence. Without entering into this latter question, I must nevertheless reject Cohen's criticism, since I nowhere attributed to Descartes and Leibniz the views that he claims they reject (and furthermore, I did refer to this element in the beliefs of Leibniz and others; cf. Chomsky [1966], p. 93). Rather, I discussed ideas of this sort that were developed

by many others, including Cartesians of varying degrees of ortho-doxy. The references to Descartes and Leibniz were relevant to other parts of my discussion and, to my knowledge, were quite accurate, contrary to what Cohen claims without argument or citation.

42. More accurately, he does make some specific suggestions, but they are hopelessly inadequate, so far as we know; e.g., his suggestion that the "multiplicity of concepts involved" in "generalizations about surface structure" can be "reduced to two primitive ones ('sentence' and 'nominal') by assuming a mode of derivation for the others like that used in categorial grammars." See Chomsky (1969c) for some comments on earlier proposals to the same effect.

43. He does offer an argument based on "Darwinian conceptions of evolution," recognizing that such explanations are "rather speculative." The latter is an understatement. Contrary to what Cohen claims, nothing we know of the mechanisms of evolution suggests that "the task of explaining the innateness of certain specifically syntactic principles, in terms of Darwinian evolution, is in principle a great deal more difficult than that of explaining the innateness of certain more general abilities." Cohen's argument is analogous to an argument that people learn to walk (rather than, say, to roll) or learn to grow arms (rather than arbitrary appendages) on grounds that the task of explaining the innateness of specific modes of locomotion (or limbs) in terms of Darwinian evolution is in principle more difficult than that of explaining the innateness of more general abilities (tendencies). If we want to pursue such speculations, consider Cohen's claim that scientific discovery proceeds by the same mechanisms as language learning. But, as noted earlier, over the past centuries or millennia there has been no selectional advantage in an ability to discover the principles of quantum theory, though there is an obvious selectional advantage in an ability to discover the language of one's speech community. Hence if one wants to give any weight to such speculations (I do not), they would hardly seem to support Cohen's conclusions.

44. Note that "comparable" is not synonymous with "identical."

45. Searle has a response to Gewirth (Searle, 1973), but I think that Gewirth's remarks stand.

46. *Meditations* (trans. Haldane and Ross, 1955), 1:191. Similar ideas were expressed by others, before and after Descartes. Cf. Chomsky (1966), pp. 79, 108, 112, and elsewhere. Cf. also chapter 1, pp. 5–7.

47. Others have indeed made a claim rather like this. Thus Vendler asserts that "Descartes envisions a 'generative' grammar, and semantics, for his language, which would correspond to the

generative structure of thought," though he did not realize "that a natural language comes close to this ideal" (1972, p. 181). He bases this conclusion on remarks by Descartes concerning an invented language presupposing "true philosophy" in which an infinity of words (and thoughts) can be enumerated. In Chomsky (1966, p. 84), I cited similar discussions by Galileo and the Port-Royal grammarians, without, however, drawing Vendler's conclusion, which seems to me questionable.

48. Cf. the discussion of "foundations of science" above and in earlier references cited there; also, Chomsky (1970) and other material that is reprinted in (1973b). Cf. also chapters 1, 3.

49. All of the following quotations are from Hume's *Enquiry Concerning Human Understanding* (ed. Selby-Bigge, 1902).

50. Compare Lord Herbert's discussion of "natural instinct" and his contention that the system of common notions is "that part of knowledge with which we were endowed in the primeval plan of Nature." For discussion in a related context, see Chomsky (1966). It is, incidentally, too strong to say that the "limited empiricism" of Hume "rejects innate knowledge" (Barnes, 1972).

51. Cf. Cooper (1972), Chomsky and Katz (1975).

Bibliography

Akmajian, Adrian. 1975. "More Evidence for an NP Cycle." *Linguistic Inquiry* 6:115–30.

Alston, William P. 1963. "Meaning and Use." *Philosophical Quarterly* 13:107–24.

Anderson, Stephen R., and Paul Kiparsky, eds. 1973. *A Festschrift for Morris Halle*. New York: Holt, Rinehart & Winston.

Armstrong, D. M. 1971. "Meaning and Communication." *Philosophical Review* 80:427–47.

Arnauld, Antoine. 1964. *The Art of Thinking: Port-Royal Logic*. Trans. J. Dickoff and P. James. Indianapolis: Bobbs-Merrill Co.

Aronoff, Mark H. Forthcoming. *Word-Structure*. Cambridge, Mass.: MIT Press.

Atherton, Margaret, and Robert Schwartz. 1974. "Linguistic Innateness and Its Evidence." *Journal of Philosophy* 71:155–68.

Austin, John L. 1940. "The Meaning of a Word." In Urmson and Warnock, 1961.

———. 1962. *How to Do Things with Words*. London: Oxford University Press.

Baker, C. Leroy. 1970. "Notes on the Description of English Questions: The Role of an Abstract Question Morpheme." *Foundations of Language* 6:197–209.

Barnes, Jonathan. 1972. "Mr. Locke's Darling Notion." *Philosophical Quarterly* 22:193–214.

Beloff, John. 1973. *Psychological Sciences: A Review of Modern Psychology*. New York: Harper & Row.

Bergling, Kurt. 1974. *The Development of Hypothetico-deductive Thinking in Children*. IEA Monograph Studies no. 3. Stockholm: Almqvist & Wiksell International.

Berlin, Isaiah. 1972. "The Bent Twig." *Foreign Affairs* 51:11–30.

Bower, T. G. R. 1972. "Object Perception in Infants." *Perception* 1:15–30.

Bracken, Harry M. 1972. "Chomsky's Cartesianism." *Language Sciences*, October, pp. 11–18.

———. 1973a. "Minds and Learning: The Chomskian Revolution." *Metaphilosophy* 4:229–45.

————. 1973b. "Essence, Accident and Race." *Hermathena*, no. 116, pp. 88–95.

————. 1974. *Berkeley*. London: MacMillan & Co.

Braine, Martin D. S. 1974. "On What Might Constitute Learnable Phonology." *Language* 50:270–99.

Bresnan, Joan W. 1970. "On Complementizers: Towards a Syntactic Theory of Complement Types." *Foundations of Language* 6:297–321.

————. 1972. "The Theory of Complementation in English." Ph.D. dissertation, MIT.

————. 1973a. "Syntax of the Comparative Clause Construction in English." *Linguistic Inquiry* 4:275–344.

————. 1973b. "Sentence Stress and Syntactic Transformations." In Hintikka, Moravcsik, and Suppes, 1973.

————. 1975. "Comparative Deletion and Constraints on Transformations." *Linguistic Analysis* 1:25–74.

Brewer, William F. Forthcoming. "There Is No Convincing Evidence for Operant or Classical Conditioning in Adult Humans." In Weimer and Palermo, forthcoming.

Bruner, J. S., and Barbara Koslowski. 1972. "Visually Preadapted Constituents of Manipulatory Action." *Perception* 1:3–14.

Bryant, Peter. 1974. *Perception and Understanding in Young Children*. New York: Basic Books.

Chomsky, Noam. 1955–56. "Logical Structure of Linguistic Theory." Mimeographed. New York: Plenum Publishing Corp., 1975.

————. 1957. *Syntactic Structures*. The Hague: Mouton & Co.

————. 1964. *Current Issues in Linguistic Theory*. The Hague: Mouton & Co.

————. 1965. *Aspects of the Theory of Syntax*. Cambridge, Mass.: MIT Press.

————. 1966. *Cartesian Linguistics*. New York: Harper & Row.

————. 1968a. "Recent Contributions to the Theory of Innate Ideas." In Cohen and Wartofsky, 1968.

————. 1968b. *Language and Mind*. New York: Harcourt Brace Jovanovich. Extended edition, 1972a.

————. 1969a. "Quine's Empirical Assumptions." In Davidson and Hintikka, 1969. Excerpted from "Some Empirical Assumptions in Modern Philosophy of Language" (1969b). In Morgenbesser, Suppes, and White, 1969.

————. 1969c. "Linguistics and Philosophy." In Hook, 1969. Reprinted in Chomsky, 1972a.

————. 1969d. *American Power and the New Mandarins*. New York: Pantheon Books.

————. 1970. "Language and Freedom." *Abraxas* 1. Reprinted in Chomsky, 1973b.

————. 1971. *Problems of Knowledge and Freedom*. New York: Pantheon Books.

———. 1972a. *Language and Mind.* Extended ed. New York: Harcourt Brace Jovanovich.

———. 1972b. *Studies on Semantics in Generative Grammar.* The Hague: Mouton & Co.

———. 1973a. "Conditions on Transformations." In Anderson and Kiparsky, 1973.

———. 1973b. *For Reasons of State.* New York: Pantheon Books.

———. 1973c. "Science and Ideology." *Jawarharlal Nehru Memorial Lectures: 1967–72,* Nehru Memorial Fund, New Delhi. Bombay: Bharatiya Vidya Bhavan.

———. 1974. "Dialogue with Noam Chomsky." In Parret, 1974.

———. 1975a. "Knowledge of Language." In Gunderson and Maxwell, 1975.

———. 1975b. "Questions of Form and Interpretation." *Linguistic Analysis* 1:75–109.

———, and Morris Halle. 1968. *Sound Pattern of English.* New York: Harper & Row.

———, Morris Halle, and Fred Lukoff. 1956. "On Accent and Juncture in English." In Halle, Lunt and MacLean, 1956.

———, and J. J. Katz. 1974. "What the Linguist Is Talking About." *Journal of Philosophy,* 71:347–67.

———. 1975. "On Innateness: A Reply to Cooper." *Philosophical Review,* 84:70–87.

Cohen, L. Jonathan. 1966. *The Diversity of Meaning.* 2nd ed. London: Methuen & Co.

———. 1970. "Some Applications of Inductive Logic to the Theory of Language." *American Philosophical Quarterly,* 7:299–310.

Cohen, Robert S., and Marx Wartofsky, eds. 1968. *Boston Studies in the Philosophy of Science,* vol. 3. Dordrecht: Reidel Publishing Co.

Cooper, David E. 1972. "Innateness: Old and New." *Philosophical Review* 81:465–83.

Cudworth, Ralph. 1838. *Treatise Concerning Eternal and Immutable Morality.* New York: Andover.

Davidson, Donald, and Jaakko Hintikka, eds. 1969. *Words and Objections: Essays on the Work of W. V. Quine.* Dordrecht: Reidel Publishing Co.

Dolgoff, Sam. 1972. *Bakunin on Anarchy.* New York: Alfred A. Knopf.

Dougherty, Ray C. 1968. "A Transformational Grammar of Coordinate Conjoined Structures." Ph.D. dissertation, MIT.

———. 1969. "An Interpretive Theory of Pronominal Reference." *Foundations of Language* 5:488–519.

———. 1970. "A Grammar of Coordinate Conjunction, I." *Language* 46:850–98.

———. 1971. "A Grammar of Coordinate Conjunction II." *Language* 47:298–399.

————. 1974. "The Syntax and Semantics of *Each Other* Constructions." *Foundations of Language* 12:1–48.

Dummett, Michael. 1973. *Frege: Philosophy of Language*. London: Duckworth & Co.

Eimas, Peter D., Einar R. Siqueland, Peter Jusczyk, and James Vigorito, 1971. "Speech Perception in Infants." *Science* 171: 303–6.

Emonds, Joseph E. Forthcoming. *Root and Structure-Preserving Transformations*.

Erteschik, Nomi. 1973. "On the Nature of Island Constraints." Ph.D. dissertation, MIT.

Estes, William K. 1972. "Reinforcement in Human Behavior." *American Scientist* 60:723–29.

Ettlinger, G., H.-L. Teuber, and B. Milner. 1975. "Report: The Seventeenth International Symposium of Neuropsychology." *Neuropsychologia* 13:125–34.

Fauconnier, Gilles R. 1974. *Coréférence: Syntaxe ou Semantique*. Paris: Editions du Seuil.

Fiengo, Robert W. 1974. "Semantic Conditions on Surface Structure." Ph.D. dissertation, MIT.

————, and Howard Lasnik. 1973. "The Logical Structure of Reciprocal Sentences in English." *Foundations of Language* 9: 447–69.

Fodor, Jerry A., Thomas G. Bever, and Merrill F. Garrett. 1974. *The Psychology of Language*. New York: McGraw-Hill Book Co.

Fodor, J. A., J. D. Fodor, and M. F. Garrett. Forthcoming. "The Psychological Unreality of Semantic Representations." *Linguistic Inquiry*.

Fraser, Bruce. 1974. "An Analysis of Vernacular Performative Verbs." In Shuy and Bailey, 1974.

Fromm, Erich. 1961. *Marx's Concept of Man*. New York: Ungar Publishing Co.

Gewirth, Alan. 1973. "The Sleeping Chess Player." *New York Review of Books*, February 22.

Glass, Andrea Velletri, Michael S. Gazzaniga, and David Premack. 1973. "Artificial Language Training in Global Aphasics." *Neuropsychologia* 11:95–104.

Goodman, Nelson. 1951. *The Structure of Appearance*. Cambridge, Mass.: Harvard University Press.

————. 1969. "The Emperor's New Ideas." In Hook, 1969.

Gramsci, Antonio. 1957. *The Modern Prince & Other Writings*. Trans. Louis Marks. New York: International Publishers.

Graves, Christina, Jerrold J. Katz, et al. 1973. "Tacit Knowledge." *Journal of Philosophy* 70:318–30.

Greenfield, Patricia M., Karen Nelson, and Elliot Saltzman. 1972. "The Development of Rulebound Strategies for Manipulating

Seriated Cups: A Parallel Between Action and Grammar." *Cognitive Psychology* 3:291–310.

Gregory, Richard. 1970. "The Grammar of Vision." *The Listener*, February 19.

Grice, H. P. 1968. "Utterer's Meaning, Sentence-Meaning, and Word-Meaning." *Foundations of Language* 4:225–42.

———. 1969. "Utterer's Meaning and Intentions." *Philosophical Review* 78:147–77.

Gunderson, Keith, and Grover Maxwell, eds. 1975. *Minnesota Studies in Philosophy of Science*, vol. 6. Minneapolis: University of Minnesota Press.

Haldane, Elizabeth S., and G. R. T. Ross, trans. 1955. *The Philosophical Works of Descartes*, vol. 1. New York: Dover Publications.

Halitsky, David. 1974. "The Syntactic Relatedness of S Extraposition and NP Postposition in English." Mimeographed, New York University.

Halle, Morris, Horace Lunt, and Hugh MacLean, eds. 1956. *For Roman Jakobson*. The Hague: Mouton & Co.

Harman, Gilbert. 1973. "Against Universal Semantic Representation." Unpublished manuscript, Princeton University.

———, and Donald Davidson, eds. 1972. *Semantics of Natural Language*. New York: Humanities Press.

Helke, Michael. 1970. "The Grammar of English Reflexives." Ph.D. dissertation, MIT.

Higgins, F. Roger. 1973. "The Pseudo-cleft Construction in English." Ph.D. dissertation, MIT.

Hintikka, Jaakko, J. M. E. Moravcsik, and Patrick Suppes, eds. 1973. *Approaches to Natural Language*. Dordrecht: Reidel Publishing Co.

Hiż, Henry. 1973. "On the Rules of Consequence for a Natural Language." *The Monist* 57:312–27.

Hook, Sidney, ed. 1969. *Language and Philosophy*. New York: New York University Press.

Hubel, D. H., and T. N. Wiesel. 1962. "Receptive Fields, Binocular Interaction and Functional Architecture in the Cat's Visual Cortex." *Journal of Physiology* 160:106–54.

Hume, David. 1902. *An Enquiry Concerning Human Understanding*. In *Enquiries Concerning the Human Understanding and Concerning the Principles of Morals*. Ed. L. A. Selby-Bigge. 2nd ed. New York: Oxford University Press.

Ishiguro, Hidé. 1972. *Leibniz's Philosophy of Logic and Language*. London: Duckworth & Co.

Jackendoff, Ray S. 1969. "Some Rules of Semantic Interpretation in English." Ph.D. dissertation, MIT.

———. 1972. *Semantic Interpretation in Generative Grammar*. Cambridge, Mass.: MIT Press.

———. 1974a. "Introduction to the X̄ convention." Indiana University Linguistics Club, Bloomington, October 1974.

———.1974b. "A Deep Structure Projection Rule." *Linguistic Inquiry* 5:481–506.

———. Forthcoming. "Eventually, an Argument for the Trace Theory of Movement Rules." *Linguistic Inquiry.*

John, E. Roy. 1972. "Switchboard Versus Statistical Theories of Learning and Memory." *Science* 177:850–64.

Kaisse, Ellen, and Jorge Hankamer, eds. 1974. *Papers* from the Fifth Annual Meeting, Northeastern Linguistic Society, Harvard University, November.

Kant, Immanuel. 1958. *A Critique of Pure Reason.* Trans. Norman Kemp. New York: Random House, Modern Library.

Kasher, Asa, ed. Forthcoming. *Language in Focus: Foundations, Methods, and Systems.* Dordrecht: D. Riedel.

Katz, Jerrold J. 1972. *Semantic Theory.* New York: Harper & Row.

———. 1975. "Logic and Language: An Examination of Recent Criticisms of Intentionalism." In Gunderson and Maxwell, 1975.

———. Forthcoming. *Propositional Structure: A Study of the Contribution of Sentence Meaning to Speech Acts.*

———, and Paul M. Postal. 1964. *An Integrated Theory of Linguistic Description.* Cambridge, Mass.: MIT Press.

Kaufman, Ellen S. 1975. "Navajo Embedded Questions and Unbounded Movement." Ph.D. dissertation, MIT.

Keenan, Edward L., and Bernard Comrie. 1973. "Noun Phrase Accessibility and Universal Grammar." Mimeographed, Cambridge University.

Kenny, A. J. P. 1973. "The origin of the soul." In Kenny et al., 1973.

———, H. C. Longuet-Higgins, J. R. Lucas, and C. H. Waddington, 1973. *The Development of Mind: The Gifford Lectures 1972–73.* Edinburgh: Edinburgh University Press.

Keyser, S. Jay. 1975. Review of Steiner, 1974. *The New Review* 2:63–66.

Kramer, P. E., E. Koff and Z. Luria. 1972. "The Development of Competence in an Exceptional Language Structure in Older Children and Young Adults." *Child Development* 43:121–30.

Kreisel, Georg. 1974. "Review of H. Wang, 'Logic, Computation and Philosophy.'" *Journal of Symbolic Logic* 39:358–9.

Kripke, Saul. 1972. "Naming and Necessity." In Harman and Davidson, 1972.

Lasnik, Howard. 1974. "Remarks on Coreference." Mimeographed, University of Connecticut.

———, and Robert W. Fiengo. 1974. "Complement Object Deletion." *Linguistic Inquiry* 5:535–72.

Leibniz, G. W. von. 1902. *Discourse on Metaphysics.* Trans. G. R. Montgomery. La Salle, Ill.: Open Court Publishing Co.

Lenneberg, Eric H. 1967. *Biological Foundations of Language.* New York: John Wiley & Sons.

Liberman, A. M. 1974. "The Specialization of the Language Hemisphere." In Schmitt and Worden, 1974.

Liberman, Mark. 1974. "On Conditioning the Rule of Subject-Auxiliary Inversion." In Kaisse and Hankamer, 1974.

————, and Alan S. Prince. Forthcoming. "The Interpretation of Scope."

Lightfoot, David. 1975. "The Theoretical Implications of Subject Raising" (review of Postal, 1974a). *Foundations of Language* 13:115–43.

Lovejoy, Arthur O. 1908. "Kant and the English Platonists." *Essays Philosophical and Psychological, in Honor of William James.* Philosophical and psychological departments, Columbia University. New York: Longmans, Green & Co.

Luce, R. Duncan, Robert R. Bush, and Eugene Galanter, eds. 1963. *Handbook of Mathematical Psychology,* vol. 2. New York: John Wiley & Sons.

Macpherson, C. B. 1962. *The Political Theory of Possessive Individualism.* London: Oxford University Press.

Malson, Lucien. 1972. *Wolf Children and the Problem of Human Nature.* New York: Monthly Review Press. Translation of *Les Enfants sauvages.* Paris: Union Générale d'Editions, 1964.

Marx, Karl. *Economic and Philosophical Manuscripts.* Trans. T. B. Bottomore. In Fromm, 1961.

McKeon, Richard P., ed. 1941. *The Basic Works of Aristotle.* New York: Random House.

Miller, George A. 1974. "The Colors of Philosophy and Psychology." Paper for Conference of Philosophy and Psychology, MIT, October 1974.

————, and Noam Chomsky. 1963. "Finitary Models of Language Users." In Luce, Bush, and Galanter, 1963.

Millikan, C. H., and F. L. Darley, eds. 1967. *Brain Mechanisms Underlying Speech and Language.* New York: Grune & Stratton.

Milner, Brenda. 1974. "Hemispheric Specialization: Scope and Limits." In Schmitt and Worden, 1974.

Milner, Jean-Claude. 1973. *Arguments linguistiques.* Paris: Maison Mame.

Moravcsik, Julius M. E. 1967. "Linguistic Theory and the Philosophy of Language." *Foundations of Language* 3:209–33.

————. 1975a. "Aitia as Generative Factor in Aristotle's Philosophy." *Dialogue.*

————. 1975b. "Natural Languages and Formal Languages: A

Tenable Dualism." Paper presented at Stanford Philosophy of Language Workshop, February 1975.

Morgenbesser, Sidney, Patrick Suppes, and M. White, eds. 1969. *Philosophy, Science, and Method: Essays in Honor of Ernest Nagel*. New York: St. Martin's Press.

Munn, Norman L. 1971. *The Evolution of the Human Mind*. Boston: Houghton Mifflin Co.

Nottebohm, F. 1970. "Ontogeny of Bird Song: Different Strategies in Vocal Development Are Reflected in Learning Stages, Critical Periods, and Neural Lateralization." *Science* 167:950–56.

Parret, Herman, ed. 1974. *Discussing Language*. The Hague: Mouton & Co.

Peirce, Charles Sanders. 1957. "The Logic of Abduction." In Vincent Tomas, ed., *Peirce's Essays in the Philosophy of Science*. New York: Liberal Arts Press.

Peters, Stanley. 1972a. "The Projection Problem: How Is a Grammar to Be Selected?" In Peters, 1972b.

———, ed. 1972b. *Goals of Linguistic Theory*. Englewood Cliffs, N.J.: Prentice-Hall.

Polanyi, Karl. 1957. *The Great Transformation: The Political and Economic Origins of Our Time*. Boston: Beacon Press.

Postal, Paul M. 1965. "Developments in the Theory of Transformational Grammar." Mimeographed, MIT. Translated as "Nový vývoj teorie transformační gramatiky." *Slovo a Slovesnost*, Československá Academie Věd, vol. 26, 1965.

———. 1971. *Cross-Over Phenomena*. New York: Holt, Rinehart & Winston.

———. 1974a. *On Raising: One Rule of English Grammar and its Theoretical Implications*. Cambridge, Mass.: MIT Press.

———. 1974b. "On Certain Ambiguities." *Linguistic Inquiry* 5: 367–424.

Putnam, Hilary. 1962. "It Ain't Necessarily So." *Journal of Philosophy* 59:658–71.

———. 1975. "The Meaning of 'Meaning.' " In Gunderson and Maxwell, 1975.

Pylyshyn, Zenon W. 1973. "The Role of Competence Theories in Cognitive Psychology." *Journal of Psycholinguistic Research* 2: 21–50.

Quine, W. V. O. 1953. *From a Logical Point of View*. Cambridge, Mass.: Harvard University Press.

———. 1960. *Word and Object*. Cambridge, Mass.: MIT Press.

———. 1968. "The Inscrutability of Reference." *Journal of Philosophy* 65:185–212.

———. 1969a. "Reply to Chomsky." In Davidson and Hintikka, 1969.

———. 1969b. "Linguistics and Philosophy." In Hook, 1969.

———. 1969c. "Response to David Kaplan." In Davidson and Hintikka, 1969.

———. 1972. "Methodological Reflections on Current Linguistic Theory." In Harman and Davidson, 1972.

———. 1974. *The Roots of Reference*. La Salle, Ill.: Open Court Publishing Co.

Reber, Arthur S. 1973. "On Psycho-linguistic Paradigms." *Journal of Psycholinguistic Research* 2:289–320.

Reinhart, Tanya. 1974. "Syntax and Coreference." In Kaisse and Hankamer, eds., 1974.

Reiss, H., ed. 1970. *Kant's Political Writings*. London: Cambridge University Press.

Rocker, Rudolph. 1938. *Anarchosyndicalism*. London: Secker & Warburg.

Rosenbaum, Peter. 1965. "Grammar of English Predicate Complement Constructions." Ph.D. dissertation, MIT.

Ross, John R. 1967. "Constraints on Variables." Ph.D. dissertation, MIT.

———. 1971. "Primacy." Mimeographed, Language Research Foundation and MIT.

———. 1972. "Primacy and the Order of Constituents." Mimeographed, MIT.

Russell, Bertrand. 1924. *Icarus, or the Future of Science*. London: Kegan Paul.

———. 1948. *Human Knowledge: Its Scope and Limits*. New York: Simon & Schuster.

Schiffer, Stephen R. 1972. *Meaning*. London: Oxford University Press.

Schmitt, Francis O., and Frederic G. Worden, eds. 1974. *The Neurosciences: Third Study Volume*. Cambridge, Mass.: MIT Press.

Schwartz, Robert. 1969. "On Knowing a Grammar." In Hook, 1969.

Searle, John. 1969. *Speech Acts*. London: Cambridge University Press.

———. 1972. "Chomsky's Revolution in Linguistics." *New York Review of Books,* June 29.

———. 1973. "Reply to Gewirth." *New York Review of Books,* February 22.

———. 1975. "A Classification of Illocutionary Acts." In Gunderson and Maxwell, 1975.

———. Forthcoming. "Indirect Speech Acts."

Selkirk, Elizabeth. 1972. "The Phrase Phonology of English and French." Ph.D. dissertation, MIT.

———. 1974. "French Liaison and the $\overline{\text{X}}$ Notation." *Linguistic Inquiry* 5:573–90.

Shuy, Roger W., and Charles-James Bailey, eds. 1974. *Towards*

Tomorrow's Linguistics. Washington, D.C.: Georgetown University Press.

Siegel, Dorothy. 1974. "Topics in English Morphology." Ph.D. dissertation, MIT.

Sperry, R. W. 1974. "Lateral Specialization in the Surgically Separated Hemispheres." In Schmitt and Worden, 1974.

Stampe, Dennis W. 1968. "Toward a Grammar of Meaning." *Philosophical Review* 77:137–74.

Steiner, George. 1974. *After Babel: Aspects of Language and Translation*. London: Oxford University Press.

Stent, Gunther S. 1975. "Limits to the Scientific Understanding of Man." *Science* 187:1052–57.

Stich, Stephen P. 1972. "Grammar, Psychology, and Indeterminacy." *Journal of Philosophy* 69:799–818.

Strawson, P. F. 1970. *Meaning and Truth*. Inaugural Lecture, University of Oxford, November 5, 1969. London: Oxford University Press.

———. 1972. "Grammar and Philosophy." In Harman and Davidson, 1972.

Suppes, Patrick. 1969. "Stimulus-Response Theory of Finite Automata." *Journal of Mathematical Psychology* 6:327–55.

———. 1973. "Semantics of Natural Languages." In Hintikka, Moravcsik, and Suppes, 1973.

Teuber, Hans-Lukas. 1974. "Why Two Brains?" In Schmitt and Worden, 1974.

Urmson, J. O., and G. J. Warnock, eds. 1967. *J. L. Austin: Philosophical Papers*. London: Oxford University Press.

Vendler, Zeno. 1967. *Linguistics in Philosophy*. Ithaca, N. Y.: Cornell University Press.

———. 1972. *Res Cogitans*. Ithaca: Cornell University Press.

Vergnaud, Jean-Roger. 1974. "French Relative Clauses." Ph.D. dissertation, MIT.

Wang, Hao. 1974. *From Mathematics to Philosophy*. London: Routledge & Kegan Paul.

Wasow, Thomas. 1972. "Anaphoric Relations in English." Ph.D. dissertation, MIT.

———. Forthcoming. *Anaphora in Generative Grammar*.

Watson, Richard A. 1968. "Cartesian Studies." Mimeographed, Washington University.

Weimer, W. B., and D. S. Palermo, eds. Forthcoming. *Cognition and Symbolic Processes*.

Weiss, Donald D. 1975. "Professor Malcolm on Animal Intelligence." *Philosophical Review* 74:88–95.

Wexler, K., P. Culicover, and H. Hamburger. 1974. *Learning-theoretic Foundations of Linguistic Universals*. Social Sciences Working Paper no. 60, University of California, Irvine, July 1974.

Whitaker, Harry A. 1971. *On the Representation of Language in the Human Mind.* Edmonton, Canada: Linguistic Research, Inc.

Williams, Edwin S. 1974. "Rule Ordering in Syntax." Ph.D. dissertation, MIT.

Wittgenstein, Ludwig. 1953. *Philosophical Investigations.* Oxford: Basil Blackwell & Mott.

Wood, C. C. 1973. "Levels of Processing in Speech Perception: Neurophysiological and Information-Processing Analyses." Ph.D. dissertation, Yale University, 1973; Haskins Laboratories, Status Report on Speech Research, SR-35/36.

————, William R. Goff, and Ruth S. Day. 1971. "Auditory Evoked Potentials During Speech Perception." *Science* 173:1248–50.

Wood, Ellen M. 1972. *Mind and Politics.* Berkeley: University of California Press.

Yolton, John W. 1956. *John Locke and the Way of Ideas.* London: Oxford University Press.

Ziff, Paul. 1967. "On H. P. Grice's Account of Meaning." *Analysis* 28:1–18.

Index of Names